Women and the Miners' Strike, 1984–1985

FLORENCE SUTCLIFFE-BRAITHWAITE
AND NATALIE THOMLINSON

OXFORD
UNIVERSITY PRESS

OXFORD
UNIVERSITY PRESS

Great Clarendon Street, Oxford, OX2 6DP,
United Kingdom

Oxford University Press is a department of the University of Oxford.
It furthers the University's objective of excellence in research, scholarship,
and education by publishing worldwide. Oxford is a registered trade mark of
Oxford University Press in the UK and in certain other countries

© Florence Sutcliffe-Braithwaite and Natalie Thomlinson 2023

The moral rights of the authors have been asserted

First published 2023
First published in paperback 2025

All rights reserved. No part of this publication may be reproduced, stored in
a retrieval system, or transmitted, in any form or by any means, without the
prior permission in writing of Oxford University Press, or as expressly permitted
by law, by licence or under terms agreed with the appropriate reprographics
rights organization. Enquiries concerning reproduction outside the scope of the
above should be sent to the Rights Department, Oxford University Press, at the
address above

You must not circulate this work in any other form
and you must impose this same condition on any acquirer

Published in the United States of America by Oxford University Press
198 Madison Avenue, New York, NY 10016, United States of America

British Library Cataloguing in Publication Data
Data available

Library of Congress Cataloging in Publication Data
Data available

ISBN 978–0–19–284309–8 (Hbk.)
ISBN 978–0–19–898076–6 (Pbk.)

DOI: 10.1093/oso/9780192843098.001.0001

Links to third party websites are provided by Oxford in good faith and
for information only. Oxford disclaims any responsibility for the materials
contained in any third party website referenced in this work.

Women and the Miners' Strike, 1984–1985

Just days into the miners' strike of 1984–1985, a few women in coalfield communities around Britain began to meet to consider how they could support the dispute, a clash with the Thatcher government over the future of the coal industry. Women ultimately formed a national network of groups that some observers saw as an 'alternative welfare state', helping to keep the strike going for just under a year. This book is the first study of this national movement, illuminating its achievements, but also telling the less well-known story of arguments and divisions with men in the National Union of Mineworkers and feminists in the women's liberation movement. Many women in the strike support movement, despite their activism, resolutely denied that they were 'political' at all, defining themselves as 'ordinary' women, housewives, mothers, and workers; and, despite some claims that women activists had been transformed for ever by their experiences, most of those involved felt they had been changed only in more subtle ways.

Women and the Miners' Strike is also the first book to look beyond the activists to study the experiences of the majority of women in mining families who did not get involved in activism. Some of these women supported the strike by going out to work themselves to keep their families going; others supported their menfolk with practical and emotional support in the home. A large number were ambivalent about the dispute. The experiences of women whose husbands or fathers worked through the strike, or returned to work early, have generally been almost entirely obscured within popular memory. This book therefore also demonstrates how some women whose husbands broke the strike refashioned concepts like democracy and community to justify their actions, and how some even formed their own support groups to aid other women in their communities who found themselves under fire for opposing the strike.

Through examining the stories of women and their varied experiences during the strike, the book sheds new light on working-class women's relationship to the 'political' and the 'ordinary', and demonstrates the ways in which gender roles, working-class lifestyles, and coalfield communities changed in Britain during the postwar period.

Florence Sutcliffe-Braithwaite is a historian of twentieth-century Britain. Her first book examined political and popular ideas about class in England between 1968 and 2000, and she is also co-editor (with Ben Jackson and Aled Davies) of *The Neoliberal Age? Britain since the 1970s* (2021). She teaches at UCL.

Natalie Thomlinson works at the University of Reading and is a historian of feminism and gender in modern Britain. Her previous works include *Race, Ethnicity and the Women's Movement in England, 1968–1993* (2016), which was named as a Choice Outstanding Academic Title for 2016.

Dedicated to all the women who spoke to us as part of this project.

Acknowledgements

We have accumulated many debts of gratitude while writing this book. First, this book literally could not have been written without the generosity of all our interviewees, and their willingness to share their stories with us. This book is for them. We have not been able to quote from every single interview in the book—we heard so many good stories—but every interview has shaped our thinking on the topic; and almost all are stored for posterity in the National Coal Mining Museum for England for the historians of the future.

Archivists at many institutions have aided us, and we must thank all those who work at the Barnsley Archives, the Bishopsgate Institute, Feminist Archive North, Glamorgan Archives, Fife Archives, Women's Library@LSE, Hull History Centre, the National Mining Museum Scotland, especially Nicola Moss and David Bell for answering many questions about holdings, Nottingham University Archive, the People's History Museum and Archive, the Keep, Richard Burton Archive, Salford Working Class Movement Library, Sheffield City Archives, the South Wales Miners' Library, London Metropolitan University Special Collections, the Archive of Market and Social Research, and the British Library's sound collection. We were also lucky enough to have access to several private collections of papers, from Gwen MacLeod (thanks to Lisa McKenzie), Janie Robertson, Maureen Coates, Poppy Peacock*, and Penny Green.

Our postdoctoral research associate, Victoria Dawson, was a brilliant interviewer, and without her excellent work this project would not have been the same.

We have also received a great deal of help from Anne Bradley and all those who work at the National Coal Mining Museum for England, Will Tregaskes at the Cynon Valley Museum, Alice Watson at the Kent Mining Museum, John Harris, who located images for us, and Paul Darlow at the NUM Archives in Barnsley. Our advisory board, Peter Mandler, Margot Finn, Lucy Delap, Jon Lawrence, and Matt Worley, have given us invaluable help and advice and have gone beyond the call of duty in reading drafts of this work. We must also thank profusely Jane Elliott, who gave us extensive help with the National Child Development Study. Jay Emery, Jörg Arnold, Lisa McKenzie, and Dave Amos have been particularly useful in illuminating the controversial history of the Nottinghamshire coalfield. Keith Gildart, Ben Curtis, and Andy Perchard have been living encyclopaedias of NUM knowledge and have answered many queries along the way. Jean McCrindle was exceptionally helpful in the early stages of this research. Roger Shannon filled in details about the Miners' Campaign Tapes. Many more historians have helped shape this work, directly and indirectly, including: Lise Butler, Laura Carter, John

Davis, David Edgerton, Matthew Hilton, Chris Jeppesen, Diarmaid Kelliher, Claire Langhamer, Gary Love, Helen McCarthy, Chris Moores, Jonathan Moss, Guy Ortolano, Senia Paseta, Charlotte Riley, Lucy Robinson, Tehila Sasson, Camilla Schofield, Jack Saunders, Gavin Schaffer, Laura Schwartz, and James Vernon. Our special thanks to Waseem Yaqoob, Daisy Payling, Laura Kounine, Jessica Hammett, Emily Robinson, Ben Mechen, and Kristen Brill, our staunch friends over many years.

We have given papers on the research at many conferences and seminar series over the years, and would like to thank all those who attended, asked questions and offered thoughts, for helping to shape our ideas, including those at: the North American Conference on British Studies in Providence, the Sorbonne, the University of Groningen's work-in-progress seminar, the University of Naples L'Orientale, the University of Lincoln, the University of East Anglia, the Oxford Centre for Gender and Identity Studies, and the Modern History Seminar at Oxford, the Economic and Social History Seminar and the Modern British History Seminar at Cambridge, the University of Portsmouth, Keele University, Anglia Ruskin University, the University of Reading, UCL's Gender Research Network, 'The End of Coal' conference at Nottingham, and Nottingham University's seminar series, the 'Minorities and Migrants in the East Midlands Coalfield' conference at Nottingham Trent University, the University of Wolverhampton, the Modern British Studies conference at Birmingham, the 'Ordinary Working-Class People?' symposium at the University of Warwick, the 'On Behalf the People: Work, Community and Class in the British Coal Industry, 1947–1994' end-of-project symposium in Loughborough, the 'Genres of Political Writing' AHRC network conferences in Cambridge and the Norwegian University of Science and Technology, Trondheim, the 'After the Factory' workshop organised at the University of Glasgow, and the 'Affect and Subjectivity in Postwar Britain' workshop at the University of California, Berkeley.

The oral history and archival research for this book was supported by an AHRC research grant. The University of Reading, University College London, and the Leverhulme Trust have also contributed resources. We are very grateful to all these bodies, without whose support we would not have been able to complete this study.

Cathryn Steele at Oxford University Press has been a huge support throughout; we would also like to thank the anonymous reviewers who offered insightful comments on the book proposal and on the manuscript.

Florence writes:

I would like to thank all my colleagues in the history department at UCL, especially Margot Finn, Rebecca Jennings, Sophie Page, Eleanor Robson, Jagjeet Lally, Cari Tuhey, and John Sabapathy, for all their support, advice, and discussions over the years, as well as colleagues beyond the department, particularly Steve Morrison, Lucy Natarajan, and John Tomaney, for intellectual and practical support. My PhD students, Finn Gleeson, Holly Smith, and Alex Hill have been a constant source of intellectual stimulation. My particular thanks are always due to Jon Lawrence. And of course, my utterly brilliant collaborator—and excellent friend—Natalie. I would also like to thank other friends: Hannah Malone, James Stafford, Zoe Strimpel, Laura Hutchinson, Howard Amos, Cat Armitage, Kitty von Bertele, Emily Craig, Matthew Evans, Lorna McGavigan, Tom Phillips, Ed Coghill, Tom and Suze Baker, Tom Crewe, Gayle Lazda, and Will Pinkney. Also Sam Tedesco. As always, I must thank my parents Karen and John Sutcliffe-Braithwaite, and my sister Emily. And finally, Edward Henderson and River Sutcliffe-Henderson.

Natalie writes:

I have many people to whom I owe thanks for their support over the long gestation period of this book.

Firstly, the history department at the University of Reading has been a very happy home since 2016, and I have received much support from my colleagues there. Everyone deserves thanking, but in particular, Richard and Rachael Blakemore, Jacqui Turner, Emily West, Matt Worley, and Donna Yamani, have been real sources of advice, wisdom, and most importantly, friendship. I owe them all more pints in Park House than they could ever hope to drink! I have also had the privilege of teaching and supervising many wonderful students there, at both undergraduate and postgraduate levels. I'd like in particular to thank my past and present PhD students Amy Gower, Emily Peirson-Webber, Jo Raineau, Michelle Tessmann, and Amy Longmuir.

Lucy Delap has remained a continual source of support and intellectual guidance; I owe her much.

My family in Doncaster have always been a source of love and strength. My mother Janet deserves particular thanks for having inspired this research project through her many gifts over the years of books about the strike found in South Yorkshire charity shops. Thank you mum—for everything. My father Mick became unexpectedly ill and died in the early stages of this research; I miss him every day. My siblings Becky, Andy, Dan, and Kate are the best anyone could hope for; the many nieces and nephews you have provided me with are a constant source of joy.

I have many friends to thank, some of whom deserve medals for putting up with what must have been at times intolerable levels of history chat. I'm not sure any of them need to read this book given how much they've heard about its making! Jo Berridge, Ruth Horswill, Josh Newton, Rachel Malkin, Lucy McIntyre, Jo Rixom, Stevie Russell, Owen Sanderson, Diana Siclovan, Chloe Stockford, Louise Stephens, Alex Stuart, Sally Taylor, and Rosie Waters—I'll try and make up for it somehow. I owe you all one.

And finally, Florence deserves huge thanks for being a truly great friend as well as research partner. Thank you!

Contents

List of Figures	xiii
List of Tables	xv
List of Abbreviations	xvii
1. Introduction	1
Britain in 1984	4
Our Sources	9
Writing the Strike	15
The Book	22
2. Before the Strike	28
21 February 1983	28
The 'Traditional' Mining Community	30
Social Change in Mining Areas after 1945	33
Conclusion	56
3. Early Days: Spring 1984	59
1 March 1984	59
Memories of the Beginning	61
COSA Women on Strike	71
The Origins of the Women's Support Movement	75
Conclusion	90
4. High Noon: Summer 1984	92
12 May 1984	92
The Growth of National Women Against Pit Closures	95
Picketing and the Politics of Gender	101
Survival Strategies	109
Conclusion	123
5. Crisis and Drift: Autumn 1984	125
18 September 1984	125
Breaking the Strike	127
The Support Movement in Autumn	130
The Politics of the Support Movement	142
The Moral Economy of the Strike	154
Conclusion	162
6. Flood Back to Defeat: Winter 1984–5	164
25 December 1984	164
The Experience of Strikers	168

Activism Under Pressure	174
Breaking the Strike	179
The End	187
Conclusion	193

7. Aftermath — 194
   - 9 March 1985 — 194
   - The Women's Support Movement — 197
   - Getting 'Back to Normal' — 207
   - Long-Term Change in Mining Areas — 210
   - Conclusion — 219

8. Remembering the Strike — 221
   - 11 September 2014 — 221
   - Writing the Story of the Strike — 222
   - Popular Culture, Public Memory, and the Strike — 227
   - Deploying the Heroic Narrative — 231
   - Complicating the Heroic Narrative — 234
   - Communities after Coal — 240
   - Conclusion — 245

Appendix 1. Details of Project Interviewees — 249
Appendix 2. Details of Key Sociological Studies of the Strike and Aftermath — 255
Appendix 3. Chronology — 257

Bibliography — 259
Index — 275

List of Figures

3.1 A striking miner and his family in County Durham watch Arthur Scargill on the television, 1984. © Keith Pattison. — 63

3.2 Jane Paxton interviewed in the *Nottingham Evening Post*, 10 March 1984. © Nottingham Evening Post. — 69

3.3 Snowdown Women's Support Group (also known as Aylesham Women's Support Group) banner. From left to right, the women are Margaret Denham, Carol Parkin, Sue Mountford, Phyllis Fraser, and Joan Phelan © Aylesham Heritage Centre and Kent Mining Heritage Foundation. — 79

3.4 A Women Against Pit Closures meeting in Oakdale, Gwent, in Wales, 26 June 1984. © Jenny Matthews/Format. — 81

3.5 Catherine Paton Black preparing food at a soup kitchen in Ollerton, Nottinghamshire. © Brenda Prince/Format. — 82

3.6 Women from Woolley Soup Kitchen wear aprons emblazoned 'I'm a souper-woman'. Betty Cook is on the far right. © Raissa Page. — 89

4.1 Inside a packed Barnsley Town Hall for the first national women's rally, 12 May 1984. © NLA/reportdigital.co.uk. — 93

4.2 Upton Ladies Miners' Support Group raise funds at Wakefield Miners' Gala, summer 1984. © Raissa Page. — 94

4.3 The huge women's march organised by National Women Against Pit Closures passes the Department of Health and Social Security headquarters in Elephant & Castle, London, 11 August 1984. © Sheila Gray/Format. — 100

4.4 A woman stands on the picket line at Bilston Glen Colliery, Scotland, 1985. © The Scotsman Publications Ltd. — 102

4.5 A mounted policeman attacks Lesley Boulton of Sheffield Women Against Pit Closures at the Battle of Orgreave, 18 June 1984. © John Harris/reportdigital.co.uk. — 108

4.6 A man and child pick up a food parcel in South Wales. © Martin Shakeshaft. — 111

4.7 Rita Wakefield, the wife of a striking miner in Nottinghamshire, gets a free haircut from a local hairdresser during the strike. © Brenda Prince/Format. — 114

5.1 Marilyn Johnson serves a meal in the miners' welfare in Easington, County Durham, 1984. © Keith Pattison. — 132

5.2 A meeting of the central Nottinghamshire Women's Support Group in Mansfield, c.1985. Betty Heathfield, a prominent WAPC activist, and wife of Peter Heathfield, NUM General Secretary, sits on the left; second from right is Gwen MacLeod, a leading activist in Ashfield Women's Support Group, and in the Nottinghamshire central group. © Brenda Prince/Format. 133

5.3 Women celebrate Brenda Greenwood's acquittal. © Brenda Prince/Format. 137

5.4 Two women talk in the street in Easington, County Durham, while police look on. © Keith Pattison. 138

5.5 Two marchers on Gray's Inn Road, London, during a miners' lobby of Parliament, June 1984. © Maggie Murray/Format. 144

5.6 Yorkshire women protest in London, February 1985. © Joanne O'Brien/Format. 160

5.7 Welsh women protest outside the Welsh Office in Cardiff, 1984. © Martin Shakeshaft. 161

6.1 Women in Kent sort clothing during the strike. © Aylesham Heritage Centre and Kent Mining Heritage Foundation. 165

6.2 Children enjoy a Christmas party at Frickley Colliery Miners' Welfare, with food donated from supporters, South Elmsall, West Yorkshire. © John Sturrock/reportdigital.co.uk. 166

6.3 A miner's wife attacks a 'scab' with her shoe after police flood the pit village of Rossington, near Doncaster, July 1984. © Peter Arkell/reportdigital.co.uk. 171

6.4 Miners' wives picketing at Yorkshire Main, Edlington, 21 February 1985. © John Sturrock/reportdigital.co.uk. 175

6.5 Rossington Women's Support Group leading the march of striking miners returning to work, March 1985. © John Harris/reportdigital.co.uk. 189

7.1 The rally organised by National Women Against Pit Closures for International Women's Day at Saltergate Football Stadium, Chesterfield, 9 March 1985. © Raissa Page. 195

7.2 Dalkeith Miners Women's Support Group float passes Canongate Kirk, en route to Holyrood Park, in Edinburgh, demonstrating against the victimisation of sacked and imprisoned miners after the end of the strike, in 1985. © National Mining Museum Scotland. 198

List of Tables

1.1	Coalfield women interviewees—involvement in activism	13
2.1	Long-term decline of coal mining	35
2.2	Accommodation of NCDS children in the mining and working-class samples, 1965	38
2.3	Working-class young women from the NCDS: marriage and childbearing in 1981 (aged 22–23)	42
2.4	Age at first marriage—coalfield women interviewees	43
2.5	Number of children—coalfield women interviewees	45
2.6	Paid labour of mothers of NCDS children, reported in 1965	47
2.7	NCDS women who were married by 1981: children and paid labour	48
2.8	Top five wards in England, Scotland, and Wales by number of workers in mining industry: proportion of married women who were economically active, 1971	49

List of Abbreviations

BMWAG	Barnsley Miners' Wives Action Group
CISWO	Coal Industry Social Welfare Organisation
CND	Campaign for Nuclear Disarmament
COSA	Colliery Officials and Staff Area
CPGB	Communist Party of Great Britain
CRT	Coalfields Regeneration Trust
DHSS	Department of Health and Social Security
LGSM	Lesbians and Gays Support the Miners
MFGB	Miners' Federation of Great Britain
NACODS	National Association of Colliery Overmen, Deputies and Shotfirers
NAFF	National Association for Freedom
NCB	National Coal Board
NCDS	National Child Development Study
NUM	National Union of Mineworkers
NWAPC	National Woman Against Pit Closures
SEAM	Save Easington Area Mines
SERTUC	Southern & Eastern Region of the Trades Union Congress
SWAPO	South West Africa People's Organisation
TGWU	Transport and General Workers' Union
UDM	Union of Democratic Mineworkers
WAPC	Women Against Pit Closures

1
Introduction

Jimmy Coates: I felt pretty proud of her really—thought, er—we [the men] did—picketed, and these [the women] did, er—

Maureen Coates: Background work.

Jimmy Coates: Well, not background, it were—you fed children didn't you, I mean, it's where you look at it, which is—background—I don't think you were in the background at all, I think, er, you—you came—you came to the forefront.

Maureen Coates: You just did it, I don't know why...

Jimmy Coates: You came to the forefront, in, er, looking after—well, in looking after families, didn't you.[1]

When we interviewed Maureen Coates and her husband Jimmy in 2014, they voiced differing views of the work of the women's support movement in the miners' strike of 1984–5. Jimmy emphasised that the women had come 'to the forefront', while Maureen initially put them more in a supportive, 'background' role. Jimmy thought that the women's activism had 'altered the way men thought of women, really'. Maureen did not disagree, but she also offered a different timeline for growing equality between men and women in mining communities, downplaying the impact of the strike: asked when she thought relationships between men and women started to change, Maureen said, 'I would say, er, late '60s, about when I were younger, it started a bit like that then—when I got married [in 1960].'[2] Where Jimmy suggested that the miners' strike had changed relationships between men and women, Maureen ascribed changes in men's attitudes to women more to gradual shifts over the generations. She suggested that the increased tendency for wives to work outside the home was particularly important, making women less dependent on their husbands. Maureen and Jimmy both agreed that Maureen's activism in the strike, as the secretary of Sprotbrough and Brodsworth Mining Families Support Group, was important—both to the family and to the community. But their interview shows how, even within the same

---

[1] Maureen Coates, b. 1942, Yorkshire, interviewed by Florence Sutcliffe-Braithwaite and Natalie Thomlinson, 11 September 2014. (In footnotes we give interviewees' strike locations as well as year of birth. In some cases husbands were present for part or all of the interview.)

[2] Ibid.

family, memories and evaluations of women's experiences in the strike could differ. This book is about the experiences of coalfield women in the strike—not just those who got involved in activism like Maureen, but also the others (the majority) who did not. Alongside traditional archival sources, we use eighty-four original interviews with just over one hundred women to examine what coalfield women went through—and how they have come to understand what they went through—during the dispute.[3] By listening to their words, we hope to uncover not simply the contours of women's experiences during the strike, but also the historical processes through which their subjectivities have been shaped; their voices are at the heart of this book.

The women's support movement sprang up within weeks of the outbreak of the strike, in March 1984. This was the first national miners' strike for a decade. Employment in the nationalised industry stood at around 196,000 on the eve of the strike, with pits in South Wales, North East England, Yorkshire, the central belt of Scotland, Nottinghamshire, and a scattering of smaller coalfields such as Kent.[4] Most members of the National Union of Mineworkers (NUM) joined the strike, but a majority in Nottinghamshire and a few smaller coalfields refused to, and by mid-April just under 20,000 miners were regularly reporting for work, fatally damaging the power of the strikers.[5] While the strikers were overwhelmingly men, a small number of women—mostly canteen workers and National Coal Board (NCB) office staff—were also part of the dispute. Support groups in the coalfields were made up of miners' wives, mothers, sisters, and other members of the community, and sometimes included men, too. Groups were set up in every coalfield, and as the strike went on—it lasted for just a few days short of a year—observers said that the women had created an 'alternative welfare system' to support striking miners and their families.[6] They set up communal food kitchens, distributed food parcels, raised funds, spoke at meetings, organised marches and rallies, and stood on picket lines beside the miners. This movement surprised most observers and excited many on the left of British politics: within just a few years of the strike's end, a number of books celebrating women's achievements had been published.[7] In 2014,

---

[3] Appendix 1 gives biographical details of all interviewees whose interviews are deposited at the National Coal Mining Museum for England, Wakefield. Some testimonies are not archived; these interviews are listed in the bibliography.

[4] Industrial Relations Section, NUM National Office, Sheffield, Bulletins of 19 November 1984, 14 February 1985, and 1 March 1985, quot. in Andrew Richards, *Miners on Strike: Class Solidarity and Division in Britain* (Oxford: Berg, 1996), 109. Jonathan and Ruth Winterton, *Coal, Crisis and Conflict: The 1984-5 Miners' Strike in Yorkshire* (Manchester: Manchester University Press, 1989), 44, puts the figure at 184,801; however, this excludes workers at coke plants and NCB workshops, which Richards includes. Their inclusion makes for a similar total.

[5] 'Strike Stalemate as Miners Wait for Talks', *The Times*, 17 April 1984.

[6] Doreen Massey and Hilary Wainwright, 'Beyond the Coalfields: The Work of the Miners' Support Groups', in Huw Beynon, ed., *Digging Deeper: Issues in the Miners' Strike* (London: Verso, 1985), 149-168, at 166.

[7] E.g. Jean Stead, *Never the Same Again: Women and the Miners' Strike 1984-85* (London: Women's Press, 1987).

thirty years after the start of the strike, celebrations of the women's support movement were perhaps even more prominent in the left-wing press, and the women's story was told in popular films such as *Pride*.[8]

Activists, journalists, and artists have told the story of the women's support movement in the strike in heroic mode, as an uprising of women fighting for community, solidarity, and socialism, transforming their lives in the process. This book tells a more complicated story. Left-wing activists had their own reasons, political and personal, for telling a heroic story about women's activism in the strike, but the dominance of this narrative has marginalised other aspects of women's experience. We show that things were not always happy for women activists: they sometimes came into conflict with each other, and with the NUM—even as they saw themselves as working to support the union. Where coalfield women met feminist supporters of the strike, they often felt sceptical of, or even hostile to, their ideas about women's liberation. We also cast our net wider than previous studies, examining, for the first time, aspects of women's experiences that have been neglected: their work within the home, in the labour force, and in the community. While the alternative welfare network provided by the women's support groups was important, help from kin and friends was also substantial, and women's paid labour was at least as significant in allowing families to remain out on strike. To understand why so many miners and their families came out on strike and stayed out for so long, it is important to understand not just the practical help activists organised, but also how they bolstered support for the strike by constructing a moral economy that demanded miners and their families strike to honour the miners of the past, and to defend the communities of the future. The benefits of being part of—but also the social sanctions that could be imposed by—a mining community were also extremely important in maintaining solidarity; but, in this context, the fact that a substantial proportion of miners had moved away from such communities in the past three decades would eventually weaken the strike. We also investigate how and why some women *opposed* the strike. In areas like Nottinghamshire, where most miners remained at work, the majority had a very different experience to those in striking coalfields: their household income was untouched, but their husbands faced picket lines made up of their fellow miners accusing them of strikebreaking, or 'scabbing'. Some women in this situation formed their own groups to defend their menfolk against the pickets. Without downplaying the achievements of women activists, then, this book provides a more comprehensive and complex picture of women's experiences during this year of struggle and conflict.

---

[8] E.g. Harriet Sherwood, 'The Women of the Miners' Strike: "We Caused a Lot of Havoc"', *Guardian*, 7 April 2014; Dawn Foster, 'Margaret Thatcher Didn't Expect it, but Miners' Wives Galvanised the '84 Strike', *Guardian*, 12 March 2014; *Pride*, dir. Matthew Warchus (2014). For more on this, see Chapter 8.

This introduction describes the state of Britain in 1984, at the outbreak of the strike; introduces our sources; sets out the state of the existing popular and scholarly literature on the strike and women's role in it, and summarises the arguments of the book. The rest of the book takes up the narrative in chronological form.

Britain in 1984

In 1984, Britain was in the middle of the Thatcher 'revolution'. As Conservative Prime Minister, Margaret Thatcher—elected in 1979 and re-elected, with an increased majority, in 1983—had declared her purpose to be the reversal of the postwar 'progressive consensus': of government maintenance of full employment, a universalist welfare state, the nationalisation of key industries, and cooperation with the powerful trade union movement.[9] In place of all this, the Thatcher governments prioritised low inflation over low unemployment, inaugurated the Right to Buy for all council tenants, eroded the value of social security, began privatising industries, and confronted the trade unions.[10] Thatcher rejected the idea of the 'social contract', where governments and unions cooperated to moderate wage demands in pursuit of low inflation, and the idea that governments should direct new employment to areas of industrial decline.[11] She set about passing legislation to curtail union power.[12] The results of the new approach were very visible by 1984: in the first three months of the year, unemployment stood at 11.8 per cent.[13]

Thatcherites thought the nationalised coal industry was inefficient, and hated its powerful and combative trade union, the NUM. National strikes in mining in 1972 and 1974 had caused power cuts, a three-day working week, a 'state of emergency', and, ultimately, the fall of Ted Heath's Tory government. Many Conservatives had never forgiven the NUM—or Arthur Scargill, who had orchestrated the miners' important victory in the mass picket that became known as the Battle of Saltley Gate, at a Birmingham coke-works, in 1972.[14] As early as 1977,

---

[9] Margaret Thatcher, speech to the Institute of SocioEconomic Studies ('Let Our Children Grow Tall'), 15 September 1975, https://www.margaretthatcher.org/document/102769.

[10] See Ben Jackson and Robert Saunders, eds., *Making Thatcher's Britain* (Cambridge: Cambridge University Press, 2012).

[11] Ewan Gibbs, *Coal Country: The Meaning and Memory of Deindustrialization in Postwar Scotland* (London: University of London Press, 2021).

[12] Peter Dorey, 'Weakening the Trade Unions, One Step at a Time: The Thatcher Governments' Strategy for the Reform of Trade-Union Law, 1979–1984', *Historical Studies in Industrial Relations*, 37 (2016), 169–200.

[13] Unemployment rate (aged 16 and over, seasonally adjusted): https://www.ons.gov.uk/employmentandlabourmarket/peoplenotinwork/unemployment/timeseries/mgsx/lms.

[14] Richard Vinen, 'A War of Position? The Thatcher Government's Preparation for the 1984 Miners' Strike', *English Historical Review*, 134 (2019), 121–50.

while Thatcher was still in opposition, a confidential annex to the report of her Nationalised Industries Policy Group (which was leaked to the *Economist* in 1978) warned that Thatcher was likely to face a confrontation with the NUM, and suggested that in order to counter the threat, the government should build up coal stocks at power plants, make plans to import coal, use non-union lorry drivers to move it, and develop 'a large, mobile squad of police who are equipped and prepared to uphold the law against the likes of the Saltley Coke-works mob'.[15] Thatcherites were far from confident they would win a confrontation with the NUM—and agreed to a large wage increase for miners in 1981 in order to head off the threat of a strike—but they longed to curtail the union's power.[16] In 1983, Ian MacGregor, who had driven 'efficiencies' and redundancies through at British Steel, was made Chairman of the NCB. He had little interest in cosy relations with the NUM: he once told Yorkshire miners that women miners in the US worked harder than they did.[17]

The industrial relations strategies that the NUM—and its forerunner, the Miners' Federation of Great Britain (MFGB)—pursued varied enormously over time, complicated by the intensely federal nature and the differing political affiliations of the constituent parts of both unions. The General Strike and subsequent seven month miners' lockout of 1926 scarred the collective psyche of miners in the pre-nationalisation era; huge hardship was endured in coalfields across the country. But, in a foreshadowing of the events of 1984–5, there was serious disagreement between different sections of the union about how to prosecute the dispute; George Spencer, Labour MP and official of the Nottinghamshire Miners' Association, negotiated a separate settlement for the miners of that county, breaking away from the MFGB in the process.[18] Industrial relations improved after nationalisation in 1947, and the newly-founded NUM, determined to make a success of the new model of ownership, cooperated with the NCB to promote productivity growth, even at the expense of the contraction of the workforce.[19] This was an era of moderate politics in the NUM, with the leadership largely associated with the Labour right. No official national industrial action was undertaken during this period, although widespread unofficial strike action over pay in 1969 and 1970 hinted at the unrest to come.[20] Coal was still vital to Britain's economy, though it was becoming less so, as other sources of energy, like nuclear and gas, were growing in importance. From the 1970s, however, a new, more combative generation of trade unionists started to come to the fore in the NUM. They were dissatisfied with the moderation shown by the leadership—a

---

[15] Report of Nationalised Industries Policy Group (leaked Ridley report), 30 June 1977, Thatcher MSS 2/6/1/37, https://www.margaretthatcher.org/document/110795.
[16] Vinen, 'War of Position?'
[17] Martin Adeney and John Lloyd, *The Miners' Strike, 1984–5: Loss without Limit* (London: Routledge & Kegan Paul, 1986), 43.
[18] Ibid., 258. [19] See Chapter 2, Table 2.1. [20] Adeney and Lloyd, *Miners' Strike*, 16.

tradition largely continued by Joe Gormley, NUM President between 1971 and 1982—and pushed for the expansion of the coal industry and higher wages.[21]

Most prominent among these dissenting left voices was Arthur Scargill, a Yorkshireman born in 1938, who became President of the Yorkshire Area in 1973, and President of the national union in 1982. Scargill was a charismatic leader, with an intransigent attachment to his principles, and a Stakhanovite work ethic.[22] Yorkshire was not the most obvious place for a militant leader to emerge from: it had long had a reputation as a mostly 'moderate' Area, with South Wales and Scotland considered the union's hotbeds of radicalism. Despite this, Scargill's political beliefs were, according to two journalists who covered the 1984-5 strike, 'a kind of communist-syndicalism'.[23] A member of the Young Communist League between 1955 and the early 1960s, he continued to believe, even after his departure from the party, in class struggle as the motor for revolution.[24] In Scargill's political worldview, militancy over wages and jobs was the foundation of successful trade unionism, and strong trade unions could eventually revolutionise politics and economics. In an interview in 1981, he argued for 'the trade union movement itself exercising power, exercising authority and compelling management, be it private or nationalised, to do certain things in terms of investment, planning, extension and development in the same way that we've been able to do on wages and conditions for many years'.[25] He was determined to oppose Thatcherism, setting out in his first conference speech as President his top priority: 'to protect the coal industry from the ravages of the market mechanism'.[26] For Scargill, industrial action was the way to achieve both his interlinked goals: promoting miners' economic interests, and propelling Britain towards socialist revolution. He was hardly alone in holding these political views; in the postwar era, many prominent positions within the NUM were held by members or ex-members of the Communist Party of Great Britain (CPGB), a group that was small in numbers but which in some ways had an outsize influence on British left politics in the 1980s—though the ability of CPGB members to influence their comrades in the NUM in the prosecution of industrial disputes was smaller than might be imagined.[27]

Scargill's strategy for any strike was to use the miners' industrial muscle and to rally other trade unionists behind the cause (in this, he was closely aligned with the traditionalist, economist faction of the CPGB that was centred around the party's newspaper, the *Morning Star*). This was what had brought Scargill victory at the Battle of Saltley Gate, in 1972, which he remembered fifty years later as 'the

---

[21] For more on this, see Chapter 2. [22] Adeney and Lloyd, *Miners' Strike*, 48.
[23] Ibid., 29. [24] Ibid., 30. [25] Ibid., 35-6. [26] Ibid., 37.
[27] Sheryl Bernadette Buckley, 'Making Miners Militant? The Communist Party of Great Britain and the National Union of Mineworkers, 1956-85', in Evan Smith and Matthew Worley, eds., *Waiting for the Revolution: The British Far Left from 1956* (Manchester: Manchester University Press, 2017), 107-24.

greatest day of my life'.²⁸ But the 1980s was a period of changing socialist politics, in which groups fighting for 'identity'-based rights (feminists, Black power activists, and gay liberationists) were becoming as important as the traditional forces of organised labour, and some doubted whether the Scargillite strategy would succeed. Many on the 'new left', including the Eurocommunist faction of the CPGB, were influenced by continental theorists like Antonio Gramsci, and hoped to secure a broad front for popular struggle. Influenced by the Gramscian idea of the war of position, they wanted to connect the miners' strike to the struggles of Black people, gays, and women, rather than relying on industrial muscle alone— trade union action on its own would be, in a Gramscian reading, a war of manoeuvre that simply could not be won before a victory in the war of position had been decisively attained, and the cultural hegemony of the state overturned.²⁹ The Labour Party was also divided over how to respond to strike action, with Neil Kinnock, the party's new leader from 1983, keen to break the association between Labour and militant trade unionism.³⁰ There were thus considerable disagreements within the NUM and on the left more broadly over how the strike should be fought. The President's power was also far from assured. Scargill wanted to centralise the NUM, whose Areas—the geographical regions upon which the NCB and consequently the NUM were based—had always retained much autonomy. His goal of uniting the union behind his leadership, however, was hampered by the Area Incentive Scheme introduced in 1977–8, which meant miners in high-productivity regions, like Nottinghamshire, which was highly mechanised and had relatively favourable conditions for getting coal, could earn more.³¹ Left-wingers within the NUM saw the scheme as an attempt to divide and rule the miners, and it probably did play a key part in 1984 in convincing many miners in Nottinghamshire that their pits were under no threat of closure and that following Scargill's lead might not be in their best interests.³² There were, thus, important strategic weaknesses and divisions in the NUM's position on the eve of the strike. The stage was set for a fight to the bitter end between Scargill and Thatcher.

Thatcher's revolution was not the only one underway in 1980s Britain, however. While Thatcher has—understandably—dominated histories of the period, long-term changes were also transforming the British economy and British society

---

²⁸ *Look North*, BBC1, 10 February 2022.
²⁹ On Eurocommunist responses, see Geoff Andrews, *Endgames and New Times: The Final Years of British Communism, 1964–1991* (London: Lawrence & Wishart, 2004), 208–10; Peter Ackers, 'Gramsci at the Miners' Strike: Remembering the 1984–1985 Eurocommunist Alternative Industrial Relations Strategy', *Labor History*, 55 (2014), 151–72. On broader new left responses, see Daisy Payling, *Socialist Republic: Remaking the British Left in 1980s Sheffield* (Manchester: Manchester University Press, 2023), ch. 2.
³⁰ Martin Westlake, *Kinnock: The Biography* (London: Little, Brown, 2001), 289–310.
³¹ Paul F. Clark, 'Introducing Productivity Incentives in the British Coal-Mining Industry', *Industrial Relations Journal*, 11 (1980), 24–36; William Ashworth, *The History of the British Coal Industry. Volume 5, 1946–1982: The Nationalized Industry* (Oxford: Clarendon Press, 1986), 373–4.
³² Richard King, *Brittle with Relics: A History of Wales, 1962–1997* (London: Faber & Faber, 2022), 263.

quite separately to the impact of Thatcherism. Perhaps foremost among these was deindustrialisation, which Jim Tomlinson has recently proposed as one of the most significant 'meta-narratives' for postwar Britain. Deindustrialisation accelerated under Thatcher because of the monetarist shock therapy she administered to the British economy, but it did not begin in 1979. Contraction of the industrial workforce set in much earlier: the proportion of employment in Britain in industry (manufacturing, mining, and construction) peaked in 1955, at 47.9 per cent, and by 1998 had declined to just 26.6 per cent.[33] The corollary of this was the rise of the service sector, including relatively well-paid and secure jobs in expanding areas like healthcare and education, but also low-paid and casualised jobs in sectors like retail, care, personal services, and domestic work. The causes of deindustrialisation lay in changing technology, the changing global distribution of industry, and the tendency for more affluent consumers to devote a larger proportion of their income to services, rather than goods. In the 1950s, 1960s, and 1970s the effects of deindustrialisation were offset by governments' efforts to direct new industrial employment to areas of the country where older industries were contracting, and by the contributions married women increasingly made to household budgets: these decades were characterised, for most working-class families, by growing affluence.[34] But in the long run, the impact of deindustrialisation would be profound: it tended to polarise incomes, and, in the harsh political climate of Thatcherism, produced growing inequality between rich and poor, as well as growing regional inequality, as many industrial heartlands struggled to reinvent themselves as industry disappeared. Polarisation of incomes had a knock-on effect on the social security system, as, from the 1970s onwards, governments found themselves increasingly under pressure to support working families on low wages as well as economically inactive households. And deindustrialisation created a less favourable climate for trade unionism, as industrial workers tended to be easier to organise than many workers in the service sector.[35]

Deindustrialisation was also inextricably bound up with a third revolution: the revolution in gender roles that took place in postwar Britain. Deindustrialisation destroyed relatively well-paid jobs that were often coded masculine, and replaced them with jobs that were more likely to be seen as 'women's work'. Where it reduced men's wages, it also created further pressures for women to contribute to family incomes through taking work. The paid labour of wives—and even of mothers with quite young children—was normalised in the period from the late

---

[33] Jim Tomlinson, 'De-Industrialization Not Decline: A New Meta-Narrative for Post-War British History', *Twentieth Century British History*, 27 (2016), 76–99, at 78.
[34] There were important limits to 'affluence': Selina Todd, 'Affluence, Class and Crown Street: Reinvestigating the Post-War Working Class', *Contemporary British History*, 22 (2008), 501–18.
[35] Tomlinson, 'De-Industrialization Not Decline'; Bernhard Rieger, 'British Varieties of Neoliberalism: Unemployment Policy from Thatcher to Blair', in Aled Davies, Ben Jackson, and Florence Sutcliffe-Braithwaite, eds., *The Neoliberal Age? Britain since the 1970s* (London: UCL Press, 2021), 112–34.

1940s onwards.³⁶ It would be reductive to suggest that deindustrialisation was simply 'good' for women: women as well as men lost jobs in this process, and they also suffered from the harm done to communities that saw the bottom fall out of them as major industries collapsed.³⁷ Nevertheless, deindustrialisation was a significant factor in a much larger and longer revolution in gender roles that saw women claim their place in politics and public life, and in the workplace. The postwar decades saw the gradual rise of a culture of 'popular individualism' in Britain, which by the 1970s was surfacing in more and more areas.³⁸ Several discourses emphasising the importance of the individual man, woman or child converged in these years—the rhetoric of equality and 'fair shares' of the postwar Labour Party and labour movement; the provision the welfare state made for the health and education of all; and the theories of the psy-sciences, which increasingly percolated into society via the mass media—and all of these encouraged women to value themselves as individuals, to demand respect, a voice and autonomy.³⁹ From the late 1960s onwards, a flourishing women's liberation movement—mainly, though not entirely, made up of middle-class women—grew up, fighting to break down the stereotypes of femininity, defending abortion rights, and arguing for free 24 hour nurseries, lesbian rights, and the right to a self-defined sexuality.⁴⁰ At the same time, working-class women in the trade union movement were mounting their own fight for equal pay, skill recognition, and the right to work, motivated not so much by feminism as by the ostensibly universal ideals of equality, autonomy and self-worth.⁴¹ In 1966, feminist Juliet Mitchell wrote an article for *New Left Review* entitled 'Women: The Longest Revolution'.⁴² By 1984, the revolution, though far from complete, was certainly well underway. The de-industrial revolution and the Thatcher revolution were both also in train. It would be Scargill's revolution that would ultimately fail to materialise.

Our Sources

This book is based on our own collection of eighty-four oral histories, undertaken with just over one hundred women from England, Scotland, and Wales between

---

³⁶ Helen McCarthy, *Double Lives: A History of Working Motherhood* (London: Bloomsbury, 2020).
³⁷ Fernando M. Aragón, Juan Pablo Rud, and Gerhard Toews, 'Resource Shocks, Employment, and Gender: Evidence from the Collapse of the UK Coal Industry', *Labour Economics*, 52 (2018), 54-67.
³⁸ Emily Robinson, Camilla Schofield, Florence Sutcliffe-Braithwaite, and Natalie Thomlinson, 'Telling Stories about Post-War Britain: Popular Individualism and the "Crisis" of the 1970s', *Twentieth Century British History*, 28 (2017), 268-304.
³⁹ Florence Sutcliffe-Braithwaite and Natalie Thomlinson, 'Vernacular Discourses of Gender Equality in the Post-War British Working Class', *Past & Present*, 254 (2022), 277-313.
⁴⁰ See Margaretta Jolly, *Sisterhood and After: An Oral History of the UK Women's Liberation Movement, 1968-Present* (Oxford: Oxford University Press, 2019).
⁴¹ Jonathan Moss, *Women, Workplace Protest and Political Identity in England, 1968-85* (Manchester: Manchester University Press, 2019).
⁴² Juliet Mitchell, 'Women: The Longest Revolution', *New Left Review*, I/40 (1966), 11-37.

2014 and 2020, as well as drawing on the work of journalists, the celebratory books and pamphlets in which women's support groups chronicled their work, and sociological studies which gathered quantitative and qualitative evidence to understand the strike. We also use archival collections—which have to date been little-utilised in studies of women in the strike—including archives from England, Scotland, and Wales, and a number of collections of papers still in private hands, which some project interviewees were kind enough to let us examine.[43]

This array of sources sheds light on the experiences of a wide range of coalfield women. Archival sources, like journalistic coverage of women's experiences in the strike, and books written and compiled by women involved in the strike, most frequently relate to the work of activists. Archives often include papers and ephemera relating to the organisation and running of women's support groups; they also sometimes include oral histories conducted during or shortly after the strike with activist women. The work of sociologists is invaluable because many sociological studies focused not just on activists but on whole communities or mining areas, generating information about miners and their family members who did not become involved in activism, as well as those who actually opposed the strike. We have also used archived sociological data, including collections of interviews conducted in coalfield areas for projects not focusing on the strike, which have been key in offering the chance to hear from coalfield women who were not involved in strike activism, who felt negatively towards the strike, and who would be unlikely to agree to be interviewed for a project centring on the strike. Finally, the key source base which allows us to reconstruct the experiences and attitudes of not only activists and supporters but also the ambivalent and the hostile is our oral history collection. While we spoke to many strike activists to research this book, we also recruited interviewees who were able to tell stories that are far less often heard in accounts of women's experiences in the strike: stories of taking on paid labour to support their families, or of accepting their husbands' strike action while remaining hostile to the political principle of the strike; or tales of supporting their husbands' or fathers' decision to return to work early, even of working through the strike in NCB jobs themselves. Our sources thus allow us to reconstruct a fuller and more complex picture of women's experiences in the strike than has previously been seen.

Our oral history collection is at the heart of this project, and is now deposited in the archive of the National Coal Mining Museum for England. We undertook the interviews alongside the project's postdoctoral researcher Dr Victoria Dawson

---

[43] Exceptions to the neglect of archival sources include: Jean McCrindle, 'The National Organisation of Women Against Pit Closures in the Miners' Strike of 1984-5' (unpublished PhD thesis, Oxford Brookes, 2001); Rebecca Davies, 'Not Just Supporting but Leading: The Involvement of the Women of the South Wales Coalfield in the 1984-5 Miners' Strike' (unpublished PhD thesis, University of Glamorgan, 2010).

between 2014 and 2020, and spoke to just over one hundred women. (We also interviewed two men, and, as our interviews were usually conducted in women's homes, a number of husbands were also present for parts of the discussions.) Project interviewees were recruited in several ways: flyers advertising the project were sent to libraries and community centres in former coalfield areas; letters were sent to local newspapers; and calls for interviewees were announced on social media. We designed the promotional material to try to appeal to more than simply activist women, as we were keen to hear from a wide range of voices. Once interviewees had been recruited, they often put us in contact with friends and relatives who also had stories of the strike to share.

Our interviewees came from Yorkshire, Nottinghamshire, Derbyshire, Staffordshire, Kent, London, North East England, the West and East of Scotland's central belt, and South Wales. Most—eighty-one in total—were what we call 'coalfield women': that is, women whose fathers were miners, and/or whose husbands were miners, and/or who were from working-class families in mining communities and remained embedded in these communities as adults. Of these, sixteen women were born between 1934 and 1944; forty-eight were from the baby boom generation, born between 1945 and 1964, and seventeen were younger, born between 1965 and 1973. Many were both daughters and wives of miners: among the forty-eight coalfield women from the baby boom generation, thirty-seven were married to miners, and twenty-one of these women were also the daughters of miners. The remainder of our interviewees—those who were not 'coalfield women'—were connected to the strike by their links to communities, and usually because they got involved in strike activism. The majority of our interviewees wanted to be known by their real names, a wish that we felt it appropriate to respect given the way in which working-class women have been marginalised in the historical record. Some, however, wished to be only known by their first name, and some wished to remain anonymous; pseudonyms within the text are denoted by the use of asterisks.

Almost all our coalfield interviewees were born into working-class families and communities, and remained within those communities as adults. As part of the shift in occupational structure that postwar Britain witnessed, many daughters of manual labourers moved into white-collar work, and into jobs that have often been seen as, at the very least, lower-middle-class; our interviewees were no different. Many also participated in the expansion of home-ownership after 1945, often taking advantage of the Right to Buy council houses or Coal Board houses in the final decades of the twentieth century. Like many in early twenty-first-century Britain, our interviewees often thought that these changes in the occupational structure and in patterns of housing tenure had blurred class boundaries in confusing and complicated ways.[44] However, the majority still identified as

---

[44] Florence Sutcliffe-Braithwaite, *Class, Politics, and the Decline of Deference in England, 1968–2000* (Oxford: Oxford University Press, 2018).

'working-class', defining class as based not just on occupation or housing tenure, but on background, values, attitudes, and the need to work. Christina Bell, for example, said that she thought she and her husband were 'lower-middle-class' now, because they owned their home and had a comfortable lifestyle, but when asked if she *felt* 'lower-middle-class' she laughed and said 'no!'—she still felt working-class.[45] All but one of our interviewees were white. Though coalfields were never places untouched by migration—in the nineteenth and twentieth centuries, the expansion and contraction of the industry in different parts of the country led to major movements of workers and their families, both within the UK and from beyond—the predominance of white interviewees reflects the fact that Britain's coalfields were, in the main, unusually white areas in the postwar decades.[46] The exception among our interviewees was Maggie Stubbs, born in Jamaica around 1950. Maggie came to the UK to study nursing, married a miner, and lived in the South Yorkshire village of Maltby during the strike.[47]

As a project team we drew up a list of biographical details and topics that we wished to cover in each interview, but we allowed our interviewees considerable latitude to discuss the events that they felt had been important in their lives. Our interviews were generally life-story interviews, lasting between two and three hours (though some were much longer), and covering everything from birth, childhood, and education to work, marriage, and family, the strike, and the years after the strike. This, importantly, allows us to place the strike in context, to show what coalfield women's lives were like on the eve of the strike, and how they changed afterwards. We use quantitative data from the census, and from the National Child Development Study (NCDS) of 1958 (a project that surveyed all children born in Great Britain in a single week in 1958, following up with them at regular intervals thereafter), to reconstruct the lives of coalfield women and coalfield communities in the postwar decades.[48] A comparison between our data and that of the NCDS shows that, as is common with oral history interviews, those from more affluent households and with higher levels of education—daughters of owner-occupiers and grammar-school girls—are overrepresented in our sample. Strike activists are also overrepresented: they were, understandably, often the most keen to share their stories, and the most likely to see the project as one that spoke to them. While sociological studies found that only a small minority of coalfield

---

[45] Christina Bell, b. 1949, North East England/Nottinghamshire, interviewed by Victoria Dawson, 27 June 2018. (Where interviewees grew up in a different place to their strike location, we give childhood location followed by strike location.)

[46] 'Ethnic Population by Local Authority' spreadsheet: https://www.ethnicity-facts-figures.service.gov.uk/uk-population-by-ethnicity/national-and-regional-populations/regional-ethnic-diversity/latest#download-the-data shows that in the 2011 census data, many coalfield areas remained predominantly white. See Chapter 2 for more on migration.

[47] Maggie Stubbs, b. c.1950, Jamaica/Yorkshire, interviewed by Natalie Thomlinson, 13 September 2018.

[48] See Chapter 2 for more detail.

Table 1.1 Coalfield women interviewees—involvement in activism

	b. 1934-44	b. 1945-64	b. 1965-73
Involved in women's support group activism	9	25	–[a]
Involved in activism more informally	1	8	3
Not involved in pro-strike activism	6	15	14
Total	16	48	17

[a] The youngest generation were mainly still at school during the strike, and were therefore not members of support groups.

women became involved in strike activism, among our interviewees activists predominated. Over 40 per cent of the coalfield women we interviewed were involved in support group activism, and a further 15 per cent were involved in activism in a less formal way—for example, through attending marches or pickets, or running occasional raffle sales to raise money for the miners. However, this does still leave us with a substantial sample of women who were not involved in activism (Table 1.1).

Our sample is certainly not representative of coalfield women, or of miners' wives, but this does not diminish its use. Oral histories help us to reconstruct, in tandem with other sources, what women *did* in the strike, but, perhaps even more importantly, they allow us to analyse how women felt, and what their experiences meant to them—at the time, and in the late 2010s. This approach to oral history goes back to the 1980s, when critiques were mounted of the new research method on the grounds that memory is highly fallible. These criticisms were answered with two lines of argument. First, the proponents of oral history pointed out, *all* sources are fallible and need to be examined critically. Second, and perhaps more importantly, oral historians argued that in fact, oral history's very *strength* lies in the insight it gives into the subjective—and the errors and distortions found in oral history testimonies give some of the most telling clues about the psychic investments individuals have in the past. As the Italian oral historian Alessandro Portelli famously wrote, 'errors, inventions and myths lead us through and beyond facts to their meanings'.[49] This analytical framework helps us to decode why women who were activists in the strike tended to frame their political involvement as novel, even when they had been involved in activism before; or why women attributed major life events to the strike even when they happened decades afterwards.

Oral historians have also shown that the stories people tell about their own pasts do not stay the same, but change over time under the influence of cultural discourses—narratives circulating in the media, political arguments, and everyday

---

[49] Alessandro Portelli, *The Death of Luigi Trastulli and Other Stories: Form and Meaning in Oral History* (Albany, NY: State University of New York Press, 1991), 2.

life—which make some stories easier to tell than others.[50] Penny Summerfield has demonstrated, for example, that women's memories of their Second World War work grew more positive over the years, with recollections of arduous, boring, and dangerous work giving way to more positive accounts that were influenced by a growing cultural script—that is to say, a widely-held perception—that linked women's paid labour with 'emancipation'.[51] A heroic narrative linking participation in strike activism to women's emancipation was evident from the time of the strike itself, and it was clear that many interviewees' testimonies had been strongly shaped by subsequent retellings of the strike in popular culture. (That this is so is unsurprising, given the mythologising of the strike; nevertheless, this insight has been largely absent in existing studies of the strike that make use of oral testimony.) Oral history theory also draws our attention to the moments when individuals are able to construct 'composed' narratives, and the moments when those narratives break down and stories become more halting, ambiguous, or contradictory.[52] It was much less easy for the small numbers of women within our interview sample whose husbands or fathers broke the strike to articulate their experiences: the moments of 'discomposure' in their accounts point to the lack of readily available cultural scripts they could use to narrate what they went through. Following the lessons of these oral historians, we are interested in reconstructing our interviewees' experiences in the strike, but we also recognise that, as Joan Scott has argued, 'experience' is not a transparent category, but discursively constructed: 'always already an interpretation and something that needs to be interpreted'.[53]

Much has been written on the power dynamics of the oral history encounter, and our interviews were, of course, shaped by the relationship between ourselves and our interviewees, and our own positionality.[54] It can be difficult to identify the *specific* ways in which these interviews were shaped by our own backgrounds and identities, given that every interview is, by its very nature, deeply personal, and that—with a few exceptions—we did not have access to recordings of the same women being interviewed by other people for comparison. Nevertheless, a few words should be said about what we brought of ourselves to these encounters. We came as university researchers and, as such, were marked as middle-class, though Victoria came from a working-class background. We were, in most senses,

---

[50] Popular Memory Group, 'Popular Memory: Theory, Politics, Method', in Richard Johnson, Gregor McLennan, Bill Schwarz, and David Sutton, eds., *Making Histories: Studies in History Writing* (London: Hutchinson, 1982), 205–52.

[51] Penny Summerfield, *Reconstructing Women's Wartime Lives: Discourse and Subjectivity in Oral Histories of the Second World War* (Manchester: Manchester University Press, 1998).

[52] Graham Dawson, *Soldier Heroes: British Adventure, Empire and the Imagining of Masculinities* (London: Routledge, 1994); Summerfield, *Reconstructing Women's Wartime Lives*.

[53] Joan Scott, 'The Evidence of Experience', *Critical Inquiry*, 17 (1991), 773–97, at 797.

[54] See Jeska Rees, '"Are You a Lesbian?": Challenges in Recording and Analysing the Women's Liberation Movement in England', *History Workshop Journal*, 69 (2010), 177–87.

outsiders to the communities we came into. Florence grew up in Berkshire, certainly not a mining area. Natalie hails from the mining town of Doncaster; while this was at times useful in helping to establish a rapport with interviewees, it would be disingenuous to suggest that her job as a lecturer positioned her as anything other than middle-class. Victoria came from Hull; though not from a mining town, she had grown up in similar socio-economic circumstances to most of our interviewees. All three of us identify as being politically on the left; we were sympathetic to the cause of the striking miners, but also aware of the complexities of the dispute, and of the need to not simplistically demonise those who broke or disagreed with the strike. As we have seen, our interviewees' class positions were often complicated; a large majority came from unambiguously working-class backgrounds, but quite a number had moved into white-collar work, with some having gone to university as mature students, and almost all now owning their own homes. Many had gained considerable political expertise through their experiences of strike activism and within the trade union movement. Our interviewees were also all older than us, usually by several decades. As such, it would be reductive to say that the interview encounter was one in which we, the middle-class researchers, held all the power, the bourgeois creators of knowledge about our working-class subjects. Most—though not all—of our interviewees had a clear idea about the stories they wanted to tell, and were able to use the framework of the interview to tell them. Nevertheless, as the creators of the project, we had the power to determine the course of questioning, to ask our interviewees 'who are you?' and expect a response (a process which itself could generate new interpretations and subjectivities). And as the writers of this book, interpretative authority ultimately lies with us.[55] Given this, while we strove to take seriously our interviewees' understandings of events, it would be a fantasy to suggest that power could be equally shared between them and us. Indeed, it is important to acknowledge that even when we directly quote the words of our interviewees, they may not always share our interpretations.

Writing the Strike

The huge literature on the miners' strike, both popular and scholarly, is testament to the continuing cultural and political resonance of the dispute, as well as the privileged place that both the coal industry and the figure of the miner have held in the national imaginary.[56] Most general studies of the strike, whether written by

---

[55] Katherine Borland, '"That's Not What I Said!" Interpretive Conflict in Oral Narrative Research', in Sherna Berger Gluck and Daphne Patai, eds., *Women's Words: The Feminist Practice of Oral History* (New York: Routledge, 1991), 63–75.

[56] Jörg Arnold, *The British Miner in the Age of De-Industrialization: A Political and Cultural History* (Oxford: Oxford University Press, 2023).

journalists or historians, focus on the activities of the NUM and the government, but almost all at least mention the women's support movement, which most authors agree was vital to the pursuit of the strike. Jim Phillips devotes a chapter to the women's movement in his book on the strike in Scotland, and concludes that women there played a 'vital' role, 'supporting and in some ways leading the strike'.[57] General studies also tend to concur that the strike transformed patriarchal coalfield communities and women activists. Political scientist Andrew Richards suggests that 'the women of the coalfields astounded' both the 'urban Left' and 'the miners themselves'; they 'entered new worlds and established links with individuals and groups with whom they had hitherto enjoyed little contact'.[58] Ben Curtis's work on the South Wales miners agrees that, '[f]or many female activists, the strike had a profound impact on their lives'.[59] Phillips finds that there is 'substance' to the 'activist emphasis on the positive and progressive reconstruction of gender relations' in 1984–5, with men taking on some activities in the home, and women more 'public' activities.[60] A similar picture emerges from Diarmaid Kelliher's study of the strike solidarity movement in London: though Kelliher contests straightforwardly heroic accounts of 'feminist transformation' through strike activism, he nevertheless comments that the scale of coalfield women's mobilisation was new, that even for those who were already politically active, it was 'often a novel experience', and that 'coalfield women developed direct relationships with feminist activists... [and] attempted to integrate concepts of gender equality with embedded notions of community and, especially, family'.[61]

This emphasis is unsurprising when we consider the source base these authors rely on in their examination of women: celebratory accounts produced by left-wing journalists and women's support groups during and shortly after the strike, as well as interviews conducted since then with prominent activists. Richards, for example, relies on interviews with *male* activists to substantiate his assertion that many women activists were transformed by the strike; Curtis cites interviews with prominent women activists like Hefina Headon, as does Kelliher, who bases his assessment on interviews with coalfield activists like Betty Cook as well as London activists, often more middle-class and involved in the new left, who in their accounts of the strike centred questions about feminism that were actually quite peripheral to most women's groups in the coalfields.[62] The accounts of left-wing journalists, middle-class supporters of the strike, and prominent activists in the

---

[57] Jim Phillips, *Collieries, Communities and the Miners' Strike in Scotland, 1984–85* (Manchester: Manchester University Press, 2012), 112, 132, 11.
[58] Richards, *Miners on Strike*, 149. See also Adeney and Lloyd, *Miners' Strike*, 222–3.
[59] Ben Curtis, *The South Wales Miners 1964–1985* (Cardiff: University of Wales Press, 2013), 209.
[60] Phillips, *Collieries, Communities*, 112, 132, 11.
[61] Diarmaid Kelliher, *Cultures of Solidarity: London and the 1984–5 Miners' Strike* (London: Routledge, 2021), 101, 96.
[62] Richards, *Miners on Strike*, 169; Curtis, *South Wales Miners*, 210; Kelliher, *Cultures of Solidarity*, 99.

women's support movement all offer important insights, but they tell only part of the story: as we will see, all these individuals had vested personal and political interests in giving their accounts of the strike in heroic mode.

During the strike, these left-wing journalists and activists established the basic pillars of a heroic narrative about the women's support movement that have remained standing until the present day. In May 1984, the *Guardian* was reporting in upbeat tones on the extent of the women's support movement—'groups have sprung up all over the country'—as well as its activities, particularly the novel sight of miners' wives taking a 'flying leap onto the picket line'.[63] Commentary from feminists began to suggest that the women's movement was profoundly changing gender roles in mining communities. In October 1984, Loretta Loach wrote in Britain's main feminist periodical, *Spare Rib*, that women in support groups had 'created a profound and unprecedented change in the essentially male culture of the mining community'.[64] The Marxist-feminist journalist and activist Beatrix Campbell claimed, similarly, that the women were 'struggling' with the 'proletarian patriarchs' of the NUM 'for their right to organise autonomously', and that their activism had taken them into 'another universe... into the world of city socialism where women's economic and social room for manoeuvre seemed to them more open-ended and where sexual and domestic mores gave them space to breathe'.[65] When interviewed in 1986 by fellow socialist-feminist Sheila Rowbotham, Jean McCrindle—who was deeply involved in women's efforts to support the strike—gave a measured assessment of the movement, but still claimed that it 'seemed like spontaneous bush fire', that there were 'only a few women who'd had organizing experience' before, and that 'there has been quite a severe rethinking of what marriage is'.[66] Probably the most fulsome statement of this view was given in *Guardian* journalist and feminist Jean Stead's book *Never the Same Again*, which painted a picture of mining communities before the strike as deeply patriarchal, and of women's mobilisation during the strike as 'spontaneous', widespread, and transformative.[67] According to Stead, women had been politicised, and gender roles had changed, with men 'taking over a share of the housekeeping', 'looking after the children', and 'queueing up for food parcels at

---

[63] Patrick Wintour, 'Woman's Place is on the Picket', *Guardian*, 17 May 1984; Maggie Brown, 'A Flying Leap onto the Picket Line', *Guardian*, 28 May 1984.

[64] Loretta Loach, 'We'll be Here Right to the End and After', *Spare Rib*, 147, October 1984.

[65] Beatrix Campbell, 'Proletarian Patriarchs and the Real Radicals', in Vicky Seddon, ed., *The Cutting Edge: Women and the Pit Strike* (London: Lawrence & Wishart, 1986), 249–82, at 252, 277. See also Susan Miller, '"The Best Thing that Ever Happened to Us": Women's Role in the Coal Dispute', *Journal of Law and Society*, 12 (1985), 355–64, esp. 355.

[66] Jean McCrindle and Sheila Rowbotham, 'More than Just a Memory: Some Political Implications of Women's Involvement in the Miners' Strike, 1984–85', *Feminist Review*, 23 (1986), 109–24, at 113, 112, 117.

[67] Stead, *Never the Same Again*, 10. The more recent journalistic account by Triona Holden, *Queen Coal: Women of the Miners' Strike* (Stroud: Sutton, 2005), follows a similar narrative: the movement was 'spontaneous'; women were 'transformed' and 'came out of the kitchen' for the first time: 4–5.

the soup kitchens'; the women had created a new, authentically working-class 'feminism'.[68] Stereotyped and often quite patronising views of 'traditional' mining communities underlay many of these accounts: Stead, for example, suggested that '[m]ost of the women were trying for the first time to control their own destinies and their own lives', and 'were no longer simply a necessary extension of the miners and the pits'.[69] In order to emphasise the apparent novelty of coalfield women's activism, such accounts also tended to overlook the long history of working-class women's involvement in politics and trade unionism, even if—as this book will argue—there were aspects of the women's support movement that *were* qualitatively new.

Some leftists went even further, suggesting that the women's support movement had not only changed women's roles, but also reinvigorated socialism and transformed the labour movement. One writer in *Socialist Action* saw it as 'the greatest turning point in working-class politics since 1926', while Beatrix Campbell suggested that 'Labourism', which had hitherto 'slept soundly in its bed in the outposts of supposedly pure working-class socialism' (i.e. mining communities), had now been overturned in those very same communities.[70] According to Campbell, an intersectional, feminist, and anti-racist socialism had been born out of the strike. Some elements within the NUM also came to emphasise the significance and novelty of women's activism in the strike— Scargill drew attention to the role of women in his speech to the Special Delegate conference that called off the strike on 3 March 1985, and a few days later when addressing the strike supporters assembled in Chesterfield for International Women's Day—and women became woven into the powerful institutional memory of the strike that the NUM continued to maintain within mining communities for decades after 1985.[71] Left-wingers, of course, had their own reasons for depicting the women's support movement in this way: in the difficult Thatcher years, some leftists hoped to bolster faith in the dynamism of the left. Socialist feminists had looked for years for a way to reach more working-class women and invested a good deal of hope in the idea that the strike was it. Uplifting accounts of the strike support movement were also propaganda in the struggle itself, and for feminist supporters, a way of convincing others to give money to a cause associated with a famously masculinist trade union. These imperatives

---

[68] Stead, *Never the Same Again*, 28, 167. See similarly Lynne Segal, *Is the Future Female? Troubled Thoughts on Contemporary Feminism* (London: Virago, 1987), 23.

[69] Stead, *Never the Same Again*, 84.

[70] James Marshall, 'Scargillise the Labour Movement', *Socialist Action*, 22 February 1985, 3, quot. in Pat McIntyre, 'The Response to the 1984-5 Miners' Strike in Durham County: Women, the Labour Party and Community' (unpublished PhD thesis, University of Durham, 1992), 44; Campbell, 'Proletarian Patriarchs', 281–2.

[71] Winterton and Winterton, *Coal, Crisis and Conflict*, 205; Barnsley Women Against Pit Closures, *Women Against Pit Closures, Volume 2* (Barnsley: Barnsley Women Against Pit Closures, 1985), 104.

underlay some of the glowing terms in which the women's support movement was depicted.

Journalists and leftists were not the only ones penning the story of the movement during and immediately after the strike: activist women from coalfield communities were compiling their own accounts, published in major works like Vicky Seddon's collection, *The Cutting Edge*, and in a plethora of short books and pamphlets produced by individual groups.[72] Some of the women involved—particularly the more prominent activists—told the story of the women's movement in triumphant mode. Betty Cook, for example, wrote in the book produced by the Barnsley Miners' Wives Action Group in 1987:

> Traditionally the women were expected to look after their husbands and families, very few were political or active in the trade union and labour movement. They had no involvement in the NUM unless they worked in NCB canteens, or as cleaners and were eligible for NUM membership. This role changed overnight with the start of the '84/'85 strike.[73]

Stories of women standing on picket lines or speaking in public for the first time emphasised the novelty and the liberating nature of the support movement. Books and pamphlets claimed that there was a 'new breed of women' in the coalfields, and that there was 'no going back' for the women involved.[74] Because they usually took the form of collage, however, interspersing writing and interviews with different women, there was space in these books for different perspectives to emerge on questions like relations with the NUM, ideas about 'feminism', or whether the mass of activists wanted to get 'back to normal' after the strike. While some women alluded to a mass politicisation, others suggested a more subtle growth in political interest and questioning, and yet other women insisted that their activism had been motivated purely by the desire to help their husbands and communities—like the activist from Cortonwood who thought women in her group were not 'that political', unlike some in other groups: '[w]e were more for the support, not for the politics'.[75] The books produced by members of the support movement in the aftermath of the strike did not offer a single 'line', but a more complex, multivocal perspective. The overall register, however, was celebratory

---

[72] Seddon, ed., *Cutting Edge*. Activist women's accounts were also included in Beynon, ed., *Digging Deeper* and Raphael Samuel, Barbara Bloomfield, and Guy Boanas, eds., *The Enemy Within: Pit Villages and the Miners' Strike of 1984-5* (London: Routledge & Kegan Paul, 1986). For more on the books produced by women's support groups, see Chapter 8.

[73] Barnsley Miners' Wives Action Group, *We Struggled to Laugh* (Barnsley: Barnsley Miners' Wives Action Group, 1987), 9.

[74] North Yorkshire Women Against Pit Closures, *Strike 84/85* (Leeds: North Yorkshire Women Against Pit Closures, 1985), 5; Barnsley Women Against Pit Closures, *Women Against Pit Closures, Vol. 2*, 87.

[75] Denise Fitzpatrick, Christine M. Nelson, May Cadwallader, and Edith Armitage, *10 Years On and Still Laughing* (Rotherham: Dearne Community Arts, 1994), 5.

and heroic: these were books, after all, produced to commemorate—to write into history—a movement with great achievements to its name; they were also mainly written in the aftermath of defeat, when it was important to many women to save some sense of meaning from the wreckage. The heroic narrative of women's strike activism contains kernels of truth—as do most of the myths we live by—but it was so popular during and after the strike for both personal and political reasons; a full historical account requires us to trace the emergence of this narrative, rather than taking it as the last word on women's experiences in the strike.[76]

If activists and journalists wrote the first draft of history, sociologists and historians soon began revising it. Sociologists often studied not only women activists, but whole coalfield communities, so that while they generally agreed on the significance of the women's support movement to the strike,[77] they also highlighted the importance of other sources of support, not least the income of working wives, the support of family and friends, and social security payments.[78] Sociological studies have also repeatedly emphasised the limits to coalfield women's activism. Jonathan and Ruth Winterton calculated what is probably the most accurate figure: they found that only 4.7 per cent of Yorkshire miners' wives and partners were involved in any form of collective action in support of the strike.[79] Sociologists and historians conducting detailed studies of individual mining communities or regions have also tended to contest the narratives of politicisation, of feminist transformation, and of lasting change in gender roles in the coalfields as a result of the strike, and we tend to concur with their findings. Many scholars have highlighted the fact that a significant proportion of strike activists—and particularly of the instigators of activism—were already politically engaged before the strike began—something that we also found among the activists we interviewed.[80] Feminist scholars have pointed out that the narrative of 'politicisation' has focused on a highly masculine view of what counts as 'political': organising, marching, picketing, public speaking, Labour Party or trade union membership. Jean Spence and Carol Stephenson, based on qualitative interviews in North East England, argued that we should see women's

---

[76] For more on the emergence of the heroic narrative, see Chapter 8.

[77] E.g. Winterton and Winterton, *Coal, Crisis and Conflict*, 128. See Appendix 2 for details of the source base of key sociological studies cited.

[78] Winterton and Winterton, *Coal, Crisis and Conflict*, 132–7; Dennis Warwick and Gary M. Littlejohn, *Coal, Capital and Culture: A Sociological Analysis of Mining Communities in West Yorkshire* (London: Routledge, 1992), 193. See also McIntyre, 'Response to the 1984–5 Miners' Strike'.

[79] Winterton and Winterton, *Coal, Crisis and Conflict*, 122; see also Fiona Measham and Sheila Allen, 'In Defence of Home and Hearth? Families, Friendships and Feminism in Mining Communities', *Journal of Gender Studies*, 3 (1994), 31–45, at 34; McIntyre, 'Response to the 1984–5 Miners' Strike', 49.

[80] Jean Spence and Carol Stephenson, '"Side by Side with Our Men?" Women's Activism, Community, and Gender in the 1984–1985 British Miners' Strike', *International Labor and Working-Class History*, 75 (2009), 68–84, at 73; Spence and Stephenson, 'Female Involvement in the Miners' Strike 1984–1985: Trajectories of Activism', *Sociological Research Online*, 12 (2007), 1–11, paras 3.4–3.5; Allen and Measham, 'In Defence', 39.

interpersonal and emotional work—before, during, and after the strike—as marking a significant continuity in women's roles. In this sense, they argued, the narrative of 'politicisation of women' obscures as much as it reveals: what was going on during the strike was a 'personalisation of the political rather than a politicisation of the personal'.[81]

The narrative of 'feminist transformation' has been challenged from two directions. First, sociologists have contested the idea that the women's support movement was struggling *against*, as much as *alongside*, the men of the NUM, and that its members were thus aiming at—and succeeding in—carving out a newly liberated role for themselves. Penny Green, for example, concluded that though the women who supported the strike in Ollerton, Nottinghamshire, did 'experience and fight sexism', they did it 'within the context of a united struggle' with the men.[82] Many scholars have also critiqued the narrative of 'feminist transformation' by highlighting the hostilities, tensions, and ambiguities in coalfield women's feelings towards feminist supporters from outside the coalfields.[83] Meg Allen's study of strike activists mounted a challenge to this revisionist position, emphasising that activists who were 'intensely involved'—women like Betty Cook in Yorkshire and Hefina Headon in South Wales—did experience a 'personal transformation': the experience of activism '"shook" them up, it changed their perceptions and beliefs, they did things they never could believe they would be able to do'.[84] But Allen did not contest the fact that the numbers of women who became so deeply involved were very small. Finally, the narrative of transformation in gender roles has also been challenged by a number of scholars. Dennis Warwick and Gary Littlejohn's study of four mining communities in West Yorkshire found that 'a highly gendered division of labour still exist[ed]' in 1986-7, and that such changes as had occurred were likely to be the effect of long-term trends in the domestic division of labour, particularly the trend towards

---

[81] Spence and Stephenson, 'Female Involvement', 4.5. See also Allen and Measham, 'In Defence', 40.

[82] Penny Green, *The Enemy Without: Policing and Class Consciousness in the Miners' Strike* (Milton Keynes: Open University Press, 1990), 190. See also Peter Gibbon, 'Analysing the Miners' Strike of 1984-5', *Economy and Society*, 17 (1988), 139-94, at 183; Peter Gibbon and David Steyne, *Thurcroft. A Village and the Miners' Strike: An Oral History by the People of Thurcroft* (Nottingham: Spokesman, 1986); Winterton and Winterton, *Coal, Crisis and Conflict*, 122; McIntyre, 'Response to the 1984-5 Miners' Strike', 111 ff., 119; John Murphy, 'Community and Struggle: A Sociological Study of a Mining Village in the 1980s' (unpublished PhD thesis, University of Warwick, 1989), 131; Monica Shaw and Mave Mundy, 'Complexities of Class and Gender Relations: Recollections of Women Active in the 1984-5 Miners' Strike', *Capital & Class*, 29 (2005), 151-74, at 163.

[83] Shaw and Mundy, 'Complexities of Class and Gender Relations', 162-3; see also Monica Shaw, 'Women in Protest and Beyond: Greenham Common and Mining Support Groups' (unpublished PhD thesis, University of Durham, 1993); Keith Gildart, *North Wales Miners, 1945-1996: A Fragile Unity* (Cardiff: University of Wales Press, 2001), 176, 185-6; Davies, 'Not Just Supporting'.

[84] Meg Allen, 'Carrying on the Strike: The Politics of Women Against Pit Closures' (unpublished PhD thesis, University of Manchester, 2001), 191, 23. See also, for somewhat anti-revisionist views of activism, Hywel Francis, *History on Our Side: Wales and the 1984-5 Miners' Strike* (London: Lawrence & Wishart, 2015), 20-1, 31-2; Steffan Morgan, '"Stand by your Man": Wives, Women and Feminism during the Miners' Strike 1984-85', *Llafur*, 9 (2005), 59-71.

women entering the labour force, itself a result of a confluence of forces, not least among them deindustrialisation.[85] Many of the women activists interviewed in the North East in the early 2000s by Monica Shaw and Mave Mundy felt that changes in gender relations since 1985 were caused by 'labour-market changes and the loss of the pits, rather than activism in the strike'.[86] Narratives of women's 'transformation' in the strike were thus overblown, and relied on an outdated stereotype of miners' wives as uniquely downtrodden. As with many of the arguments advanced about women and the miners' strike, the reality was more complex.

The Book

This book advances a number of key arguments. We start by describing the world of mining communities on the eve of the strike. Where mining villages had once been 'a world apart', by 1984, mining areas and mining families were in many important ways similar to other working-class areas and working-class families. While there were still some 'traditional' pit villages, built around and centred on a working colliery, many miners now travelled to work and lived outside of such communities. Mining families had been impacted by many of the forces that had tended to develop a more national culture in the postwar period, like the development of the welfare state, and of national media. Mining families were more likely to live in tied housing and less likely to be owner-occupiers than other working-class households, and they were also more likely to live in houses rather than flats. But they were not, as they had been in the interwar period, likely to be living in poverty and in substandard housing. The children of miners had similar educational experiences to other working-class children, and ages of marriage and childbearing were only slightly lower. Married women's work—which had been rare in mining communities before 1945—was now common, though less so for women living in the most isolated mining settlements, where it was harder to access jobs. All this would have implications for experiences in the strike and for levels of solidarity. Many middle-class outsiders to mining communities, however, still relied on outdated stereotypes about mining communities as isolated bastions of patriarchy in 1984, and this, too, would have implications for perceptions of coalfield women's activism in the strike.

The book gives the first scholarly overview of the women's support movement across England, Scotland, and Wales, drawing on much of the excellent sociological and historical research that has been conducted on individual

---

[85] Warwick and Littlejohn, *Coal, Capital and Culture*, 194, 199. See also Allen and Measham, 'In Defence', 41–2; David Waddington, Maggie Wykes, and Chas Critcher, *Split at the Seams? Community, Continuity and Change after the 1984–5 Coal Dispute* (Milton Keynes: Open University Press, 1991), 28; Davies, 'Not Just Supporting', 206; Spence and Stephenson, 'Side by Side'.

[86] Shaw and Mundy, 'Complexities of Class and Gender', 167.

communities and regions. The support movement involved a minority of coalfield women—probably around 5 per cent of miners' wives and partners. A significant proportion, particularly of the instigators of the movement, had pre-existing political experience, and these women were also likely to be the most involved, and to take on the most 'political' of the jobs, such as speaking at meetings, or going on picket lines. Most groups, particularly those that formed early in the strike, also contained some women who were not part of mining families, but drawn into activism by their political principles. Groups were heterogeneous: food provision was the main activity for almost all groups, though this was sometimes via soup kitchens, sometimes food parcels, and sometimes vouchers. The numbers of women involved were usually low, somewhere between a handful and several dozen, though a few groups reached larger numbers. From the summer of 1984, a nation-wide umbrella organisation, National Women Against Pit Closures (NWAPC), also developed, with the aspiration of connecting groups all across the country—though in practice, not all groups joined, and some were not even particularly aware of NWAPC. The national organisation was started by a small group of deeply political women, several of whom were close to Arthur Scargill. Their personal and ideological connections to Scargill would be one source of tension within the movement, and would also make NWAPC a pawn within intra-NUM power struggles. Nevertheless, after the sequestration of the NUM's assets in October 1984, NWAPC would prove invaluable as a channel for donations, and thus helped keep the strike—and the NUM itself—going. NWAPC continued to organise for several years after the end of the strike, though most local support groups disbanded almost immediately, unsurprisingly given that they saw their purpose as being nothing more or less than supporting miners and their families in the dispute.

The 'heroic' narrative about women's activism—which held that women's organisation was spontaneous, widespread, and transformative, challenging the traditional gender order in the coalfields—was cemented very early on in the strike. As we have seen, it was powerful and widely promulgated partly for political reasons: it was extremely useful in soliciting support from many on the left, including trade unionists, but also feminists, who might well otherwise have seen the NUM as a masculinist and even misogynist trade union they had little interest in supporting. The heroic narrative also served several purposes in the aftermath of the strike, as a tool of political education and inspiration, a means of maintaining bonds between activists in the dispute, and a way of salvaging a sense of achievement from the ruins of defeat. This discourse, which has become culturally dominant, profoundly shaped how some activist women recounted their lives in our interviews. Many drew on the narrative of transformation in the strike as a resource to frame their own life stories, a way to show how they became the women they are today. This narrative was never entirely hegemonic, however, and other interviewees drew on alternative discursive resources to tell their stories, framing themselves, for example, not as heroic strike activists but as stoic working-class wives and mothers who were able to take good care of their families in times of externally-imposed hardship, or as 'respectable', self-reliant families opposed to industrial militancy.

Like other academics who have written on the subject, we argue against the notion of a 'feminist' transformation in the coalfields during or after the strike. Some women's groups experienced conflict with local NUM branches over the activities they wanted to undertake, but the majority of activists saw their goal as supporting the union's struggle, and had little engagement with the (feminist) politics of women's autonomous organisation. In many ways groups were a product of the traditional gender order, with women taking on a supportive role, backing their menfolk, backing the union, and focusing on the provision of food. Even picketing—widely mentioned as the most novel and radical of women's activities in the strike—often relied on traditional gender roles to give it its symbolic power. As we show, picketing women often implied that their very presence on the picket lines demonstrated a rupture in the normal order of things, implying that working miners had forfeited their masculinity and forced women into action. For some women—though doubtless a minority, even among the activists—strike activism *did* propel them into new roles. More commonly, it instigated more subtle shifts in women's sense of self. In addition, the heroic narrative of transformation became, in itself, a resource for some women to understand their own experiences, and thus itself came to play a role in bringing about further changes in women's self-understanding. But for the vast majority of mining families, any changes seen during the strike in areas like the domestic division of labour disappeared soon after the end of the dispute, with both women and men keen to get 'back to normal'. The media spotlight that suddenly shone on mining communities during the strike certainly helped to create the impression of change, particularly as so many outsiders brought with them outdated ideas about what 'traditional' mining communities were like. But changes in gender roles were occurring gradually before 1984 and continued after 1985 in coalfield communities, when they were given further impetus by the sharp deindustrialisation that hit the coalfields in the decade after the loss of the strike.

The book also moves away from the tendency in accounts of the strike to focus on activist women, examining the experiences, attitudes, and decisions of all women in mining families caught up in the strike, including those who did not support, or even actively opposed, the dispute. It is important to recognise the messiness and ambiguity of women's attitudes: it can be difficult to put women into the binary categories of supporter or opponent of the strike. Many (including activists) fluctuated in their feelings. Some who initially opposed the strike subsequently became committed supporters. Others supported their husbands' decisions to come out, but never agreed with the strike. So why did so many women offer their support to striking husbands? Women supported their husbands, in the main, not because they were domineering patriarchs who demanded obedience, but because women knew their husbands had little choice but to go on strike in majority-striking coalfields, and because they shared dominant cultural understandings of marriage as teamwork. Many women also saw their economic interests as tied to their husbands', and linked to the success of the strike. Furthermore, community was an important factor pushing men to come out and stay out, and women to support their menfolk. Communities provided moral and practical support, but could also inflict serious social sanctions on strikebreakers and their families. The idea of being part of a mining community was an important resource for many strikers, giving the dispute larger psychic dimensions stretching into the past and the future. Strike activists, both men and women, worked hard to construct a moral economy during the strike which demanded that mining families back the NUM to honour the sacrifices of mining communities past and to defend the interests of future generations and future communities. The importance of community to support for the strike, however, gave a heightened significance to the fact that many miners in the 1980s did not live in 'traditional' mining communities: such families were more likely to feel distant from the arguments for the strike, and from the support and coercion communities could offer. Finally, our research shows how important emotions could be in sustaining the strike: the feelings generated by collective action—whether the angry release of shouting on picket lines, or the joyous enactment of solidarity on marches—buoyed up and sustained supporters of the strike when their spirits flagged.

In understanding how striking families kept going for as long as they did, we revise the centrality of the women's support groups. While undoubtedly highly significant, both in the practical support they organised, and in the proof they offered that not all coalfield women opposed the strike, support groups were far from the main source of sustenance for most mining families. Their help probably reached around 60 per cent of miners' households. One factor that meant many mining families were reluctant to take help from support groups (and sometimes from the state, too) was the stigma associated with taking 'charity' or 'handouts', of being a 'scrounger' rather than self-reliant. For many mining households, support from family and friends was just as important as support group help, as were social security benefits and other forms of support from local authorities, and—less happily—taking on debt. Perhaps the most underestimated factor in maintaining strike solidarity was women's paid labour; this has probably been underplayed in part because of the strength of stereotypes about miners' wives being 'trapped in the kitchen' before the strike. If these stereotypes had been true, the strike simply would not have been able to last for the length of time that it did. Substantial numbers of miners' wives were in paid labour, or took on jobs during the strike, and their wages were vital in keeping many families afloat.

Finally, this book is the first study of women's experiences in the strike to include the voices of women who opposed the strike, and whose husbands or fathers worked through the dispute or returned to work early. Some of these women explained that neither they nor their family members had opposed the strike, but that by the final months, they felt that what was being asked of strikers was too much: their families were desperate and this simply overrode the demands of the union. Others had never supported the strike ideologically or politically: they backed their husbands in joining the action because they knew the consequences that men would face at work and families would face in the community if they broke the strike. However, these women felt that in the final months, when the mass return to work was evident, the calculus changed, and it was no longer necessary to go along with the striking majority: it was time to make decisions for themselves. In areas where working miners were the majority, some women drew on the same rhetoric of community as strikers did, and deployed arguments about the importance of trade union democracy, in order to endorse their position of opposition to the strike. In the majority-working area of Nottinghamshire, some women even gathered into their own groups to publicly protest against flying pickets from other areas coming to their villages. These groups were, ironically, a mirror-image of the women's support movement—though much smaller and less significant. These women sometimes found it hard to articulate their stories in their interviews, because of how far they diverged from the 'heroic' narrative of women's support for the strike, which has been so culturally dominant, and because of the stigma still associated in many mining areas with 'scabbing'. But understanding their feelings about the dispute is vital if we are to understand not only why the strike remained strong in so many places for so long, but also why solidarity ultimately broke down.

The book tells the story of the strike in chronological form: we begin, in Chapter 2, by setting the scene with an account of the lives of coalfield women and communities in the forty years before the strike. Four chapters follow, examining the early, confusing months of the dispute; the long summer, when the strike seemed winnable to many and when activism solidified around the country; the difficult run-up to Christmas, when more and more miners returned to work, and, finally, the early months of 1985, when the flood back to work swelled and the failure of the strike began to seem inevitable. Two final chapters trace, first, the aftermath of the strike, and how it impacted women—whether or not they had been caught up in activism—and, second, how the strike has been remembered, and the impact of the end of coal upon communities.

The story of women and the strike is a messy and complicated one. Every single person affected by the dispute has their own story to tell; we can never hope to represent all of these in one short book. We have had to leave out many of the fascinating tales that we heard in the course of this research; there will be many more that we do not even know about. The strike remains capable of generating enormous emotion and political passion, and we have been conscious of the burdens of history as we have written this book, of trying to do justice to the stories that the women we interviewed so generously shared with us. These are not events that either of the authors lived through; they are 'history' to us in a way that they are not to those who were there. Nevertheless, as we became absorbed in the research for this book, we began to feel immersed in the world of the strike, to understand something of the hardship and the passion and the drama (and sometimes the mundanity) of it all; to glimpse something of the texture of the lived experience of those who went through it; of how it did—and did not—shape women's understandings of themselves. What follows in these pages is our attempt to convey all this as we have come to understand it.

2
Before the Strike

21 February 1983

On 21 February 1983, twenty-seven men descended 1,500 feet below ground at the Tymawr-Lewis Merthyr colliery, in Rhondda, South Wales, and began a sit-in. The National Coal Board (NCB) had announced the closure of the pit, which employed 539 people: the occupiers were determined to contest the closure.[1] Two days later, the South Wales National Union of Mineworkers (NUM) decided to ballot on a strike, and soon the entire Area was out.[2] A national ballot was proposed, and many expected it to return a mandate for a national strike. NUM President Arthur Scargill and other militants were warning that if the closure of Merthyr was allowed to go ahead without a fight, many more pits would soon be slated for closure. A national miners' strike—the first since the strike of 1974 that brought down Ted Heath's Tory government—threatened. South Wales sent flying pickets to Yorkshire to urge miners there to vote 'yes'.[3] But the national vote was overwhelmingly against.[4] Only two areas passed the 55 per cent threshold for action: South Wales and Kent (both on 68 per cent). Yorkshire, Scargill's own power base, fell 1 per cent short. Nationally, only 39 per cent voted to strike: precisely the same proportion that had voted to take action in the previous national ballot, in October 1982.[5] Then, too, Scargill had argued for strike action, and then, too, he had lost. On 14 March 1983, the Welsh miners returned to work, and the spectre of a national miners' strike receded.[6]

Why had the ballot failed? On 21 March, Jean McCrindle, a lecturer at Northern College, a trade union college near Barnsley, in Yorkshire, wrote to Arthur Scargill (who had been involved in the College's governance) with some ideas. McCrindle had conducted a straw poll of twenty miners attending courses at the college, mostly from Yorkshire and mostly under 30. The miners attending Northern College tended to be at the very least politically aware, if not outright militants, and McCrindle's sample set out a series of reasons why they thought

---

[1] Tim Jones, 'Close Result Likely in Welsh Pit Strike Call', *The Times*, 25 February 1983.
[2] Tim Jones, 'Strike Ballot by Welsh Miners', *The Times*, 24 February 1983.
[3] Jean McCrindle, 'The National Organisation of Women Against Pit Closures in the Miners' Strike of 1984–5' (unpublished PhD thesis, Oxford Brookes, 2001), 71.
[4] Paul Routledge, 'Miners Vote "No" and Push Union into Policy Crisis', *The Times*, 9 March 1983.
[5] Tim Jones, 'Anger and Despair at Doomed Pit', *The Times*, 11 March 1983.
[6] Tim Jones, 'Bitter Strikers Set to Go Back', *The Times*, 12 March 1983.

other miners at their pits might have voted 'no'. At the top of the list: fear that a dispute was unwinnable, and the divisive nature of the incentive scheme (introduced in 1977–8), which had delivered high wages for miners in high-productivity coalfields like Nottinghamshire.[7] Then came several other suggestions:

> Younger men with families were worried about a protracted strike given mortgages, cars, holidays, etc...
>
> The break-up of pit communities means less loyalty to the Union from both younger men and women who no longer identify with the 'collective ethos' of previous generations...
>
> women...cannot be relied on automatically to support their husbands' decisions.[8]

McCrindle suggested to Scargill that at the very least, the NUM should actively include women in their communications strategy. One miner had told McCrindle that at the rally held in Sheffield in October 1982 to boost support for a strike vote, 'women connected to the mining communities were not encouraged to attend and some were actually turned away from the door'.[9] There were some 4,000 people at this rally, but one of those present said she only saw 'maybe a dozen or so women'.[10] McCrindle, an activist of long pedigree with connections across the old and new lefts—including as an early member of the women's liberation movement—told Scargill, 'I know you may think this is insignificant but maybe it does have some bearing on the problems the Union now face.'[11]

Jean McCrindle was not the only woman urging Scargill to take miners' wives seriously. In the summer of 1983, Nell Myers, a journalist on the NUM paper *The Miner*, and Scargill's personal assistant (and, after the strike, his long-term partner), raised the issue too. She started by noting a 'disturbing fact':

> a decline or diminishing of 'traditional' support for the Union from the mineworker's most immediate source of physical and emotional nourishment: the family. In the ballot campaigns of October, 1982, women married to miners captured media space in, for example, Nottinghamshire, with their own

---

[7] On the incentive scheme, see William Ashworth, *The History of the British Coal Industry. Volume 5, 1946–1982: The Nationalized Industry* (Oxford: Clarendon Press, 1986), 373–4.
[8] Letter from Jean McCrindle to Arthur Scargill, 21 March 1983, 7JMC/A/22/07, papers of Jean McCrindle, Women's Library@LSE, London (hereafter McCrindle papers).
[9] Ibid.
[10] Beatrix Campbell, *Wigan Pier Revisited: Poverty and Politics in the Eighties* (London: Virago, 1984), 112.
[11] Letter from Jean McCrindle to Arthur Scargill, 21 March 1983, 7JMC/A/22/07, McCrindle papers.

campaign *against* the NUM: their husbands, they claimed, were earning good money; their jobs were safe. 'Go away', they more or less said to the Union— 'leave us alone.'[12]

Myers asked, '[h]ow deep, how widespread is this sort of feeling?' Neither she nor Jean McCrindle knew, but they wanted to find out.

With this in mind, in January 1984 McCrindle led a survey of women in pit villages near Northern College. Though the survey was small, the results were not hopeful. Only one woman expressed complete solidarity with the NUM, and she was married to an activist NUM branch official. Most disliked Scargill and Thatcher equally. McCrindle wrote in her diary that the interviews found '[o]utright anger amongst most wives about the overtime ban', which the NUM had introduced the previous October in order to run coal stocks down in preparation for a possible future strike. Some families had had to cancel mortgages and holidays because of the ban. Women, McCrindle wrote, 'don't care that the industry is closing; they think they never win anyway and that the Union is useless. Scargill is anathema.'[13] Right-wing media continued to publicise anti-NUM women's feelings: in the same month that McCrindle was conducting her survey, the *Daily Mail* found one miner's wife, a mother of three, calling for Scargill to be sued for lost miners' wages: 'we had a rotten Christmas because of this man', she said.[14] Thus, in early 1984, Myers and McCrindle worried that, under the influence of women's growing independence from their husbands, consumerism, home-ownership, and the break-up of pit communities, the 'traditional' support women had given to their menfolk in coal strikes was waning. Were they right to be concerned? In this chapter, we examine the contours of 'traditional' mining communities pre-1939, and survey the changes that affected miners, their wives, families, and communities in the decades after 1945, in order to answer that question.

The 'Traditional' Mining Community

Life in nineteenth-century mining communities has been summed up as: '[d]anger and drudgery; male solidarity and female oppression'.[15] Unlike the manual workers swept into Britain's large towns and cities by industrialisation,

---

[12] Nell Myers, 'Notes for Hilary Cave, and All Members of the Campaign Committee: Family and Community Involvement in the Fight to Save and Expand the Coal Industry', 2 August 1983, 7JMC/A/22/01, McCrindle papers.
[13] McCrindle, 'National Organisation of Women Against Pit Closures', 74.
[14] 'Scargill Should be Sued for Overtime, Says an Angry Wife', *Daily Mail*, 10 January 1984.
[15] Linda McDowell and Doreen Massey, 'A Woman's Place?', in Doreen Massey and John Allen, eds., *Geography Matters! A Reader* (Cambridge: Cambridge University Press, 1984), 128–47, at 129.

miners often lived in small, semi-rural communities, near the deposits of coal they worked. They frequently lived in tied housing provided by colliery owners, and the quality of this and of much other housing in mining districts was very low: in 1919 the Sankey report called the houses in some mining areas 'a reproach to our civilisation', and there were only limited improvements in the following two decades.[16] For most of the interwar period, mining areas also had an 'unenviable reputation' for poverty.[17] After 1920-1, miners' real wages per shift fell substantially, only beginning to rise in a sustained—though modest—way in the mid-1930s. Unemployment was at least as significant as a cause of poverty: from 1928 to 1936, 24 per cent or more of British coalminers were partly or wholly unemployed.[18] It was not surprising that George Orwell headed to mining districts to write *The Road to Wigan Pier*.[19] Paid labour for women was often scarce: women were banned from working underground by the Mines and Collieries Act 1842, and had been excluded from pit work in some parts of the country for much longer.[20] In 1921, almost half of all miners lived in areas dominated by mining (that is, areas with 53-78 per cent of adult men employed in the industry), and in almost all these areas, the female proportion of the labour force was less than half of the national average of 26 per cent.[21] The daily work of a miner's wife was all-consuming: there was a constant battle against dirt and pollution, and meals and hot water to wash in had to be prepared for husbands and sons as they returned from shifts. In 1926, only 2 per cent of miners in Britain had access to pithead baths.[22]

In part due to the low levels of employment of married women, and the availability of tied housing, in the early twentieth century miners' wives married young in comparison with other working-class women, and miners had the highest fertility of any occupational group in the country.[23] The 1911 census actually separated miners out into their own, special social class—Class VII—because of their distinctively high fertility.[24] Miners forged strong bonds in the face of the dangers of working underground, and they socialised above ground in sex-segregated leisure activities: sport, betting, working men's clubs, miners' welfares, and pubs. The stereotype of the nineteenth- and early twentieth-century

---

[16] Barry Supple, *The History of the British Coal Industry. Volume 4, 1913-1946: The Political Economy of Decline* (Oxford: Clarendon Press, 1987), 457.
[17] Ibid., 448. [18] Ibid., 443-8.
[19] George Orwell, *The Road to Wigan Pier* (London: Victor Gollancz, 1937).
[20] Jane Humphries, 'Protective Legislation, the Capitalist State, and Working-Class Men: The Case of the 1842 Mines Regulation Act', *Feminist Review*, 7 (1981), 1-35, at 7.
[21] Supple, *History of the British Coal Industry*. Vol. 4, 480. In Nottinghamshire and Lancashire, women's employment in the principal mining towns was similar to the national average, however.
[22] Ibid., 474.
[23] Simon Szreter, *Fertility, Class and Gender in Britain, 1860-1940* (Cambridge: Cambridge University Press, 1996), figure 7.1, 312, 354.
[24] Simon Szreter, 'The Genesis of the Registrar-General's Social Classification of Occupations', *British Journal of Sociology*, 35 (1984), 522-46, at 533-4.

miner was a patriarch, and the stereotypical mining community was tight-knit and insular.²⁵ The ideal-type of mining community was thought in the mid-twentieth century to be a key reason for the high levels of industrial militancy found in collieries, and miners were seen as the 'shock troops' or 'Praetorian guard' of the labour movement.²⁶ The Miners' Federation of Great Britain (MFGB) was an organisation of men, as was its successor, the NUM; the Labour Party was also, in mining areas as elsewhere, dominated by men, though from the early twentieth century, small numbers of women *did* get involved in labour movement politics in the coalfields—often in organisations like the Women's Co-operative Guild, or Labour Party Women's Sections.²⁷

Britain's coalfields were highly differentiated. North East England saw the earliest development of an extensive mining industry, in the eighteenth century, while the Kent coalfield only opened up in the interwar period.²⁸ Different coalfields mined different types of coal, for different markets, and had different work practices and trade union traditions.²⁹ While some miners were 'archetypal proletarians', others saw themselves as 'independent colliers'.³⁰ Mining communities were not all the same, despite the stereotype. But that stereotype of 'traditional' mining communities—as tight-knit, patriarchal, insular, and militant—persisted after 1945, and was perhaps even more deeply entrenched in works of sociology from the 1950s and 1960s. In 1966, David Lockwood described the miner as the prime example of the 'proletarian' worker, embedded in a working-class community, and holding an oppositional ('them v. us') view of class.³¹ Lockwood was heavily influenced by the classic community study *Coal is Our*

---

²⁵ See e.g., Huw Beynon and Terry Austrin, *Masters and Servants: Class and Patronage in the Making of a Labour Organisation: The Durham Miners and the English Political Tradition* (London: Rivers Oram Press, 1994), 154–84.
²⁶ Clark Kerr and Abraham Siegel, 'The Interindustry Propensity to Strike: An International Comparison', in Arthur Kornhauser, Robert Dubin, and Arthur M. Ross, eds., *Industrial Conflict* (New York: McGraw-Hill, 1954), 189–212; Gareth Rees, 'Coal, Crisis and Conflict: The 1984–85 Miners' Strike in Yorkshire', *Sociology*, 27 (1993), 307–12, at 307; Roy Gregory, *The Miners and British Politics, 1906–1914* (Oxford: Oxford University Press, 1968), 178.
²⁷ Pamela M. Graves, *Labour Women: Women in British Working-Class Politics, 1918–1939* (Cambridge: Cambridge University Press, 1994); Valerie Gordon Hall, 'Contrasting Female Identities: Women in Coal Mining Communities in Northumberland, England, 1900–1939', *Journal of Women's History*, 13 (2001), 107–31.
²⁸ Michael W. Flinn, David Stoker, and Roy A. Church, *The History of the British Coal Industry. Volume 2, 1700–1830: The Industrial Revolution* (Oxford: Clarendon Press, 1984), table 1.2, 26; Alan Booth, 'The Economy of Kent: An Overview', in Nigel Yates, ed., *Kent in the Twentieth Century* (Woodbridge: Boydell Press, 2001), 27–58, at 30 ff.
²⁹ See Martin Daunton, 'Down the Pit: Work in the Great Northern and South Wales Coalfields, 1870–1914', *Economic History Review*, 34 (1981), 578–97; Supple, *History of the British Coal Industry. Vol. 4*, 450–1; Alan Campbell, Nina Fishman, and David Howell, *Miners, Unions and Politics, 1910–47* (Aldershot: Scholar Press, 1996).
³⁰ Royden Harrison, ed., *Independent Collier: The Coal Miner as Archetypal Proletarian Reconsidered* (Hassocks: Harvester Press, 1978).
³¹ David Lockwood, 'Sources of Variation in Working-Class Images of Society', *Sociological Review*, 14 (1966), 249–67. See also Martin Bulmer, 'Sociological Models of the Mining Community', *Sociological Review*, 23 (1975), 61–92, which sets out an ideal-type of mining communities at 85–8.

Life, which examined the Yorkshire pit village of 'Ashton' (Featherstone) in West Yorkshire, in the 1950s. The study, whose findings were echoed in other sociological studies of mining published around the same time, painted a picture of families—and, indeed, of an entire community—profoundly divided by gender.[32] Husbands and wives were supposed to move 'in different spheres'; to live 'separate, and... secret, lives'.[33] Marriage was more often a contract than an intimate relationship, and few married women worked outside the home.[34] Women grumbled during strikes that the men's actions were 'determined by quite other considerations than those of their families' welfare', but they did not defy their husbands, instead supporting them against the common 'enemy'.[35]

Yet *Coal is Our Life* should not be taken as the last word on mining communities in the 1950s. When Dennis Warwick and Gary Littlejohn returned to Featherstone in the late 1970s and 1980s, they noted that the earlier study had already been subject to sociological criticism.[36] One of their interviewees, a trade unionist and local Labour councillor, complained that the earlier researchers had come with 'firmly fixed stereotypes' and 'preconceived ideas', and naturally found what they were looking for: '[t]he place was represented as a cultural desert, full of drunken, wife-beating miners who only thought of beer, baccy and betting'.[37] *Coal is Our Life* almost certainly exaggerated the 'traditionalism' of the community. However, the book quickly became a 'foundational text' of postwar sociology, and was still influential decades later.[38] The assumption that coalfield communities were static places led, in fact, to a remarkable dearth of sociological studies of these communities in the years between the 1950s and the 1984–5 strike.[39] But the idea that mining communities were untouched by social change in these decades is highly misleading.

Social Change in Mining Areas after 1945

Changes in the Mining Industry

Britain's mines were nationalised on 1 January 1947. The Attlee government argued that 'the nation's most precious raw material' had been 'floundering

---

[32] Norman Dennis, Fernando Henriques, and Clifford Slaughter, *Coal is Our Life: An Analysis of a Yorkshire Mining Community* (London: Eyre & Spottiswoode, 1956). For other sociological/quasi-sociological statements along the same lines, see: Kerr and Siegel, 'Inter-Industry Propensity to Strike'; Ferdynand Zweig, *Men in the Pits* (London: Victor Gollancz, 1949); Mark Benney, *Charity Main: A Coalfield Chronicle* (London: George Allen & Unwin, 1946).
[33] Dennis et al., *Coal is Our Life*, 170, 228.   [34] Ibid., 228 and passim.   [35] Ibid., 227.
[36] Dennis Warwick and Gary M. Littlejohn, *Coal, Capital and Culture: A Sociological Analysis of Mining Communities in West Yorkshire* (London: Routledge, 1992), 31.
[37] Ibid., 32.
[38] Tim Strangleman, 'Mining a Productive Seam? The Coal Industry, Community and Sociology', *Contemporary British History*, 32 (2018), 18–38, at 19.
[39] Rees, 'Coal, Crisis and Conflict'.

chaotically under the ownership of many hundreds of independent companies'; nationalisation would bring 'great economies' by modernising technology and rationalising labour.[40] Britain now had a developmental state concerned to build up the national economy, and coal was vital to this project: it was used to heat houses and water, cook, drive trains and steam ships, generate electricity, produce town gas, power industry, and smelt iron. The new NCB was responsible for providing this coal, and, along with a new Coal Industry Social Welfare Organisation (CISWO), for ensuring the welfare of miners, providing pithead baths, medical facilities, canteens, and much else.[41] The industry became safer—the rate of fatal injury was cut in half in the 1950s and 1960s, in comparison with the 1920s and 1930s—and a new pension scheme was established.[42]

Three trends shaped the mining industry after nationalisation: mechanisation, rationalisation, and contraction. The NCB immediately set about closing small, unproductive pits, transferring miners who wanted to remain in the industry to larger ones, and investing in new technology, boosting productivity, and allowing output to expand between 1947 and 1958 despite a small fall in the workforce.[43] More serious contraction set in in the late 1950s, when oil and then gas and nuclear became more attractive sources of energy for many purposes. More pits began to close, and the workforce was concentrated in larger and more productive coalfields and pits (see Table 2.1). The 'central' coalfields (Yorkshire, Nottinghamshire, and Derbyshire), oriented towards the domestic market and producing coal ideally suited to electricity generation, did relatively well. Nottinghamshire lost only 778 mining jobs between 1947 and 1974.[44] The 'peripheral' coalfields saw much more significant decline. In Scotland, employment fell from 86,000 in 1957 to just 36,000 in 1967.[45]

The bargain between the miners and the state in the 1950s and 1960s was that though job losses would occur, those miners who wanted to remain in the industry would be offered transfers to other collieries; the state would guarantee full employment, and would encourage the growth of other industries to replace mining jobs. The NUM leadership, schooled in the hard lessons of the interwar period with its strikes, lockouts, and dole queues, was deeply invested in making a

---

[40] Labour Party General Election Manifesto, 1945, quot. in Ewan Gibbs, *Coal Country: The Meaning and Memory of Deindustrialization in Postwar Scotland* (London: University of London Press, 2021), 26.

[41] Jim Phillips, *Scottish Coal Miners in the Twentieth Century* (Edinburgh: Edinburgh University Press, 2019), 28–9.

[42] Ibid., 81, 85, 22.

[43] 'Historical Coal Data: Coal Production, Availability and Consumption 1853 to 2020', Department for Business, Energy & Industrial Strategy, 22 January 2013: https://www.gov.uk/government/statistical-data-sets/historical-coal-data-coal-production-availability-and-consumption.

[44] Jay Emery, 'Belonging, Memory and History in the North Nottinghamshire Coalfield', *Journal of Historical Geography*, 59 (2018), 77–89, at 82; Royce Turner, 'Post-War Pit Closures', *Political Quarterly*, 56 (1985), 167–74, at 167.

[45] Phillips, *Scottish Coal Miners*, 31.

Table 2.1 Long-term decline of coal mining

Year	Collieries	Employment (000s)	Output (million tonnes)
1947	958	704	187
1957	850	699	213
1967	483	456	177
1977	238	242	108
1987	101	115	90
1997	15	8	39

Source: Katy Bennett, Huw Beynon, and Ray Hudson, *Coalfields Regeneration: Dealing with the Consequences of Industrial Decline* (Bristol: Policy Press, 2000), 3.

success of nationalisation and accepted the bargain.[46] As a result, the link between pit and pit village was increasingly broken, and more and more miners travelled to pits, either in buses, often laid on by the NCB, or, as car ownership came within the reach of more families, in their own vehicles. By 1982, there was just one 'traditional' pit village in Scotland (Polmaise, in Stirlingshire).[47] Many pit villages had been isolated and inaccessible: when a new road to Ludworth, in County Durham, opened in 1927, a county councillor remarked that the village had, until now, been like the South African town of Mafeking, where British troops were besieged for seven months in the Second Boer War: 'all hemmed in with no road out and a bad road in'.[48] The increasing mobility offered by buses and cars thus made a significant difference to the lives of many miners and their families.[49]

In the postwar decades, miners also migrated across the country from contracting to expanding coalfields like Nottinghamshire and North Yorkshire. This was nothing new: coalfield communities had a long history of migration, sometimes over quite long ranges. Booming areas—such as South Wales in the late nineteenth century, and Nottinghamshire and Kent in the interwar period—sucked in miners from other regions, and workers from other industries.[50] Irish miners were found in many pits, and from the late nineteenth century there were settlements of Germans and Poles in certain parts of the Scottish coalfields, and of Spaniards and Italians in parts of South Wales.[51] After 1945, further groups of migrants joined the workforce, including Black migrants from the Caribbean, who particularly gravitated towards Nottinghamshire, and Poles who came to Britain

[46] Gibbs, *Coal Country*.
[47] Jim Phillips, *Collieries, Communities and the Miners' Strike in Scotland 1984-85* (Manchester: Manchester University Press, 2012), 46.
[48] Margaret Hedley, *Women of the Durham Coal Field in the 20th Century: Hannah's Daughter* (Cheltenham: The History Press, 2020), 146.
[49] For discussion of the impact of car-ownership and mobility, see Simon Gunn, 'People and the Car: The Expansion of Automobility in Urban Britain, c.1955-70', *Social History*, 38 (2013), 220-37.
[50] Supple, *History of the British Coal Industry. Vol. 4*, 488.
[51] Roy Church, *The History of the British Coal Industry. Volume 3, 1830-1913: Victorian Pre-Eminence* (Oxford: Clarendon Press, 1986), 224.

during and immediately after the Second World War, who were directed to work in mining and other essential industries facing labour shortages.[52] Flux, rather than stasis, was often a defining characteristic of coalfield areas.

By the 1970s, Britain was no longer run on coal in the way it had been in 1945, but coal was still the main fuel used for electricity generation by a significant margin.[53] As younger generations took over the NUM leadership in the late 1960s and 1970s, the union grew more critical of pit closures, and of the way miners' pay had been held down by the NCB relative to the wages of other manual workers. (In 1955, miners' weekly earnings were the highest of all manual workers; by 1970, they were in sixteenth place.)[54] Cold winters, rising oil prices, and crises in the Middle East led to a bounce-back in demand for coal, setting the scene for the first national coal strikes since nationalisation, in 1972 and 1974. Electricity shortages led to power cuts and a three-day working week; Ted Heath's Tory government fell; miners won a record pay increase, and secured the future of their industry with the new Labour government's *Plan for Coal* in 1974. Miners were now actively recruited to work in pits deemed particularly productive, and this meant further migration, particularly to the expanding collieries of Yorkshire and Nottinghamshire. The strikes of 1972 and 1974 catapulted miners up the wages table: Carol Willis, from Ashington, recalled that the consequence was 'not great wealth, but... wages became decent... [miners] could afford holidays and extensions to the house. For about twelve years, it was a boom town.'[55] By 1984, miners were, thus, well paid but less likely than ever to live in a 'traditional' pit village.

Childhood, Housing, Education, and Young Womanhood

Girls born in coalfield communities in the 'baby boom' generation (1945–64) grew up in a very different world to that into which their mothers had been born: a world with the NHS, compulsory secondary education, full employment, mass council house building, and an increasingly national culture. In this period, the lives of miners and their families grew more comfortable, and miners' families also grew more similar to the rest of the working class. Both these developments are

---

[52] See Norma Gregory's research on Black miners: https://blackcoalminers.com/oral-history-archives/; Andrew Nocon, 'A Reluctant Welcome? Poles in Britain in the 1940s', *Oral History*, 24 (1996), 79–87, at 80; Diana Kay and Robert Miles, 'Refugees or Migrant Workers? The Case of the European Volunteer Workers in Britain (1946–1951)', *Journal of Refugee Studies*, 1 (1988), 214–36.

[53] David Edgerton, *The Rise and Fall of the British Nation: A Twentieth Century History* (London: Penguin, 2019), 292 ff.

[54] Alan A. Carruth and Andrew J. Oswald, 'Miners' Wages in Post-War Britain: An Application of a Model of Trade Union Behaviour', *Economic Journal*, 95 (1985), 1003–20, at 1010.

[55] Carol Willis, b. 1952, North East England/Manchester, interviewed by Victoria Dawson, 3 April 2019.

illuminated in the National Child Development Study (NCDS) begun in 1958.[56] This study surveyed all 17,414 children born in Great Britain in a single week in 1958; in 1965, a follow-up survey identified those with fathers (or other male heads of household) working in mining. This allows us to locate the NCDS children (526 of them) whose father was a working-class miner when they were aged 7 (we call this the 'mining sample'), and to compare them to the larger cohort of 9,093 NCDS children whose father was doing *any other* working-class job at the same point in time (the 'working-class sample').[57] We can also compare the NCDS mining sample with our sample of oral history interviewees who were 'coalfield women'—that is, the eighty-one women whose fathers were miners, and/or whose husbands were miners, and/or who were from working-class families in mining communities and remained embedded in these communities as adults.[58] The NCDS mining sample is not a perfect comparator group for our oral history interviewees, but it does help place them in context.

The NCDS data shows that the fathers of the mining sample were overwhelmingly skilled or semi-skilled: only 1.1 per cent were unskilled, whereas in the working-class sample it was 10.2 per cent. The NCDS also suggests that where, in the early twentieth century, miners had distinctive patterns of nuptiality and fertility, in the postwar period these differences diminished. The average age of the mothers of children in the mining sample at their birth was 27.9 years; this compared with 27.1 years for the working-class sample. (It should be remembered that the NCDS children were not necessarily the first-born children in their families.) There were differences in the housing situation of the two groups, but these diminished over time. In 1958, 45 per cent of children in the mining sample were in overcrowded housing, compared with only 38 per cent in the working-class sample.[59] By 1965, the children of miners were, however, *more* likely than children in the working-class sample to live in an entire house (Table 2.2). This was related to the distinctive geography and history of the coalfields. Mining settlements were usually in rural or semi-rural areas and small towns; there was a long history of the building of tied housing, and council properties in the coalfields

---

[56] National Child Development Study: Childhood Data from Birth to Age 16, Sweeps 0–3, 1958–1974 (data collection), 3rd Edition, National Children's Bureau, National Birthday Trust Fund (original data producer), Institute of Education, Centre for Longitudinal Studies, University of London (2020), UK Data Service, SN: 5565; National Child Development Study: Age 23, Sweep 4, 1981, and Public Examination Results, 1978 (data collection), 2nd Edition, National Children's Bureau (original data producer), Institute of Education, Centre for Longitudinal Studies, University of London (2020), UK Data Service, SN: 5566. For information on the study, see Chris Power and Jane Elliott, 'Cohort Profile: 1958 British Birth Cohort (National Child Development Study)', *International Journal of Epidemiology*, 35 (2006), 34–41; and see https://cls.ucl.ac.uk/cls-studies/1958-national-child-development-study/.

[57] Taking 'working-class' to mean Registrar-General's social class III manual, IV manual or V, as recorded in 1965.

[58] Of these, sixteen women were born 1934–44; forty-eight were from the baby boom generation, and seventeen were born 1965–73.

[59] Using the measure of having over 1 person per room in the household.

were generally substantial suburban houses with indoor bathrooms and gardens (though in some parts of Scotland maisonettes or flats were more common). In both the working-class and the mining samples, about half of the NCDS children were living in council housing in 1965 (Table 2.2); however, mining children were less likely to live in privately rented accommodation (usually the worst standard of housing), and more likely to live in tied housing. Colliery owners began to build tied housing for their workers in the nineteenth century, and it remained common, particularly in County Durham; this accounts for the high proportion of the NCDS mining sample whose tenure was recorded as 'other' (Table 2.2).[60] The housing of children in mining families in 1965 was, thus, distinctive, but by this point, children in the mining sample had similar access to key amenities like bathrooms as children in the working-class sample did (Table 2.2).

Our coalfield women interviewees who were born in the baby boom generation had a similar pattern of housing to the children in the NCDS mining sample: sixteen out of forty-eight lived in council housing as children, while ten lived in coal board houses, nine in privately owned houses, and only two in privately rented accommodation.[61] Owner-occupiers seem to be slightly overrepresented in our sample, which tallies with the well-known tendency of oral history projects to attract participants from more comfortable backgrounds.

Table 2.2 Accommodation of NCDS children in the mining and working-class samples, 1965

		Mining sample (%)	Working-class sample (%)
Type of accommodation	Whole house	95.4	85.9
	Flat	2.9	10.0
	Rooms	1.0	2.3
Tenure of accommodation	Owner occupied	22.1	32.1
	Council rented	51.1	49.8
	Private rented	9.5	13.2
	Rent free	2.5	1.7
	Other	14.7	2.9
Amenities	Sole use of bathroom	84.6	84.8
	Sole use of indoor lavatory	76.7	79.5
	Sole use of hot water supply	91.0	89.3

[60] In the mid-1980s, the Coal Board still owned 165,000–170,000 houses in coalfield areas: Hansard, HC Deb 16 July 1997 vol. 298 cc329–50.
[61] The remaining ten lived in a mixture of tenures, or their housing tenure as children was not clear.

While some of our interviewees recalled childhood poverty and unhappy families, many—no doubt to some extent influenced by widespread nostalgia for the 'good old days'—described happy childhoods in relatively comfortable homes, in working-class communities where everyone was 'the same', and where playing out with friends all day was common.[62] Many interviewees remembered an assumption that children should be 'seen but not heard', though a few thought their parents took a more 'modern' approach to parenting, encouraging their children to develop and voice their opinions.[63] Over the postwar decades, working-class parents gradually shifted towards more child-centred parenting styles, based on trusting their own judgement as parents and responding to their children as individuals.[64] Many of our interviewees also recalled, however, that as children, they were treated differently to their brothers, allowed less freedom, or given different chores to do. Lorraine Walsh and Linda Finnis, sisters from Kent, born in the 1950s, felt their brothers were treated as 'special'; as 'golden boys'.[65] Kay Case, born in 1948, from South Wales, recalled that as a child, she 'always felt that my mother favoured my brother', though looking back now, she thought 'it was more a case of, well women are brought up to do this and not the other'.[66] Carol*, twenty years younger than Kay, recalled that though both she and her brothers were expected to do well at school, it was only she who had to help around the house—it was just 'what was expected' at the time, she said, though even as a girl this struck her as 'not fair'.[67] Most of our interviewees' primary socialisation within the home was, thus, deeply gendered.

School was no different.[68] Before the Second World War, few girls (or boys) from mining families had anything beyond an elementary education, but the 1944 Education Act changed this, introducing free secondary education for all, at first in the tripartite system of grammars, technical schools, and secondary moderns, and, from the 1960s, in comprehensives. When they were surveyed at age 16, in 1974, of the NCDS mining sample who were attending local authority schools, 64

---

[62] See Mathew Thomson, *Lost Freedom: The Landscape of the Child and the British Post-War Settlement* (Oxford: Oxford University Press, 2013).
[63] E.g. Christine Worth, b. 1952, Derbyshire, interviewed by Natalie Thomlinson, 2 August 2018; Janie Robertson, b. 1955, East Scotland, interviewed by Florence Sutcliffe-Braithwaite, 20 November 2018.
[64] Florence Sutcliffe-Braithwaite and Natalie Thomlinson, 'Vernacular Discourses of Gender Equality in the Post-War British Working Class', *Past & Present*, 254 (2022), 277–313; David Cowan, '"Modern" Parenting and the Uses of Childcare Advice in Post-War England', *Social History*, 43 (2018), 332–55.
[65] Lorraine Walsh, b. 1959, and Linda Finnis, b. 1952, both Kent, interviewed by Florence Sutcliffe-Braithwaite, 3 July 2018.
[66] Kay Case, b. 1948, South Wales, interviewed by Florence Sutcliffe-Braithwaite, 13 August 2018.
[67] Carol*, b. 1968, South Wales, interviewed by Natalie Thomlinson, 19 June 2018.
[68] For more on education, see Natalie Thomlinson, '"I was Never Very Clever, but I Always Survived": Educational Experiences of Women in Coalfield Communities in Post-War Britain', in R. Simmons and K. Simpson, eds., *Education, Work and Social Change in Britain's Former Coalfield Communities: The Ghost of Coal* (Basingstoke: Palgrave Macmillan, 2022), 173–96.

per cent were at comprehensives, 6 per cent grammars, and 29 per cent secondary modern schools, similar proportions to those in the working-class sample.[69] Among our coalfield women interviewees, grammar-school girls are overrepresented: in the baby boom generation, twelve out of forty-eight of our interviewees attended grammar schools, while seventeen attended secondary moderns and ten comprehensives.[70] (Again, this tallies with the well-known tendency for oral history projects to attract those with higher levels of education.) Even after the 1944 Act, there were important limits to the expansion of opportunity: grammar schools often had lower expectations of their working-class students, and secondary moderns generally prepared working-class young women for unskilled labour and housewifery.[71] The curriculum in almost all the schools our interviewees attended was heavily gendered, with boys taking subjects like woodwork while girls learned cooking and sewing.[72] Aggie Currie, from Doncaster (born in 1950), remembered that gardening was a 'feller's job', while the girls were expected to 'sweep the path after they'd finished'.[73] But the very fact of secondary education meant something: the expansion of state education (and the welfare state in general) proclaimed the value of young people and implied that opportunity was to be distributed more democratically in postwar Britain.[74] Secondary schooling also meant most children from pit villages travelled out of the village daily during term time, meeting new people and widening their horizons. Though some schools had low expectations of working-class girls, others encouraged self-expression, an interest in learning, and a critical approach to the world, and these developments must have impacted to some extent on how young women in the coalfields saw themselves.[75]

---

[69] In the working-class sample, of those children in Local Educational Authority schools, 64 per cent attended a comprehensive, 8 per cent a grammar, and 24 per cent a secondary modern school. Very similar proportions were attending non-Local Educational Authority schools in the two samples (12–13 per cent).

[70] In the generation above, secondary modern education predominated, with eleven out of sixteen interviewees attending secondary moderns; in the generation below, we see the effects of comprehensivisation: fifteen out of seventeen interviewees attended comprehensives.

[71] Brian Jackson and Dennis Marsden, *Education and the Working Class: Some General Themes Raised by a Study of 88 Working-Class Children in a Northern Industrial City* (London: Routledge & Kegan Paul, 1962). Some interviewees commented on these lower expectations, e.g., Jean Shadbolt, b. 1948, Nottinghamshire, interviewed by Natalie Thomlinson, 23 July 2018. Qualification levels for secondary modern students were low: see George Smith, 'Schools', in A. H. Halsey and J. Webb, eds., *Twentieth Century British Social Trends* (London: Routledge, 2000), 179–220, at 212.

[72] Two of our interviewees attended the progressive Minsthorpe school in Yorkshire where boys and girls did the same lessons.

[73] Aggie Currie, b. 1950, Yorkshire, interviewed by Victoria Dawson, 22 June 2018.

[74] Carolyn Steedman, *Landscape for a Good Woman: A Story of Two Lives* (London: Virago, 1986); Peter Mandler, 'Educating the Nation I: Schools', *Transactions of the Royal Historical Society*, 24 (2014), 5–28; Peter Mandler, *The Crisis of the Meritocracy: Britain's Transition to Mass Education since the Second World War* (Oxford: Oxford University Press, 2020).

[75] Carolyn Steedman, 'State Sponsored Autobiography', in Becky Conekin, Frank Mort, and Chris Waters, eds., *Moments of Modernity: Reconstructing Britain, 1945–1964* (London: Rivers Oram, 1999), 41–54; Christopher Hilliard, *English as a Vocation: The Scrutiny Movement* (Oxford: Oxford University Press, 2012), ch. 4.

Most working-class young people from the baby boom generation left school at the earliest possible age and found work easily, regardless of qualifications.[76] The 1958 NCDS children were the first cohort for whom the school leaving age was raised from 15 to 16; 79 per cent of girls in the working-class sample left at the earliest possible point (in 1974), compared with 84 per cent in the mining sample. The picture was similar for the coalfield women who we interviewed from the baby boom generation: sixteen (out of forty-eight) left school at 15, and twenty left at 16.[77] They went straight into work, in factories, shops, or offices (the latter was the largest employer of young women by 1951).[78] Few working-class women of this generation went into domestic service, which in 1931 had been the most common job for a girl.[79] A handful of our interviewees went into nursing, an attractive option for some as nurse training usually came with accommodation away from home. Demand for workers was high in most parts of the country in the 1950s, 1960s, and 1970s, and many interviewees told us that it was easy to leave one job on a Friday and have a new one by Monday.[80] This phrase was well-known and much-repeated, and was deployed particularly to emphasise the contrast with the 2010s, when our interviewees were speaking. Though it was clearly a trope, it captured how relatively easy it was to find work in this period: as Rita Wakefield (born in 1943) put it, when she was young, 'all the jobs were laid out for you'.[81]

In the context of high demand for labour, young people's wages improved relative to adults' (in 1939, girls under 18 earned a quarter of an average adult male's weekly wage; by 1949, they earned one third).[82] In addition, before the Second World War, it was common for young women working full-time to 'tip up' their entire pay packet to their mothers and receive pocket money back. This practice continued after the war. When Marie Price, born in 1935, left school aged 15, she had to give her mother her whole wage packet from the yarn factory where she went to work.[83] But over time, more and more mothers just took a set amount for 'board'—Linda Conway, born twenty years after Marie, in Dunfermline, called it 'dig money'—or even let their daughters keep all of their wages.[84] Many

---

[76] Ingrid Schoon, Andrew McCulloch, Heather E. Joshi, Richard D. Wiggins, and John Bynner, 'Transitions from School to Work in a Changing Social Context', *YOUNG*, 9 (2001), 4–22, at 5.
[77] Among the generation above, twelve out of sixteen left school aged 15; in the generation below, six out of seventeen left aged 16.
[78] Selina Todd and Hilary Young, 'Baby-Boomers to "Beanstalkers": Making the Modern Teenager in Post-War Britain', *Cultural and Social History*, 9 (2012), 451–67, at 455.
[79] Ibid.
[80] See Janice Bartolo, b. 1957, Kent, interviewed by Florence Sutcliffe-Braithwaite and Natalie Thomlinson, 5 March 2016; Joyce Boyes, b. 1955, Yorkshire, interviewed by Victoria Dawson, 21 November 2018; Mandy Slater, b. 1937, Yorkshire, interviewed by Victoria Dawson, 8 August 2018; Carole Hancock, b. 1938, Yorkshire, interviewed by Victoria Dawson, 26 June 2018.
[81] Rita Wakefield, b. 1943, Nottinghamshire, interviewed by Natalie Thomlinson, 20 August 2018.
[82] Todd and Young, 'Baby-Boomers', 455.
[83] Marie Price, b. 1935, Nottinghamshire, interviewed by Natalie Thomlinson, 29 May 2019.
[84] Linda Conway, b. 1955, Scotland, interviewed by Victoria Dawson, 28 August 2018.

working-class young people thus had relatively high disposable incomes—this was the era of the invention of the 'teenager'—and young women used their wages to buy clothes, records, and magazines, to go to the cinema, to dances, and on holiday.[85] The mass media encouraged them to seek out romance and marriage, but it also encouraged them to see marriage as a relationship based on love, not an institution based on convention; marriage was supposed to help each partner develop as an individual.[86] From the late 1950s, young women's magazines emphasised independence, experience, and opportunity (though the expectations thus raised were often not entirely met).[87] Working-class women born into mining communities in the mid-twentieth century were thus *both* being socialised with particularly gendered expectations, *and* also encouraged to some extent by parents, school, and the wider culture they found themselves in to see themselves as individuals with the right to opportunities for self-development, even if that self-development was to take place within marriage.

Marriage, Homemaking, Children, and Work

From the end of the Second World War to the early 1970s, marriage grew in popularity and average age at first marriage fell; by 1971, it was just 22.6 years for women.[88] Within the NCDS, data collected in 1981 shows that the young women in the mining sample married and had children slightly earlier than other working-class girls (Table 2.3). Of course, we do not know how many of these young women married miners, but, given that many of our interviewees (twenty-one

Table 2.3 Working-class young women from the NCDS: marriage and childbearing in 1981 (aged 22–23)

	Mining sample	Working-class sample
% who were married	65.2	58.8
% who had children	45.9	38.7
N (100%)	207	3,407

---

[85] Todd and Young, 'Baby-Boomers'.

[86] Claire Langhamer, *The English in Love: The Intimate Story of an Emotional Revolution* (Oxford: Oxford University Press, 2013).

[87] Penny Tinkler, '"Are You Really Living?" If Not, "Get with It!"', *Cultural and Social History*, 11 (2014), 597–619.

[88] Jane Elliott, 'Demographic Trends in Everyday Life, 1945–87', in David Clark, ed., *Marriage, Domestic Life and Social Change: Writings for Jacqueline Burgoyne (1944–88)* (London: Routledge, 1991), 85–110, at 88.

Table 2.4 Age at first marriage—coalfield women interviewees

	b. 1934–44	b. 1945–64	b. 1965–73
15–19	9	18	2
20–24	4	21	4
25–29	2	3	3
30+	1	1	1
Never m.	–	2	–
Unclear	–	1	7
N	16	48	17

out of the forty-eight coalfield women we interviewed from the baby boom generation) were both daughters and wives of miners, this helps contextualise our sample. Almost all the coalfield women we interviewed married, usually in their late teens or early twenties; the average age grew in each generation (see Table 2.4).

Joyce Boyes, who was born in Leeds in 1955 and grew up in nearby Castleford, was 18 when she got married. She recalled asking her mother whether she thought Joyce was too young:

> And she says, 'Well yeah, I do think you are—but he's alright, he's got his chairs at home.' That's what she said—which meant he were sensible, and they liked him—they always did, and they knew he were a good lad, so they didn't mind. Plus t'fact, again, I'm going back—but your parents expected you to get married then, specially girls... this sounds awful, they didn't want rid of you, but they didn't want—everybody were expected to get—to leave home and either get married or work away somewhere, it were nearly always get married.

Later Joyce commented that if she had her time again, she'd have 'a few years on my own, pursuing other things', before marrying—though she emphasised that she would still marry her husband. Like several interviewees, Joyce recognised that the fact that most working-class women of her generation 'went straight from home life then to married life' meant that they missed an opportunity to develop independently, something seen as common for young people in the twenty-first century.[89] In fact, like many women of the baby boom generation, several of our interviewees had to 'live in' with their parents or in-laws for several months when they first married, but they generally found it relatively easy to find their own family home soon after.[90]

---

[89] Joyce Boyes; see also Linda Finnis and Lorraine Walsh.
[90] E.g. Jeanette McComb, b. 1953, Midlands/Scotland, interviewed by Victoria Dawson, 26 September 2018.

The ideology of companionate marriage was powerful in postwar Britain—backed up by the state and endorsed by mass media—and this view of marriage as a partnership based on love which should support and fulfil both husband and wife clearly impacted women in mining communities.[91] Companionate marriage was an ideal-type constructed by sex reformers, progressive Christians, and social scientists in the late nineteenth and early twentieth centuries: the spread of this ideal was uneven and its realisation in practice often incomplete.[92] Some of our interviewees described unequal, unhappy, or abusive marriages (and women with traumatic experiences in their marriages were probably less likely to come forward to be interviewed for the project). But, strikingly, many of our interviewees contrasted their own marriages with those of their parents or grandparents, which they perceived as being more patriarchal and based on strict gender roles. Sue, born in 1956, from Kent, thought that for her grandparents' generation, 'it was a man's world, and—and what the man said went'; but, she said, 'I didn't want it to be like that.'[93] Linda Chapman, born in 1958, recalled her father 'telling my mum that he could hand her notice in at work if he wanted to—he was very old-fashioned', but said she and her husband had always been 'fifty-fifty kinds of people'.[94] Some miners did little or no housework. Maggie Stubbs's husband, a miner in South Yorkshire, had no problem with Maggie working as a nurse, but still 'expected' her 'to do everything else'.[95] But others were happy to help out around the house. David Waddington, Maggie Wykes, and Chas Critcher's study of three mining villages in Yorkshire, Derbyshire, and Nottinghamshire, conducted in 1987–8, found that before 1984, there was 'a degree of male involvement in domestic life at variance with the stereotype of the traditional miner'.[96] Almost every one of our coalfield women interviewees took the main responsibility for housework and childcare for most of their marriages; this, however, did not seem, to most, to denote an 'unequal' relationship. Indeed, mining was a particularly dangerous and exhausting job, and some of our interviewees, like Wendy Minney (a self-described feminist), felt this justified miners' wives' taking the main responsibility for the home.[97] What was important to most of our interviewees was not the division of household labour, but rather that they had autonomy, a voice, and respect within their marriages.[98]

---

[91] Langhamer, *English in Love*.
[92] Marcus Collins, *Modern Love: An Intimate History of Men and Women in Twentieth-Century Britain* (London: Atlantic, 2003).
[93] Sue, b. 1956, Kent, interviewed by Florence Sutcliffe-Braithwaite, 14 July 2018.
[94] Linda Chapman, b. 1958, North East England, interviewed by Victoria Dawson, 18 July 2018.
[95] Maggie Stubbs, b. c.1950, Jamaica/Yorkshire, interviewed by Natalie Thomlinson, 13 September 2018.
[96] David Waddington, Maggie Wykes, and Chas Critcher, *Split at the Seams? Community, Continuity and Change after the 1984–5 Coal Dispute* (Milton Keynes: Open University Press, 1991), 82.
[97] Wendy Minney, b. 1964, Nottinghamshire, interviewed by Natalie Thomlinson, 20 August 2018.
[98] Sutcliffe-Braithwaite and Thomlinson, 'Vernacular Discourses'.

In the postwar decades, most working-class women expected to have children fairly soon after marriage, and this was certainly the case for most of our interviewees. The fact that families expecting children were prioritised for council housing encouraged young couples to begin their families sooner rather than later. Indeed, when Lorraine Walsh and her husband decided to delay having children for several years after marriage so they could continue enjoying their youth and freedom, they decided it made sense to buy their own home rather than wait on the council list.[99] Very large families were now the exception rather than the rule, and families grew smaller over the generations (Table 2.5).

Sociologists and historians have argued that in the postwar period, and particularly from the 1960s, working-class parenting changed, with parents adopting a closer, more friend-like relationship with their children, and focusing less on discipline.[100] Fathers became more involved in child-rearing, with the rise of what Laura King has called 'family-centred masculinity'.[101] The NCDS data suggests that 'family-centred masculinity' had hit the coalfields by the mid-1960s: in the mining sample, in 1965, 62 per cent of mothers reported that the child's father took a 'big part, or equal part' in 'managing the child', in comparison with 58 per cent in the working-class sample. Even if such reports cannot be taken as a wholly accurate impression of what fathers were doing, the similarity in what mothers *claimed* about their husbands' attitudes to child-rearing is striking. The trend towards child-centred parenting can be seen in our interviewees' testimonies, too. Mary Hole, born in 1935, from South Wales, described her parents as distant, saying that parents then 'didn't show any love to you'. She recalled of her father,

Table 2.5 Number of children—coalfield women interviewees

	b. 1934–44	b. 1945–64	b. 1965–73
0	–	5	1
1	4	5	3
2	5	28	11
3	6	6	–
4	–	1	–
6	1	–	–
Unclear	–	3	2
N	16	48	17

[99] Lorraine Walsh.
[100] John Newson and Elizabeth Newson, *Patterns of Infant Care in an Urban Community* (Harmondsworth: Penguin Books, 1965), 237–49; Newson and Newson, *Four Years Old in an Urban Community* (London: Allen & Unwin, 1968), 556–7.
[101] Laura King, *Family Men: Fatherhood and Masculinity in Britain, 1914–1960* (Oxford: Oxford University Press, 2015).

'he'd sit in his chair in the corner and he'd smoke his pipe', and she remembered her mother constantly working: she had had nine children, one of whom died as an infant. Mary concluded, 'I can't remember really being really involved with my parents much, like I've been with—with ours.'[102] Rita Wakefield (born in 1943) and her daughters contrasted the way that Rita's husband had played a hands-on role with the girls with Rita's own father.[103] Many interviewees thought the assumption that children should be 'seen and not heard', common when they were growing up, had faded over the decades.[104] Many also emphasised that they had consciously treated their sons and daughters in a more equal way, and had gone further than their own parents had in encouraging their children—both boys and girls—to develop as individuals and to set high aspirations for themselves. Alison Anderson, born in 1959, for example, recalled that while she was just expected to 'be a mum and keep house...now, cor blimey, when I was bringing mine up I was saying to them, oh—you can—the world's your oyster, you can go and do what you want and be who you want'.[105] Thus, between 1945 and the early 1980s, working-class family life—including in the coalfields—became more focused on the home, with less emphasis on hierarchy and more on openness and warmth, and fathers playing more of a role in children's lives.

Women's participation in paid labour was also, as is well-known, increasing in Britain from the late 1940s. In this period, women began to concentrate their childbearing in a shorter period than earlier generations, and to return to paid work when their children were younger: 79 per cent of working-class mothers of children in the 1958 NCDS returned to work before their child was 11, compared with 66 per cent of working-class mothers of children in the 1946 birth cohort study.[106] While some mothers have always participated in the paid labour force, working motherhood became a cross-class norm over the second half of the twentieth century,[107] and this pattern held good in the coalfields as elsewhere. Most of our interviewees grouped the births of their children together in a short window soon after marrying. This meant that after a period of five to ten years, their children had all begun school, leaving women with their days free. More modern housing and labour-saving devices also made it easier and more attractive for them to contemplate taking up work, often part-time work, as did the greater mobility offered by buses and cars—in the postwar decades, buses were often sent to coalfield

---

[102] Mary Hole, b. 1935, South Wales, interviewed by Victoria Dawson, 2 September 2018.
[103] Rita Wakefield, b. 1943, Kim Hickling, b. 1962, and Wendy Minney, b. 1964, all Nottinghamshire, interviewed by Natalie Thomlinson, 20 August 2018.
[104] Sutcliffe-Braithwaite and Thomlinson, 'Vernacular Discourses'.
[105] Alison Anderson, b. 1959, Scotland, interviewed by Victoria Dawson, 29 August 2018; see also Linda Conway.
[106] This figure is calculated using only final-born children from the studies. Heather Joshi and P. R. Andrew Hinde, 'Employment after Childbearing in Post-War Britain: Cohort-Study Evidence on Contrasts within and across Generations', *European Sociological Review*, 9 (1993), 203–27, at 208.
[107] Helen McCarthy, *Double Lives: A History of Working Motherhood* (London: Bloomsbury, 2020).

villages to pick up women for shifts at nearby factories. Even the authors of *Coal is Our Life* noted that miners' wives in Featherstone in the 1950s were working more as greater employment opportunities for women opened up.[108]

The NCDS allows us to compare the employment levels of miners' wives and other working-class wives by examining the work situation of the NCDS children's mothers in the 1950s and 1960s.[109] The 1958 survey shows that the mothers of 73 per cent of children in the mining sample had no paid job during pregnancy; in the working-class sample, it was 61 per cent—a difference of 12 percentage points. By 1965, the mothers of 59 per cent of children in the mining sample had not worked since the child started school; in the working-class sample, it was 51 per cent—a difference of 8 percentage points (Table 2.6). Miners' wives did work outside the home less frequently than other working-class wives, but the difference was not vast. Following the girls in the NCDS to young adulthood, we find that in 1981, the year in which they turned 23, it was *motherhood*, and not marriage, which prompted most women to give up work, and that the pattern was very similar for young women from mining backgrounds and from other working-class backgrounds. Of the miners' daughters who were married with children, 81 per cent were not working; in the working-class sample it was 83 per cent (Table 2.7).

Table 2.6 Paid labour of mothers of NCDS children, reported in 1965

	Mining sample		Working-class sample	
	Mother worked before child at school (%)	Mother worked since child started school (%)	Mother worked before child at school (%)	Mother worked since child started school (%)
Don't know/inapplicable	4.3	1.9	3.6	1.6
Part-time or temporary	15.3	26.2	21.7	37.5
Full-time	7.2	13.2	9.6	10.0
Has not worked	73.3	58.7	65.1	50.9
Total	100.0	100.0	100.0	100.0

[108] Dennis et al., *Coal is Our Life*, 233.
[109] Because we select the two samples based on the recorded work and social class of the father or other male head of household in 1965, we can be confident that none of the women in question were single mothers in 1965. However, some might have been unmarried, and some may have been single in 1958. Given the high levels of marriage in the period, however, this seems unlikely to be a major distortion in the data.

Table 2.7 NCDS women who were married by 1981: children and paid labour

	Mining sample		Working-class sample	
	Has children	Childless	Has children	Childless
Not working (%)	81.3	18.3	82.8	12.4
Full-time work (%)	4.0	76.7	5.1	82.8
Part-time work (%)	14.7	5.0	12.1	4.7
Total (%)	100	100	100	100
N (100%)	75	60	1,142	996

Census data from 1971 gives further insights into the pattern of women's work in the coalfields (Table 2.8). In several of the areas with the highest levels of employment in mining, levels of married women's work were just as high as the national average, or higher (Llantrisant, in Glamorgan, Dalkeith, in Midlothian, and North Mansfield, in Nottinghamshire). These were places that were relatively close to nearby cities and large towns (Cardiff, Edinburgh, and Mansfield) with job opportunities for women. By contrast, levels of women's work were below average in places like Horden, a relatively isolated mining village on the coast in County Durham, where there were likely to be fewer jobs easily available to women. This tallies with Jim Phillips's analysis of the 1981 census data in Scotland: Phillips found that women in mining areas were as likely to work as women from across Scotland more broadly (around 56 per cent), but women worked more where convenient job opportunities were available.[110] While before 1945 it was considered undesirable—even taboo—for working-class wives in many communities, and *particularly* in mining communities, to take on paid labour, in the postwar decades, miners' wives, like other working-class women, broke with this pattern.

As historians have shown, working-class women took up paid labour in the 1950s and 1960s because they needed the money for essentials, but also because they wanted to be able to buy 'extras' for the family, to get out of the house and meet people, and to do something 'for themselves'.[111] These reasons all came out in our interviews. In fact, the need for essentials and the desire for 'extras' could not be entirely separated out as things like televisions and holidays came to be expected parts of life in working-class communities, as Kay Case (born in 1948) made clear. Kay married aged 18, and was looking forward to being a housewife and mother, but once her older son was in school, she ended up taking a part-time job:

---

[110] Phillips, *Miners' Strike*, 168.
[111] Dolly Smith Wilson, 'A New Look at the Affluent Worker: The Good Working Mother in Post-War Britain', *Twentieth Century British History*, 17 (2006), 206–29; Laura Paterson, '"I Didn't Feel Like My Own Person": Paid Work in Women's Narratives of Self and Working Motherhood, 1950–1980', *Contemporary British History*, 33 (2019), 405–26; McCarthy, *Double Lives*, 30.

Table 2.8 Top five wards in England, Scotland, and Wales by number of workers in mining industry: proportion of married women who were economically active, 1971

	Ward	% of married women economically active
England	Hirst, Ashington Urban District, Northumberland	36
	Warsop, Warsop Urban District, Notts.	33
	North, Mansfield Metropolitan Borough, Notts.	43
	Shirebrook, Blackwell Rural District, Derbyshire	35
	Horden, Easington Rural District, Durham	32
	England average	**43**
Scotland	Dalmellington South, Ayr	32
	Dalkeith, Midlothian	48
	Culross, Dunfermline, Fife	37
	Stair and Ochiltree, Cumnock, Ayr	34
	Old Cumnock, Cumnock, Ayr	34
	Scotland average	**41**
Wales	Llantrisant, Glamorgan	38
	Llanguicke, Glamorgan	34
	Hengoed, Glamorgan	34
	Ferndale, Glamorgan	31
	Cwmtillery, Monmouthshire	31
	Wales average	**35**

Note: 1971 census, UK Data Service, https://casweb.ukdataservice.ac.uk/. The category of 'mining' in the 1971 census included coalmining as well as other forms of mining and extraction (stone, slate, chalk, slate, gravel, petroleum, natural gas, ore, and salt); however, we can be confident that coalmining made up the largest proportion of the category in the fifteen wards shown in this table, all of which were associated with coalmining.

I went to work, at the end of the summer holidays, because I wanted money for Christmas for the children... I thought, 'once Christmas is over I'll give it up'. Then I thought, 'if I keep working, we'll have a summer holiday. I'll keep working a bit longer—I'll work till the summer, we'll have an 'oliday'. Then, 'Christmas'll be round the corner'. And I honestly was never out of work after. But it didn't go with any need to be independent. It didn't go with any need to show that I could do it. It was just a case of—Colin wasn't earning big wages, kids were coming, getting bigger, they wanted dearer things, and... I heard about, a friend of mine said, 'oh, there's part-time factory jobs going down on Treforest estate, and there's a bus going from the square'. I said, 'I think I'll go—I'll ask my mother-in-law if she can help out with the kids'.[112]

---

[112] Kay Case.

Not all miners were happy with their wives working outside the home: patriarchal attitudes were still to be found in some households. In the late 1950s, Marie Price found her husband Alan waiting outside her workplace one day, where he told her, 'one of us isn't going to work, it's either me or you'. She therefore stopped working.[113] But such opposition became less common over time. Women's wages were key to the achievement of 'affluent' lifestyles in working-class communities, and this was one important factor convincing some miners that they should support their wives taking paid work.[114] Margaret Davis, born in 1949, recalled that 'the first time we went for a fitted carpet—and that came out of my wages, really', she and her husband 'felt like the king and queen of England...the men did realise then, if two of you worked hard, you got more stuff!'[115]

Working-class women across Britain in the postwar period tended to do part-time jobs, often with little status and low pay. Our interviewees' jobs certainly were not thought of—by themselves or their families—as important in the same way their husbands' were: when Jeanette McComb got married to a miner from East Ayrshire, in 1974 (they met on holiday in Spain), it was assumed she would give up her job in Marks & Spencer and move from Wolverhampton to Scotland. Looking back, she said:

> it's funny, when I think about it, there was never a debate about it...it was always, I would give up my work and move to live in Scotland. We never really had much debate about it: I don't know if that was just part of the culture that, you know, women's work—and I didn't have a high-flying job, and he was the main breadwinner, so that's where we went.[116]

However, this did not mean that women's work had no impact on the balance of power within marital relationships.[117] Many of our interviewees associated paid labour with being a 'modern' woman, more independent and confident. Kay Case summed this up well: though she was keen to point out in her interview that she had *not* taken paid work in order to try to assert her independence from her husband, she nevertheless associated married women's work with a change in the culture of the family, arguing that where, when she was young, 'what the men in the family said, went', in more recent years women had 'liberated themselves' and 'made their own independence'. This, she thought, had 'a lot to do with the fact that we went out and earned our own money, because years ago they didn't work. They had hordes of kids, stayed home, brought the kids up. Had to lean towards

---

[113] Marie Price.   [114] Smith Wilson, 'A New Look'.
[115] Margaret Davis, b. 1949, Kent, interviewed by Florence Sutcliffe-Braithwaite and Natalie Thomlinson, 5 March 2016.
[116] Jeanette McComb.
[117] Helen McCarthy, 'Women, Marriage and Paid Work in Post-War Britain', *Women's History Review*, 26 (2017), 46–61.

their husbands for everything.'[118] Married women's paid labour thus gave many women a feeling that they had more independence and autonomy within their marriages than previous generations.[119] It also gave some women their own experience of trade unionism (Kay was a member of the NUM in 1984, as a canteen worker at the same pit where her husband worked). Thus, by the 1970s and 1980s, mining communities were not 'traditional' places where women deferred to their husbands: as a result of a growing emphasis on love and self-fulfilment in marriage, relationships between husbands and wives changed gradually over the course of the postwar decades, and more and more married women were working outside the home, a fact which contributed both to mining families' comfortable lifestyles and to women's sense of their own independence.

Community and Politics

Some of our interviewees lived in pit villages centred on a mine that was still functioning, and these were usually described as tight-knit communities. Sue evoked the daily and weekly rhythms of life in one of Kent's pit villages before 1984:

> The men worked at the pits, the women worked at one factory, or another factory, or on the fields; you communicated every weekend, Friday, Saturday, Sunday, in the club. I worked with the same women as I socialised with; 'cause I drove, I used to pick 'em up and take 'em food shopping, and I used to pick 'em up and take 'em to skittles, I used to take 'em to darts. We used to play skittles on a Wednesday, darts on a Tuesday, shopping on a Saturday morning, club Friday night, Saturday night, Sunday dinner, Sunday night, in them days, that was life! So you was with the same people all the time. All the time. And they weren't—they weren't friends, they were your family.[120]

Maggie Stubbs, who was born in Jamaica around 1950, and moved to Rotherham, in South Yorkshire, to start nurse training in the mid-1960s, loved the area she lived in. When she and her husband moved briefly to Hertfordshire, she found it friendly, but 'not the—the sort of community, look after each other type friendship', and they soon moved back to Maltby, near Rotherham, where Maggie's husband followed his father down the pit. Though there 'weren't many black faces' in Maltby in the 1970s, Maggie found her husband's family extremely welcoming, and become very involved in the local community. Although she had since moved,

---

[118] Kay Case.
[119] For a fuller statement of this argument, see Sutcliffe-Braithwaite and Thomlinson, 'Vernacular Discourses', 291 ff.
[120] Sue.

she said the village was still her 'spiritual home' today. There were two sides to tight-knit communities, though: when Jeanette McComb moved from Wolverhampton to Auchinleck, in East Ayrshire, in 1974, she found it oppressive that 'everybody knew who you were, where you were going, what you did, if you'd been out the night before, what time you'd got in'; but realised 'the flip side to that was, you know, if you were in trouble, or whatever, then they were there'.[121]

Pubs, miners' welfares, and working men's clubs were central institutions in many of these communities. Drinking spaces were heavily gendered—all-male bars were, like the pit, places where men could use 'pit talk', or 'blue' language—but this changed, albeit slowly and patchily, over the postwar decades.[122] The assumption—common in interwar mining communities—that respectable women did not go to pubs gradually relaxed. Hugh Dixon, born in 1950, recalled that in the village of Sacriston, in County Durham, when he was growing up 'women would never, ever come in [to a pub] on their own', only with their husbands, but by the time he was in his late twenties, 'you'd start to see groups of women coming in on their own'.[123] Working men's clubs increasingly catered for the whole family, with concert spaces, activities like bingo, and facilities for children.[124] The rules, however, excluded women from participating in management, and women's presence was often restricted to particular times and areas of the club.[125] Sue recalled that in Kent, 'when I first got married [in the early 1970s], you was—women was allowed in the club, but only 'cause your husband was a member—but you was only allowed in the big room, with the children, you wasn't allowed in the men's room, in the snooker room'.[126] Clubs often had rigid communal rules. At the working men's club in Auchinleck, Jeanette McComb found that 'you had to be there by six o'clock—if you weren't there by six you didn't get a seat—and you daren't sit in anybody else's seat'.[127] While the gendering of space within pubs, clubs, and miners' welfares had shifted over time, on the eve of the strike, these were still generally places run by men, with rules demarcating when and where women could participate.

With the rise of the travelling miner, however, fewer miners lived and worked in pit villages, and they were increasingly seen as 'traditional' or 'old-fashioned'. Some actively wanted to avoid such communities: Adrienne C. (born in 1956), for example, said that when moving to the Selby area—where her husband had a job in the expanding pit complex—in 1983, she 'definitely, definitely' did not want to live in a 'massive mining community', one of the 'big new estates in those areas

[121] Maggie Stubbs; Jeanette McComb.
[122] For discussions of men's 'blue' language/swearing, see: Jean Shadbolt; Sue.
[123] Hugh Dixon, interviewed by Florence Sutcliffe-Braithwaite, 21 February 2020.
[124] Richard Hall, 'Being a Man, Being a Member: Masculinity and Community in Britain's Working Men's Clubs, 1945–1960', *Cultural and Social History*, 14 (2017), 73–88, at 83.
[125] Ibid., 80.   [126] Sue.   [127] Jeanette McComb.

where there was, like, a massive influx of miners'.[128] She was disappointed to find that in the village they moved to, there was a street with many mining families, and 'it turned out they were all like, staunch, er, union, and all living in each other's pockets, all very close-knit, and erm, did everything together'. This was precisely the sort of network Adrienne and her husband did not want to be part of: 'we'd never been people who'd lived in neighbours' pockets, you know what I mean, we'd always wanted to come home from work, and do us own thing... we'd always minded us own business so we wanted to carry on like that really'. Adrienne was not from a mining community: her father was a hospital manager (though his father had been a miner) and her mother was a nurse, and growing up they lived in a small village south of Leeds. Adrienne's husband was the son of a miner, but did not immediately go into the industry on leaving school: he trained as a mechanic, then worked for an oil company before going into mining because of the higher wages on offer. In her interview, Adrienne said she saw herself as having been born into the working class, but as being 'upper-working-class, lower-middle class, maybe, on that boundary' today.[129] Adrienne and her husband's choices placed them firmly within a long-established paradigm of working and lower-middle-class 'respectability' which emphasised 'keeping ourselves to ourselves'.[130] As working-class incomes went up in the postwar period, it was increasingly easy for families like Adrienne's to choose this sort of affluent, privatised lifestyle.[131]

It was not only women like Adrienne from outside close-knit mining communities who preferred not to live in such areas. Theresa Gratton* (born in 1955) and her husband moved away from the pit village where he worked (and where both had extensive family networks) after a few years of marriage, to a former pit village about ten miles away. Theresa explained that though her husband did not particularly want to move, 'I felt I wanted to live life the way I wanted to live it, I felt a bit constrained, that's all I can say. I just thought I didn't want to go to the club every Saturday night; I didn't want this to be the rest of my life.' Theresa's mother-in-law was 'traumatised, absolutely traumatised' that her son was moving: to her 'it was the ends of the earth'—and though Theresa stressed that it was only ten miles, she acknowledged that it 'felt like a massive break'.[132] Theresa had family in the village to which she moved, and a community effort in support of the strike *did* develop there in 1984–5. As we will see in the final chapter, Jon Lawrence has suggested that, although many working-class people chose a more

---

[128] Adrienne C., b. 1956, Yorkshire, interviewed by Victoria Dawson, 26 June 2018.
[129] Ibid.
[130] Robert Roberts, *The Classic Slum: Salford Life in the First Quarter of the Century* (Manchester: Manchester University Press, 1971); Elizabeth Roberts, *A Woman's Place: An Oral History of Working-Class Women 1890–1940* (Oxford: Blackwell, 1984).
[131] J. H. Goldthorpe, D. Lockwood, F. Bechhofer, and J. Platt, *The Affluent Worker in the Class Structure* (Cambridge: Cambridge University Press, 1969).
[132] Theresa Gratton*, b. 1955, North East England, interviewed by Florence Sutcliffe-Braithwaite, 22 February 2020.

arm's-length approach to community in the postwar period, this did not mean the abandonment of community ties, but rather their reformulation.[133] In villages like the one Theresa moved to, community was not absent, but was less intense.

The decline in the number of miners and their families who lived in 'traditional' pit villages was one factor changing the politics of the coalfields. In the early and mid-twentieth century, mining constituencies were 'in theory... the safest single reservoir of working-class seats in the country', and the miners' trade union was a powerful player in local Labour parties.[134] In 1931, thirty-nine of Labour's fifty-two MPs were sponsored by the MFGB. From the 1970s, however, the 'dealignment' in class-based voting that was visible at a national level was also evident in mining constituencies (taking class as typically measured by sociologists and market researchers).[135] Two examples suggest the scale of the shift: the constituencies of Easington, in County Durham, and Don Valley, in South Yorkshire, both of which existed for the entire period 1950–92, and both of which were represented by NUM-sponsored MPs throughout that time. In Easington between 1950 and 1970, 79–81 per cent of the vote went to Labour. By contrast, between 1970 and 1992, Labour's vote share fell from 80 to 60 per cent and then rose again to 73 per cent. In Don Valley between 1945 and 1970, 70–75 per cent of votes were for Labour. Between 1970 and 1992, Labour's vote share fell to 45 per cent, then rose to 55 per cent. In the later period, Labour's vote share was lower, and also much less stable, a pattern that continued after 1992, the last election where the NUM sponsored MPs.

Our interviewees registered this shift: many recalled that growing up, they were instructed by their parents that working people voted Labour, and absorbed the knowledge that in their communities, 'everyone' voted Labour. Jean Shadbolt did not see herself as particularly political growing up, but she said that, 'I suppose when I was old enough to vote, I was always going to vote for the Labour Party, and that really—yeah, that's down to me background, down to me dad saying, "you vote Labour", you know.'[136] Labour voting was less an expression of political belief, and more a community habitus—a taken-for-granted mode of being in the world. But by the late 2010s, the strong link between class, community, and voting had been attenuated, even in communities that were still safe seats for Labour. Some of our interviewees critiqued the older model of electoral choice: Joyce Boyes, who, tellingly, had chosen to live in a non-mining village in the Selby area, commented that:

---

[133] Jon Lawrence, *Me, Me, Me? The Search for Community in Post-War England* (Oxford: Oxford University Press, 2019).

[134] Ross McKibbin, *The Evolution of the Labour Party, 1910–1924* (Oxford: Oxford University Press, 1975), 24.

[135] On the national picture, see Bo Särlvik and Ivor Crewe, *Decade of Dealignment: The Conservative Victory of 1979 and Electoral Trends in the 1970s* (Cambridge: Cambridge University Press, 1983).

[136] Jean Shadbolt. See also Janet Slater, b. 1954, Nottinghamshire, interviewed by Natalie Thomlinson, 3 August 2018; Ann, b. 1942, Yorkshire, interviewed by Victoria Dawson, 25 July 2018.

I'm not like some of these staunch Labour people, and a lot of miners fell into this trap, 'oh me dad's voted Labour all their life, me granddad did'—I'm not like that, I vote for who I think is the most appropriate person and who's going to look after me, and the country as a whole. I can't see the point in keep voting for somebody just because your predecessors voted, it's just not politics, that.[137]

High levels of political engagement were far from typical among miners' wives (or, indeed, miners) in the years before the strike, but many did go further than simply voting Labour: some were involved in their local Labour parties,[138] or in social movements like the Campaign for Nuclear Disarmament (CND),[139] while other women were trade union activists in their own right.[140] As we will see in the next chapter, many of these women were the first movers in the strike support movement.

None of our coalfield interviewees had been part of the women's liberation movement, perhaps unsurprisingly: the movement predominantly attracted middle-class supporters and had its base in cities and in university towns.[141] In the late 1980s, Beverley Skeggs found that working-class women in North East England were hostile to 'feminism', valuing instead traditional markers of femininity.[142] Many of the coalfield women we interviewed, in the late 2010s, were likewise reluctant to call themselves 'feminists'. Importantly, however, almost every interviewee told us that she strongly believed in the equality of men and women. They constructed a vision of equality for women that focused on voice, autonomy, and respect, and this version of equality was one that most felt they had achieved over the course of their own lives.[143] Maureen Coates, for example, felt that her marriage was equal because, though she took the main responsibility for the home and children, her husband 'always backed me, whatever I wanted to do... he wouldn't stop me, 'cause he agrees that women should be equal'.[144] Like Maureen, many of our interviewees identified a (rather whiggish) progress over the generations, with a growing equality, openness, and emphasis on self-fulfilment. These new attitudes extended to children, too. As one miner's wife from Upton, interviewed shortly after the end of the strike, said, '[i]t's like, if there's a chop, Bob and his mother would think he ought to have it. But me,

---

[137] Joyce Boyes.   [138] E.g. Theresa Gratton*.
[139] E.g. Siân James, b. 1959, South Wales, interviewed by Florence Sutcliffe-Braithwaite, 5 February 2019.
[140] E.g. Margaret Holmes, b. 1942, Kent, interviewed by Florence Sutcliffe-Braithwaite, 26 July 2018.
[141] See Margaretta Jolly, *Sisterhood and After: An Oral History of the UK Women's Liberation Movement, 1968–Present* (Oxford: Oxford University Press, 2019), 21–5.
[142] Beverley Skeggs, *Formations of Class and Gender: Becoming Respectable* (London: Sage, 1997).
[143] For a fuller statement, see Sutcliffe-Braithwaite and Thomlinson, 'Vernacular Discourses'.
[144] Maureen Coates, b. 1942, Yorkshire, interviewed by Florence Sutcliffe-Braithwaite and Natalie Thomlinson, 11 September 2014.

I'd give it to the children if there wasn't enough to go round for everybody.'[145] This woman contested the assumptions made by her husband and mother-in-law, and in her insistence on the rights of children to have some of the good stuff in life, we can see the influence of changing assumptions about the value of each individual—including women and children. Coalfield women were not immune to the growing culture of 'popular individualism' that developed in Britain in the postwar decades.[146] Coalfield communities were not hotbeds of women's liberation in the early 1980s, but nor were they places of unreconstructed patriarchy.

Conclusion

In the summer of 1984, Joanna Head wrote in the *New Statesman* that 'of all women, miners' wives are the most firmly rooted in their traditional role of housewives and mothers. The sexual apartheid of mining communities is almost as pronounced as in the days before pit baths and canteens.'[147] This was probably how many leftists from outside the coalfields imagined miners' wives; indeed, some coalfield women were annoyed by these assumptions, as a poem by Lynne Dennet suggests. 'Here she is, come and see her / The pet miner's wife, she's over there', wrote Dennet:

> It's amazing, isn't it,
> The way she's so articulate?
> She really knows what she's about.
> It's not just grunt, scream and shout.[148]

It may seem like a banal—even a self-evident—point, to emphasise that by the early 1980s, miners and their families led a variety of different lifestyles; but it is an important one, because of the strength and persistence of stereotypes about miners, their wives, and their communities. In the late nineteenth and early twentieth centuries it might have been the case that most miners lived in tight-knit communities where poverty was never far away, gender roles were rigid, and married women's lives focused on the home. By the early 1980s this was simply not true. Miners had been affected by general trends tending to reduce regional

---

[145] Martin Adeney and John Lloyd, *The Miners' Strike: Loss without Limit* (London: Routledge & Kegan Paul, 1986), 222.

[146] Emily Robinson, Camilla Schofield, Florence Sutcliffe-Braithwaite, and Natalie Thomlinson, 'Telling Stories about Post-War Britain: Popular Individualism and the "Crisis" of the 1970s', *Twentieth Century British History*, 28 (2017), 268–304.

[147] Joanna Head, 'Miners' Wives', *New Statesman*, 107, 15 June 1984, 13; see, similarly, Beatrix Campbell, 'The Other Miners' Strike', *New Statesman*, 108, 27 July 1984, 8.

[148] Lynne Dennet, 'The Pat on the Head', in Joan Witham, *Hearts and Minds: The Story of the Women of Nottinghamshire in the Miners' Strike, 1984–1985* (London: Canary, 1986), 143.

differences in working-class cultures after 1945—increasingly national mass media, centralised government, mobility, and consumerism.[149] Miners' lives had been affected by the affluence that had come (albeit slowly and unevenly) to Britain in the postwar decades; as Jean McCrindle highlighted to Arthur Scargill in her memo of 1983, many had regular holidays, cars, and mortgages to pay. Some miners still lived in pit villages with long-established communities, where work and leisure were organised around the pit, the miners' welfare, the working men's club, and the pub. But many did not: rationalisations and the rise of car-ownership meant that many travelled to work. Others had moved across the country to new communities in search of work in the coal industry. Though some valued their tight-knit communities, others had chosen to live differently.

Our interviewees grew up expecting to marry and to invest a major part of their lives—and of their sense of themselves—in taking care of their families: and they had, indeed, in most cases done so. But they had also experienced secondary education, and even if the schools they attended often had low expectations of them as working-class students *and* as girls, the expansion of education was nevertheless associated with an increasingly pervasive belief in the importance of the democratic distribution of opportunity throughout the population.[150] Our interviewees grew up in a culture where people had higher and higher expectations of what the state and society should do for them as individuals.[151] Even where these expectations were not fulfilled, the expectations themselves were important. Many miners' wives were working, even when they still had children at home, and they often drew an important sense of independence from this. They had smaller families than their mothers and grandmothers, and their homes were easier to run. The increase in mining families' living standards since the interwar period had been astonishing. Many of our interviewees also emphasised that their relationships with their husbands were very different to those of their mothers and grandmothers. These relationships might not have involved equal sharing of housework and paid labour, but many miners' wives saw them as egalitarian in important ways: many felt they had a voice, respect, and autonomy within their marriages; though we should not forget that others had unhappy and unequal marriages, and some experienced domestic violence. None of our interviewees from the coalfields were involved in the women's liberation movement—but they were also not, in the main, 'trapped at the kitchen sink' or 'under the thumb' of their husbands. We need to dispense with old stereotypes about what miners'

---

[149] Helen Smith, 'Working-Class Ideas and Experiences of Sexuality in Twentieth-Century Britain: Regionalism as a Category of Analysis', *Twentieth Century British History*, 29 (2018), 58–78.
[150] Mandler, *Crisis of the Meritocracy*.
[151] See Elizabeth Roberts, *Women and Families: An Oral History, 1940–1970* (Oxford: Blackwell, 1995), 14; Glen O'Hara, *Governing Post-War Britain: The Paradoxes of Progress, 1951–1973* (Basingstoke: Palgrave Macmillan, 2012), 174–5; Alistair Kefford, 'Housing the Citizen-Consumer in Post-War Britain: The Parker Morris Report, Affluence and the Even Briefer Life of Social Democracy', *Twentieth Century British History*, 29 (2018), 225–58.

wives were like in the early 1980s. Given all this, the concerns that Jean McCrindle and Nell Myers raised with Arthur Scargill in late 1983 and early 1984 about how social change might be reducing miners' wives' support for strikes certainly seemed like pressing ones. As it turned out, however, a committed minority of coalfield women stepped forward to actively support the strike, and it seems likely that the majority of miners' wives offered their striking husbands vital support in the home and family over the course of the dispute. In fact, some social and cultural changes impacting on women's position in the home and community—most notably the rise of companionate marriage, and of married women's paid labour—gave women a strong incentive to back their partners, and the material resources to do so.

3
Early Days: Spring 1984

1 March 1984

On 1 March 1984, the National Coal Board (NCB) unexpectedly announced the closure of Cortonwood Colliery, in Brampton Bierlow, at a South Yorkshire Area general colliery review meeting. While the pit had been loss-making for a while, and the appetite of the NCB for pit closures under the chairmanship of Ian MacGregor was clear, the announcement came as a surprise to the workforce: the closure was supposed to take place in just five weeks' time, yet miners had been transferred from nearby Elsecar just weeks before, and £1 million had recently been invested in new machinery. Moreover, the procedure for announcing a pit closure had not been followed.[1] Jackie Keating, whose husband Paul worked at Cortonwood, recalled that, '[t]he news spread like wildfire. A lot of my friends and neighbours gathered in groups in Dearne Road, Brampton, after taking their little ones to school. Everyone was dumbfounded.'[2] Five days later, on 6 March, the official announcement came, outlining the details of major national reductions in output.[3] Around twenty pits would have to close and 20,000 jobs disappear in the next year.[4] The premature announcement of the Cortonwood closure on 1 March, however, meant that miners in South Yorkshire had had the weekend to organise. In Brampton Bierlow, over 500 people (almost certainly overwhelmingly men) gathered in the parish hall on Sunday 4 March, and voted unanimously for immediate strike action. On Monday 5 March, other collieries in the South Yorkshire National Union of Mineworkers (NUM) Area walked out in support or were picketed out.[5]

The strike spread quickly across the Yorkshire coalfield, helped along by the other disputes that were current in the area: nearby Manvers Main was in a dispute about 'snap' (meal) times, and there was a stoppage at Goldthorpe pit,

---

[1] Jonathan and Ruth Winterton, *Coal, Crisis and Conflict: The 1984–5 Miners' Strike in Yorkshire* (Manchester: Manchester University Press, 1989), 66–7.
[2] Jackie Keating, *Counting the Cost: A Family in the Miners' Strike* (Barnsley: Wharncliffe Publishing, 1991), 10.
[3] Winterton and Winterton, *Coal, Crisis and Conflict*, 69.
[4] David Felton, 'Coal Strike Threat Spreads as NCB Insists on Closures', *The Times*, 7 March 1984.
[5] Winterton and Winterton, *Coal, Crisis and Conflict*, 67–9; David Gibbon and Peter Steyne, *Thurcroft. A Village and the Miners' Strike: An Oral History by the people of Thurcroft* (Nottingham: Spokesman, 1986), 44–5.

only four miles from Cortonwood.⁶ There were also disputes in other coalfields: as Jim Phillips has noted, 50 per cent of Scottish miners were *already* in dispute with the NCB *before* the national strike began, and in some cases had been so for several months.⁷ Indeed, disputes in the mining industry had been growing for several years, especially over the winter of 1983–4. Most significantly, in autumn 1983, the union had instigated a national overtime ban: the NCB relied heavily on overtime, and running down coal stocks would increase the NUM's leverage in any potential future dispute.⁸ The strike could have started at any number of pits. But the shock announcement of Cortonwood's closure, within the context of the dense and restive Yorkshire coalfield, made it the tinder box that lit the fuse of a national strike. As the NUM Cortonwood delegate successfully argued at the Yorkshire Area council meeting on 5 March, if Cortonwood pit was not safe from closure, neither were many others.⁹ Within a week, miners in Kent and Scotland also walked out. South Wales followed suit, though reluctantly, still sore about the failure of miners across the country to support them in proposed strike action the year before.¹⁰ By 12 March, ninety-nine pits employing more than 96,000 men had shut down production.¹¹ However, most miners in the extensive and productive Nottinghamshire coalfield, plus a few small mining regions like Staffordshire and Leicestershire, did not come out, or quickly returned to work. Despite this, NUM President Arthur Scargill quickly declared the dispute a national stoppage on the basis that a majority of Areas were already striking. But a national ballot was never held—a source of much contention during and after the dispute, giving political ammunition to opponents of the strike.¹²

The early days of the strike were confused, and the important decisions and actions were mainly taken by men (though, as we discuss later in this chapter, there *were* women in the NUM Colliery Officials and Staff Area (COSA) on strike). But the strike would also be sustained by the work of women, in two distinct forms: first, in the everyday support given to male family members on strike, and, secondly, by the swift development of women's support groups, which played a vital role in facilitating the strength of the strike. Despite the fears of some close to Arthur Scargill that it would be difficult to get miners and their wives to support a national strike—after all, national ballots for strike action had failed in 1982 and 1983, and the right-wing press carried regular features on anti-Scargill wives—in the event, the dispute generated its own momentum.¹³ Many who lacked enthusiasm at first were nevertheless reluctant to see picket lines crossed;

---

⁶ Winterton and Winterton, *Coal, Crisis and Conflict*, 64–9.
⁷ Jim Phillips, *Collieries, Communities and the Miners' Strike in Scotland, 1984–85* (Manchester: Manchester University Press, 2012), 1.
⁸ Winterton and Winterton, *Coal, Crisis and Conflict*, 61–4.   ⁹ Ibid., 67.
¹⁰ See Chapter 2.
¹¹ Paul Routledge, 'Militant Picketing Spreads Coal Strike to 100 Pits', *The Times*, 13 March 1984.
¹² Winterton and Winterton, *Coal, Crisis and Conflict*, 70–2.
¹³ For more on 1982 and 1983 see Chapter 2.

and it was partly anxieties about miners' wives opposing the strike that led already-political coalfield women to organise in support of the dispute from its very first days. This chapter examines why, in these early days, women supported or opposed the strike, and how they did it.

Memories of the Beginning

Not all women we interviewed for this project had clear memories of the strike's beginning. The pre-existing local stoppages at some collieries, and the fact that different Areas were called out at different times, meant that there was no clear, single start date. The confusion that marked the first few days and weeks of the strike has often been smoothed over retrospectively, but it is important to remember that it was not immediately clear that the dispute would become national, or that it would go on so long. Short, local disputes were common in mining, and even the national strikes of 1972 and 1974 only lasted a matter of weeks or months. As Ann Robertson from Kent remembered, 'there'd been the odd talk—to tell you the truth, I didn't take very much notice at the time. I mean— strikes had come before and strikes had gone.'[14] Many interviewees were aware of the poor industrial relations of recent years. Adrienne C., who had recently moved to a village near Selby when her husband transferred to the super-pit complex there, remembered, 'there started to be nigglings from when we moved in, really... they seemed to have a heck of a lot of days where he used to get there and it—"oh they're on strike", "oh they disagreed with this, they've disagreed with that"'.[15] Jeannette McComb, who had moved from Wolverhampton to Ayrshire with her Scottish miner husband in the 1970s, told us:

> There were rumblings... There was always a lot of speculation about what was happening. And you kinda had the feeling that something was going to happen... But you never really thought that it would happen. So when it *did* happen—although it wasn't a total shock, you thought, 'oh god, oh they are on strike, you know, actually, this is it, kind of thing'.[16]

As Jeanette suggests, there was a difference between the anticipation and the reality of a strike.

Most of our interviewees assumed that this would be another short strike; annoying, perhaps, but not life-changing. In Fife, Alice Samuel remembered her

---

[14] Ann Robertson, b. 1934, London/Kent, interviewed by Florence Sutcliffe-Braithwaite, 5 November 2018.
[15] Adrienne C., b. 1956, Yorkshire, interviewed by Victoria Dawson, 26 June 2018.
[16] Jeanette McComb, b. 1953, West Midlands/Scotland, interviewed by Victoria Dawson, 26 September 2018.

husband had 'been on strike before, but it had usually been for a day or something like that, so I wasnae too worried about it'.[17] Kay Case, from Treharris, in South Wales, remembered, 'we thought, "oh it'll be a couple of weeks, or, what have you, oh it won't be long"... we thought, "oh they'll be back at work before the holidays", you know, for the summer holidays'.[18] A few people claimed to know that the strike would be a long one. In Kent, Liz French recalled that her husband said, 'this is gonna last forever'.[19] Lynne Dennet, from Church Warsop, Nottinghamshire, also claimed that, 'I expected it to be about a year.'[20] But such voices were in a minority. The confusion of the first few weeks, and the fact that a concerted support movement only began to emerge in late spring, suggests that these testimonies were informed by a significant measure of hindsight. As Siân James remembered, 'people will say to you now, "oh I knew we were in for a long one"—well I didn't!'[21] Very little suggests that many coalfield women foresaw how long the strike would last, or how significant it would become as a turning point, not just for coalfield communities, but for industrial relations in Britain more broadly.

Many women whose husbands were active supporters of the strike felt strong personal and political motivations to back them. They were exhorted to do so by Kay Sutcliffe of Aylesham Women's Support Group when she was filmed for the popular ITV documentary strand *World in Action* telling the crowds at a rally in Mansfield in April 1984, 'we are going to stand by our men, and make sure they have got all the backing they can get'.[22] This was one of a number of high-profile television programmes shown early in the strike which gave women a chance to air their opinions, and which probably helped shape pro- and anti-strike discourses—indeed, the strike was rarely out of the news (see Figure 3.1). The rhetoric of standing 'by' or 'behind' one's man recurred again and again on strike banners (see Figure 5.6), in memoirs and in our interviews. Pat Smith, whose husband was President of the NUM branch at Dinnington, in South Yorkshire, remembered:

> I knew, because of his political persuasions, that I'd either be standing with him, or that I'd be totally—you know, we'd be—we'd be opposite end of the room on these things. So there wasn't a choice, really, it was stand—stand shoulder-to-shoulder... I had no qualms.[23]

Marie Price, who was married to one of the few striking miners at Silverhill, in Nottinghamshire, similarly reminisced:

---

[17] Alice Samuel, b. 1958, Scotland, interviewed by Natalie Thomlinson, 1 August 2018.
[18] Kay Case, b. 1948, South Wales, interviewed by Florence Sutcliffe-Braithwaite, 13 August 2018.
[19] Liz French, b. 1950, Kent, interviewed by Florence Sutcliffe-Braithwaite, 6 July 2018.
[20] Joan Witham, *Hearts and Minds: The Story of the Women of Nottinghamshire in the Miners' Strike, 1984–1985* (London: Canary, 1986), 140.
[21] Siân James, b. 1959, South Wales, interviewed by Florence Sutcliffe-Braithwaite, 5 February 2019.
[22] 'Women on the Line', *World in Action*, ITV, 16 April 1984.
[23] Pat Smith, b. 1949, Yorkshire, interviewed by Victoria Dawson, 8 June 2018.

Figure 3.1 A striking miner and his family in County Durham watch Arthur Scargill on the television, 1984. © Keith Pattison.

When he came to us and talked it over, he said that I'm coming out on strike. 'Yeah.' He says, 'well I think like this Marie. I know I've got a job here', he says. 'But there's an Alan Price in Yorkshire, and an Alan Price in Wales, and everywhere else, that hasn't', he says. 'So I've got a job. They should have a job as well.' He says, 'what do you think of me coming out on strike?' I said, 'I wouldn't have any respect for you if you didn't.'[24]

Alan told her, 'that's it, if you're behind me, I'm out on strike'.[25] When asked if she believed in the strike, Margaret Whitaker, who kept her family afloat through the dispute by taking on more hours at work, said, 'I thought it was a just cause at the time, erm, I didn't believe it would ever be successful, deep down... I believed that we had a job to do... we've always been a partnership, if anything happens, we're in together'.[26]

For these women, backing their husbands in their strike action was not just a chance to display their commitment to the cause, but also an opportunity to demonstrate the strength of their marriages—both at the time, and in the retelling of the story. Here we can discern the influence on many (though not all) coalfield couples of the ideology of companionate marriage, which emphasised the marital relationship as a team effort, and which, as we suggested in Chapter 2, had a

---

[24] Marie Price, b. 1935, Nottinghamshire, interviewed by Natalie Thomlinson, 29 May 2019.
[25] Ibid.
[26] Margaret Whitaker, b. 1942, Yorkshire, interviewed by Victoria Dawson, 6 September 2018.

significant impact on working-class culture, including in the coalfields, in the postwar decades. Reconfiguring gender and marital relations was not a priority for most women when they gave their support to their husbands' decision to strike. Rather, many wanted to be seen visibly *standing by their men*. Indeed, while men often discussed their decision to strike with their wives, they had usually taken it already, and mainly wanted their wives' endorsement and support. Neither of the two major sociological studies of the strike published shortly after the dispute's end even considered the role of wives in their discussions of how men made the decision to come out, although wives were seen as key in the decisions taken by individual men to break the strike.[27] It should be remembered, though, that it would have been difficult for many men to even consider going against the decision of the local lodge, or to cross picket lines, particularly given the intense camaraderie of miners: for many men, the 'decision' to join the strike was less a personal than a collective one.[28]

Though most women supported their husbands' strike action, unsurprisingly, few were enthusiastic at the prospect of a huge cut to household income. Some families had savings, but these would very rarely be enough for more than a few weeks. Some women remembered being frightened, unsure, or even angry when they heard about the strike. Maureen, from Lothian Women's Support Group, said she was 'fuming': her family was only just getting over a recent eight-week strike at Monktonhall pit in 1983.[29] Women were still generally tasked with responsibility for making ends meet within the family budget week by week. Jeanette McComb remembered that, 'you're aware that things are going to be difficult, you're aware that things are going to be tight, and your budget's, you know, slashed'.[30] In Washington, Tyne and Wear, Linda Chapman remembered that:

> He said, 'no, we're on strike, that's it'. And me, like, 'oh god, what happens now—we're gonna?' ... I mean, they earned really good money then. I mean, he worked six, maybe six and a half days a week, and I mean he was probably earning twenty-five, maybe thirty grand a year then, it was a lot of money... we'd moved house, we had quite a big house, with a mortgage, we had a car, which we were borrowing money for. And then suddenly I was thinking 'what are we gonna do?'[31]

---

[27] Gibbon and Steyne, *Thurcroft*, 43–60; Winterton and Winterton, *Coal, Crisis and Conflict*, 53–78.

[28] See Emily Peirson-Webber, 'Masculinity and Mining in the British Coal Industry: From Nationalisation to Pit Closures' (unpublished PhD thesis, University of Reading, 2022), ch. 4, for an extended discussion of male camaraderie in the pit.

[29] Lothian Women's Support Group, *Women Living the Strike* (Dalkeith: Lothian Women's Support Group, 1986), 9.

[30] Jeanette McComb.

[31] Linda Chapman, b. 1958, North East England, interviewed by Victoria Dawson, 18 July 2018.

These were precisely the sentiments that women close to Arthur Scargill, like Jean McCrindle and Nell Myers, had been concerned about in 1983.[32] But miners' wives like Linda, despite their anxiety, generally felt little or no inclination to pressure their husbands to break the strike; for some, this was a matter of political principle, but for others it was more obviously about supporting their husbands, who would face major social pressure from workmates and community to stay solid. Linda herself turned to a different strategy for coping with the strike—as we will see in a later chapter, she went full time at work to ensure the family could survive.

Other women worried about the effect that not going into work would have on their husbands. Adrienne C. said, 'I honestly remember it—more than money, I mean money's a worry, but more than money, I was worried about [him] being off work more than anything. He'd—he'd hate that, being at home all day... it was more him being around the house all day.'[33] Similarly, Ann Robertson remembered her worries about her husband Rob at the beginning of the strike: he'd 'never been idle in his life; he'd never been unemployed in his life, and he was one of these people who needed, if you like, to work'.[34] Neither Ann nor Adrienne, nor their husbands, supported the dispute personally, but both men came out on strike and stayed out: they knew the social costs that strikebreakers would incur (although Adrienne's husband did eventually return to work after Christmas). In Adrienne and Ann's memories, we can hear echoes of a contemporaneous discourse that, as Jack Saunders has shown, portrayed strike-prone industrial workers as lazy and as wreckers of the economy.[35] Indeed, two Nottinghamshire women with striking husbands talked about hearing, while at work, their own colleagues condemning 'lazy idle strikers' who 'should get back to work and keep their families'.[36] Adrienne and Ann were implicitly rebutting these sorts of allegations when they spoke of their own husbands' need to work, as well as picking up on discourses which linked the successful performance of masculinity with work. Unsurprisingly, given their personal disagreement with the strike, neither Adrienne's nor Ann's husbands became actively involved in supporting the dispute, and nor did Adrienne and Ann. For some strikers, rather than the occasion for idleness, the strike provided a stage upon which masculine fantasies of 'going into battle' could be heroically enacted; but there were probably many men like Ann and Adrienne's husbands whose masculinity was realised through other means.[37]

Perhaps surprisingly, in the coalfield that was to become strongest for the strike, South Wales, there was hostility to the action at its beginning. In the initial

---

[32] See Chapter 2.   [33] Adrienne C.   [34] Ann Robertson.
[35] Jack Saunders, *Assembling Cultures: Workplace Activism, Labour Militancy and Cultural Change in Britain's Car Factories, 1945–82* (Manchester: Manchester University Press, 2019), ch. 1.
[36] Lynn Beaton, *Shifting Horizons* (London: Canary, 1985), 76.
[37] Peirson-Webber, 'Masculinity and Mining', 173–4.

meetings called to discuss the strike, the Area lodges voted by eighteen to thirteen against it.[38] South Wales miners were reluctant to support South Yorkshire when the Area had failed to support them in a similar crusade just a year previously, as Carol*, who was 16 and still at school when her father went on strike, recalled:

> A lot of the South Wales miners were pretty pissed off. They were pretty pissed off, because it was seen as, well, hang on, where was everybody when our mines had been picked off?... So in fact they went to work, the majority of them went on the Monday, but there were pickets, and it was the—the thing, you do not cross the picket line. So they didn't. And everybody's out. Even though at that time, there was a lot of anger as to why it had happened when it happened, and not earlier. Not that they didn't agree with the principle of the strike, because we really, really did. But there was quite a bit of resentment.[39]

The complexity of Carol's—and the wider community's—feelings about the strike is evident here: support for the strike could coexist with 'resentment' of the Yorkshire miners, and a belief in the political objectives of the strike could coexist with fatalism about the future of the pits. Yet despite the reluctance of many miners to come out at the beginning of the dispute, many nevertheless ended up doing so, and their wives tended to support them. This was true not just in South Wales, but across the country.

Two overarching imperatives framed the decision to support the strike for both men and women. The first was an *individual* moral or political imperative, probably most keenly felt by those who were already politically committed: *that to strike was the right thing to do to prevent pit closures*. The second was a *collective* community imperative *that a picket line must never be crossed*, and that solidarity should be shown with the decision of the trade union. The acceptance of this imperative by many—even when they disagreed with, or had doubts about, the strike—was part of a collective habitus that was located in a shared, if declining, recognition of the legitimate role that trade unions played in public life.[40] There was also a negative side to the community imperative: families living in close-knit mining communities could face the prospect of social ostracism if men broke the strike. As Alison Anderson remembered of her community in Fife, to 'scab' would be 'life changing... you would have lost everything'.[41] This, of course, had less impact on families living outside close mining communities, which, as shown in Chapter 2, was a significant proportion of the total by 1984. For many women,

---

[38] Martin Adeney and John Lloyd, *The Miners' Strike, 1984–5: Loss without Limit* (London: Routledge & Kegan Paul, 1986), 96.
[39] Carol*, b. 1968, South Wales, interviewed by Natalie Thomlinson, 19 June 2018.
[40] Saunders, *Assembling Cultures*, ch. 1.
[41] Alison Anderson, b. 1959, Scotland, interviewed by Victoria Dawson, 29 August 2018.

added to these imperatives was the strong sense that they wanted to 'stand by' their men.

However, the community imperative could also be a strong factor bolstering the decision *not* to strike, as in Nottinghamshire, where the majority of miners stayed in work for the whole dispute. Here, community pressure helped *keep miners in work*. Polly*, who was married to a working miner in Calverton, remembered how her husband felt:

> In hindsight, if he had had a vote, then he would have probably have followed. But because he didn't have a vote, and they came out, and they came down here to tell us 'this is what you're going to do'. Oh no. You don't tell—you're dealing with a group, you're dealing with a community which has got a bond—all mining villages have got a—are bonded—not like you're dealing with an individual, and you go, 'oh no. Nobody [is] coming down here to tell us.' That's how we felt.[42]

Ironically, the discourse of 'solidarity', 'community', and 'togetherness' in the face of a common enemy—generally associated with striking areas—could also be used by those in areas that resisted the strike to defend their decision. Polly's arguments echoed the points made by Nottinghamshire women in the April 1984 *World in Action* documentary. In the film, two Nottinghamshire women insisted that while they and their husbands did not disagree with the injunction not to cross a picket line, this only held good if it was a picket line of their workmates: otherwise, it was simply bullying.[43] The film also demonstrated the significance of the ballot argument: for those who questioned the strike, the absence of a national vote became totemic, representing what they saw as a lack of democratic process.[44] Rather than drawing on explicitly anti-trade union discourses, these women's support for their husbands' 'right to work' was couched in the language of the defence of community, trade union democracy, and peaceful picketing. These were the mainstays of the anti-miners' strike arguments.[45] Within coalfields where the majority worked through the strike, women who supported the 'right to work' often saw themselves simply as 'ordinary' women supporting their menfolk, in much the same way that many women involved in supporting striking miners did.

One woman featured in the *World in Action* documentary was Jane Paxton, a miner's wife from Eastwood. Paxton's husband was a surface worker at Moorgreen pit, which was scheduled for closure in 1985; she made a media splash early in the strike when the *Nottingham Evening Post* ran an article entitled

---

[42] Polly*, b. 1944, Lincolnshire/Nottinghamshire, interviewed by Natalie Thomlinson, 7 November 2018.
[43] 'Women on the Line', *World in Action*.
[44] Winterton and Winterton, *Coal, Crisis and Conflict*, 70–2.
[45] Diarmaid Kelliher, *Cultures of Solidarity: London and the 1984–5 Miners' Strike* (London: Routledge, 2021), 164–5.

'Petticoat Pickets', about Paxton and other working miners' wives who were organising 'to take on Scargill's men': Paxton was pictured with a child on her hip, drawing from the popular visual iconography of working-class matriarchs (see Figure 3.2).[46] The article also noted that Scargill had received 'a noisy reception in Sunderland by women protesting at the decision to call their husbands out on strike without a ballot'.[47] Two days later, the *Daily Mail* ran a piece on 'Why Women are Against the Strikes', centred on Paxton, emphasising her credentials as a miner's wife with 'coal-dust in her veins', whose own father and father-in-law were miners too. According to the *Mail*, Paxton had gathered seventeen other miners' wives who were sympathetic to her point of view to protest the flying pickets from Yorkshire.[48] Paxton complained in the press and in the *World in Action* documentary about the lack of a ballot, displaying a detailed grasp of the political issues involved, and the money that her husband and other Nottinghamshire miners earned. She also told the *Daily Mail* that she spoke as one 'who isn't union-bashing', implying she was situating her critique of the NUM *within* rather than *against* the values of trade unionism.[49] In her outspokenness and political knowledge, Paxton was remarkably similar to those miners' wives who most prominently *supported* the dispute. Like some women in the support movement would be, Paxton was also accused of having her husband 'under the thumb'.[50]

Polly*, like Jane Paxton, also gathered a group of local women to protest flying pickets. She told us she had been concerned about the intimidation that her husband and other working miners faced on the picket line at Calverton. The colliery there had very few strikers and was thus a focus for flying pickets early on in the strike. Polly recalled:

> I remember going charging up there, we had a little Robin Reliant at the time, and I remember charging up there going through the gangs of men, shouting at them, telling them to 'fuck off home', you know, and you know, 'how dare you come here?' And then the women—we eventually got a little women's group together... we actually decided to walk up together with the children and walk through all these men to go to the top club, to show them we weren't afraid, and we weren't going to take [it].[51]

While Polly disapproved of the women's groups that were being set up to support the strike all over the country, it is clear that the group in Calverton was in some ways their mirror image. Polly identified as a feminist, and was keen to support women: she formed the group, she said, to 'tell other women, this group's here if

---

[46] 'Petticoat Pickets', *Nottingham Evening Post*, 10 March 1984. [47] Ibid.
[48] Stephen Oldfield, 'Why Women are Against the Strikes', *Daily Mail*, 12 March 1984.
[49] Ibid.   [50] 'Women on the Line', *World in Action*.   [51] Polly*.

Figure 3.2 Jane Paxton interviewed in the *Nottingham Evening Post*, 10 March 1984. © Nottingham Evening Post.

you need us, we'll come and help if you've got problems in the family'.[52] Like women activists who supported the strike, Polly stressed the importance of women's agency, mutual support, and involvement in the dispute.

While—as we discuss in Chapter 5—some of the women who would become leaders of the official back-to-work campaign were not deeply embedded in mining communities, and were motivated by Conservative political beliefs and staunch anti-trade union ideology, other women who publicly opposed the strike were not. Most wives of miners who continued to work in coalfields like Nottinghamshire probably supported their husbands because of a complex mixture of factors. Their immediate economic interests clearly lay with their husbands continuing to work: as Jane Paxton told the *Daily Mail*, '[w]e wives have to hold house and home together...a strike would devastate us'.[53] Many felt buoyed up by the support they received from their immediate communities, where most continued to work. Some probably felt distant from, and hostile to, NUM decision-making processes; as Jack Saunders has suggested in relation to the Cowley wives' back-to-work campaign in the 1970s, this could bolster anti-strike feeling among women.[54] Women like Polly* and Jane Paxton rejected the idea that they were anti-trade union, but their respect for the foundational conventions of trade unionism had clear limits: they insisted on the need for a national ballot— which they considered to be proper democratic process—and the illegitimacy of flying pickets from outside the community.

At the start of the strike, coalfield women thus asserted their agency in a variety of political directions, not all of them supportive of the dispute, or retrospectively amenable to a 'heroic' reading. There have been various attempts to quantify coalfield women's attitudes towards the strike, both while it was ongoing and afterwards. Fiona Measham and Sheila Allen found in their small study of a coalfield area in West Yorkshire in the late 1980s that 47 per cent of women declared themselves in favour of the dispute, and 42 per cent against, with the rest undecided; women from mining households expressed more support for the dispute (56.5 per cent) than those from non-mining households (41.6 per cent).[55] The impetus to measure women's support for the strike came from an established discourse, prevalent in both the media and academia, that women tended to act as a conservative brake on the tendencies of their more militant husbands.[56] But such attempts to quantify support for the strike in binary terms fail to capture the messy reality of many women's mixed feelings about the dispute. While there were women who were strongly for or against the strike from the beginning, for most, feelings were much more ambivalent.

---

[52] Ibid. [53] Oldfield, 'Why Women are Against the Strikes'.
[54] Saunders, *Assembling Cultures*, 221.
[55] Fiona Measham and Sheila Allen, 'In Defence of Home and Hearth? Families, Friendships and Feminism in Mining Communities', *Journal of Gender Studies*, 3 (1994), 31–45, at 34.
[56] E.g. Gibbon and Steyne, *Thurcroft*, 187.

COSA Women on Strike

At the start of the strike, Roni Chapman faced a dilemma. Roni was a librarian at Coal House, the administrative headquarters for the NCB in Doncaster, and a member of NUM-COSA, the section of the union that represented administrative staff, canteen workers, and underground chargehands.[57] She was also a Labour Party councillor on Doncaster council. When the strike broke out, the COSA branch at Coal House voted to remain at work until a national ballot was held. Roni therefore continued working, walking past pickets at Coal House until she was moved to another nearby building. As a local politician, Roni's stance attracted some publicity, and an article ran in a local newspaper with the headline 'Councillor Defies Pickets'.[58] In light of this, the NUM wrote Roni a letter asking her to explain her position. In her interview for this project, Roni discussed her split loyalties, and her confusion about what she, as a member of COSA, was supposed to be doing at this point, remembering that 'we never had any sort of proper notice or anything of anything':

> Initially I went in, because nobody was striking at Coal House. You know—there was nobody else striking. But then there was a more militant member of the union in Coal House so he struck. And then it got to the point—you know, you've got your colleagues, who you've got a loyalty to...[59]

In the first days of the dispute, Roni felt that by not going to work in Coal House, she was letting down her colleagues, and not honouring the result of the vote at her local branch.

Roni, however, was well aware of the wider position of the NUM, and of the cause of striking miners. As she told us, 'it was a case of, who do I owe my loyalties to? That was the problem, always the problem.' She also faced significant pressure from her fellow councillors in the Labour Party (many of whom were in the NUM), who ostracised her: she was put 'in a polling station out in the sticks' on election day, and one even wrote 'blackleg' on her desk in the council chamber.[60] The tension became so much that Roni had a minor breakdown:

> It was like a depression. I—I just couldn't get out of bed. I can't describe the feeling, you know, it was pretty horrible... Because I knew whatever I did, I wasn't going to do right by everybody. But in the end, that's when I decided, after I'd been in bed a couple of days.[61]

---

[57] It had 16,500 members: Paul Routledge, 'Colliery Officials may Quit NUM', *The Times*, 18 January 1985.
[58] Roni Chapman, b. 1941, Yorkshire, interviewed by Victoria Dawson, 11 June 2018.
[59] Ibid.   [60] Ibid.   [61] Ibid.

Roni came out on strike, and became involved in efforts to support other striking COSA members. Her tale illustrates the dilemma that many NCB administrative workers faced; indeed, it has echoes of the dilemma faced by miners in areas like Nottinghamshire where most miners were working.

The vast majority of clerical workers for the NCB, however, chose not to strike. Christine Wooldridge, an administrative worker at Coal House, explained her reasons for continuing to work thus: 'the clerical union, management, had voted not to strike. So a lot of people felt they had a right to work because they had voted not to strike. And of course, yes we were paid because, you know, we went in to work.' Christine vividly remembered crossing the picket lines at Coal House during the first few weeks of the strike, when the attempts to picket out COSA were at their most intense:

> The initial few weeks was awful, but of course it tapered off. And we used to have to gather behind Coal House—with the—because the police station was next to Coal House—with the police guard all the way down—and there were hundreds [of pickets]... There was the police guard all the way down, and there were hundreds. It was the most horrendous thing, and it was terrifying. You know, because all these people baying at you, you know, shouting, spitting at you, throwing things at you, we used to have to wipe ourselves down because we had all spit all over us when we got into Coal House.[62]

Yet even Christine—who during the strike went to court to testify against one of the picketers—was not entirely unsympathetic to the striking miners, commenting that she thought the pickets had 'just been so, if you like, worked up, that it wasn't them, if you know what I mean'.[63] She also noted that many people in Coal House were from mining families, and that many administrative workers' wages were going to support striking husbands, fathers, or sons. The early days of the strike were messy, and in the absence of a national ballot, it was not entirely clear whether authority—legal and moral—lay with the NUM at national level, or the decisions of local branches. The affective bonds that workers had with colleagues were often significant, and could trump the more abstract calls to solidarity with other, unknown, Coal Board employees. Neither was the prospect of losing pay attractive.

Despite the sizeable literature on the 1984–5 strike and the women's support movement, very little has been written about the small numbers of women—NUM-COSA members such as canteen workers and administrative staff—who were on strike themselves. The position of COSA in relationship to the strikes of colliery workers was historically ambiguous; though part of the NUM, it often

---

[62] Christine Wooldridge, b. 1941, Nottinghamshire, interviewed by Victoria Dawson, 25 May 2018.
[63] Ibid.

functioned as a de facto separate union, in a structure that allowed significant autonomy to Areas, of which COSA—despite not being a geographical region—was one. During the 1972 strike, despite union instructions to allow COSA members to continue working, they had been unofficially picketed out of their jobs.[64] This happened to some women in 1984, too. Kay Case, who worked in the canteen at Treharris colliery, in South Wales, recalled the confusion about the status of COSA workers in the early days of the strike: at first, neither the National Association of Colliery Overmen, Deputies and Shotfirers (NACODS), nor COSA came out, so Kay was 'still working in the canteen... Then of course, the men would be picketing on the gates. Well we wouldn't walk through the pickets to go to work, so we were sort of not getting into work. And eventually our union called us out as well, so we were all out.'[65] In fact, though, COSA never did officially call its members out.

Like Roni and Kay, Barbara Drabble, President of the COSA branch at the NCB's Pensions and Insurance office in Sheffield, recalled the start of the strike for COSA members as confused and demoralising.[66] Trevor Bell, the President of COSA, had initially called for members to strike alongside the miners, but knew that this would be unpopular with his members and downplayed his calls for solidarity. Drabble recalled the 'utter chaos' that resulted on Monday 5 March as she tried to persuade workers in her Sheffield office to go out on strike, chaos that was exacerbated by the announcement mid-morning that Roni Chapman's COSA branch in Coal House had voted *not* to come out. Approximately 140 workers out of over 1,000 in the Sheffield office initially took strike action, but a few days later, Bell backtracked and they returned to work.[67] Bell then issued a statement saying COSA should support the NUM, *without* going as far as to say COSA members should go on strike (he even appeared on television calling for a national ballot).[68] At this point Drabble and a few others from the Sheffield office returned to striking, but their numbers dwindled from forty to nine in a week, and remained at this level for the rest of the strike.[69] Drabble described attempting to picket in these circumstances as 'soul-destroying'.[70] It seems likely that Bell, as Drabble suggested, 'wanted to ride two horses': he was certainly ambiguous in his communications with COSA members, essentially leaving up to them the decision about whether or not to strike.[71] The testimonies of women like Roni Chapman, Kay Case, and Barbara Drabble reveal the confusion and ambivalence that characterised the early days of the strike. As we have seen in South Wales, many who

---

[64] Ralph Darlington, 'There is No Alternative: Exploring the Options in the 1984–5 Miners' Strike', *Capital & Class*, 87 (2005), 71–95, at 73.
[65] Kay Case.
[66] Barbara Drabble, 'Office Workers Take Action', in Vicky Seddon, ed., *The Cutting Edge: Women and the Pit Strike* (London: Lawrence & Wishart, 1986), 109–23.
[67] Ibid., 114–15. [68] Winterton and Winterton, *Coal, Crisis and Conflict*, 71.
[69] Drabble, 'Office Workers Take Action', 115. [70] Ibid., 119. [71] Ibid., 113.

later became staunch supporters of the strike were initially lukewarm. The battle lines had yet to harden in the early spring of 1984, and were more in flux than many retrospective histories of the strike suggest.

While there are no statistics available for the number of COSA members who took strike action, it appears that canteen workers were more likely to strike than office staff, perhaps because of their daily personal contact with the men, and because many were deeply embedded in their local mining communities—indeed, many were married to miners. Liz Marshall, a striking canteen worker from Killoch, Ayrshire, suggested:

> It was just the canteen workers who came out, the office staff and the cleaners didn't come out. They worked in the office right through the strike. And the cleaners who are NUM members refused point-blank to come out. In the canteen you are in constant contact with the men, you know them, you are friendly with them. On the picket line you can see them and think 'Och, I ken that man,' you are meeting them every day. The office staff didn't have that daily, but still I could never understand why they didn't come out.[72]

And Catherine Paton Black, who worked in the canteen at the Nottinghamshire pit where her husband was a miner, wrote in her memoir that the couple 'both instantly decided we'd support any strike. We knew if we didn't we'd both be likely to lose our jobs anyway.'[73]

But—as Christine Wooldridge suggested to us—many who worked in NCB offices were also related to miners by blood or by marriage, and, ironically, money from administrative staff who did not join the dispute kept some striking miners and their families afloat financially. Among our interviewees, Jean Shadbolt continued working in her office job at Annesley colliery, despite the fact that her husband was a militant striking miner, a rare thing in Nottinghamshire. Yet Jean supported her husband and he supported her. She remembered:

> The offices weren't picketed often, but I had to cross a picket line to go to work, and every time they were there, somebody shouted, 'why are you at work, your husband's on strike!' And I didn't say—I just used to think, 'oh leave me alone'. And we were told—and you know, they couldn't do it now—the office staff were told, 'if you go on strike, you will not have a job to come back to'. We were told that... And that was one element of it. And the other one was, I suppose, if I'm perfectly honest, is—I'd got two kids and I didn't want them

---

[72] Liz Marshall, 'A Canteen Worker on Strike', in Seddon, ed., *Cutting Edge*, 97–108, at 98.
[73] Catherine Paton Black, *At the Coalface: My Life as a Miner's Wife* (London: Headline, 2012), 251.

to suffer. You know, it was bad enough only having one wage—my wage, which wasn't anything like a miner's wage. But, you know—this is perhaps the wrong thing to say, the wrong point of view, but why should my girls suffer if I can go and earn some money? That's how I looked at it.[74]

Nevertheless, Jean very much saw herself as a supporter of the strike—though she conceded she was perhaps 'a lone voice' in her office—even attending the women's rally in Barnsley in May alongside her sister Janet, who was active in Annesley and Newstead Women's Support Group.[75] In a reflection of the ambiguity that attended the question of whether or not COSA members should strike, neither Jean's husband, nor her daughters or sister, all of whom were strong supporters of the strike, saw any great contradiction in Jean's position; though in suggesting that what she was saying was 'perhaps the wrong thing to say, the wrong point of view', it is clear that Jean herself was aware of a 'correct' political stance from which her own narrative deviated.[76] Support for the strike could coexist with actions that appeared to undermine it. Manichean narratives—promulgated both at the time and afterwards—in which people were simply either for or against the strike, have obscured the complexity of attitudes that were in existence.

The Origins of the Women's Support Movement

Before 1945, miners' wives' support in coal strikes came in two main forms: first, practical and moral support in the home, and, secondly, collective action, such as picketing shops that sold to blacklegs' wives, or community shaming of strike-breakers, by shouting abuse, or using tactics like 'white shirting'—parading a nightdress on a broom behind a 'scab' as he made his way through the streets, in order to indicate that he was less than a man.[77] In the 1926 strike and miners' lockout, there was also a major organisation led by women to support the strike: the Relief Committee for the Miners' Wives and Children. This, however, was led by women from the labour movement, and was not a mass movement of miners' wives.[78] Soup kitchens, at least in County Durham and South Wales, were mainly

---

[74] Jean Shadbolt, b. 1948, Nottinghamshire, interviewed by Natalie Thomlinson, 23 July 2018.
[75] Ibid.
[76] Rachel Johnson, b. 1970, and Kerry Smith, b. 1972, both Nottinghamshire, interviewed by Natalie Thomlinson, 23 July 2018; Janet Slater, b. 1954, Nottinghamshire, interviewed by Natalie Thomlinson, 3 August 2018.
[77] Hester Barron, *The 1926 Miners' Lockout: Meanings of Community in the Durham Coalfield* (Oxford: Oxford University Press, 2010), 158; J. J. Gier-Viskovatoff and A. Porter, 'Women of the British Coalfields on Strike in 1926 and 1984: Documenting Lives Using Oral History and Photography', *Frontiers*, 19 (1998), 199–230, at 200; Angela V. John, *By the Sweat of their Brow: Women Workers at Victorian Coal Mines* (London: Croom Helm, 1980), 124–5.
[78] Barron, *1926 Miners' Lockout*, 153.

run by men, with women in general taking no more than supportive roles.[79] In the postwar decades, small numbers of wives organised opposition to strikes, and the right-wing press sought out women willing to go on the record opposing strikes, in order to bolster attacks on the legitimacy of trade unionism.[80] This drove some miners' wives to organise, and to speak out, in support of the national strikes of 1972 and 1974 (which lasted for seven weeks and sixteen weeks respectively).[81] Women in Calverton, Nottinghamshire, negotiated lower prices with local shops, bought in bulk and made food parcels for striking families.[82] In Rugeley, Staffordshire, women left their children at the Social Security office in protest until the administration agreed to pay them the benefits they were entitled to, and occupied the Stafford County Council offices to demand food, money, and coal.[83] Miners' wives joined picket lines at Kilnhurst colliery, near Rotherham, and in Battersea, West Ham, Stepney, Woolwich, and Dagenham.[84] Women in Aylesham, Kent, set up the Aylesham Ladies Action Group, catering for supporters visiting the village, and travelling to London.[85] In many places, however, feeding centres were still the affair of men. In Blidworth, Nottinghamshire, in 1972, a soup kitchen in the Youth Club served snacks, chip butties, bacon cobs, and soup, rather than cooked meals, with a small charge for food, and only men and children went.[86] There was, thus, limited—though not zero—precedent for coalfield women's organisation in support of strikes before 1984.

Unsurprisingly, given the fact that few anticipated such a long strike, many women's support groups only got underway later in spring. In Barnsley, however, a small group of women, centred around the trade union educational centre Northern College, quickly began to plan how they could support the strike, building on Northern College tutor Jean McCrindle's efforts (described in Chapter 2) to understand miners' wives' attitudes to industrial disputes. These women formed a group within days of the announcement of Cortonwood's

---

[79] Ibid., 158; Sue Bruley, 'The Politics of Food: Gender, Family, Community and Communal Eating in the General Strike and Miners' Lockout in South Wales in 1926', *Twentieth Century British History*, 18 (2007), 54–77, at 65, 67. Alan Campbell, *The Scottish Miners, 1874-1939, I: Industry, Work and Community* (Aldershot: Ashgate, 2000), 241 suggests this was not true in Scotland.

[80] E.g. Gill Martin, 'Cowley Militants "Gag Moderates"', *Daily Mail*, 2 May 1974; 'Striking Miner's Wife Defies the Pickets', *Daily Mail*, 24 January 1972. See Saunders, *Assembling Cultures*, ch. 1.

[81] Anthea Disney, 'We're Not Asking for Damn Cake', *Daily Mail*, 16 February 1972.

[82] 'Housing Crisis—Women's Offensive', supplement, 'Women in Struggle', 5ERC/2/3, papers of the Essex Road Women's Centre, Women's Library@LSE, London (hereafter ERWC papers). Nottinghamshire women's organisation in 1972 and 1974 is also mentioned in Witham, *Hearts and Minds*, 9.

[83] 'Housing Crisis—Women's Offensive', supplement, 'Women in Struggle', 5ERC/2/3, ERWC papers.

[84] Joseph Mullins, 'Fury as the Picket Line Wives go into Action', *Daily Mail*, 8 February 1972, 12–13; 'Housing Crisis—Women's Offensive', supplement, 'Women in Struggle', 5ERC/2/3, ERWC papers.

[85] Kay Sutcliffe, b. 1949, Janice Bartolo, b. 1957, and Margaret Davis, b. 1949, all Kent, interviewed by Florence Sutcliffe-Braithwaite and Natalie Thomlinson, 5 March 2016.

[86] Beaton, *Shifting Horizons*, 16–17.

closure. Witnessing news reports on 10 March of women demonstrating against Scargill in the Durham coalfield, some of the women who were to become involved in the group wrote to the *Barnsley Chronicle*:

> We, as women, would like to express our support for the strike... we wish to object to the assumption made in some sections of the popular press that all miners' wives oppose the decision to strike. We suspect that the vast majority of miners' families realise that the only other alternative is to bury our heads in the sand and hope that our pit won't be next.[87]

The letter was unsigned, but a few days later, the *Barnsley Chronicle* listed Jean Miller as a contact for anyone interested in joining the group to support the strike. Miller was a miner's wife and a prominent local leftist—an active member of the Communist Party of Great Britain (CPGB), she had spent time in the Young Communist League alongside Arthur Scargill in her youth. McCrindle notes that all the women in the Barnsley group were on the left, and several were in the CPGB.[88] To attract a broad base of support, they deliberately downplayed their political connections to pose as 'everywomen' who simply wanted to stand by their menfolk. But the name they chose—Barnsley *Women* Against Pit Closures—was explicitly chosen over the more conservative nomenclature of 'wives' or 'ladies', and was a signal of desire for autonomy from the NUM.[89]

The Barnsley group was the most prominent of the early women's groups (and, as we shall see, spearheaded the development of National WAPC), but it was not the only group to form early on in the dispute. In nearby Sheffield, another chapter of WAPC also began to form, after some of the organisers spoke to Jean Miller about the work of the Barnsley group; Sheffield WAPC was dominated by women who were politically active on the left (as in the Barnsley group), a number of whom were not miners' wives.[90] As with the Barnsley group, Sheffield WAPC came to act as an umbrella group for others in the area, holding weekly meetings in which money collected centrally would be distributed, and issues discussed.[91] Few women's groups were so dominated by self-avowedly 'political' women as

---

[87] *Barnsley Chronicle*, 16 March 1984, quot. in Jean McCrindle, 'The National Organisation of Women Against Pit Closures in the Miners' Strike of 1984-5' (unpublished PhD thesis, Oxford Brookes, 2001), 78–9.
[88] Ibid., 78–9, 255. For more on the role of the CPGB in the NUM and in British politics in the 1980s, see Chapter 1.
[89] See Jean Miller, 'Barnsley', in Seddon, ed., *Cutting Edge*, 227–40.
[90] Kath Mackey, 'Women Against Pit Closures', in Seddon, ed., *Cutting Edge*, 50–62, at 51; Janet Hudson, 'Holding it Together', in Seddon, ed., *Cutting Edge*, 63–78; and see Caroline Poland, b. 1949, South East England/Yorkshire, interviewed by Natalie Thomlinson, 5 February 2019.
[91] Sheffield Women Against Pit Closures, *We are Women, We are Strong* (Sheffield: Sheffield Women Against Pit Closures, 1987); Betty Cook and Pat Smith attended the Barnsley and Sheffield groups respectively as delegates from their own local groups: Betty Cook, b. 1938, Yorkshire, interviewed by Natalie Thomlinson, 16 March 2019; Pat Smith.

Barnsley and Sheffield WAPC; but many—perhaps even most—groups contained one or more women who were active trade unionists, Labour Party members, or politically active in some other way. As Theresa Gratton*, a miner's wife and an active trade unionist in her own right, who played a key role in the support group in her village in County Durham, remembered:

> It was just ordinary people coming together to do that and some played bigger roles than others, but if I'm honest, it wasn't people who had no background in anything who were at the core of organising it, it was people who had some form of either trade union or political background.[92]

Politically experienced women were often the driving forces behind groups' formation: twenty-eight out of forty-five of Meg Allen's interviewees, all of whom were active in the women's support movement, had been involved in political activity of some description before the strike, and she found that 'seasoned activists' were 'prime movers in the campaign's first weeks'.[93]

Some women's support groups grew directly out of existing political groups. In Chesterfield, a women's action group had been formed by Betty Heathfield (wife of NUM General Secretary Peter Heathfield and a longstanding political activist, She had been a member of the Young Communist League, the CPGB, and the Co-operative Women's Guild),[94] and Caroline Benn (wife of Tony Benn) to canvass on Tony Benn's behalf in the by-election for the Chesterfield seat in February 1984. On 22 March, this group held its first meeting in support of the strike, in Duckmanton Miners' Welfare.[95] In County Durham, Save Easington Area Mines (SEAM), set up a year before the strike to campaign for mines in the area, formed the basis of strike support activities in the village.[96] In Kent, the Aylesham Ladies Action Group, which had been formed to show support for the strikes of the 1970s, had 'waned' after 1974, as Kay Sutcliffe remembered, 'but we still had the background sort of organisation of it, and when the strike started in '84, a couple of us actually got together and called a meeting'.[97] This time, they called themselves Aylesham Women's Support Group, or Snowdown Women's Support Group, after the pit the village served (see Figure 3.3).

The impetus for re-forming the Aylesham support group came not just from the fact that the women involved had pre-existing experience, but also from anger

---

[92] Theresa Gratton*, b. 1955, North East England, interviewed by Florence Sutcliffe-Braithwaite, 22 February 2020.

[93] Meg Allen, 'Carrying on the Strike: The Politics of Women Against Pit Closures' (unpublished PhD thesis, University of Manchester, 2001), 71–3; Pat McIntyre argued similarly in her work on County Durham: McIntyre, 'The Response to the 1984–5 Miners' Strike in Durham County: Women, the Labour Party and Community' (unpublished PhD thesis, University of Durham, 1992), 50.

[94] McCrindle, 'National Organisation of Women Against Pit Closures', 252.   [95] Ibid., 82.

[96] Allen, 'Carrying on the Strike', 71; McIntyre, 'Response to the 1984–5 Miners' Strike', 50.

[97] Janice Bartolo, Margaret Davis, and Kay Sutcliffe.

Figure 3.3 Snowdown Women's Support Group (also known as Aylesham Women's Support Group) banner. From left to right, the women are Margaret Denham, Carol Parkin, Sue Mountford, Phyllis Fraser, and Joan Phelan © Aylesham Heritage Centre and Kent Mining Heritage Foundation.

at seeing anti-strike women in the media. As Kay recalled, 'it made us all really, really cross, thinking, how can women not support their men, wanting to keep their jobs'. The women spoke to the local NUM, who told them that flying pickets travelling to the Midlands needed food and bedding: providing this was their first goal. But the opportunity soon arose to take a coachload of women to Coalville for a march, and the group jumped at the opportunity to demonstrate publicly that women were supporting the strike: 'so, we got together with the other pit villages, and, erm, Betteshanger and Tilmanstone, they, they sent women along. The NUM provided the bus for us, a BBC reporter got on the bus with us... so we were on the news'.[98] Kent women were also among the most visible at an early rally held by miners and their women supporters in Mansfield in April 1984: this rally, though not as big as later events, was filmed for the April *World in Action* programme about women in the strike, which noted in a voiceover that the march 'attracted miners' wives from all over the country'.[99] That such a march occurred points to the speed with which some women within mining communities organised; that it was deemed television-worthy suggests the coverage that such activism was

[98] Ibid.   [99] 'Women on the Line', *World in Action*.

receiving relatively early on in the strike, and that it was perceived as novel. The media coverage these early groups received in turn stimulated activism in other communities.

There was a clear snowball effect in the formation of groups: women who were already active encouraged others to join the effort, and women who heard about support groups were inspired to set up their own. In Thurcroft, South Yorkshire, one woman remembered:

> I'd never heard of Women's Action Groups. I think they'd been on strike a few weeks and I was bored. My daughter (she lives on the east coast) came over. She said 'Get an Action Group going and get some people involved'. So she wrote out a poster and I put it in a shop window.[100]

Margaret Coulson remembered that Upton Ladies' Action Group formed after attending a meeting of a group in nearby Fitzwilliam (see Figure 4.2 for an image of the group).[101] Jean Miller of Barnsley WAPC visited other mining communities in the area to encourage women to form their own groups,[102] and Nell Myers, press secretary at the NUM, compiled a list of miners' wives (such as Kay Sutcliffe in Kent) who she thought would be sympathetic to the cause and who might be able to drum up support for the NUM.[103] The formation of some groups was encouraged or suggested by local NUM branches. In Oakdale, in South Wales (see Figure 3.4), Jane Davies and Sheila James recorded that '[i]t was the men at the lodge, the NUM branch, who first called the women together'.[104] Other groups evolved from what had been relatively small-scale attempts to provide food for picketing miners. Kay Case, for example, a striking canteen worker at Treharris pit, in South Wales, got together with a few other striking women several weeks into the dispute, 'and we said, "why don't we try and do something to help?"' They decided to make sandwiches and hot drinks for men acting as flying pickets; they 'put notices up or spread the word around', and soon more women got involved, with the group's activities expanding beyond simply feeding men.[105]

There were, thus, in the earliest days of the strike, three different goals that drove the formation of groups. Some came together because deeply political women wanted to support the strike and to campaign against pit closures; some were formed because women were angry that anti-strike miners' wives were

---

[100] Gibbon and Steyne, *Thurcroft*, 54.
[101] Margaret Coulson, unpublished memoir, n.d., FAN/JP Box 2, papers of Jill Page, Feminist Archive North, Leeds (hereafter Page papers).
[102] Miller, 'Barnsley', 227.   [103] Ibid.
[104] Jane Davies and Shirley James, 'Women from the Valleys Turn Activist', in Seddon, ed., *Cutting Edge*, 16–29, at 17.
[105] Kay Case; see also Bob Hume, 'The Hatfield Main Welfare Organisation', in Raphael Samuel, Barbara Bloomfield, and Guy Boanas, eds., *The Enemy Within: Pit Villages and the Miners' Strike of 1984-5* (London: Routledge & Kegan Paul, 1986), 128–38, at 129.

Figure 3.4 A Women Against Pit Closures meeting in Oakdale, Gwent, in Wales, 26 June 1984. © Jenny Matthews/Format.

gaining a more prominent hearing in the national media, and wanted to publicly show their support; and some formed because pickets needed feeding. These goals shaped groups' activities in the early days. It was only as the weeks wore on, and mining households began to experience more hardship, that women's support groups increasingly diversified from feeding pickets to feeding families too, via soup kitchens, food parcels, and supermarket vouchers. These feeding activities tended to get going towards the end of spring—often in later April or May—as it became clear that the dispute would be a long one.[106] Striking canteen workers like Kay Case and Catherine Paton Black often deployed their skills in such feeding activities (see Figure 3.5). While women who got involved in strike activism in the earliest days of the dispute tended to be those who were more politically minded, as activism broadened out to focus on providing sustenance to families, a more diverse range of women became involved, many of whom—as we will see in Chapter 5—never saw themselves as 'political' at all.

---

[106] The account books for the Woolley women's group and the Aberdare Miners' Relief Fund begin in May: Woolley Account Book, A308-G/2/1/1, papers of Barnsley Women Against Pit Closures, Barnsley Archives, Barnsley; Cashbook, D1432/1, papers of Aberdare Miners' Relief Fund, Glamorgan Archives, Cardiff. The first meeting of the Swansea, Neath and Dulais Valleys Miners' Support Fund recorded in the minute book was on 6 May 1984, but activities had clearly been going on for some time already, as a treasurer's report from 26 April–6 May was heard: minutes of meeting 6 May, Neath and District Miners' Strike Support Fund minute book, 6 May–22 September 1984, SWCC/MND/25/1, box 4 of 8, South Wales Coalfield Collection, Richard Burton Archive, Swansea.

Figure 3.5 Catherine Paton Black preparing food at a soup kitchen in Ollerton, Nottinghamshire. © Brenda Prince/Format.

In many cases, it can be difficult to unpick precisely how groups began: often there was a multiplicity of forces at work, and the formation of local groups could be overdetermined by a number of factors. In Bolsover, where there was already a local activist network from the recent by-election in the area, Toni Bennett remembered that having already organised 100 food parcels to distribute, she 'heard that Joyce and Carol Clare were already planning a group so it seemed like common sense to get together'.[107] Neat origin stories were constructed after the dispute, and smoothed over the often more chaotic and unplanned processes that led to women joining forces and forming groups. In the same way, the NUM committee structure which most groups quickly adopted often served to make them appear more formal and stable in their organisation than they in reality were: as Meg Allen argues, such structures were often adopted in order 'to appear as a serious organisation to their fellow strikers', where 'the reality was often one of informal leadership and constantly negotiated decision-making'.[108] It is also important to note that not all coalfield-based support groups were women-only. Some groups were mixed from the beginning (though even these tended to be

---

[107] Witham, *Hearts and Minds*, 132. [108] Allen, 'Carrying on the Strike', 101.

dominated by women),[109] but even some of those which had 'women's' or 'ladies' in their names included male volunteers, often men who were unable to picket due to previous arrests or to health problems.[110] Unlike in the women's liberation movement, the concept of 'women's only' space was rarely central to the politics of support groups. Many of Allen's interviewees 'stated that they would have been happy to work in mixed groups had that been practical or "allowed"'.[111]

What motivated women to join these groups? Clearly, many were compelled to action by their political convictions. But joining the support movement also provided a way of combating boredom and anxiety, and gave women a sense that they were doing something to help the strike. As Anne Kirby from Fife told us, 'you have to either get involved or sit at home, doing nothing'; Janie Robertson of Stirling remembered that 'it kept us sane'; and in response to a question about how she coped during the strike, Pat Smith simply responded by saying, 'getting involved'.[112] Getting involved was not just about politics; it also gave many women a sense of agency in a situation where they were to a large extent powerless.

Most miners' wives who became heavily involved in support work had partners who were also very active in supporting the strike. The Wintertons calculated that, of the miners' wives and girlfriends who got involved in support activities, 76 per cent were the partners of men who were spending at least five days a week on strike-related activities.[113] This is not to say that such women were simply doing their husbands' bidding; as we have already seen, many women involved in groups were themselves trade unionists or involved in other forms of activism. Nevertheless, women were probably more likely to know about support groups if their husbands were heavily involved in NUM politics: Marie Price, for example, only became involved in Ashfield Women's Support Group after her husband, a militant trade unionist, volunteered her services at a meeting at which Marie was not even present.[114] Anne Kirby recalled her then husband, a strike activist, telling her to go down to the local strike centre in Cowdenbeath.[115] Other women we interviewed, such as Pat Smith, Liz French, and Janet Slater, also had husbands who were well-known activists, and attributed their activism partly to their

---

[109] E.g. the Aberdare Miners' Relief Fund: see Anne Watts, b. 1949, South Wales, interviewed by Florence Sutcliffe-Braithwaite, 23 May 2019.

[110] E.g. the Ynyswen group involved five women and five men: Rebecca Davies, 'Not Just Supporting but Leading: The Involvement of the Women of the South Wales Coalfield in the 1984–5 Miners' Strike' (unpublished PhD thesis, University of Glamorgan, 2010), 162; men were involved in the support groups in Aylesham, Mill Hill, Scawsby, and at Hatfield Main: Kay Sutcliffe; Liz French; Maureen Coates, b. 1942, Yorkshire, interviewed by Florence Sutcliffe-Braithwaite and Natalie Thomlinson, 11 September 2014; Hume, 'Hatfield Main Welfare Organisation', 128.

[111] Allen, 'Carrying on the Strike', 118.

[112] Anne Kirby, b. 1955, Scotland, interviewed by Victoria Dawson, 26 November 2018; see also Janie Robertson, b. 1955, Scotland, interviewed by Florence Sutcliffe-Braithwaite, 20 November 2018; Pat Smith; Beaton, *Shifting Horizons*, 81.

[113] Winterton and Winterton, *Coal, Crisis and Conflict*, 121. This figure is adjusted for the over-representation of activists among respondents to the Wintertons' questionnaire.

[114] Marie Price. [115] Anne Kirby.

partners' involvement (though Liz French was a shop steward in her own union).[116] Women were less likely to be in trade unions than were men, and trade unions were often the primary arena in which an education in left-wing politics could be gained in working-class communities: to suggest that for some women, husbands *could* be a source of political influence and education is not to traduce their intelligence or capacity for independent thought.

There was a spectrum of activism in support of the strike. Between the hardcore of committed organisers who were active in a range of support activities most days, and those who supported their husbands but did not become involved in any formal support group activities, were a range of women who occasionally helped out in a local kitchen, volunteered at events like jumble sales or parties, or shook a bucket to raise funds. These women were often reluctant to see themselves as activists; in oral history interviews, it would sometimes take time for their involvement in such activities to emerge. Christina Bell, for example, told us that she 'never really went into that full on—I was more concerned about what was happening in my own home at the time'. Nevertheless, she went on to describe how she had got involved in organising car boot sales and pie and pea suppers, as well as hosting many visiting activists invited by her militant husband George to stay at their house. Likewise, Joan Holden told us that she 'tried not to get involved' with the strike, but would sometimes go to the local community centre to help with activities such as redistributing second-hand clothes. Some women's groups grew out of more informal support activities: Maureen Coates, for example, recalled that although the first meeting of the Sprotbrough and Brodsworth Mining Families Support Group (of which she was the secretary) was only held in November, the women were 'doing bits before then'.[117] This sort of informal strike support was much more common than formal activism. In Warwick and Littlejohn's 1986 survey of four Yorkshire mining communities, two out of 123 women interviewed reported involvement in support groups, but nearly a quarter of the sample said that they had been active in support of the strike or strikers.[118]

Despite both popular and scholarly portrayals of the women's support movement as 'widespread',[119] in fact, only a small minority of women in coalfield communities ever became deeply involved. The Wintertons estimated that only 4.7 per cent of miners' wives or partners in Yorkshire were ever active in support efforts.[120] Sheila Allen and Fiona Measham found, based on interviews with

---

[116] Pat Smith; Liz French; Janet Slater.   [117] Maureen Coates.
[118] Dennis Warwick and Gary M. Littlejohn, *Coal, Capital and Culture: A Sociological Analysis of Mining Communities in West Yorkshire* (London: Routledge, 1992), 174.
[119] Ben Curtis, *The South Wales Miners 1964–1985* (Cardiff: University of Wales Press, 2013), 209; see also e.g. Jean Stead, *Never the Same Again: Women and the Miners' Strike 1984–85* (London: Women's Press, 1987), passim.
[120] Winterton and Winterton, *Coal, Crisis and Conflict*, 122.

women from four coalfield communities in North Yorkshire, that 19.6 per cent of women from mining households were involved in any kind of support activity.[121] Given that they adopted a 'very broad definition of support activities', and that they studied coalfield *communities*, where the Wintertons surveyed all striking miners and their partners in Yorkshire (and controlled their figures for the greater tendency of strike activists to respond to the survey), it is unsurprising that Allen and Measham's figure is higher. In fact, Allen and Measham found that women in the four coalfield communities they studied from non-mining families were *more likely* to get involved in support group activities than were women from mining families (26.7 per cent compared with 19.6 per cent).[122] The Wintertons' study showed that miners' wives who lived in mining communities were far more likely to be involved in the support movement than were miners' wives living outside such communities; organising strike relief was therefore particularly difficult in areas like Selby, where no one community was associated with the pit.[123] Stress, frustration, busy lives, and political apathy kept many women from participating in activism. Allen and Measham found that of the women they interviewed who did not get involved, 31 per cent mentioned as reasons, 'caring for small children and elderly relatives, pregnancy, being too busy supporting their own immediate and extended family to be involved in support activities outside the home'. Their interviewees made comments such as:

I never thought about it. I just thought about my own family being able to get through, without either involving others or depending on others.

I... couldn't be there [at the food kitchen] at meal times. I had to look after my own family who were affected by the strike.[124]

Accounts that focus on the novelty of women's groups—and their undoubted achievements—tend to obscure the fact that the vast majority of women in coalfield communities did not join them.

Most groups were small. In Askern, South Yorkshire, the women's group never had more than about sixteen members, despite Askern colliery employing over 1,200 miners.[125] Local activist Joan Witham listed the membership for twenty-two groups in Nottinghamshire, with numbers ranging from five (in the Calverton Women's Support Group), to forty-two (in the Welbeck Women's Action Group—comprising twelve committee members and thirty further members).

---

[121] Measham and Allen, 'In Defence', 33–4. See also McIntyre, 'Response to the 1984–5 Miners' Strike', 49.
[122] Measham and Allen, 'In Defence', 34.
[123] Winterton and Winterton, *Coal, Crisis and Conflict*, 122, 124. Similar problems were encountered in Mansfield, not associated with any one pit, by the group there: Witham, *Hearts and Minds*, 178.
[124] Measham and Allen, 'In Defence', 34.
[125] Jane Thornton, *All the Fun of the Fight* (Doncaster: Doncaster Library Service, c.1987), 18.

Eighteen of the groups had between eleven and twenty-six members listed, though often a small 'core' did the main work.[126] Membership fluctuated: Liz French recalled of her support group in Mill Hill, in Kent, that 'the group didn't have exactly a kind of, fixed membership, it wasn't like, well these twelve people are...'; she recalled that if there was 'summat going on, it'd be packed'.[127] Guerrilla tactics sometimes had to be used to get women to come to meetings: one of the women who set up the group in Grimethorpe recalled that, after leafleting the women in the village whom she believed to be militant, they 'played it crafty... we advertised welfare rights to get 'em there', a ploy that worked, given that over 200 women came to the initial meeting.[128] Other groups never got off the ground, as the account of the attempt to start a women's group in Cowie, in Stirlingshire, suggests.[129]

Women had to overcome practical barriers to activism, often on the most basic of levels: one common challenge was finding a suitable venue where hot food could be prepared. The women's group in South Kirkby, Yorkshire, used a tent without mains water or standard kitchen facilities to produce 570 meals a day.[130] Working men's clubs and miners' welfare halls were frequently used, but they did not always have adequate facilities; and in areas where communities were divided over the strike, using such venues was contentious. In Bilsthorpe, Nottinghamshire, the support group 'tried the village hall, the Scout hall, the St John's Ambulance Hall, no good, nobody wanted to know. We felt like outcasts.'[131] Sometimes groups had to use several locations. Pat Smith recalled that the Dinnington group started 'in a little hut on [the] market' that the women got for free; later on in the year, as winter arrived, they moved into a local club to pack and distribute food parcels, and they were then given the use of the Lyric Theatre, owned by the town council, where they opened a soup kitchen.[132] The Dinnington group provided both food parcels and soup kitchens; some groups tended to focus on one or the other, while a few concentrated on the provision of food vouchers for local shops.[133] In Nottinghamshire, according to Witham twenty groups out of thirty distributed food parcels; twenty groups set up soup kitchens, eight were unable to, and the final two seem to have been able to find a venue to provide meals only occasionally.[134] In South Wales, the support effort centred mainly around the distribution of food parcels, rather than soup

---

[126] Witham, *Hearts and Minds*, 114–213.   [127] Liz French.

[128] Guy Boanas, 'Interviews at Grimethorpe', in Samuel, Bloomfield, and Boanas, eds., *Enemy Within*, 202–15, at 207.

[129] Steve McGrail and Vicky Patterson, *For as Long as it Takes: Cowie Miners in the Strike, 1984–5* (Cowie: S. McGrail and V. Patterson, c.1985), esp. 34.

[130] Winterton and Winterton, *Coal, Crisis and Conflict*, 123.

[131] Witham, *Hearts and Minds*, 23. Harworth also encountered significant issues: ibid., 163.

[132] Pat Smith.

[133] Theresa Gratton* discussed the switch from providing food parcels to food vouchers in her local support group.

[134] Witham, *Hearts and Minds*, 114–213.

kitchens,¹³⁵ partly because of the geography of the valleys, and partly because soup kitchens had been the 'symbol' of the 1926 lockout, and might evoke painful memories.¹³⁶ This was also the case in Easington, where activists used the term 'café' rather than 'soup kitchen' as they 'weren't going to be forced back to the 1930s'.¹³⁷ In areas where miners were not concentrated in pit villages, food parcels rather than soup kitchens predominated, such as in the Selby area of North Yorkshire.¹³⁸

Whether or not a group was primarily centred on soup kitchens, food parcels, or food vouchers, methods of raising money had to be thought up. Funding was at first often a rather ad hoc affair. In many (though certainly not all) areas, the local NUM donated some funds to women's groups to help start a kitchen or food parcel distribution.¹³⁹ Women sometimes went round local housing estates asking for money or tins of food, or bucket-shaking on the street.¹⁴⁰ In the Cynon valley, Ann Wilson and Elizabeth Ann* recalled knocking on doors asking for donations of food to the support group: Ann recalled that almost everyone contributed, apart from two people who told her that 'the miners chose to do this and put their families in peril, so it's up to the miners to feed their families and not us'.¹⁴¹ Coffee mornings, raffles, and jumble sales were also popular.¹⁴² Askern women's group undertook their first fundraising in a pub in nearby Pontefract, where they collected £64.¹⁴³ Only as it became clear that the dispute was going to last a long time did more systematic fundraising—such as twinning arrangements with local Labour parties, trade union branches, and other groups, or media appeals, public events, and fundraising trips—become the main locus of money-raising activity. Local shops and businesses were canvassed for donations of food or money, or

---

¹³⁵ Though some groups did run kitchens, e.g. in Maesteg: see exercise book with names of miners and their relatives using the Maesteg kitchen, D/DX/960/10/5, papers of Violet John, Glamorgan Archives, Cardiff.
¹³⁶ Bruley, 'Politics of Food', 63; Richard King, *Brittle with Relics: A History of Wales, 1962–1997* (London: Faber & Faber, 2022), 292. Hywel Francis suggested this to us in a portion of the interview with his wife, Mair, that he was present for: Mair Francis, b. 1948, South Wales, interviewed by Florence Sutcliffe-Braithwaite, 17 July 2018.
¹³⁷ Keith Pattison and Huw Beynon, *Easington August 1984*, n.p., 'The Miners' Strike Papers', People's History Museum and Archive, Manchester.
¹³⁸ Winterton and Winterton, *Coal, Crisis and Conflict*, 123 ff.
¹³⁹ E.g. the Oakdale group in South Wales and the Warsop Action Group in Nottinghamshire: Davies and James, 'Women from the Valleys Turn Activist', 17; Witham, *Hearts and Minds*, 203.
¹⁴⁰ Carole, 'How We Started', n.d., mentions collecting for food: FAN/JP Box 2, Page papers. An account of street collecting is given in Janine Head, Mavis Watson, and Teresa Webb, *Striking Figures: The Story of Normanton and Altofts Miners Support Group 1984-5* (Huddersfield: Artivan and Striking Figures, 1986), 4.
¹⁴¹ Ann Wilson, b. 1945, South Wales, interviewed by Victoria Dawson, 11 August 2018; Elizabeth Ann*, b. 1943, South Wales, interviewed by Victoria Dawson, 12 August 2018.
¹⁴² See the account of the Carlton in Lindrick group: Witham, *Hearts and Minds*, 136. Jumble sales are also mentioned by Joan Holden, b. 1937, Lancashire/Yorkshire, interviewed by Victoria Dawson, 23 July 2018; Kay Case; and Theresa Gratton*.
¹⁴³ Thornton, *All the Fun of the Fight*, 9.

offers to supply food at discount prices.¹⁴⁴ But, as Ann and Elizabeth's experience shows, while the public was often supportive, fundraisers also encountered hostility to the strike.

Perhaps the most surprising quarter of opposition to the women's support groups came from some in the NUM itself. The provision of food by women, rather than men, could challenge men's status as breadwinner; and the refusal of some women to accept the right of men to tell them what to do was a direct challenge to the power of the NUM. As such, the very existence of women's support groups could destabilise the gender order. Reactions to groups varied between locations: while some NUM lodges actively encouraged women to get involved in supporting the dispute, others were positively obstructionist. Theresa Gratton* described varied experiences with different NUM lodges in County Durham: 'Sacriston was old school, Dawdon was old school, Easington was more forthcoming, Wearmouth, they had activists there who were younger.'¹⁴⁵ In Woolley Edge, near Barnsley, Betty Cook encountered resistance from the local NUM lodge in her early attempts to organise a support group. Betty was married to a miner at Woolley pit, and alongside a neighbour had begun collecting food for the community. After having found a building and funding to support a soup kitchen, she remembered:

> I got summoned to a meeting at the miners' welfare, with the union men, and it set off first of all that we couldn't have a soup kitchen. I said, 'of course we can'. 'You've nowhere to have it'. I said, 'we have'. 'You've no cutlery or crockery', I said 'we've got everything we need'. 'You can't have a soup kitchen'. I said, 'it's going ahead'.¹⁴⁶

The kitchen ended up feeding around forty people a day when open (see Figure 3.6).¹⁴⁷

In Dinnington, the women in Pat Smith's support group also encountered hostility from some members of the local NUM lodge. Pat's husband was President of the lodge and supportive of the women's activism; ultimately he suggested that the women picket a union meeting in order to force the men to allow them to organise in support of the strike. Pat remembered, 'we just said to them, all we wanted to do were raise money to—to support them, like all t'other communities were doing'. That this was contentious for some of the men is indicative of what Pat described as the chauvinism of some in Dinnington NUM.¹⁴⁸ While the

---

[144] See e.g. Gwen MacLeod, 'Ashfield Women's Support Group Appeal', 10 May 1984, form letter, papers of Gwen MacLeod, private collection.
[145] Theresa Gratton*. [146] Betty Cook.
[147] Betty Cook, interviewed by Rachel Cohen, 29 August 2012, C1420/60, Sisterhood and After, British Library, London.
[148] Pat Smith.

Figure 3.6 Women from Woolley Soup Kitchen wear aprons emblazoned 'I'm a souper-woman'. Betty Cook is on the far right. © Raissa Page.

'wifely' activities of providing food were often tolerated to a greater extent than the more explicitly political activities of picketing and marching, even feeding could sometimes be seen as too challenging of the NUM's dominance. In some strike centres in Scotland, for instance, the men did the cooking rather than the women. Jim Phillips has seen the activities of such men as evidence of 'the particularly progressive character of gender relations in the Scottish coalfields', but it is probably more appropriate to understand some of these actions as stemming from the men's desire to retain control of strike-related activities, as Grace Millar found in her study of male-organised strike relief during the 1951 Auckland dockers' dispute.[149]

In other places, tensions with the NUM were more subtle, but still centred around local NUM men's assumption that they would direct the activity of the women's groups. When asked about the relationship between the Treharris support group and the NUM, Kay Case answered:

> We obviously had to work alongside them and some of the husbands that were on the union, their wives did work with support groups. But as a whole I felt the

---

[149] Phillips, *Collieries, Communities*, 5; Grace Millar, 'This is Not Charity: The Masculine Work of Strike Relief', *History Workshop Journal*, 83 (2017), 176–93. Similarly, in Carlton in Lindrick, and Langold in North Nottinghamshire, the men organised all food parcels in the area: Witham, *Hearts and Minds*, 136, 176.

NUM felt that it was their job to make all decisions and for us to go along with them, basically, even though it was the women's support group that in the majority kept the children and the wives fed, clothed to a certain extent.[150]

As this suggests, a desire to keep focused on the main task of supporting strikers and their families could work to prevent hostilities being aired too openly. Furthermore, as Theresa Gratton* recalled, an acceptance of women's organising could often be as rooted in pragmatism as in a progressive model of gender relations. Theresa recalled another female activist commenting that an NUM lodge official who was well-known to Theresa was 'wonderful, he never tries to control'; Theresa only partly agreed, though, suggesting of the NUM official in question that:

> Why would he want to bother sorting out the running of the kitchen, if somebody else was gonna go and do it for him, if women were there to do it, so while he was progressive...he wasn't that progressive, I know, from his own attitudes—but his view was, 'if there's people there to do it, let them get on with it. I've got other things to do, running the union'.[151]

As this suggests, where local women's groups accepted the authority of the NUM, relationships between the two tended to be harmonious; when, however, women questioned the power of the NUM to control their activities, things could become much more fractious. This was an issue that, as we will see in Chapter 5, led to splits in the support movement. Such tensions had to be delicately navigated by women involved in the support movement throughout—and, indeed, after—the strike.

Conclusion

The first two months of the strike were more confused, and feelings about it generally more ambivalent, than most accounts have suggested. The beginning of the strike provoked a range of responses from women: shock, fear, resignation, and, occasionally, a willingness to do battle. Such emotions were perhaps even more heightened for those women who worked for the NCB, who had to make decisions about whether or not to strike themselves. It was not at first apparent that the dispute would last so long, and many of those who initially opposed—or were ambivalent about—industrial action nevertheless came out on strike due to

---

[150] Kay Case. See also Lynne Dennet's account of the Church Warsop Group in Witham, *Hearts and Minds*, 130.
[151] Theresa Gratton*.

strong local cultures that stigmatised crossing a picket line. The strike drew its strength from this as much as from mass political or ideological support for the dispute. In other areas, notably Nottinghamshire, a desire to keep working, and anger with the NUM's tactics, trumped the stigma of 'scabbing', and men and women here *also* drew strength from feeling that they were acting with the 'community' by continuing to work and by supporting the men's 'right to work'. For some women who became active in the support movement, these early days were the crucible in which their activism was formed; more would join them as the months drew on. The contradictions and tensions that characterised the support groups—a movement largely of women that was set up to support men, and that did not always have the support of the very union it was fighting on behalf of—were present from the very start. The next chapter tells the story of the support movement's growth as spring turned into summer, and of the other survival strategies employed by women, as savings ran out and many were forced to fall back on networks of kith and kin.

4
High Noon: Summer 1984

12 May 1984

By the end of April 1984, the role of women in the strike was attracting the attention of both the media and the NUM President himself. A plan for a national rally in Barnsley where women could gather to publicly display their support for the strike was born, according to Jean McCrindle, in 'the Scargill home'.[1] Yet not everyone was so enthusiastic: Barnsley Area secretary Owen Briscoe refused to hire out Barnsley miners' hall to the women, a signal of the difficulties that would dog relationships between some men of the NUM and the women's movement.[2] The organisers of the march were worried that they would fail to fill any of the possible venues,[3] with only a fortnight to plan the event; and a disappointing turnout would be a blow to morale and a gift to the right-wing media, which was still heavily invested in a narrative of miners' wives being against the strike.

But the panic turned out to be premature. Saturday 12 May dawned 'red hot',[4] and the organisers looked on in gratified astonishment as coach after coach full of women arrived in central Barnsley.[5] The organisers estimated that 10–12,000 women from support groups across the country arrived—success not imagined in their wildest dreams.[6] Women from as far field as Ammanford in South Wales and Aylesham in Kent made the long journey.[7] The massed women marched through the centre of Barnsley, led by girl majorettes who were 'overwhelmed' to be taking the place of the brass bands and miners, who usually came first; for once, men stuck to the side-lines as stewards, and the only men allowed to march were

---

[1] Jean McCrindle, 'The National Organisation of Women Against Pit Closures in the Miners' Strike of 1984–5' (unpublished PhD thesis, Oxford Brookes, 2001), 90.
[2] Letter from Owen Briscoe to Jean McCrindle, 1 May 1984, quot. in ibid., 91.
[3] Ibid., 91–2.
[4] Aggie Currie, b. 1950, Yorkshire, interviewed by Victoria Dawson, 22 June 2018.
[5] Jean Stead, *Never the Same Again: Women and the Miners' Strike 1984–85* (London: Women's Press, 1987), 19.
[6] McCrindle, 'National Organisation of Women Against Pit Closures', 93, and see 91–6. Lynn Beaton, *Shifting Horizons* (London: Canary, 1985), 123–4, discusses the huge turnout.
[7] McCrindle, 'National Organisation of Women Against Pit Closures', 92; report on Barnsley trip, 12 May 1984, in Neath and District Miners' Strike Support Fund minute book, 6 May–22 September 1984, SWCC/MND/25/1, box 4 of 8, South Wales Coalfield Collection, Richard Burton Archive, Swansea (hereafter SWCC papers).

Women and the Miners' Strike, 1984–1985. Florence Sutcliffe-Braithwaite and Natalie Thomlinson, Oxford University Press.
© Florence Sutcliffe-Braithwaite and Natalie Thomlinson 2023. DOI: 10.1093/oso/9780192843098.003.0004

NUM leaders Arthur Scargill, Peter Heathfield, and Mick McGahey.[8] The march finished with a rally in Barnsley Town Hall, an imposing neo-classical building from the 1930s that was a monument to civic pride, and which dominated the local landscape. It was a fitting location for such a momentous occasion.

Contemporary accounts emphasise the joyfulness and exuberance of the packed hall (see Figure 4.1). Jean McCrindle remembered in her diary that, '[t]he actual rally was indescribably exciting—electric, unconventional, joyful, exuberant—chanting, [sic] witty, ebullient'.[9] Several of our interviewees were in attendance. Aggie Currie recalled, 'I was dumbstruck, I loved it'.[10] Janet Slater remembered that as the wife of a striking miner from Nottinghamshire, it was particularly important:

> [There was] definitely a feeling of pride, y'know, to be a part of this... because we were so isolated from all these gatherings and solidarity... we were just isolated from that, so to get among people where you're all of the same thought, y'know, was really uplifting, definitely.[11]

Figure 4.1 Inside a packed Barnsley Town Hall for the first national women's rally, 12 May 1984. © NLA/reportdigital.co.uk.

---

[8] Jean McCrindle and Sheila Rowbotham, 'More than Just a Memory: Some Political Implications of Women's Involvement in the Miners' Strike, 1984–85', *Feminist Review*, 23 (1986), 109–24, at 113; McCrindle, 'National Organisation of Women Against Pit Closures', 92.
[9] McCrindle diary entry, 21 May 1984, quot. in McCrindle, 'National Organisation of Women Against Pit Closures', 96.
[10] Aggie Currie.
[11] Janet Slater, b. 1954, Nottinghamshire, interviewed by Natalie Thomlinson, 3 August 2018.

Her sister Jean was also there and recalled it was 'amazing': when Arthur Scargill began to speak, 'everybody was jumping up and down—the floor was bouncing!'[12] Thirty-five years later, women still recalled the heady feelings that being at rallies and marches often evoked; for those who attended such events, they were often a high point of the dispute. McCrindle attributed the large turnout partly to the press coverage of rallies in support of the strike the previous May Day weekend, which often emphasised the role of women.[13] The success of the march underlines the fact that the women's movement was already beginning to establish itself and create networks, as well as demonstrating the efficacy of the NUM machine in getting its supporters out on to pickets, rallies, and demonstrations.

The success of the rally catalysed the formation of more local groups, and of an official national organisation: McCrindle and others used it as a moment to get other women enthused and spread ideas and practice.[14] The movement began to further develop the diverse array of feeding, fundraising, and picketing activities that it had already begun in the spring (see Figure 4.2). The Barnsley rally proved there was breadth and depth in the women's support movement, and confirmed

Figure 4.2 Upton Ladies Miners' Support Group raise funds at Wakefield Miners' Gala, summer 1984. © Raissa Page.

---

[12] Jean Shadbolt, b. 1948, Nottinghamshire, interviewed by Natalie Thomlinson, 23 July 2018.
[13] McCrindle, 'National Organisation of Women Against Pit Closures', 92.
[14] E.g. women from the Swansea, Neath and Dulais Valleys met Anne Scargill and Jean McCrindle, among others, at Northern College as part of their trip: report on Barnsley trip, 12 May 1984, in Neath and District Miners' Strike Support Fund minute book, 6 May–22 September 1984, SWCC/MND/25/1, box 4 of 8, SWCC papers.

for Scargill its potential. It also brought to light more generally the role of women in the strike, and how the dispute affected them. Summer 1984 was the high noon of the strike, the point at which it became clear that this was a once-in-a-generation industrial dispute. Mass returns to work lay in the future; morale was still (relatively) high; many still thought the strike winnable. This chapter traces the growth of the national support movement in this period, the decision of some women to join the picket lines—often seen as the most novel aspect of women's strike activism—and the survival strategies employed by women to help their families survive as hardship began to really hit.

The Growth of National Women Against Pit Closures

In the aftermath of the Barnsley rally, Betty Heathfield, wife of NUM General Secretary Peter Heathfield and a committed activist in her own right, set up a meeting between women's groups in Nottinghamshire, Derbyshire, and Yorkshire. She argued that a national coordinating committee and register of groups would be useful during the strike. Jean McCrindle's notes from the meeting recorded that Heathfield thought that '[t]he women's groups had released an enormous amount of creative energy in mining communities', and hoped this could be 'sustained beyond the present crisis in our lives': even at this early stage, some women were thinking of what the afterlife of any such organisation would be.[15] Ad hoc structures were already beginning to link together support groups at a regional level. Now more women thought a national organisation should be formed, too. Due to their close proximity to NUM headquarters in Sheffield, their personal links to key NUM personnel, and their potentially useful connections to left activists and feminists across the country, women in the Barnsley group—which included McCrindle as well as Anne Scargill—were in an ideal position to put these ideas into action.

The success of the Barnsley rally helped convince the NUM leadership that the women's movement could be an important weapon in the strike. This perception was further bolstered by Anne Scargill's arrest on the picket line two days later at Silverhill in Nottinghamshire. Rather than being eviscerated in the press, as so many male miners (including, of course, her husband) were, Anne was feted for her pluck, down-to-earth manner, and good looks. The *Daily Mirror* recorded that:

> with her blonde-streaked brown hair, her well-tailored trousers, her neat black sweater with its shining white shirt peeping over the collar, she hardly looked like

---

[15] McCrindle notes from 21 May 1984, quot. in McCrindle, 'National Organisation of Women Against Pit Closures', 106–7.

an arch-criminal. Mrs Scargill, in fact, is a nice-looking woman. The sort you'd notice—and Arthur is lucky to have a gutsy wife like this.[16]

The *Daily Mail* commented on the 'language' used by the women, but also reported on how 'passionately' Anne, 'wearing slacks, a dark blue sweater and white blouse...a part-time co-operative society office worker', supported her husband, and pointed out the mass movement of women in support of the strike that was growing up.[17] The 'ordinariness' and respectability of women like Anne Scargill meant they garnered very different media coverage to that of the NUM. Anne was presented as existing within a more middle-class mode of femininity that was implicitly contrasted with the 'rough' hypermasculinity of striking miners, who were coded as archetypally working-class. She, and other women like her, were the respectable face of the strike; not industrial dinosaurs but 'modern' women.

The positive press stories, the success of the Barnsley rally, and the impressive work of the women's groups meant that Arthur Scargill, alongside women from the support movement, now moved to set up an official umbrella national support group—called, after some debate, National Women Against Pit Closures (NWAPC)—which would be closely tied to NUM structures. At a meeting in late June, Betty Heathfield, Anne Scargill, Jean McCrindle, and Debbie Allen (a Northern College student and Barnsley WAPC member) discussed plans for a new office for the women at the NUM headquarters in Sheffield, as well as a memo that Arthur Scargill had prepared on the subject. In it, Scargill praised the women's groups as a development 'without parallel in an industrial dispute', but argued that their 'most essential weakness' stemmed from the 'fact that they are established on an ad hoc basis': national coordination and a 'formalised structure' were needed.[18] Scargill hoped that after the strike, 'a National Conference of all delegates from all over Britain, ie 2000, could be held', enabling groups 'to continue their development and involve more and more women in the activities of the Union and help to "politicize them"'.[19] As this suggests, Scargill was deeply involved in NWAPC on a day-to-day level from the very beginning.[20] His involvement was facilitated by the fact that he knew several of the women involved extremely well on a personal basis—including his wife, Anne, Jean McCrindle, whom he knew through Northern College, and Nell Myers, the NUM press secretary, for whom

---

[16] *Daily Mirror*, 17 May 1984, quot. in McCrindle, 'National Organisation of Women Against Pit Closures', 201.
[17] '"I'm Proud of Her"—Scargill', *Daily Mail*, 17 May 1984.
[18] 'Women Support Groups', 7JMC/A/01, papers of Jean McCrindle, Women's Library@LSE, London (hereafter McCrindle papers).
[19] Ibid.
[20] For more detail, see Florence Sutcliffe-Braithwaite and Natalie Thomlinson, 'National Women against Pit Closures: Gender, Trade Unionism and Community Activism in the Miners' Strike, 1984–5', *Contemporary British History*, 32 (2018), 78–100, at 87–8.

he later left his wife. These women were not controlled by Scargill—rather, they shared his goal of winning the strike—but it is important to recognise his involvement in shaping the organisation's structure and goals.

An 'inner circle' of women organised an inaugural conference for NWAPC in July 1984 at Northern College.[21] Though the conference was supposedly convened to arrange a national women's march in London in August, the 'inner circle'—plus NUM leaders—had, in fact, already planned this event. Approximately fifty women from support groups across the country were at the conference.[22] Most were unaware of the fact that the 'inner circle' met with Arthur Scargill and Peter Heathfield on the Saturday night—while the social was going on—for a private discussion to determine the future of the organisation. The two men wanted to keep an eye on NWAPC, and, in particular, to ensure that anti-Scargillites in the Eurocommunist faction of the Communist Party of Great Britain (CPGB) would be excluded from positions of influence.[23] This included women such as Jean Miller and Lorraine Bowler, key movers in Barnsley WAPC. These women were, like other Eurocommunists—and many others in the new left—sceptical about Scargill's strategy of mass picketing during the strike, and wanted to place more emphasis on building a popular front. Given the deep divisions in the NUM over key strategic questions relating to the strike, Scargill and his allies saw activists aligned to this faction of the CPGB as a challenge to his authority.[24]

Notes taken by Kath Slater show that Scargill insisted that the women's groups,

> should be organised and run in the main by miners [sic] wives and female dependents. Initially the union are giving substantial financial aid and support which they are concerned we do not abuse. It is necessary that the media do not have the opportunity to say that political parties of any shade are running the womens [sic] organisation... support group leaders should always be aware of the safety and security of the NUM, and see this as a main priority in this vital struggle.[25]

Scargill wanted the organisation to be dominated by miners' wives, not by women who were already active in left politics, who might be more likely to challenge his strategy for the strike. A motion suggesting that all women on the NWAPC

---

[21] Nell Myers, Betty Heathfield, Anne Scargill, Kath Slater, Debbie Allen, and SERTUC (Southern & Eastern Region of the Trades Union Congress) members Kate Bennett and Shelley Adams: McCrindle, 'National Organisation of Women Against Pit Closures', 119–23.

[22] This figure has been derived from a headcount of a photograph of all the women at the conference outside the steps to Northern College, 7JMC/A/01, McCrindle papers.

[23] McCrindle, 'National Organisation of Women Against Pit Closures', 119–23.

[24] See Dave Feickert, *Britain's Civil War Over Coal: An Insider's View* (Newcastle: Cambridge Scholars Publishing, 2021), 73–6, on how the split within the CPGB spilled over into NUM politics; and on the influence of the CPGB and the factions within it, see Chapter 1 of this book.

[25] Notes in Kathryn Slater's handwriting from 21/22 July 1984, 7JMC/A/01, McCrindle papers.

committee should be miners' wives passed at the conference, despite opposition from Eurocommunist women like Kath Mackey (not, herself, a miner's wife). But non-miners' wives were, in fact, appointed to the committee, without consultation: Kath Slater, as national organiser, and Jean McCrindle, as treasurer.[26] Given his longstanding relationships with both Anne Scargill, who was also appointed to the committee, though without voting rights, and Jean McCrindle, Arthur Scargill would have privileged access to NWAPC.[27] Further cementing the Scargillite position, the conference decided that 75 per cent of delegates to national conferences must be miners' wives.[28] But the association between NWAPC and Arthur Scargill was to prove consistently controversial during and after the strike.

The connections between NWAPC and local groups were always complicated, and its reach exceeded its grasp. The organisation was shaped by the NUM's desire to exert influence over the grassroots women's support movement, and Scargill's desire to use the women as a bulwark in his own factional struggles within the union. Many women resented the attempts of NWAPC to direct individual groups. Some deliberately stayed out of the national organisation; some activists in groups like Save Easington Area Mines (SEAM) saw (correctly) the establishment of NWAPC as an attempt to centralise power, and were keen to retain their autonomy.[29] One County Durham woman suggested that NWAPC was 'just trying to make a structure of themselves', a complaint that mirrored much of the unease with the organisation.[30] Similar dynamics were also at play in the South Wales coalfield, where Siân James recalled that although the South Wales Women's Support Group was happy to be aligned to NWAPC, they also 'wanted to do our own thing'; she felt that to NWAPC, 'the be all and end all was Sheffield'.[31] Some local groups seem not to have affiliated to NWAPC because they were not aware of its existence; several activists we spoke to seemed to be unfamiliar with the organisation.[32] NWAPC never represented all women's support groups, yet it was not simply a shell organisation: it held many meetings, had a lively network of delegates, organised several conferences and rallies during the course of the strike, and continued to do all these things after the dispute ended. Most importantly, given its official presence, office, and bank account, it was where many of those from outside the coalfields directed their money.[33] As such,

[26] McCrindle, 'National Organisation of Women Against Pit Closures', 121.
[27] Ibid., 116, 117.
[28] Ibid., 120–3; minutes of NWAPC committee meeting, 6 October 1984, DWSG4/1, papers of the South Wales Women's Support Group, Glamorgan Archives, Cardiff (hereafter SWWSG papers).
[29] Meg Allen, 'Carrying on the Strike: The Politics of Women Against Pit Closures' (unpublished PhD thesis, University of Manchester, 2001), 99–100.
[30] Monica Shaw, 'Women in Protest and Beyond: Greenham Common and Mining Support Groups' (unpublished PhD thesis, University of Durham, 1993), 190.
[31] Siân James, b. 1959, South Wales, interviewed by Florence Sutcliffe-Braithwaite, 5 February 2019.
[32] E.g. Maureen Coates, b. 1942, Yorkshire, interviewed by Florence Sutcliffe-Braithwaite and Natalie Thomlinson, 11 September 2014. See also Allen, 'Carrying on the Strike', 99.
[33] McCrindle, 'National Organisation of Women Against Pit Closures', 109, 118–19.

NWAPC had significant access to funds over the course of the strike, and played an important role in trying to ensure resources were more evenly distributed across the country.

The women's rally in central London on 11 August was NWAPC's first major public event, and further heightened its profile. NWAPC claimed that 20–23,000 people attended.[34] The march attracted groups from across the country and, due to its location, a wide section of the metropolitan left (Figure 4.3). McCrindle described it as more 'traditional' and 'less spectacular' than the Barnsley rally, with many trade union-style banners and far-left groups selling newspapers.[35] Marchers donned 'black scarves, and arm bands and wore black flowers in memory of Davy Jones and Joe Green who had died on picket lines'.[36] They averted their eyes as they passed 10 Downing Street,[37] and threw black petals on the ground.[38] Events like these, which were deliberately dramatic and aimed to rouse emotion, were central in the formation and cohesion of a sense of group belonging, and in facilitating a sense of investment in the cause.[39] Women from the support movement in Kent recalled the rally and the work of NWAPC positively, suggesting that the national movement encouraged women to join in and brought them together. Kay Sutcliffe recalled that 'it worked really well, I think it brought a lot of areas together that wouldn't have come together, and I think it encouraged a lot of women that might not have been full supporters to join in'.[40]

The 11 August marchers also handed in a petition to the queen. This was Arthur Scargill's idea, and he himself revised McCrindle's original text, which he thought was too political.[41] The petition appealed 'directly' to the queen to support the 'women of mining communities' in their crusade to save their industry and their communities, pointing out that '[w]e have, over recent years, seen the horrors of mass unemployment cripple other industries; we have witnessed the slow death of communities dependent on them, and the tragedies that fall on families and individuals'.[42] Not all women were happy with the petition,

---

[34] 20,000 estimate in: minutes of NWAPC committee meeting, 29 August 1984, 7JMC/A/01, McCrindle papers. 23,000 estimate in partial transcript of NWAPC conference, 17 August 1985, DWSG4/1, SWWSG papers.

[35] McCrindle, 'National Organisation of Women Against Pit Closures', 129.

[36] Gwen Newton, ed., *We are Women, We are Strong: The Stories of Northumberland Miners' Wives 1984–85* (Northumberland: The People Themselves, 1985), 87, 88.

[37] Ibid.

[38] Barnsley Women Against Pit Closures, *Women Against Pit Closures, Volume 2* (Barnsley: Barnsley Women Against Pit Closures, 1985), 35.

[39] See Jeff Goodwin, James M. Jasper, and Francesca Polletta, eds., *Passionate Politics: Emotions and Social Movements* (Chicago: University of Chicago Press, 2001).

[40] Kay Sutcliffe, b. 1949, Janice Bartolo, b. 1957, and Margaret Davis, b. 1949, all Kent, interviewed by Florence Sutcliffe-Braithwaite and Natalie Thomlinson, 5 March 2016.

[41] McCrindle, 'National Organisation of Women Against Pit Closures', 117.

[42] Pat McIntyre, 'The Response to the 1984-5 Miners' Strike in Durham County: Women, the Labour Party and Community' (unpublished PhD thesis, University of Durham, 1992), 238, 239.

Figure 4.3 The huge women's march organised by National Women Against Pit Closures passes the Department of Health and Social Security headquarters in Elephant & Castle, London, 11 August 1984. © Sheila Gray/Format.

however. One woman from Eppleton, Florence Anderson, recalled her anger on receiving it:

> we had to sign a bloody petition to go to the Queen! The Queen! Well I got the petition and I tore it up and I said you can take that back to Durham because

the Eppleton women are not signing no petition to no Queen, this is the establishment and we're not begging to no establishment. I tore it up and sent it back.[43]

The petition drew on a centuries' old tradition of petitioning the monarch when appeals to Parliament had failed. But it was, consciously or not, playing into a populist strategy, and irritated some left-wing, republican, or anti-establishment women in the support movement. The framing of the strike and support movement as being in defence of 'community' also angered some feminists, who saw this language as celebrating a reified version of mining communities where traditional gender roles reigned supreme.[44] Yet many—probably most—women in the support movement *did* see the strike as a battle to retain their way of life, rather than as a moment to question the gender order. Tensions over the alignment of NWAPC with Scargill, and over whether it was a movement in defence of community or a broader political movement—radical, socialist, even feminist— would continue to dog the organisation. As we will see in the next chapter, many women in the support movement were profoundly ambivalent about whether their activism was 'political' at all.

Picketing and the Politics of Gender

Perhaps the single biggest challenge to gender roles during the strike was the presence of women on picket lines. Women started picketing early in the strike: on 13 March, pro-strike Nottinghamshire Area officials were urging 'miners' wives' to stay away from picket lines, arguing that outsiders (Yorkshire miners, women, and non-miners) on Nottinghamshire picket lines were harming the cause.[45] Women's picketing continued throughout the dispute, though only a small minority of women ever participated. In the early months, it was only in coalfields where the majority of miners were working—principally Nottinghamshire, as well as smaller coalfields like Leicestershire—that picket lines were routinely needed outside pits. Elsewhere, after the very early days, there was limited need for pickets because of the solidity of the strike. Pickets from coalfields where the strike was solid were, therefore, mainly *flying* pickets, travelling to coalfields where the strike was weak, or picketing power stations or other places where coal was being

---

[43] Allen, 'Carrying on the Strike', 96–7.
[44] Jean Spence and Carol Stephenson, '"Side by Side with Our Men?" Women's Activism, Community, and Gender in the 1984–1985 British Miners' Strike', *International Labor and Working-Class History*, 75 (2009), 68–84.
[45] David Amos, 'The Nottinghamshire Miners, the Union of Democratic Mineworkers and the 1984–5 Miners' Strike: Scabs or Scapegoats' (unpublished PhD thesis, University of Nottingham, 2011), 333.

moved. In some cases, this meant a daily journey—as with pickets from South Yorkshire travelling into Nottinghamshire. In other cases, it meant a trip away: pickets from South Wales travelling to picket Didcot Power Station stayed at Ruskin College, for example, while Christine Worth, a supporter of the strike in Derbyshire, put up men from South Wales travelling to the area, until the local support group decided to fund a house for them to stay in.[46] In the early weeks and months of the strike, women sometimes went to the picket lines to take food or hot drinks for pickets, but quite quickly, women began organising their own pickets, or joining mixed, local pickets. Sometimes picket lines could erupt into violence, but often they were sites of mundanity as well as drama (see Figures 4.4 and 6.4).

Picketing could be scary, but it was a very public way for women's groups to show their support for the strike, and, as was proven after Anne Scargill's arrest at Silverhill on 14 May, a good way to get coverage in the national media. On 16 May, 120 women from Yorkshire, Derbyshire, and Nottinghamshire picketed seven pits in Nottinghamshire.[47] A woman interviewed by sociologist Penny Green in Ollerton, Nottinghamshire, described a mass picket of the pit there in May:

Figure 4.4 A woman stands on the picket line at Bilston Glen Colliery, Scotland, 1985. © The Scotsman Publications Ltd.

---

[46] Angela, b. 1958, Kent/Oxford, interviewed by Florence Sutcliffe-Braithwaite, 9 July 2018; Christine Worth, b. 1952, Derbyshire, interviewed by Natalie Thomlinson, 2 August 2018.
[47] Claire Higney, *Notts Women Strike Back*, WAIN/1 file 12, papers of Hilary Wainwright, People's History Museum, Manchester (hereafter Wainwright papers).

All we wanted to do was just to show our presence—not to cause any disturbance, just to see what they would really do with us; well we got the shock of our life that morning, because we got pulled, pushed, dragged, I myself got dragged by three [policemen].[48]

Women's pickets were frightening but exhilarating. An anonymous account of an all-women picket described travelling to Calverton in a car and white van—'no seats inside, women crowded in and sat on the floor'—evading the police, who were 'on the motorway bridges, cars and figures watching us', by 'making up stories...about where we were going and for what purpose'. Later, on the picket line, the women were 'frightened': '[t]he ring of men is closing in & we cannot walk about in our own space, only stand together. It is getting dark. Then there is some shouting & a struggle.'[49]

Sometimes women simply joined in mixed pickets of a local pit. Lorraine Walsh and her sister Linda Finnis joined local pickets at Betteshanger—while Lorraine was heavily pregnant—during the occupation of the pit between 17 and 20 June 1984. The occupation was staged to refute management's statements that the mine was becoming unsafe due to gas, and to ensure that the two strikebreakers at the pit, Robert McGibbon and Alec Stuart, would desist from going into work.[50] (Robert McGibbon's wife, Irene, would later emerge as the leader of the 'Miners Wives Back to Work Campaign'.)[51] When large numbers of police were brought in to confront the occupation, Lorraine and Linda joined the picket lines, though only when their husbands were present to keep them safe. They conceptualised their actions within a paradigm of defending jobs and community rather than as a 'political' act. Both agreed it was a positive experience: as Linda put it, it felt like they were 'doing something', when generally they felt 'so useless': 'it was scary but it was good. Standing up for what you think is right.'[52] Similarly, Mig Weldon, from Fife, remembered going picketing for pragmatic reasons, 'just when it was needed—I mean, there was enough men that were doing it'. Nevertheless, she enjoyed picketing, and gave an insight into the emotional release it could provide: 'all that aggravation that's been building up inside you... it had to come out!'[53]

Women on picket lines were not just metaphorically, but also quite literally, intruding on traditionally male space. Their presence brought into question ideas

---

[48] Interviewee 5, interviewed by Penny Green, 15 June 1984, papers of Penny Green, private collection (hereafter Green papers).
[49] Anonymous account of Calverton Women's Picket, FAN/JP/Box 2, papers of Jill Page, Feminist Archive North, Leeds (hereafter Page papers).
[50] *Betteshanger Occupation Strike 1984–5* (Brussels: Socialist Solidarity, n.d.), WAIN/1 file 12, Wainwright papers; P. Keel, 'Pit Sit-in Ends as Two Miners Quit Work', *Guardian*, 21 June 1984.
[51] See Chapter 5.
[52] Lorraine Walsh, b. 1959, and Linda Finnis, b. 1952, both Kent, interviewed by Florence Sutcliffe-Braithwaite, 3 July 2018.
[53] Mig Weldon, b. 1950, Scotland, interviewed by Victoria Dawson, 29 August 2018.

about the proper place for women: by standing on picket lines, women were claiming their right to be seen as legitimate actors in the strike, and their presence could be disturbing to striking miners. Picketing was often the occasion for disputes between women's support groups and local NUM branches, and between women and their husbands. One woman remembered shortly after the strike that 'one thing my husband was dead against—me going on picket lines. I could do meetings. I could go on Rallies and demonstrations... He had seen the violence.'[54] In Fife, Anne Kirby's husband, Frank, was worried about her wish to go to a local picket line: Anne was pregnant, and he insisted she should not go to what he described as—using military language—the 'front line':

> So I stood right back, I didn't take the children either... It was quite frightening how violence can reach a height—escalate—because from a peaceful protest, a peaceful picket line, to then when the buses came in, with scabs, to throwing the stones, and banging on the buses, and you know, young men climbing on the buses, and banging them, and the shouting and everything... it was frightening. It was frightening... At that point, Frank was aware that I was there, and he wasn't happy, because he was sacred I'd get hurt. But I wanted to see for myself.[55]

Picket lines were often seen as rough and dangerous: no place for women.

There were several reports of NUM men 'refusing' to let women go picketing. Women in Oakdale, South Wales, interviewed in August 1984, suggested that some women acquiesced in this: they said that the men would not 'let' them go picketing, but that the women 'don't mind' about this, having seen picket line violence.[56] On other occasions, however, this was a source of tension. Beatrix Campbell thought picketing 'seemed to cause most differences between men and women', though Campbell was notably hostile towards the NUM, which she saw as implacably patriarchal.[57] Liz Marshall, who was involved in the women's pickets at Barony pit, remembered that 'initially' the men would not allow the women to be involved in picketing, instead expecting to be fed by them after a picketing shift.[58] Margo Thorburn in Scotland recalled: '[i]t was different at different strike centres. Our men wouldn't let us go. We wanted to go. I wanted to go and experience picketing... We asked at the centre one day, but they

---

[54] Interviewee 15, unpublished book manuscript, 7BEH/1/2, papers of Betty Heathfield, Women's Library@LSE, London (hereafter Heathfield papers).
[55] Anne Kirby, b. 1955, Scotland, interviewed by Victoria Dawson, 26 November 2018.
[56] Women's Support Committee, Oakdale, interviewed by unknown person, 6 August 1984, AUD/676, South Wales Coalfield Collection, Welsh Council for Civil and Political Liberties Study, South Wales Miners' Library, Swansea (hereafter SWCC, WCCPL Study).
[57] Beatrix Campbell, 'Proletarian Patriarchs and the Real Radicals', in Vicky Seddon, ed., *The Cutting Edge: Women and the Pit Strike* (London: Lawrence & Wishart, 1986), 249–82, at 270.
[58] Liz Marshall and Barney Menzies, interviewed by unknown person, 8 January 2004, National Coal Mining Museum for Scotland, Newtongrange.

wouldn't let us.'⁵⁹ Many women, however, did not wait for permission, and went without the blessing of local NUM men.⁶⁰ In other villages, such as Askern, in South Yorkshire, it appeared that if picketing was done under the direction of NUM men, it was acceptable.⁶¹ The opposition to picketing was not just rooted in patriarchal understandings of the need to protect women, but also in larger disputes between the NUM and the women's groups about the NUM's right to direct them.

Many women did get hurt on picket lines, and a number were arrested. Aggie Currie remembered vividly the first time she was arrested after picketing a Nottinghamshire pit. She had attended with her elderly mother and aunt, and had already had an altercation with the police over abuse directed at them on the picket line. When she went to the toilet, two policemen insisted on accompanying her: she shouted, 'first time they've been on piss duty!', and was promptly arrested for insulting a police officer. Aggie was treated roughly, hit, put into a police wagon, taken to a local police station and put into a cell with about a dozen men, where she had to spend the night. She remembered that 'they do clobber you, they don't give a shit whether you be male or female, they don't give a shit'. The men she was in a cell with (all striking miners arrested for picketing) turned their backs when she needed to go to the toilet to help her preserve some privacy, but Aggie believed she was put in the mixed cell deliberately by the police: 'they tried to degrade me, I think... they really tried to break us'.⁶² This was the first of many arrests for Aggie, but she was released the next morning without charge, as she would be every time. Aggie believed that she was not charged because 'they would have made women martyrs, wouldn't they, and that's something they didn't want to do'—although, as we will see in Chapter 5, a number of women *were* charged.⁶³ There are many accounts of police brutality towards women arrested on picket lines.⁶⁴ Two women recounted not being allowed to go to the toilet after being arrested and wetting themselves.⁶⁵ Others told tales of police violence that had sexualised overtones.⁶⁶ All this strongly suggests that the tactics of the police were as much about the psychological violence of humiliation and degradation as they were about the physical violence of dragging and hitting: the police were

---

⁵⁹ Suzanne Corrigan, Cath Cunningham, and Margo Thorburn, 'Fife Women Stand Firm', in Seddon, ed., *Cutting Edge*, 30–49, at 39.

⁶⁰ Ibid., 39; Jean Miller, 'Barnsley', in Seddon, ed., *Cutting Edge*, 227–40, at 239.

⁶¹ Jane Thornton, *All the Fun of the Fight* (Doncaster: Doncaster Library Service, c.1987), 7–8, 15–17.

⁶² Aggie Currie. ⁶³ Ibid.

⁶⁴ See, e.g., North Yorkshire Women Against Pit Closures, *Strike 84/85* (Leeds: North Yorkshire Women Against Pit Closures, 1985), 34–6.

⁶⁵ Janet Kay and Kila Millidine, 'Intruders not Peacekeepers', in Seddon, ed., *Cutting Edge*, 176–202, at 190.

⁶⁶ Iris Preston, 'A Strike Diary: Brookhouse, South Yorkshire', in Raphael Samuel, Barbara Bloomfield, and Guy Boanas, eds., *The Enemy Within: Pit Villages and the Miners' Strike of 1984–5* (London: Routledge & Kegan Paul, 1986), 100–17, at 105.

weaponising the traditional gender order to try to tell women that their place was not on the picket line. When the arrested miners in the cell with Aggie turned their backs to allow her to use the toilet, they were resisting the effects of such treatment.

Jean Crane noted that the first time Askern Women's Support Group went picketing, the women were not as outspoken or abusive as they became later.[67] Stewart B., a striking miner in Lancashire, remembered similarly:

> when I first went to the picket line and they was bringing women on [the] picket line, well there was maybe about half a dozen women turned up, and the women were first time on a picket line, were quite loud and God knows what like, you know shouting what men shout like 'scab' and a bit of all this like... The very next day we had maybe thirty to forty women on the picket line, let me tell you they were rougher than the men. And for that reason I did not want my wife mixing with er these women. 'Cause I'm telling you, they was as rough as cowboys.[68]

His wife, Stewart emphasised, was a 'lady'. Some women felt the same. Jackie Keating, of Cortonwood Women's Action Group, went to rallies with her mother—both wanted to 'be seen showing our support for our husbands'—but they soon realised rallies were

> totally out of our league. Listening to the abuse of some of the women to the police made my toes curl, appalled is an understatement. We had both been brought up to be polite, civil, and at all times courteous to all members of the police force. Some of the pit language used against them made me ashamed.[69]

Among our interviewees, Carol Willis recalled similarly that when she took her mother on a demonstration in Blythe, the slogan used by some of the demonstrators—'Maggie Thatcher's got one, Ian McGregor is one'—shocked her mother, who said she hoped no one saw them there.[70]

Feminist historians have pointed to the ways in which respectability has long been fundamentally linked to the maintenance of the gender order.[71] This was a link that women like Carol Willis's mother and Jackie Keating, as well as men like Stewart B., certainly made. While feminist scholars have rightly challenged the

---

[67] Jean Crane, interviewed by unknown person, 14 January 1986, SY689/V/9/2, papers of Askern Women's Support Group, Sheffield City Archives, Sheffield (hereafter Askern WSG papers).

[68] Stewart B., interviewed by Emily Peirson-Webber, 26 August 2020.

[69] Jackie Keating, *Counting the Cost: A Family in the Miners' Strike* (Barnsley: Wharncliffe Publishing, 1991), 21.

[70] Carol Willis, b. 1952, North East England/Manchester, interviewed by Victoria Dawson, 3 April 2019.

[71] For the most famous statement of this position, see Leonore Davidoff and Catherine Hall, *Family Fortunes: Men and Women of the English Middle Class* (London: Routledge, 1988).

notion that the ideology of 'separate spheres' was ever truly hegemonic,[72] there was still a sense for these men and women that the passage from the relatively hidden 'backstage' role of making food to the much more public one of attending picket lines or demonstrations marked a transgression of women's 'natural' association with the private or domestic sphere. Maureen Coates, who described herself as a feminist and was involved in a women's support group, laughed when we asked her whether she had ever been on a picket line, and said, 'I weren't that feminist!'[73] Even for a woman like Maureen, who was comfortable describing herself as a feminist, being present on picket lines represented a transgression greater than she was comfortable with.

NUM picket lines were masculine spaces not only because they were peopled by men, but also because many of their distinctive practices were coded as male: solidarity, violence, and 'pit language', or swearing. When women appeared on picket lines, in some places men and women worked together to make their presence less threatening to the sanctity of masculine space and feminine respectability by changing how they behaved. On the picket line at Grimethorpe, for example, a no-swearing rule was instigated.[74] However, few picket lines seem to have changed substantially to accommodate the presence of women, and some women *did* feel altered by their experiences on the picket lines in quite profound ways. 'K', from Thurcroft, in South Yorkshire, remembered that later in the strike when picketing in the village she would not stand near her husband: 'I thought "If he hears me swearing like this, he'll say 'Oh, shut up'." But when I was on my own I didn't care. It's alright to use it on a picket line, but not in the home. You're a different person on the picket line.'[75] 'K' was not alone in taking up swearing during the strike: Aggie Currie, who was given the nickname 'gobshite' during the strike for her outspokenness, did not swear prior to 1984.[76] Women's incursion into the male space of the picket line—and the heightened atmosphere and anger of picket lines—had a powerful effect on some. As 'K' said, she felt like a 'different person': the rules of female behaviour were rewritten or temporarily in abeyance.

However, the power of women on the picket lines could sometimes *rely on* conservative understandings of gender roles that striking miners, female picketers, and strikebreakers all shared. The famous image of Sheffield WAPC member Lesley Boulton (see Figure 4.5) narrowly missing being struck on the head with a truncheon by a mounted policeman at the Battle of Orgreave (a huge

---

[72] See Amanda Vickery, 'From Golden Age to Separate Spheres: A Review of the Categories and Chronologies of English Women's History', *Historical Journal*, 36 (1993), 383–414.
[73] Maureen Coates.
[74] Barnsley Women Against Pit Closures, *Women Against Pit Closures*, Vol. 2, 92.
[75] David Gibbon and Peter Steyne, *Thurcroft. A Village and the Miners' Strike: An Oral History by the People of Thurcroft* (Nottingham: Spokesman, 1986), 171.
[76] Aggie Currie; Ruth, a Denby Grange picket, said the same: Barnsley Miners' Wives Action Group, *We Struggled to Laugh* (Barnsley: Barnsley Miners' Wives Action Group, 1987), 23.

Figure 4.5 A mounted policeman attacks Lesley Boulton of Sheffield WAPC at the Battle of Orgreave, 18 June 1984. © John Harris/reportdigital.co.uk.

confrontation between mass pickets and large numbers of police at the coking plant at Orgreave, South Yorkshire) on 18 June draws its power from the officer's transgression in hitting a woman. When they first went to a picket line, at Creswell, in Derbyshire, the Askern Women's Support Group made a banner reading, 'Askern Women will fight for your jobs, why won't you?'[77] With this slogan the group challenged the masculinity of the strikebreakers, and implied that women were forced onto the picket line simply because men could not act as men. Similarly, in a picket undertaken by Derbyshire women, Betty Savage recalled bringing frilly knickers to wave at the strikebreakers, saying 'they're not really men, are they?'[78] Women in Thurcroft shouted at strikebreakers, '[y]ou're not a man, you're a mouse, at least our men are men!'[79] Rather than challenging the gender order, these women were suggesting that *the inverted gender order that their presence on the picket line demonstrated represented the inverted morality of working miners*. Without shared conservative understandings of gender, protests like these would not have made sense. As such, the presence of women on picket lines could work as much to reinscribe the patriarchal gender order as to destabilise it.

Survival Strategies

From the early summer onwards, more and more striking miners' families began to experience significant hardship. One of Penny Green's interviewees in Nottinghamshire reported on 20 June that she had finished all her savings and had written to her brother in Ireland to ask if he could send money: if he did not, she did not know what she would do.[80] By August, one woman in Oakdale, in South Wales, said that the impact on living standards was 'heartbreaking': families were 'experiencing the collapse of everything they've been working for for years'.[81] Warwick and Littlejohn's survey of twenty-five striking miners' families in 'Ashby', Yorkshire, in late summer 1984 found that households had income levels at about a third or a quarter of pre-strike levels.[82] Linda Finnis and Joyce Boyes's memories captured the feelings of many:

> It was things like the electric—you were too scared to put the electric on, weren't you? You had no telly. You didn't buy anything.[83]
>
> Everything stopped... we just stopped going out, we stopped socialising... Holidays obviously stopped. Eventually, the car, it ran out of its tax and its insurance and things, so although we still had a car we couldn't drive it, we just went everywhere on our pushbikes.[84]

---

[77] Thornton, *All the Fun of the Fight*, 8.   [78] Beaton, *Shifting Horizons*, 82.
[79] Gibbon and Steyne, *Thurcroft*, 169.
[80] Interviewee 8, interviewed by Penny Green, 20 June 1984, Green papers.
[81] Interview with Women's Support Committee, Oakdale, interviewed by unknown person, 6 August 1984, AUD/676, SWCC, WCCPL Study.
[82] Dennis Warwick and Gary M. Littlejohn, *Coal, Capital and Culture: A Sociological Analysis of Mining Communities in West Yorkshire* (London: Routledge, 1992), 168.
[83] Linda Finnis.
[84] Joyce Boyes, b. 1955, Yorkshire, interviewed by Victoria Dawson, 21 November 2018.

South Kirkby miner's wife Irene Pattison wrote bluntly in an unpublished memoir, '[w]e keep struggling every day. I don't know how we carry on, we get desperate for an end to it all.'[85] In the face of growing hardship, women turned to a variety of survival strategies, all of which would only became more and more significant as the months wore on and summer turned to autumn and then winter.

Support groups were one source of help. While many—perhaps the majority—formed in April and May, groups continued to form throughout summer and autumn, until close to Christmas.[86] Groups that formed later probably had fewer overtly political activists in comparison with those formed earlier in the strike. In some places, a late-forming group was a sign of a lack of enthusiasm for the strike, and foretold difficulties, as in Cynheidre, the first place in South Wales to see a major return to work, where the late formation of the support group was one factor making it less effective.[87] However, other groups formed later in the strike because of a surfeit of support, as with the Upton and North Elmsall Mining Dispute Infant Support Group, which came together in May, and was the third group in the area; it was formed partly because there were 'too many women' and 'not enough for all the women to be fully involved' in the other two groups.[88] The new group aimed to fulfil the unmet needs of the infant children of miners, who were too young to be receiving free school meals, though while the group's parcels included provisions such as powdered milk and rusks, other supplies—such as five pounds of potatoes—were potentially of use to all the family.[89] Food parcels varied considerably from place to place, and from week to week, dependent on the funds that were available. But they rarely provided enough to keep a family fed for an entire week: in May 1984, the Swansea, Neath and Dulais Valleys Support Group provided eight potatoes, six carrots, one tin each of peas, meat, and beans, one loaf of bread, a packet of cereal, and one piece of fruit for a whole family.[90]

Not all households received help from support groups. A MORI poll of a representative quota sample of 591 miners in Derbyshire, carried out in September 1984, found that 60 per cent had accepted food parcels or other such

---

[85] Irene Pattison 'Eighty-Four to Eighty-Five', unpublished memoir, FAN/JP/Box 2, Page papers.

[86] Joan Witham's survey of Nottinghamshire support groups suggests that most groups probably formed in April or May: Joan Witham, *Hearts and Minds: The Story of the Women of Nottinghamshire in the Miners' Strike, 1984–1985* (London: Canary, 1986), 114–213. See also Labour Research Department, *Solidarity with the Miners* (London: LRD, 1985).

[87] This is discussed in minutes of meeting 25 November 1984, Neath and District Miners' Support Group minute book, 23 September 1984–17 February 1985, SWCC/MND/25/1, box 4 of 8, SWCC papers; and in Hywel Francis, *History on Our Side: Wales and the 1984-5 Miners' Strike* (London: Lawrence & Wishart, 2015), 51.

[88] Iris Knight, 'Upton, the Infants' Support Group', in Samuel et al., eds., *Enemy Within*, 122–6, at 122.

[89] Ibid., 124.

[90] Minutes of meeting 6 May 1984, Neath and District Miners' Strike Support Fund minute book, 6 May–22 September 1984, SWCC/MND/25/1, box 4 of 8, SWCC papers.

aid (92 per cent were on strike).[91] This tallies with the findings of sociologists. Warwick and Littlejohn's research in four Yorkshire mining communities found that only 63 per cent of mining households received help from support groups.[92] The Wintertons' study of Yorkshire showed that levels and type of support received varied: use of soup kitchens was higher among strike activists, among those in pit communities, and among single miners, or miners with non-working wives. Among households containing a strike activist and living in a pit community, 83 per cent used kitchens. Among households containing no strike activists and living outside a mining community it was only 29 per cent.[93] Food parcels or money were received by 55 per cent of respondents (see Figure 4.6); these were targeted more at 'outsiders' (those not living in mining communities), to compensate for their lack of easy access to soup kitchens. But they were more successful in reaching activists: among 'outsiders', 72 per cent of activists received support, but only 59 per cent of non-activists.[94] Help from support groups was important, but it was far from the only source of support strikers and their families

Figure 4.6 A man and child pick up a food parcel in South Wales. © Martin Shakeshaft.

[91] *British Public Opinion*, 6 (September 1984), 5, Archive of Market and Social Research, https://www.amsr.org.uk/.
[92] Warwick and Littlejohn, *Coal, Capital and Culture*, 173.
[93] Jonathan and Ruth Winterton, *Coal, Crisis and Conflict: The 1984–5 Miners' Strike in Yorkshire* (Manchester: Manchester University Press, 1989), 136.
[94] Ibid., 137.

depended on, and was less likely to reach those from outside traditional pit villages.

Individual survival strategies relying on help from family, friends, and local businesses mirrored, in many ways, the collective survival strategies of support groups: they involved drawing on community networks built up over many decades. Of utmost importance was the support provided by kith and kin. Gibbon and Steyne suggested that in Thurcroft, '[h]elp from relatives was almost universal'; it was 'distinguished from other help of this kind by the fact that it occurred on a regular basis', and from the summer, 'became the most important source of support in the wider community'.[95] The Wintertons found that 42 per cent of their respondents in Yorkshire received loans or gifts from friends and family; Measham and Allen found that 61 per cent of respondents in the four West Yorkshire locales they studied had received assistance from their families.[96] Most of our interviewees had grown up in the communities in which they lived as adults, and had extensive networks of family and friends. In fact, for many of our interviewees, that they received support from family and friends seemed so obvious that it was only mentioned in passing. Kay Case, from South Wales, remembered that, 'I did get various help off family or friends . . . You sort of lived off what came in your parcel or other people gave you.'[97] Linda Chapman, in North East England, remembered, 'I mean both of our parents bought us shopping every week, slip you a fiver for a treat, and bought shoes for Daniel [Linda's son] when he needed them and that sort of stuff.'[98] In Midlothian, Connie Dixon remembered: 'Jock's sister was good, every now and again would come down with a baggy of messages [food]'.[99] Tanya Dower's grandmother helped out her family from her savings.[100] Even Adrienne C., who refused to accept food directly from her mother, let her parents cook for her several times a week.[101]

Local shops and other organisations also gave support on an individual basis, as well as in many cases helping support groups, something also seen in the 1926 miners' lockout.[102] Many local business-owners were embedded in the community, and sympathetic to the miners as a group, and to longstanding customers. Mary Hole remembered the generosity of a butcher in Aberdare to her husband:

---

[95] Gibbon and Steyne, *Thurcroft*, 211.
[96] Winterton and Winterton, *Coal, Crisis and Conflict*, 135; Fiona Measham and Sheila Allen, 'In Defence of Home and Hearth? Families, Friendships and Feminism in Mining Communities', *Journal of Gender Studies*, 3 (1994), 31–45, at 38.
[97] Kay Case, b. 1948, South Wales, interviewed by Florence Sutcliffe-Braithwaite, 13 August 2018.
[98] Linda Chapman, b. 1958, North East England, interviewed by Victoria Dawson, 18 July 2018.
[99] Connie Dixon, b. 1948, Scotland, interviewed by Victoria Dawson, 7 December 2018.
[100] Tanya Dower, b. 1967, South Wales, interviewed by Florence Sutcliffe-Braithwaite, 13 August 2018.
[101] Adrienne C., b. 1956, Yorkshire, interviewed by Victoria Dawson, 26 June 2018.
[102] Hester Barron, *The 1926 Miners' Lockout: Meanings of Community in the Durham Coalfield* (Oxford: Oxford University Press, 2010), 37–42.

He was passing the butchers, and he'd gone there, oh, for years, to this butchers... and the chap inside who was running it, he stopped him, he waved by hand, called him in like, and he didn't tell him that he was, er, on strike, or anything, but obviously he knew, and then he said, 'oh come in', he said, and he got a box, and he'd put tins in there, and I think he'd given some meat, and Den said, 'oh don't be soft, I don't want it', but he was quite adamant, for him to have it, because he knew he was such a good customer, always going there, so that was it.[103]

This gift was hard to accept: Den had always said he did not want 'charity', and Mary told us that they collected a food parcel from the support group 'only once—I think we only ever went at the very end'.[104] Many shopkeepers lowered prices or donated goods: one of Brian Hill and Lesley Sutcliffe's interviewees for their book on the politics of social security in the strike said that '[l]ocal shopkeepers have regularly been giving us fresh vegetables and cheap meat such as liver and sausage. There's a local butcher who supplies sausage at twenty pence a pound just for strikers.'[105] Connie Dixon remembered that '[in the] barber shop, he decided you could take your bairns for a haircut. And you just had to make a donation, could be 10 pence or anything.'[106] Men and women, too, sometimes received cheap or free haircuts (see Figure 4.7).

There was a pragmatic side, too, to some businesses' support. Many business-owners knew that in areas of high occupational homogeneity, the entire local economy rested on the continuation of the coal industry; many, therefore, had a vested interest in the success of the strike. The slogan, 'Close a pit, kill a community' was understood to be only too true. In Armthorpe, a woman remembered:

The electric shop in the village where I got my video has been good. I went to school with him. I went to take it back. He said 'Keep it'. I said 'I can't pay'. He said 'Pay me when you go back'. He's done that with three parts of the whole village. He said 'If I take all the videos back, I'm out of business.'[107]

There was also, in places, pressure on local shopkeepers to support the strike, with, for example, reports of shops that served policemen being boycotted, again a tactic women had used during the 1926 lockout.[108] Shopkeepers were also doubtless

---

[103] Mary Hole, b. 1935, South Wales, interviewed by Victoria Dawson, 2 September 2018.
[104] Ibid.
[105] Brian Hill and Lesley Sutcliffe, *Let them Eat Coal: The Politics of Social Security during the Miners' Strike* (London: Canary, 1985), 22–3.
[106] Connie Dixon.
[107] 'Woman Factory Work, Married to Miner', in 'Interviews at Armthorpe, December 1984', in Samuel, Bloomfield, and Boanas, eds., *Enemy Within*, 166–202, at 168.
[108] Ibid., 167. Anne Watts noted the boycott by striking miners of a market stall holder in Aberdare who had abused those who had tried to collect money: Anne Watts, b. 1949, South Wales, interviewed by Florence Sutcliffe-Braithwaite, 23 May 2019.

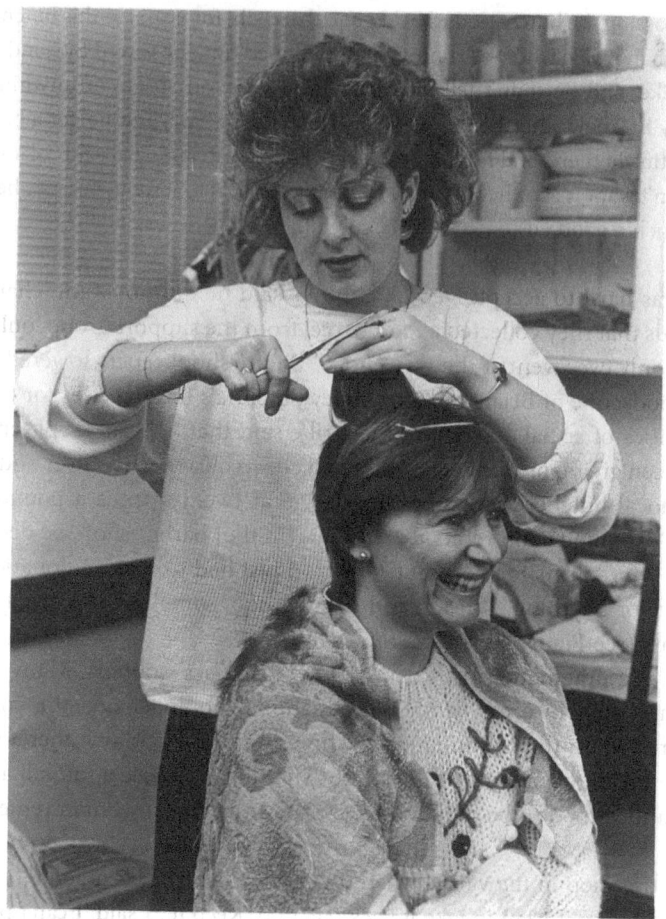

Figure 4.7 Rita Wakefield, the wife of a striking miner in Nottinghamshire, gets a free haircut from a local hairdresser during the strike. © Brenda Prince/Format.

aware that those who had been generous to miners would be more likely to keep their customer base after the dispute's end.

Schools were at the centre of communities, and teachers in mining areas often seem to have helped children and families during the strike on a personal basis, or to have helped coordinate support. In Oakdale, South Wales, a box was placed outside the local school, from which the children of striking miners could take home tinned food.[109] A group of teachers from the Rossington area of Doncaster recalled that it was common to buy things for their classes even in normal times. During the strike they extended this help, with Diane remembering that as the

---

[109] Richard King, *Brittle with Relics: A History of Wales, 1962–1997* (London: Faber & Faber, 2022), 295.

year went on they 'noticed quite a difference in the children and the parents'. The group recalled bringing in fruit, or baked goods, or ingredients to bake with the children; Judy* recalled that 'the need was there, you got on with it—you were earning, they weren't'.[110] Churches also played their part in some areas; the vicar at Rossington was remembered as particularly helpful, and allowed the women's group to use the church hall to put on a disco every Saturday night; 'he wouldn't take a penny off us', remembered one woman from the group.[111]

Nevertheless, help from family, friends, and local organisations and businesses—who were often in straitened circumstances themselves—could only go so far. In many families, women's wages were vital. As we saw in Chapter 2, despite the persistent perception that women from mining communities were less likely to work outside the home, a large proportion of women in mining families were already in paid employment on the eve of the strike. In the Wintertons' sample—which included single miners—44 per cent of respondents had working wives, and for more than two thirds of these respondents, their wives' earnings were the 'major source of income' during the strike.[112] Of our interviewees, approximately thirty of about fifty women with striking partners were in the paid labour force during the strike, though it was not possible to tell in every case.[113] Those who were already in work when the strike started unsurprisingly reported less hardship than those who were not. Indeed, the fact that so many miners' wives were already in paid work was undoubtedly one of the main factors that enabled the strike to go on as long as it did. But the lack of money still made a difference. Maggie Stubbs, who continued her work as a health visitor while her husband was on strike, remembered, 'the bills got paid, but we didn't have the, the extra, you know, we had food, we were alright, but of course with my husband not getting a salary, of course that's gonna make a difference'.[114]

A number of our interviewees took on more hours or an extra job during the strike. In Washington, Tyne and Wear, Linda Chapman told us that:

> I had quite a good job working two days a week, so you can imagine...we'd moved house, we had quite a big house, with a mortgage, we had a car which we

---

[110] Mary*, Victoria*, Judy*, Diane Jarratt, and Val, Yorkshire, interviewed by Victoria Dawson, 20 November 2018.
[111] Interview with Rossington Women's Support Group, SY748/V2/1, papers of Rossington Women's Support Group, Sheffield City Archives, Sheffield.
[112] Winterton and Winterton, *Coal, Crisis and Conflict*, 134.
[113] Where women were working, it was not always clear when they had started jobs. Furthermore, it was not always straightforward to categorise our interviewees by whether or not their partner had gone on strike, because some women we interviewed had partners who were on strike but returned to work during the dispute. We also interviewed a small number of women who were in their late teens during the strike and still living with their parents, but had boyfriends and fathers who were striking; the position of these women in relation to the family economy was particularly difficult to disentangle.
[114] Maggie Stubbs, b. c.1950, Jamaica/Yorkshire, interviewed by Natalie Thomlinson, 13 September 2018.

were borrowing money for, and then suddenly I was thinking...'What are we gonna do?' We had an interest-only mortgage, because everybody had been talked into having them, so building society's saying, 'there's nothing really we can do to help you', because you must pay the interest otherwise your, y'know, you're gonna be, they'd have to foreclose on yer, type of thing... He said, 'not last long, they'll sort it out', but then as things progressed, and we realised it was likely to go on and obviously...you could see it was becoming this political battle of wills. I said to him, 'I'm going to ask if I can go full-time at work', I said, 'I think there's a job coming up I can apply for'.[115]

This course of action was not without sacrifice for Linda, whose son was 14 months old: she recalled, 'I worked in Newcastle, and we lived in Washington, by the time I got home, he was like, bathed, ready for bed, I'd get a little cuddle, I'd sit and cry, what am I missing out on, he was having all the fun with him, you know, and I was just like devastated'—though she also found that she enjoyed work and wanted to 'see how I could progress my career'.[116]

Linda's husband was not the only one who took on more domestic labour and childcare in order to support a wife working more hours. Pippa Morgan*, in South Wales, took two extra jobs to support her striking husband and young son: already working for a mail order catalogue, she found additional work as a home help and in a local supermarket.[117] Her husband took on the majority of childcare and housework for the period of the strike, though this was not sustained after the dispute's end. Such experiences gave the seed to popular strike narratives of gender role-reversal in striking families; while, as we will see later in the book, this idea was overblown, some men *did* do more at home—though generally for pragmatic rather than progressive reasons. Regardless of whether or not their husbands contributed more to domestic labour, many women became extremely busy: in Maltby, South Yorkshire, Ann McCracken—who had recently moved down to the area from Scotland—took on night shifts in a local pub in addition to the part-time job she already had in a hospital, as well as looking after her children, and studying at night-school.[118] Given this, it is perhaps not surprising that in some cases, as more women took on jobs, the pool of labour available for support group work diminished: in Rhodesia, Nottinghamshire, for example, when '[s]ome of the previously active women found jobs...an even greater strain fell on those who stayed in the group'.[119]

Men also picked up odd jobs. Ann Robertson's husband Rob did some painting and decorating; Erica Stevenson's* partner went fruit-picking in Wisbech; Lorraine

---

[115] Linda Chapman. [116] Ibid.
[117] Pippa Morgan*, b. 1962, South Wales, interviewed by Natalie Thomlinson, 13 August 2018.
[118] Ann McCracken, b. 1954, Scotland/Yorkshire, interviewed by Victoria Dawson, 6 December 2018.
[119] Witham, *Hearts and Minds*, 197.

Walsh's husband Steve got a 'little electrical job' for two weeks.[120] Sara C. remembered her father's efforts in this respect, but also pointed to how some miners could be exploited in their desperation for cash:

> He did odd jobs for neighbours and things, just to try and get a bit of money... just, I think, to get him... something to do. I remember we'd... he took me with him, cause we did some painting for the house next door and I always remember that and even then it was, like, the woman said, 'do you want to paint?'... I can't remember how many rooms we did and we spent a whole day doing this and she gave him five pounds and even then, that was like... [laughs].[121]

But in areas that were already economically depressed, there could be little spare labour to go around, or fewer people willing to pay for jobs they could do themselves.[122] Furthermore, some men considered taking jobs on the side to be a form of scabbing.[123] The Wintertons found that, across the strike, in Yorkshire, 27 per cent of strike activists found casual work, compared with 36 per cent of non-activists. Those living outside mining communities were also more able to find casual work: the highest levels were among non-activists outside mining communities, 47 per cent of whom had casual earnings.[124] In addition to casual earnings, some of our interviewees had savings they could turn to, or insurance policies they could cash in, but the sums involved were generally small.[125] Some, particularly in rural and semi-rural areas, undertook self-provisioning. Alison Anderson recalled women gleaning (gathering leftover crops) from farmers' fields; Lorraine Finnis and Linda Walsh remembered local landowner Lord Northbourne allowing striking miners to help themselves to trees that had fallen over.[126] Mandy Slater and her husband had a smallholding on the rural outskirts of Barnsley; others, like Mary Hole, had allotments.[127]

Despite all these survival strategies, many—perhaps most—in the coalfields were forced to take on debt, often significant amounts. As the summer went on and it became clear the strike would be long, many women began to worry about the mounting burden of what they owed. In August, one woman in Ammanford said:

[120] Ann Robertson, b. 1934, Kent, interviewed by Florence Sutcliffe-Braithwaite, 5 November 2018; Erica Stevenson*, b. 1959, Yorkshire, interviewed by Victoria Dawson, 1 August 2018; Lorraine Walsh.
[121] Sara C., b. 1971, Yorkshire, interviewed by Victoria Dawson, 25 June 2018.
[122] Carol*, b. 1968, South Wales, interviewed by Natalie Thomlinson, 19 June 2018; Claire*, b. 1969, South Wales, interviewed by Natalie Thomlinson, 11 August 2018.
[123] Connie Dixon.   [124] Winterton and Winterton, *Coal, Crisis and Conflict*, 134–5.
[125] Joyce Boyes discussed savings (though she was under the impression that many miners did not save); Mandy Slater, b. 1937, Yorkshire, interviewed by Victoria Dawson, 8 August 2018, recalled her husband cashing in a life-insurance policy.
[126] Alison Anderson, b. 1959, Scotland, interviewed by Victoria Dawson, 29 August 2018; Lorraine Walsh and Linda Finnis.
[127] Mandy Slater; Mary Hole.

I've gone through the first half [of the strike] now and I don't owe anything at the moment. Now I'm coming in now as if I've started like some people from the beginning. Now if it goes on another 6 months I'm going to be six months in debt with everything because I haven't got no more money left. And the people who are in six months debt, they're going to be a year in debt, and it'll take them about three years to get on their feet.[128]

As we will see in Chapter 7, this was a perceptive insight into the future costs of the strike. Some women recalled simply not paying bills. As Mig Weldon succinctly put it: 'we were not getting money in, we couldnae give them it'.[129] Pat Smith recalled that of all the bills they did not pay, only one company—Reader's Digest—took them to court; she also recalled a local business-owner who remortgaged his own house so he did not have to 'torment the miners'.[130] But many recollected struggles; Pippa Morgan* recalled that she 'broke down in tears' in front of a 'horrible' woman who refused to accept she could not pay her electricity bill (though she did later manage to set up a payment plan after she spoke to someone more sympathetic), and Jeanette McComb remembered 'scrabbling about for money' for the slot meter they had to have installed as they could no longer afford to pay electricity bills in the usual way.[131] Many striking families who owned their homes reported going on a mortgage holiday. As Linda Chapman observed, 'the building societies that just froze everybody's mortgage, were they gonna repossess hundreds of homes?'[132] Nevertheless, for some, the threat of repossession felt very real: Jeanette McComb recalled her building society being 'very unsympathetic' and her brother stepping in to ensure that she and her husband did not lose their home.[133] The Wintertons found in Yorkshire that among their respondents who owned their homes, 55 per cent suspended mortgage payments, and 3 per cent ultimately lost their homes because of debts.[134] Many of our interviewees talked of the fear of losing their homes: it was widely felt that this was a motivating factor for many of those who returned to work early.

Local authorities gave significant—though variable—support to striking families. Those who lived in council-owned properties in local authorities that were sympathetic to the strike were often allowed to go into arrears without facing punitive action. Labour-controlled authorities in areas where the NUM dominated local politics, such as South Yorkshire and South Wales, were often deeply sympathetic to the strike—and aware of their need for miners' votes—and did

---

[128] Ammanford Women's Support Group, interviewed by Jill Evans, 14 August 1984, AUD/587, SWCC, WCCPL Study.
[129] Mig Weldon.
[130] Pat Smith, b. 1949, Yorkshire, interviewed by Victoria Dawson, 8 June 2018.
[131] Pippa Morgan*; Jeanette McComb, b. 1953, West Midlands/Scotland, interviewed by Victoria Dawson, 26 September 2018.
[132] Linda Chapman.   [133] Jeanette McComb.
[134] Winterton and Winterton, *Coal, Crisis and Conflict*, 136.

much to support the dispute. In Barnsley, miners were quickly reclassified as 'dependants', which reduced the rents of those in council housing and the rates of those who were not; Barnsley council also paid single miners living with their parents £8.20 a week in lodging allowance. Rent and rates rebates were the most common form of assistance from local authorities: the Wintertons found in their study of the strike in Yorkshire that 52 per cent of striking miners received such assistance.[135] Support from sympathetic local councils also extended to the provision of free meals (particularly for children in schools) and clothing and food vouchers; Rotherham council provided £268,095 worth of assistance to striking miners in the first seven months of the strike alone.[136] In Wales, Blaenau Gwent moved quickly to give food vouchers to every miner within the authority, while Torfaen suspended rent for miners during the dispute.[137] Strathclyde council provided daily meals for the children of striking miners in Lanarkshire and Ayrshire during the holidays as well as during term.[138] It was different, however, for those in local authorities not sympathetic to the strike, as was the case in much of Nottinghamshire, Conservative-controlled Kent, and North Yorkshire, where the Selby pits were located. Here, a lack of support from local authorities compounded an already difficult situation for striking families, who tended to be more isolated from other forms of support, and who were often located in communities where support for the dispute was weaker (though this was less true for the militant Kent coalfield).

State benefits also played a key part in the survival strategies deployed by families on strike. A central—though not particularly well-known—component of the support movement during the strike focused on ensuring that the families (especially the wives) of striking miners were able to navigate the benefits and taxation system and demand what they were entitled to from often hostile Department of Health and Social Security (DHSS) officials. 'Anyone who thinks that the days of the means test ended forever in 1944', wrote Jean McCrindle in the *Guardian*, in May, 'should look at the forms which people on strike have to fill in'.[139] In August, women from Ystrad Mynach complained about the 'condescending and disapproving' attitude of the local DHSS office.[140] Mig Weldon remembered of her encounters with the DHSS during the strike that 'you were made to feel as if you were begging'.[141] Pamphlets and leaflets were produced (sometimes by sympathetic councils themselves), and talks and surgeries were held in order to publicise the help to which miners' families were legally

---

[135] Ibid., 133. [136] Ibid.
[137] Ben Curtis, *The South Wales Miners 1964–1985* (Cardiff: University of Wales Press, 2013), 211.
[138] Jim Phillips, *Collieries, Communities and the Miners' Strike in Scotland, 1984–85* (Manchester: Manchester University Press, 2012), 116.
[139] Jean McCrindle, *Guardian*, May 1984, quot. in Hill and Sutcliffe, *Let them Eat Coal*, 6.
[140] Women's Support Committee Ystrad Mynach, interviewed by unknown person, 13 August 1984, AUD/669, SWCC, WCCPL Study.
[141] Mig Weldon.

entitled.[142] Alan Booth and Roger Smith thought that child benefit, meagre though it was (it was set at the rate of £6.50 per week per child during the dispute) was 'crucially important' and one of the main sources of income for families with children; the Wintertons also found that, for miners with young children, child benefit was a 'major' source of income for 80 per cent of respondents, and the 'most important' source of income for 22 per cent.[143] While striking miners themselves were not entitled to benefits, their families were entitled to supplementary benefit if their household income fell below the threshold. It was also possible under certain conditions for women to transfer tax allowances from their husbands to themselves, or for women on unemployment, sickness, maternity, or disability benefits to claim extra because their husbands were now their dependants.[144] The effort to get advice to families clearly had a useful effect: the *Financial Times* estimated that over 80 per cent of the wives of striking miners with families claimed supplementary benefit during the strike.[145] Nevertheless, this was still a minority of miners' households: Sutcliffe and Hall calculated that only 42,000 out of approximately 180,000 miners were in households that were receiving supplementary benefit. The remainder were single miners, working miners, miners with wives earning too much to be eligible, or miners whose wives were also out on strike.[146]

The level of supplementary benefit to which the families of striking miners were entitled was the subject of much controversy throughout the dispute. Before the advent of the Thatcher government, supplementary benefit had been set at relatively generous rates, but legal changes—specifically targeted at weakening the ability of trade unions to strike—meant that such supplementary benefit would now have strike pay deducted. This was the case even if strike pay was never received, as in the 1984–5 dispute. A much-reproduced piece of strike art was a fake five pound note with an image of Margaret Thatcher, bearing the legend, 'The capitalist state owes you 16 pounds': this was the 'strike pay' that was deducted at source from the supplementary benefit strikers' families received.[147]

---

[142] See, e.g., pamphlet produced by West Yorkshire County Council informing striking miners of the benefits they were entitled to, SY689/V6/1, Askern WSG papers; Nottingham Centre for the Unemployed photocopied note about how supplementary benefit claimants can claim extra fuel allowance from the DHSS in cold weather, papers of Gwen MacLeod, private collection; Ida Hackett interview, tape 207C, Working Class Movement Library, Salford.

[143] Alan Booth and Roger Smith, 'The Irony of the Iron Fist: Social Security and the Coal Dispute of 1984–5', *Journal of Law and Society*, 12 (1985), 365–74, at 369, 370; Winterton and Winterton, *Coal, Crisis and Conflict*, 133.

[144] See, e.g., letter from Nigel Wheatley, Walsall Citizens' Advice Bureau, to Maureen Coates, Sprotbrough and Brodsworth Miners' Support Group, February 1985, enclosing information sheet and leaflet delineating tax allowance rights of working wives of striking miners, papers of Maureen Coates, private collection.

[145] *Financial Times*, 2 January 1985, quot. in Booth and Smith, 'Irony of the Iron Fist', 369.

[146] Hill and Sutcliffe, *Let them Eat Coal*, 6.

[147] Examples of these five pound notes can be found in several places; there is one preserved in A-3590/G/6/, papers of Barnsley Women Against Pit Closures, Barnsley Archives, Barnsley.

At the women's rally in London in August, marchers carried a banner in the form of an 'invoice' to the DHSS demanding the payment of the £49,500,000 they calculated had been withheld (see Figure 4.3). This deduction had a profound effect on families; indeed, it was one of the main factors that necessitated the growth of the support movement. In June, Kent women who were involved in the support movement staged a sit-in at DHSS offices in Dover in protest at the deduction. A delegation marched to the office with their children, and after being there for a while, walked out 'as a gesture to say "We can't afford to feed them. You feed them."'[148] This action (which drew on a long tradition of similar protests in mining and other working-class communities)[149] revealed part of the moral economy that structured strike activism: women invoked what they saw as the state's ultimate responsibility to see that children did not go hungry, contesting the punitive actions of the DHSS. The struggle of miners' families to receive the benefits to which they were entitled has rarely been foregrounded in retrospective discussions of the strike, but the question of just how much they were entitled to demand from the authorities struck at the heart of what was politically at stake in the dispute: what the responsibilities of the state were to ensure the wellbeing of its citizens.

Receiving support was not, for many striking families, psychologically straightforward. Many were unwilling to take the help offered by support groups, the NUM, local councils, the DHSS, or even family and friends. The shame of taking charity loomed large. Adrienne C. refused to accept the food even her family offered because she 'didn't want to be a charity case'.[150] Claire*, from South Wales, remembered that, for her mother, receiving food parcels was an 'indignity'; she recalled her mother crying when she received vouchers from the council to pay for Claire's school uniform, which Claire thought was due to the shame of receiving social security for the first time.[151] Jeanette McComb remembered that the soup kitchen in Auchinleck was a 'friendly' place and that she appreciated the free food there, but that there was still 'a wee bit of shame' attached to going.[152] In South Kirby, Irene Pattison remembered it was 'difficult at first, having to cadge a meal and feel embarassed [sic]', recalling that her husband preferred to 'make do' as 'he's too proud'.[153] And as a teenager with a striking father, Sara C. went to a soup kitchen in Mapplewell, South Yorkshire, with a friend whose father was also on strike, but recalled:

---

[148] Chrys Salt and Jim Layzell, *Here We Go: Women's Memories of the 1984–5 Miners Strike* (London: Co-operative Retail Services Ltd, 1985), 18.
[149] See Barron, *1926 Miners' Lockout*, 155, 158; 'Housing Crisis—Women's Offensive', supplement, 'Women in Struggle', 5ERC/2/3, papers of the Essex Road Women's Centre, Women's Library@LSE, London.
[150] Adrienne C.   [151] Claire*.   [152] Jeannette McComb.
[153] Irene Pattison, 'Eighty-Four to Eighty-Five', unpublished memoir, FAN/JP/Box 2, Page papers.

I didn't dare tell my mum I'd been, she would have gone mad, 'cause it was just the shame. So even though my mum was really poor and everything, she just believed in working and had a work ethic and not relying on any handouts or anything like that, but I did do that and then was worried that somebody had seen me and would tell mum and dad that I'd been.[154]

Ann Robertson, whose husband was on strike in Kent, recalled being 'incensed' by being offered food parcels from the local branch of the union, and told them 'you know where you can take that'.[155]

The anonymity of the food parcel was preferable to a public appearance at the soup kitchen for some. One woman in Nottinghamshire remembered that:

I think many people thought they could manage, they thought the strike would soon be over. A lot of people were too proud or embarrassed. But after two or three months things changed. Money very soon started to run out. Pantries were empty. We were doing 450 parcels every week before long, but even then some folks wouldn't come for one.[156]

Another activist told Brian Hill and Lesley Sutcliffe that her group produced 'well over 500 meals a day and about 410 food parcels a week because there's some people who just won't come to the soup kitchen, I don't know whether it's pride or what'.[157] In South Wales and North East England, some groups' decisions to focus relief efforts on food parcels, or to exclude 'outsiders... or professional do-gooders' from the kitchens, were based in part on the perception that some miners' families would find going to a 'soup kitchen' or taking help from 'outsiders' psychologically difficult due to the perceived stigma of taking charity.[158] Groups also tried to frame the help they were offering as 'solidarity' rather than 'charity'. Margaret Vallins, of Chesterfield Women's Action Group, told the makers of the film *Not Just Tea and Sandwiches* that, 'when they come, they feel very humble that they've got to ask for this. And I've said to people, "it's not charity. Charity is what rich people give to poor people as a token. This is what working-class people are doing to help other working-class people."'[159] But that Vallins felt the need to explicitly state that support groups were not offering charity is revealing of the difficulties that strike activists had in convincing people that this was the case.

None of this is surprising given the long history of the stigmatisation of charity and of social security. Stigma has long been recognised as a major factor

---

[154] Sara C.   [155] Ann Robertson.   [156] Witham, *Hearts and Minds*, 139.
[157] Hill and Sutcliffe, *Let them Eat Coal*, 25; see also Layzell and Salt, *Here We Go*, 32.
[158] Mair Francis, b. 1948, South Wales, interviewed by Florence Sutcliffe-Braithwaite, 17 July 2018; Stead, *Never the Same Again*, 29.
[159] *The Miners' Campaign Tapes 1. Not Just Tea and Sandwiches*, dir. Birmingham Film/Video Workshop and Platform Films, 1984.

preventing those in need taking up either state benefits or charity;[160] it seems likely that the same psychic dynamics were at play even when the help offered was from trade unions or support groups. Grace Millar found similar feelings of shame in the five-month waterfront lockout in Auckland, New Zealand, in 1951, where there was a huge union-organised support effort.[161] Here, the union also felt it imperative to stress that the relief efforts were 'not charity' in order to persuade those entitled to support to claim it.[162] It may seem counterintuitive that networks of friends and family were often crucial in providing support to striking families, but in fact, many found it easier to accept help from these sources, because there was a much greater chance that such help could be reciprocated after the strike, or that it had been offered by the recipient to the giver before the strike; it is being unable to return the 'gift' of charity that is precisely what makes it humiliating.[163] As one interviewee told Sutcliffe and Hill, 'I've got no money coming in. I'm living on friendship at the moment. If I didn't have friends I'd be up the creek. *I was always free with my money when I was working and it's coming back now*' (italics ours).[164] Old divides of 'rough' and 'respectable', while not necessarily voiced explicitly, also informed the shame many women felt about receiving help.[165] Those who saw receiving food parcels or other help as particularly 'unrespectable' also tended to be those with the most conservative political views; Adrienne C. and Ann Robertson implied that receiving 'charity' would have placed them into a category of 'shirkers'—dependants, not self-reliant—that they had always defined themselves against. For such women, taking what they saw as 'charity' threatened their very sense of self.[166] Understanding these dynamics is crucial in comprehending why so many were reluctant to receive the support to which they were entitled. This made the work of the support movement even more challenging as the strike wore on.

Conclusion

By May, it was clear that the strike would be lengthy and that the majority in Nottinghamshire would not come out. The Barnsley rally at the start of May was a sign of the support movement's growing strength, and itself stimulated the growth

---

[160] See Jonathan Bradshaw and Alan Deacon, *Reserved for the Poor: The Means Test in British Social Policy* (Oxford: Blackwell, 1983) for extensive discussion.
[161] Grace Millar, 'This is Not Charity: The Masculine Work of Strike Relief', *History Workshop Journal*, 83 (2017), 176–93.
[162] Ibid., 176.
[163] Marcel Mauss, *The Gift: The Form and Reason for Exchange in Archaic Societies* (London: Routledge, 2001; originally published Paris, 1925).
[164] Hill and Sutcliffe, *Let them Eat Coal*, 23.
[165] On respectability, see Robert Roberts, *The Classic Slum: Salford Life in the First Quarter of the Century* (Manchester: Manchester University Press, 1971); Elizabeth Roberts, *A Woman's Place: An Oral History of Working-Class Women 1890–1940* (Oxford: Blackwell, 1984).
[166] Bradshaw and Deacon, *Reserved for the Poor*, 135.

of further groups. Over the summer, NWAPC established itself, though it was not without controversy, both over its relationship to Scargill, and its relationship to grassroots groups. Not all groups were affiliated to NWAPC, and its oversight of those which were affiliated was always limited; it would, however, prove extremely important as a central clearing-house for large donations. Women's picketing, which had begun early in the strike, grew over the summer. This was seen at the time, and has been frequently seen since, as one of the most powerful ways in which women transgressed traditional gender roles in the strike. While this is partly true, the full picture is more complex: many women deployed the traditional gender order as a weapon on the picket lines, accusing strikebreakers of having forfeited their masculinity. Their actions could reinforce as well as challenge traditional gender roles. Participation in pickets, marches, rallies, and soup kitchens gave women a way to feel they were doing something, as well as to develop networks of friends to combat isolation and anxiety: the powerful emotions generated by these collective activities were important in bolstering the morale of women who took part in them.

Hardship began to bite for many striking families over the summer: while the aid provided by women's groups was one important bulwark against destitution, however, it was far from the only significant source of support. Help from family, friends and local businesses, social security, support from local authorities, debt, men's casual jobs, and self-provisioning were all important. For a large number—probably a majority—of striking families, women's wages were also important, far more so than the stereotype of mining communities would suggest. Women's wages were particularly key given that large numbers of miners and their wives felt a reluctance to take up support from family, friends, support groups, and the state, their attitudes shaped by the stigma that had long been attached to 'charity' and the emphasis that working- and lower-middle-class cultures of respectability placed on hard work and self-reliance. As the summer moved into autumn, however, it became ever harder for those caught up in the strike to survive without outside help, and the first signs of a return to work in previously strong coalfields began to appear.

5
Crisis and Drift: Autumn 1984

18 September 1984

On 18 September, Margaret Thatcher met with Irene McGibbon, Mrs Linton, and Jane Fjaelberg, the wives of working miners in Kent, Derbyshire, and South Wales, respectively, who had started what they called the 'Miners Wives Back to Work Campaign'. When the women first got in touch with the Prime Minister's Office to request a meeting, the Department of Energy suggested that Thatcher should politely tell them she was too busy. Thatcher herself, however, overruled this advice—though the meeting was not briefed to the press.[1] The women received a sympathetic hearing. They voiced their concerns that men who had returned to work were being intimidated; that 'shops were being blackmailed into supplying strikers and into withholding supplies from working miners', and that 'active pickets were not short of money or supplies' while 'non-militant miners were being left to fend for themselves'.[2] The women complained that not enough had been done to notify miners of the National Coal Board's (NCB's) 'plans for investment in new capacity', that 'rumours about imminent closures were able to thrive', and that 'while talks were going on or in prospect, it was difficult to persuade men to return to work'.[3] The deputation argued, therefore, that more information must be got to striking miners, that all talks should cease, that the NCB should protect working miners after the end of the dispute, and that legal action should be taken against the National Union of Mineworkers (NUM).[4] Thatcher wrote in her autobiography that she was 'moved by the courage of these women, whose families were subject to abuse and intimidation', and she stayed in touch with them.[5]

---

[1] Letter from J. S. Neilson to Andrew Turnbull, 11 September 1984, including handwritten annotation noting Thatcher's response, and 'Miners' Wives Back To Work Campaign', n.d., both in PREM/19/1333, Records of the Prime Minister's Office, Part 19: Correspondence and Papers 1979–1997: Nationalised Industries: Financial Position of the Coal Industry; Miners' Strike; Power Station Endurance; Daily Coal Reports; part 12, The National Archives, Kew (hereafter Records of the Prime Minister's Office).

[2] Letter from Andrew Turnbull to Michael Reidy, 19 September 1984, PREM/19/1333, Records of the Prime Minister's Office.

[3] Ibid. [4] Ibid.

[5] Margaret Thatcher, *The Downing Street Years* (London: HarperCollins, 1993), 364, 371.

Irene McGibbon was subsequently invited to speak at the Conservative Party Conference in October. Many party bigwigs were in attendance: according to one press report, most of the cabinet 'joined in the applause'.[6] Just hours after she survived the IRA bombing of the Grand Hotel, which had killed five people and was intended to kill her, Thatcher found time in her speech to Conference to praise McGibbon's contribution:

> we heard—unforgettably—from the incomparable Mrs. Irene McGibbon—who told us what it is like to be the wife of a working miner during this strike. She told us of the threats and intimidation suffered by herself and her family and even her 11-year-old son, but what she endured only stiffened her resolve. To face the picket line day after day must take a very special kind of courage, but it takes as much—perhaps even more—to the housewife who has to stay at home alone.[7]

Thatcher was personally determined to defeat the NUM. She depicted mining communities as places of violent coercion, and McGibbon as an ordinary housewife, despite her political activism—a rhetorical move that Thatcher often made about herself.

In September and October, Thatcher and her ministers were optimistic about an apparent shift in the coalfields. More miners were returning to work around the country. On 18 September, when Thatcher met McGibbon, Fjaelberg, and Linton, some men had reported for work in the once-solid coalfields of Scotland, North East England, Yorkshire, North Derbyshire, and Kent. Forty-two pits were working normally, eight turning some coal, seventeen had some men present, four were on their annual closure weeks, and 103 were on strike or picketed out.[8] After talks broke down between the NUM and NCB, the National Association of Colliery Overmen, Deputies and Shotfirers (NACODS) refused to join the NUM on strike; the NUM's funds were then sequestered, when, on 25 October, the High Court ruled the strike illegal due to the lack of a national ballot.[9] On 31 October, after another round of talks between the NUM and NCB collapsed, the NCB changed tack, shifting to the very strategy McGibbon and Fjaelberg had suggested to Thatcher.[10] There were to be no more talks; instead the NUM would be ground into surrender. The NCB announced generous 'Christmas bonuses' to miners returning to work before 19 November, a canny strategy given that few wanted to see their children go without Christmas presents. By 20 November, forty-five pits

---

[6] 'Miner's Wife Wins Cheer with Tales of Harassment', *Globe and Mail* (Toronto), 10 October 1984.
[7] Margaret Thatcher, Speech to Conservative Party Conference, Brighton, 12 October 1984, Margaret Thatcher Foundation, https://www.margaretthatcher.org/document/105763.
[8] 'Daily Coal Report—Tuesday 18 September 1984', PREM/19/1333, Records of the Prime Minister's Office.
[9] Martin Adeney and John Lloyd, *The Miners' Strike: Loss without Limit* (London: Routledge & Kegan Paul, 1986), 172–3.
[10] Ibid., 20.

were working normally, fourteen turning some coal, sixty-eight had some men present, and only forty-seven were on strike or picketed out.[11]

The autumn months were when the strike started to crumble, and many activists began to fear defeat. The breakdown of talks, the NACODS vote, and the sequestration were huge blows to the NUM, but would only increase the importance of the women's support movement. This chapter examines what drove some women to support a return to work—including the Thatcherite true believers like McGibbon, but also those women who were not motivated mainly by ideology or politics, who were certainly in a majority in families where men returned to work. It also looks at how the support movement responded to the unfolding crisis, and what kept so many activists united in the cause. It examines the moral economy structuring the activism of those who supported the strike, and how the politics of that activism was framed, both by the women who were involved in it, and left-wing supporters and the press.

Breaking the Strike

Women like McGibbon, Fjaelberg, and Linton were explicitly rooted in a right-wing anti-trade union politics: the fact that they were willing to put their heads above the parapet in majority-striking communities points to the depth of their ideological convictions. Irene McGibbon and her husband Robert had, in fact, been involved in anti-trade union politics for years. In 1974 at British Leyland's Cowley Plant they led a campaign against an elected Transport and General Workers' Union (TGWU) shop steward, ending with his removal from office; the campaign was spearheaded by Irene, and mainly involved 'collecting signatures, agitating, and spreading despondancy [sic] amongst the wives of striking men'.[12] In 1976 Robert McGibbon, who was originally from Kent, moved to Betteshanger colliery.[13] Like McGibbon, Jane Fjaelberg's husband had also been a miner for only a relatively short time: Gordon Fjaelberg had been in the RAF and only started working at Cwm colliery about a year before the strike.[14] In addition to their ideological stance, the fact that these women were not deeply embedded in mining areas was undoubtedly significant in enabling them to disregard the moral

---

[11] 'Daily Coal Report—Tuesday 20 November 1984', PREM/19/1335, Records of the Prime Minister's Office.
[12] 'The Enemy Within', photocopied sheet, n.d., in HD 9551.6, 'Miners' Strike 1984/5 Leaflets and Cuttings', TUC Collection, London Metropolitan University Library (hereafter TUC Collection). A copy is also held in PREM/19/1333, Records of the Prime Minister's Office. See Jack Saunders, *Assembling Cultures: Workplace Activism, Labour Militancy and Cultural Change in Britain's Car Factories, 1945–82* (Manchester: Manchester University Press, 2019), 221, on the Cowley wives' campaign.
[13] 'The Enemy Within', photocopied sheet, n.d., HD 9551.6, TUC Collection; Adeney and Lloyd, *Miners' Strike*, 222–3.
[14] Ben Curtis, *The South Wales Miners 1964–1985* (Cardiff: University of Wales Press, 2013), 233.

pressure exerted by communities like those in the militant Kent and South Wales coalfields to back the strike.

Jane Fjaelberg reported that she had started her group in South Wales about two months before she and McGibbon met with Thatcher in September, in order to encourage men to return to work and to 'act as a mutual support group of wives, giving help to those who are suffering under the strain and exchanging practical ideas on how to face shared problems'.[15] In Kent, Irene McGibbon similarly 'agitat[ed] amongst the miners' wives, with offers of help, providing you can convince your man to cross picket lines'.[16] These women linked up across the country, though it is not clear whether their local groups, or the national 'Miners Wives Back to Work Campaign' (for which McGibbon was soon calling herself the 'national organiser') had many, or indeed any, members beyond themselves. The women told Thatcher they had raised 'a small sum of money' and received 'some assistance from the National Working Miners Association'.[17] This was almost certainly the National Working Miners' Committee, a group which put a great deal of pressure on the NUM in autumn 1984 by giving individual working miners help in bringing legal cases against the NUM, and which drew on the help of prominent Thatcherites.[18] Both Irene and Robert McGibbon also acknowledged they had connections to the National Association for Freedom (NAFF), a pressure group formed in 1975 to directly confront the power of trade unions; Robert McGibbon, appearing on Radio 4's 'Decision Makers' alongside NAFF's chairman, said he had been in touch with the Association during the Cowley dispute, and was 'regularly' in touch with them during the miners' strike.[19]

Challenged about her connections to the Thatcher government in September 1984, Irene McGibbon claimed that, '[n]o way are we lovers of Maggie Thatcher. All we want to see is miners have the right to decide their future for themselves through the ballot box.'[20] Given her meeting with Thatcher earlier in the month, and her candidacy as a Tory councillor in 1983, this was clearly disingenuous.[21] Making an argument about trade union democracy was the most widely-acceptable means of denouncing the strike: it was so powerful because it did not contest the idea of trade unionism, but merely insisted unions must be controlled

---

[15] 'Miners' Wives Back to Work Campaign', n.d., PREM/19/1333, Records of the Prime Minister's Office.

[16] 'The Enemy Within', photocopied sheet, n.d., HD 9551.6, TUC Collection.

[17] Letter from Andrew Turnbull to Michael Reidy, 19 September 1984, PREM/19/1333, Records of the Prime Minister's Office.

[18] David Amos, 'The Nottinghamshire Miners, the Union of Democratic Mineworkers and the 1984-5 Miners' Strike: Scabs or Scapegoats' (unpublished PhD thesis, University of Nottingham, 2011), 94.

[19] 'The Enemy Within', photocopied sheet, n.d., HD 9551.6, TUC Collection; 'Diary', Guardian, 18 September 1984.

[20] Mark Hollingsworth, 'Using Miners to Bust the Union', New Statesman, 108, 14 December 1984.

[21] Ibid.

by their members to have legitimacy. McGibbon consistently implied that the NUM was making illegitimate and immoral use of bullying and intimidation to curtail the basic freedoms of its members, and traducing their 'right to work'. She also implied that far from representing its members, the union had been taken over by 'anarchist and communist agitators'.[22] After her appearance at the Conservative Party Conference, McGibbon had a letter published in *The Times* in which she argued that 'in a ploy typical of his Marxist mentors, Mr Scargill issued an impossible demand: that no pit be closed, however uneconomic to mine, until total exhaustion of its resources'. She claimed Scargill was trying to *deliberately* prolong the strike as 'a political manoeuvre to challenge democratic process'.[23] In all this, McGibbon and her husband precisely echoed Thatcherite beliefs: Thatcher always insisted that trade unions must be in the democratic control of individual members through secret ballots, argued that militant union behaviour was the result of extreme left groups hijacking organisations, and opposed the closed shop as coercive.[24]

Few women who opposed the strike were as ideological as McGibbon and her group, however. In South Shields, Joanne's* father returned to work in autumn 1984, driven by anger with the strike and despair at the hardship it was causing. He was enticed by the NCB's Christmas bonus: Joanne's family had not been well off even before the strike; now they had huge rent arrears and no money coming in except for Joanne's child benefit. Her parents had no savings, and her mother did not want to admit how much they were struggling; she told Joanne, 'don't you dare tell anyone we've had mince' for Sunday dinner.[25] Joanne recalled that her mother hated Scargill during the strike: if he came on TV, she would 'always have choice words' for him. Her father, Joanne said, 'went back early for the money. Purely and simply the only thing he'd gone back for was the money. To—to start earning again.' Joanne recalled that it transformed how her parents felt:

> All of a sudden, there was like a—oh, hope... oh finally we're going to have some money, oh, we can start paying this, we can start—we can start living again, we can start buying the normal shopping again, you know... They were really hopeful and excited.

Her mother told Joanne that she would have a Christmas present (she had had no present or card for her birthday in September).[26] But the decision also had painful

---

[22] 'Diary', *Guardian*, 18 September 1984.
[23] Irene McGibbon, 'Talks as Bar to Return to Pits', *The Times*, 24 October 1984.
[24] Florence Sutcliffe-Braithwaite, *Class, Politics, and the Decline of Deference in England, 1968–2000* (Oxford: Oxford University Press, 2018), 160–1.
[25] Joanne*, b. 1973, North East England, interviewed by Victoria Dawson, 16 July 2018.
[26] Ibid.

consequences. Joanne recalled hearing her father describe the experience of travelling through picket lines to work for the first time:

> I can remember on the night time every—all my sisters and that coming round and he was sitting in his chair and he was recounting this story about what had happened that day and he was actually crying and shaking, that was the only time I've ever, ever seen him cry or—you know, react emotionally to anything.[27]

The whole family was also subject to insults and social ostracism in the community.[28]

Joanne's recollections make clear just how wearing financial struggle was, particularly for women who did not want to receive what they saw as 'charity'. It was not deeply-held anti-trade union ideology but sheer misery, anger, and despair that led Joanne's father to return to work, and her mother to support him—though it is also significant that Joanne's mother felt angry at Scargill, and perceived the union's actions not as defending the family's wellbeing, but as destroying it. Though they lived in a mining community, Joanne's parents decided returning to work would be worth the social repercussions. Joanne's experience was repeated up and down the country during the autumn, as men drifted back to work. Yet many coalfields remained relatively strong in support of the strike in late 1984, testament to the power of ideological support for the cause, respect for the picket line, community solidarity, and fear of being ostracised. As we will see in Chapter 6, crossing a picket line began to become more thinkable during the final months of the strike as desperation grew; and as more strikers returned to work, the calculation of whether or not it was worthwhile staying out began to change. These, then, would be difficult times for the strike support movement.

The Support Movement in Autumn

On 30 September, the Swansea, Neath and Dulais Valleys Miners' Support Group gathered for its weekly meeting. The support group was a mixed umbrella group representing nine support groups in the three valleys, most of which were organised solely or largely by women. Over the last seven days, it was reported, they had distributed a record number of food parcels—998—and the impact of the strike on local families was clearly showing.[29] 'The building societies are beginning to put the screws on', reported one woman.[30] Another noted the mass pickets of

---

[27] Ibid.   [28] For more on this, see Chapter 6.
[29] Minutes of meeting 20 September 1984, Neath and District Miners' Strike Support Fund minute book 6 May–22 September 1984, SWCC/MND/25/1, box 4 of 8, South Wales Coalfield Collection, Richard Burton Archive, Swansea (hereafter SWCC papers).
[30] Ibid.

the Electricity Board in Barnsley, a form of protest seen in several parts of the country, as the Board began to threaten to cut off supplies to those who had not paid their bills.[31] The strike was becoming more difficult to sustain, though South Wales did not see a single strikebreaker until November.[32]

As the needs of strikers and their families only grew over time, new support groups continued to form in autumn. In suburban Doncaster, miner's wife Maureen Coates helped form the Sprotbrough and Brodsworth Miners' Support Group in November. Living in the suburb of Scawsby (part of Sprotbrough and Brodsworth parish), Maureen realised that the many miners of the district, living a couple of miles from the nearby pit villages of Bentley and Woodlands, were isolated from much of the support offered in those areas.[33] She had been involved in informal support work, but the trigger for the formation of the group—which held its first meeting on 24 November, and which had around sixteen members—seems to have been the donation of £4,000 from Sprotbrough Parish Council and £2,000 from Brodsworth Parish Council, necessitating the formation of an official group; the women used the money to distribute vouchers for the budget supermarket Kwik-Save to about 200 miners.[34] There was continuing concern in the women's support movement that such dispersed and suburban miners were most likely to break the strike: they had less access to the support of groups, which were strongest in close-knit mining communities, and more insulated from community sanctions against strikebreakers, too.

Most women's support groups, however, were well-established by the start of autumn, and were probably assisting as many people as could be reached. It can be difficult to pinpoint exactly how many people groups were feeding at this point: not all kept records, account books often documented the overall money spent rather than the number of meals served or food parcels or vouchers delivered, and the numbers helped fluctuated substantially from week to week. Unsurprisingly, few of our interviewees remembered precise details. Nevertheless, some groups did keep records which give a sense of the overall picture. The Swansea, Neath and Dulais Valleys support group, for example, went from distributing 408 food parcels in the week to 13 May, to over 900 a week by July; numbers stayed around this level, rising slightly in the latter months of 1984, until on 31 December it was reported that 1,072 parcels had been given out.[35] In Hatfield, South Yorkshire, the support group was providing 300 dinners every day at the miners' welfare by

---

[31] Ibid. See also, e.g., Theresa Gratton*, b. 1955, North East England, interviewed by Florence Sutcliffe-Braithwaite, 22 February 2020.
[32] Curtis, *South Wales Miners*, 227.
[33] Maureen Coates, b. 1942, Yorkshire, interviewed by Florence Sutcliffe-Braithwaite and Natalie Thomlinson, 11 September 2014.
[34] Minutes of meeting 24 November, Sprotbrough and Brodsworth Miners' Support Group minute book, papers of Maureen Coates, private collection.
[35] Neath and District Miners' Strike Support Fund minute books, 6 May–22 September 1984, and 23 September 1984–17 February 1985, both in SWCC/MND/25/1, SWCC papers.

Figure 5.1 Marilyn Johnson serves a meal in the miners' welfare in Easington, County Durham, 1984. © Keith Pattison.

June; by August, the group was giving out 273 food parcels a week on top of this, and by November, the women were serving 500 dinners a day and distributing over 700 food parcels a week.[36] In Easington, a village with a very high density of miners, 500 meals were served every day (see Figure 5.1).[37] In Nottinghamshire, the size of the local operations varied enormously. In Manton, the food kitchen initially tried to provide for nearly 800 striking miners and their dependants, but by the end, only 187 miners were left. The group cooked an average of 70–150 meals a day, and also provided food parcels.[38] At the other end of the spectrum, Newark Miners' Support Group—which covered an area which had few striking miners—provided for seventeen miners at the beginning of the strike, falling to just seven at the end; most of the funds the group raised were used to support groups elsewhere in Nottinghamshire.[39] As this suggests, food provision varied significantly from group to group, and across the strike.

Account books give some insight into the finances of the support movement. In the soup kitchen at Woolley, in Yorkshire, accounts suggest that the kitchen was

---

[36] Bob Hume, 'The Hatfield Main Welfare Organisation', in Raphael Samuel, Barbara Bloomfield, and Guy Boanas, eds., *The Enemy Within: Pit Villages and the Miners' Strike of 1984-5* (London: Routledge & Kegan Paul, 1986), 128–38.
[37] Keith Pattison and Huw Beynon, *Easington August 1984*, n.p., 'The Miners' Strike Papers', People's History Museum and Archive, Manchester (hereafter 'Miners' Strike Papers').
[38] Joan Witham, *Hearts and Minds: The Story of the Women of Nottinghamshire in the Miners' Strike, 1984–1985* (London: Canary, 1986), 180–1.
[39] Ibid., 184–7.

spending anything between £11 and £150 a week by autumn, and even more by the end of the strike; items were often bought in bulk, which could result in large discrepancies in expenditure between weeks.[40] This was a relatively small operation, reflecting the small size of the village; Betty Cook, one of the organisers, thought that 'on average we were feeding thirty-six people plus six people in the kitchens' on the days they were active.[41] In the much larger settlement of Aberdare, in South Wales, the Miners' Relief Fund consistently spent over £200 a week by autumn, though it is difficult to gauge how many people were being fed; Anne Watts thought they made up about 150 parcels per week.[42] The umbrella group for all the Nottinghamshire support groups (see Figure 5.2) reported on 23

Figure 5.2 A meeting of the central Nottinghamshire Women's Support Group in Mansfield, c.1985. Betty Heathfield, a prominent WAPC activist, and wife of Peter Heathfield, NUM General Secretary, sits on the left; second from right is Gwen MacLeod, a leading activist in Ashfield Women's Support Group, and in the Nottinghamshire central group. © Brenda Prince/Format.

[40] Woolley Account Book, A308-G/2/1/1, papers of Barnsley Women Against Pit Closures, Barnsley Archives, Barnsley.
[41] Betty Cook, interviewed by Rachel Cohen, 29 August 2012, C1420/60, Sisterhood and After, British Library, London (hereafter Cook, interviewed by Cohen).
[42] Cashbook, D1432/1, papers of Aberdare Miners' Relief Fund, Glamorgan Archives, Cardiff; Anne Watts, b. 1949, South Wales, interviewed by Florence Sutcliffe-Braithwaite, 23 May 2019.

November 1984 that in the past week its income was £4,552.09 and its expenditure £1,375.60.[43]

Huge amounts of money were being raised across the country to support the strike by autumn. National Women Against Pit Closures (NWAPC) had raised £39,814 by 6 October, and in total, between July 1984 and September 1985, the group raised over £710,000.[44] The Scottish area of the NUM raised about £60,000 a month over the course of the strike, and in London, about £40,000 a month was being raised and channelled through the official London NUM support committee—though, as Diarmaid Kelliher has noted, this was only a 'tiny fraction' of the total raised.[45] Local support groups set up outside the coalfields also raised impressive (if variable) amounts: the Labour Party Research Department found that groups from the Isle of Wight and Kirby raised £1,000 a week, though the average was closer to £230 a week.[46] In the run-up to Christmas, the Mining Families Christmas Appeal, instigated by NWAPC, brought in nearly £400,000.[47] Significant donations were also made to striking miners and their families from abroad, both from trade unions and from communist Warsaw Pact countries, particularly the Soviet Union. Support for the strike was local, national, and international.[48]

International support was made tangible through donations of food and other goods from abroad, something several interviewees remembered. Tanya Dower recalled that in South Wales, 'we were eating welfare packages from Russia, you know, that's how stark it was'.[49] Maxine Penkethman, from Staffordshire, remembered:

> we were having them from France for some reason... I do remember, we used to love it when the food parcels come... but—obviously we didn't know what we were getting, and I do remember we had this tube, like toothpaste, was what we

---

[43] The Notts Women's Support Groups (incorporating Mansfield Solidarity Support Committee), Treasurer's Report w/e 23 November 1984, papers of Gwen MacLeod, private collection (hereafter MacLeod papers).

[44] Minutes of NWAPC committee meeting, 6 October 1984, DWSG4/1, papers of the South Wales Women's Support Group, Glamorgan Archives, Cardiff (hereafter SWWSG papers); 'Women Against Pit Closures Reports and Accounts 1985', 7JMC/A/06, papers of Jean McCrindle, Women's Library@LSE, London (hereafter McCrindle papers) (unfortunately figures that only take into account money raised before the end of the strike are not available).

[45] Jim Phillips, *Collieries, Communities and the Miners' Strike in Scotland, 1984-85* (Manchester: Manchester University Press, 2012), 117; Diarmaid Kelliher, *Cultures of Solidarity: London and the 1984-5 Miners' Strike* (London: Routledge, 2021), 5.

[46] Labour Research Department, *Solidarity with the Miners* (London: LRD, 1985), 11, quot. in Maroula Joannou, '"Fill a Bag and Feed a Family": The Miners' Strike and its Supporters', in Jonathan Davis and Rohan McWilliam, eds., *Labour and the Left in the 1980s* (Manchester: Manchester University Press, 2017), 172-91, at 178.

[47] £394,678 at a cost of £17,300 for adverts in the national press: Jean McCrindle, 'The National Organisation of Women Against Pit Closures in the Miners' Strike of 1984-5' (unpublished PhD thesis, Oxford Brookes, 2001), 179.

[48] See Jonathan Saunders, *Across Frontiers: International Support for the Miners' Strike* (London: Canary, 1989).

[49] Tanya Dower, b. 1967, South Wales, interviewed by Victoria Dawson, 13 August 2018.

thought it was, and erm, on it it said 'crème de taches' [sic] and erm, I remember we're all like saying, 'well what is it? It's gotta be toothpaste'... and when we opened it, it was shoe polish!⁵⁰

This was a humorous story, but Maxine also reflected that 'when you look back on that, the French miners, when sending over stuff, were like, people are still proud, so people still want to have shoes that are clean, and I just thought that was really lovely'.⁵¹ There was an emotional as well as a material importance to these donations. The international expressions of solidarity were psychologically sustaining: the gift of shoe polish was a recognition of the dignity and humanity of striking miners and their families.

At the local level, women across the country mobilised in autumn to try to counter the drift back to work. Some became involved in community action targeting strikebreakers. In Kent, Sue remembered picketing the houses of strikebreakers in September:

> The green house was the first one back up. And we decided to go up there picketing as the women's support group, because a lot of the men would be down the pit picketing... So because the women wanted to get active, there was a group of us that decided we would walk the village. And we would hang around, perhaps, for, twenty minutes outside that house. And then we'd walk, and then when the next one went back—on the corner down the bottom—we may hang about there for twenty minutes.⁵²

The police imposed a curfew on the village in an effort to stamp out this activity, and Sue recalled police vans being stationed outside the family home to intimidate her, her husband and daughter. In South Wales, Siân James also remembered picketing strikebreakers' houses with other women, singing hymns such as 'What a Friend We Have in Jesus';⁵³ footage from the film *Smiling and Splendid Women* shows a group of women (including Siân) outside the house of a strikebreaker, banging drums and tambourines.⁵⁴ These actions drew on a long tradition of women shaming strikebreakers using community-based actions and ostracism, as Angela John showed in her study of pit brow lasses, and as Hester Barron demonstrated in her work on the 1926 lockout in County Durham, where women were involved in several rowdy protests against 'blacklegs'.⁵⁵ The singing

---

⁵⁰ Maxine Penkethman, b. 1967, Staffordshire, interviewed by Victoria Dawson, 2 August 2018.
⁵¹ Ibid.   ⁵² Sue, b. 1956, Kent, interviewed by Florence Sutcliffe-Braithwaite, 14 July 2018.
⁵³ Siân James, b. 1959, South Wales, interviewed by Florence Sutcliffe-Braithwaite, 5 February 2019.
⁵⁴ *Smiling and Splendid Women*, dir. Gail Allen, 1986.
⁵⁵ Angela V. John, *By the Sweat of their Brow: Women Workers at Victorian Coal Mines* (London: Croom Helm, 1980), 124–5; Hester Barron, *The 1926 Miners' Lockout: Meanings of Community in the Durham Coalfield* (Oxford: Oxford University Press, 2010), 151–7.

of hymns and banging of drums echoed traditions of 'rough music' stretching back into the early modern period.[56]

Some women also stepped up their militancy on the picket lines, and police responses to picketing women seem to have become harsher as the strike wore on. Many women arrested on picket lines were ultimately released without charge, but this was not always the case. Dianne Hogg of Askern Women's Support Group was arrested after an all-women's picket at Calverton, Nottinghamshire, on charges of obstructing police and threatening behaviour. In November 1984, she was put on trial and found guilty; she received an absolute discharge but was ordered to pay £100 towards the prosecution's costs, which was covered by the NUM. While her punishment was relatively light, Hogg found the whole process stressful and upsetting.[57] In the same month, miner's wife Brenda Greenwood became the first woman to be imprisoned for her strike activism, in Ollerton, in Nottinghamshire. Greenwood was first arrested for refusing to move from the corner of the pit lane, a spot from which police had banned pickets. Greenwood was cautioned and told not to demonstrate at Ollerton pit again. Defiant, she returned the following day, and was arrested, charged with obstruction, and taken to Mansfield Magistrates Court, where she was released on bail, with the same condition. Nevertheless, she returned again the following day, though her solicitor warned her she would probably be remanded, and her husband and children begged her not to go. 'I appreciated everyone's concern for me', Greenwood recalled, 'but something inside me kept telling me not to give up, it was very important to me that I should fight to the bitter end, in defence of my rights and the rights of my class'. This time, the magistrates remanded her in custody for seven days in Risley Remand Centre: the 'shattering experience of being sent to prison', she recalled, 'will be etched on my memory for as long as I live. But I am in no way deterred, nor has my spirit been broken.'[58] Greenwood was put on trial three times during the strike, but won each time (see Figure 5.3).[59] As the policing of the strike grew more and more intense—with aggressive outside forces brought in, whole pit villages flooded with police (see Figure 5.4), and the intimidation of miners and their families in their own homes—many women got used to a constant police presence in their communities, and some were propelled by their outrage and sense of injustice to ever-stronger protests.

Some of the most dramatic scenes of women's activism took place at Cynheidre, in South Wales. The colliery's position on the western edge of the coalfield, with its workers spread out over a large area, made it particularly vulnerable to

---

[56] Barron, *1926 Miners' Lockout*, 156–7. See also E. P. Thompson, 'Rough Music', in Thompson, *Customs in Common* (London: Merlin Press, 1991), 467–531.

[57] 'Legal Papers', SY689/V3/1, and Dianne Hogg, interviewed by unknown person, 14 January 1986, SY689/V9/1, both in papers of Askern Women's Support Group, Sheffield City Archives, Sheffield.

[58] *Women's Fightback. Paper of the Women's Campaign Labour Movement Fightback for Women's Rights*, 37 (dated February 1984 but evidently from 1985), 'Miners' Strike Papers'.

[59] Witham, *Hearts and Minds*, 86.

Figure 5.3 Women celebrate Brenda Greenwood's acquittal. © Brenda Prince/Format.

strikebreaking, and on 5 November it was one of the two pits where the strike was first broken in South Wales, when sixteen men reported for work.[60] In response, women undertook two occupations of the pit. Early in November, twenty-one women took over the pithead baths for seventeen hours.[61] Unhappy with how the occupation had ended, seventeen women occupied the colliery offices later in the month, this time for several days.[62] Edwina Roberts, one of the participants, reported that the women climbed into the manager's office at 11.30 p.m.; the next morning, they 'shouted abuse to the scabs passing under the window'.[63] Siân James recalled that 'the goal of the occupation was to gain publicity, keep the story alive', and that 'we just wanted to show that we would take action if men were drifting back'.[64] The women were able to get away with things that miners would not have been able to; at one point, they found a list of NCB contacts, telephoned Ian MacGregor's secretary and actually asked to speak to him.[65] Siân, however, left the occupation early because her husband asked her to leave, citing 'family pressures': domestic responsibilities still

---

[60] Curtis, *South Wales Miners*, 227.
[61] Minutes of meeting, 11 November, Neath and District Miners' Support Group minute book 23 September 1984–17 February 1985, SWCC/MND/25/1, SWCC papers.
[62] Ibid.
[63] 'Report on Cynheidre', 12 November, Neath and District Miners' Support Group minute book 23 September 1984–17 February 1985, SWCC/MND/25/1, SWCC papers.
[64] Siân James.
[65] Siân James, interviewed by Hywel Francis, 5 November 1986, AUD/503, '1984–85 Miners' Strike Study', South Wales Miners' Library, University of Swansea.

Figure 5.4 Two women talk in the street in Easington, County Durham, while police look on. © Keith Pattison.

had a strong claim on most women involved in the support movement, even those like Siân who were strongly political, and had supportive husbands.⁶⁶

Siân was not the only woman whose activism was curtailed by domestic duties. Pat Smith, from Dinnington, South Yorkshire, also recalled that 'one of t'miners kept saying, "you need to go to London, you need to go to London", and I says, "easier said than done, we've got kids. You know, you go to London!" So eventually, what we did, the money we had raised we funded them for *them* to go to London.'⁶⁷ It did not appear to have occurred to anyone in Pat's group that the men could have taken on the childcare temporarily, and domestic duties did not stop male strike activists sometimes leaving for extended periods, either as flying pickets or fundraisers. (Here again, women often did the work of hosting; among our interviewees, Kath Court—an active trade unionist originally from a mining community—hosted two Northumberland miners in her home in Croydon for much of the strike.)⁶⁸ And while Betty Cook's husband did take over cooking meals and washing-up, her mother 'used to come and do the washing and ironing, and clean windows and things like that'.⁶⁹ While some husbands did undoubtedly take on more housework, as we saw in Chapter 4, narratives of domestic role reversal during and after the strike have been exaggerated. As Maggie Stubbs said when asked if her (now ex-) husband had done more around the house during the strike, 'no! [laughs] What kind of a silly question are you asking me? ... It doesn't change the culture. The wives, they had to do it.'⁷⁰

During the autumn, NWAPC continued its UK-wide organising, holding a national conference in Chesterfield in November. Representatives were present from all NUM Areas, with delegates chosen on the basis of these Areas, and in adherence to the rule that 75 per cent must be miners' wives.⁷¹ There were controversial debates over strategy, with Betty Heathfield arguing for a close working relationship with the NUM, while Ella Egan and Ida Hackett—two of the three delegates who were not miners' wives, and both of whom were aligned with the Eurocommunist faction in the Communist Party of Great Britain (CPGB)—called for 'links with the peace movement and progressive women's organisations'.⁷² In line with the Eurocommunist aim of generating a 'popular front', Egan and Hackett hoped the women's support movement would not just bolster Scargill and the NUM, but help remake working-class politics, and centre the needs of women and other minoritised groups alongside those of the

---

⁶⁶ Ibid. ⁶⁷ Pat Smith.
⁶⁸ Kath Court, b. 1943, Yorkshire/London, interviewed by Florence Sutcliffe-Braithwaite, 26 April 2019.
⁶⁹ Cook, interviewed by Cohen.
⁷⁰ Maggie Stubbs, b. c.1950, Jamaica/Yorkshire, interviewed by Natalie Thomlinson, 13 September 2018.
⁷¹ McCrindle, 'National Organisation of Women Against Pit Closures', 151. ⁷² Ibid., 153.

archetypal proletarian male trade unionist.[73] The aims the conference agreed on for the organisation demonstrated, however, the influence of Scargillite women—and of Arthur Scargill himself, who suggested, behind the scenes, amendments to the original draft aims, most of which were accepted.[74] The agreed aims were: to 'consolidate the National Women's Organisation and ensure victory to the NUM in their present struggle to prevent pit closures and protect mining communities for the future'; to develop the relationship between the NUM and women's groups at all levels; to strengthen the groups and to promote the national organisation's work; to campaign on issues affecting mining communities, and to 'promote and develop education for working class women'.[75] The conference also heard a treasurer's report from Jean McCrindle—though delegates were sworn to secrecy about this—stating that, due to the sequestration of NUM funds, NWAPC's fundraising and distribution networks were now vital to the strike.[76]

The conference was felt to have gone well, but its success hid tensions in groups across the country.[77] Sometimes, these were simply the result of personal animosities, as Jackie Keating's account of her falling-out with the Cortonwood support group makes clear; the acute stress of the strike provided fertile conditions for disagreements to erupt.[78] Sometimes, though, tensions were rooted in political differences.[79] Siân James remembered that 'South Wales was riddled with schisms'.[80] Sheffield WAPC also saw political disputes break out between various left factions.[81] Perhaps the most notable example of a breakdown in groups' relations came in Barnsley, where many key activists in NWAPC were based. In November, tensions bubbled over into outright hostilities, and the group split in two. One group, containing Eurocommunist women like Jean Miller and Lorraine Bowler, retained the original name, Barnsley WAPC. The breakaway group, Barnsley Miners' Wives Action Group (BMWAG), included those closest to Arthur Scargill personally and politically, like Jean McCrindle, Anne Scargill, and her friend Betty Cook, none of whom were in the CPGB.[82] The split ostensibly

---

[73] See Jean Miller, 'Barnsley', in Vicky Seddon, ed., *The Cutting Edge: Women and the Pit Strike* (London: Lawrence & Wishart, 1986), 227–40; Beatrix Campbell, 'Proletarian Patriarchs and the Real Radicals' in Seddon, ed., *The Cutting Edge*, 249–82, for two extended reflections by prominent Eurocommunists on the purpose of the women's movement.

[74] McCrindle, 'National Organisation of Women Against Pit Closures', 154. For discussion of the CPGB and its factions, see Chapter 1 of this book.

[75] Notes on All Women National Conference 9–11 November, Neath and District Miners' Support Group minute book 23 September 1984–17 February 1985, SWCC/MND/25/1, SWCC papers.

[76] Ibid.   [77] Ibid.

[78] Jackie Keating, *Counting the Cost: A Family in the Miners' Strike* (Barnsley: Wharncliffe Publishing, 1991), 17–20.

[79] Meg Allen, 'Carrying on the Strike: The Politics of Women Against Pit Closures' (unpublished PhD thesis, University of Manchester, 2001), ch. 4.

[80] Siân James.

[81] Janet Hudson, 'Holding it Together: Strategies for Broad-Based Work', in Seddon, ed., *Cutting Edge*, 63–8.

[82] McCrindle, 'National Organisation of Women Against Pit Closures', 144.

took place over the participation of women who were not related to miners. Cook remembered that:

> there was striking miners, wives and mums and aunties and cousins, then you'd got women that didn't have any connection with the mining industry as such but living in a mining area they needed to support it. And then we got a lot of students from college that were coming along and supporting. But as time went on it—it seemed to [us] that the students were taking over and we were—we didn't agree with that, we were the miners' wives and we were sort of organising the group and they were welcome, they were welcome to come and support us. But they weren't welcome to say that, 'oh if there's any speaking to be done we'll go and if there's any meetings we'll go', because we needed to involve the women that were actually going through the strike, that knew what the problems were and [had] experience of the difficulties.[83]

Yet this reasoning masked deeper political tensions about the group's purpose and its relations with the NUM.[84] BMWAG's members were not—despite the group's name—all miners' wives. They were, however, Scargill loyalists, and saw the purpose of the support groups primarily as being to help the NUM win the strike. Many of the 'students' (some of whom were, in fact, miners' wives) were associated with the CPGB Eurocommunist faction: they wanted the women's groups to be part of a broad 'popular front' for social and political change, disagreed with Scargill's tactics, and resented any NUM attempts to control the women.[85]

Scargill's behind-the-scenes influence on NWAPC was kept quiet at the time, but it was widely believed that women in the support movement tended to be pro-Scargill. Siân James laughingly said that the women in South Wales called themselves 'Scargill's Angels'.[86] While Scargill did envisage the women's groups taking on a political education role, this was within the framework of a traditional left politics which essentially placed the women's groups as auxiliaries to the (male-dominated) NUM. Even so, this limited vision for the women's groups still gave women a new degree of agency and recognition within coalfield politics, given the almost complete lack of space for coalfield women's voices in the NUM prior to 1984. There was little room for the remaking of gender relations in Scargill's vision of the women's groups; but, as we will see, this was not the main motivation for most women who took part in them. The central question relating to gender that concerned most women involved in the support movement

---

[83] Cook, interviewed by Cohen.
[84] Allen, 'Carrying on the Strike', ch. 2; McCrindle, 'National Organisation of Women Against Pit Closures', 163–6.
[85] See Allen, 'Carrying on the Strike', ch. 2; Miller, 'Barnsley'.
[86] Siân James; Jean McCrindle interviewed by Louise Brodie, 13 March 2012, National Life Stories, British Library, London (hereafter McCrindle, interviewed by Brodie).

was whether to place themselves in a purely supportive role in relation to the male-dominated NUM, or instead to demand more organisational and political autonomy. Feminism was, for most, a marginal issue.

The Politics of the Support Movement

In October 1984, feminist magazine *Spare Rib* hit the newsstands of Britain with a cover that loudly proclaimed 'Women Winning the Strike', superimposed over a picture of women from coalfields involved in the support movement.[87] Inside, there was an extended feature on Bobby and Sue, sisters involved in the support movement in the village of Bentley, South Yorkshire. The article focused particularly on the sense of personal emancipation that political involvement could bring:

> Until the moves to safeguard their livelihoods, Bobby and Sue have never been involved in anything even distantly political. Their action, like those of other women in the coalfields, grew out of the practical needs of the community, but through their energy and initiative they and the other women who make up Bentley Women's Action Group have created a profound and unprecedented change in the essentially male culture of the mining community.[88]

This was indicative of the way that the support movement was covered in the radical press; it suggested the curiosity of many in the women's liberation movement about the new movement in the coalfields, and their desire to help their sisters who lived there. Many women who identified as feminists got involved in supporting the strike, and their accounts, as we saw in Chapter 1, helped produce the influential idea of a newly politicised—even feminist— cohort of coalfield women.[89] But in fact, few coalfield women met feminists during the strike, and very few were converted to 'feminism'; after the strike, there was little long-term change in gender roles that was attributable to strike activism.[90] Indeed, the prominence of the narrative of feminist transformation in media and scholarly accounts of the strike speaks to the power of middle-class activists and intellectuals to create the paradigms through which the dispute is understood.

For many socialist-feminists, the development of the women's support movement was exciting because it suggested that feminist politics had a constituency beyond

---

[87] *Spare Rib*, 147, October 1984.
[88] Loretta Loach, 'We'll be Here Right to the End and After', *Spare Rib*, 147, October 1984.
[89] On metropolitan support for the strike, see Kelliher, *Cultures of Solidarity*.
[90] See Chapter 7 for more on this.

middle-class, educated women.[91] Long-time feminist activist Lesley Boulton (see Figure 4.5), who was part of Sheffield WAPC, emphasised in 1986 that she was 'very interested in, in encouraging women to act politically and from that point of view it was very exciting'.[92] Radical feminists involved in the Greenham Common Peace Camps built reciprocal links with women's support groups for similar reasons (see Figure 5.5).[93] Many women active on the left were involved in a number of causes, like Karmen Thomas, who had co-founded 'Women for Life on Earth' in 1981, and was involved in CND as well as Ammanford Trades Council in South Wales. She connected her involvement with the strike support movement to both her labour movement and peace movement work.[94] Long-time left activist Jean McCrindle recalled in one interview that:

> It was exciting, it was exhausting, it was putting in practice what I thought I'd learnt all my life from the political campaigning that I'd always been doing amongst women...I'd had years and years of discussing how to make our ideas sort of relevant to most women, not just to us, as a university-educated group of women.[95]

McCrindle went on to discuss how she had the 'skills ready' to do this work, but that it was 'difficult organising, because most miners' wives had never been in any organisation, ever': in large meetings, there was 'often quite a lot of quarrelling and interrupting, and inability to keep order. People didn't know about having minutes of the decisions that were being taken.'[96] As this suggests, there was perhaps more than a hint of missionary zeal and class condescension in the way some middle-class feminists approached support work, echoing the way middle-class women had long seen it as their duty to politically educate their working-class 'sisters'.[97] They positioned themselves as the facilitators of working-class women's emancipation, and dictated the terms through which it could be achieved. Of course, some women were sensitive to this dynamic; Sheffield WAPC member Caroline Poland—from a middle-class background but the partner of a striking miner—was self-aware about her class privilege, remembering, 'the coming together of women [is] what we want to see, but we want to see it in a way that

---

[91] See George Stevenson, *The Women's Liberation Movement and the Politics of Class in Britain* (London: Bloomsbury Academic, 2019).
[92] Lesley Boulton, interviewed by unknown person, 3 March 1986, SY729/V/5/1, papers of Lesley Boulton, Sheffield City Archives, Sheffield.
[93] See 'Mines not Missiles: Links with the Peace Women', in Seddon, ed., *Cutting Edge*, 149–75.
[94] Karmen Thomas, b. 1956, South East England/South Wales, interviewed by Florence Sutcliffe-Braithwaite, 12 August 2018.
[95] McCrindle, interviewed by Brodie.   [96] Ibid.
[97] See Natalie Thomlinson, *Race, Ethnicity and the Women's Movement in England, 1968–1993* (Basingstoke: Palgrave Macmillan, 2016), ch. 1.

Figure 5.5 Two marchers on Gray's Inn Road, London, during a miners' lobby of Parliament, June 1984. © Maggie Murray/Format.

doesn't underestimate class differences, privilege differences'.[98] But differences of financial, social, and cultural capital made unequal power relationships difficult to avoid, and clashing political orientations caused tensions.

---

[98] Caroline Poland, b. 1949, South-East England/Yorkshire, interviewed by Natalie Thomlinson, 5 February 2019.

Some feminists also took to task their 'brothers' in struggle, criticising miners for sexism and chauvinism. Perhaps the most high-profile example was Marxist-feminist journalist Bea Campbell, who wrote an essay after the strike in which she labelled the miners 'proletarian patriarchs', severely criticising what she saw as the male chauvinism of the NUM, and the fetishisation of the miners' heroic masculinity.[99] Angela, who was originally from Kent but who was attending Ruskin College, Oxford, during the strike, recalled that when miners from Maerdy staying in the college's common room put up a nude calendar, 'one of the more strident feminists' told them they would not be getting any more deliveries of food, as they could not be socialists and hold such attitudes towards women. Angela recalled that the calendar 'quickly came down'.[100] But such clashes highlighted the ways that sexual politics could divide activists who wanted to work side by side.

Some women from mining communities recalled difficult interactions with feminists. Kent activist and striking miner's wife Liz French responded, when asked about feminism:

Oh, yes, I'm there and I'm not there...I think you can take it too far, sometimes...I mean, how many times I've got told off in the strike for— cause I wasn't politically correct... Don't ask me their names. I just remember [them] standing afterwards, saying, 'you shouldn't sort of say that', 'cause I used to say, 'Liz French, miner's wife', and they used to, that's one of the things they used to pick me up on—'no, you were Liz French...Women Against Pit Closures'. I said, 'but, I wouldn't be Women Against Pit Closures, if I weren't married to a miner, and I'm his wife', and, I can't...I can't waste time picking nitty-gritty things up like that.[101]

Anne Kirby, from Fife, also recalled being patronised by feminist activists after she did not speak up at a meeting when an NUM official angered her: 'when I came off the stage, I had two feminists at me: "why didn't you say something? You're a woman!"'[102] As Bev Skeggs has argued, for working-class women, feminism could be just another standard by which they were judged by middle-class women and found wanting.[103]

Moreover, the domestic sphere was often a key source of pride, respectability, and identity for working-class women, and one which feminism was seen to disrupt.[104] Lisa McKenzie, whose mother Gwen MacLeod founded the Ashfield

---

[99] Campbell, 'Proletarian Patriarchs'.
[100] Angela, b. 1958, Kent/Oxford, interviewed by Florence Sutcliffe-Braithwaite, 9 July 2018.
[101] Liz French, b. 1950, Kent, interviewed by Florence Sutcliffe Braithwaite, 6 July 2018.
[102] Anne Kirby, b. 1955, Scotland, interviewed by Victoria Dawson, 26 November 2018.
[103] Beverley Skeggs, *Formations of Class and Gender: Becoming Respectable* (London: Sage, 1997).
[104] Ibid.; Florence Sutcliffe-Braithwaite and Natalie Thomlinson, 'Vernacular Discourses of Gender Equality in the Post-War British Working Class', *Past & Present*, 254 (2022), 277–313.

Women's Support Group and was the Nottinghamshire delegate for NWAPC, was 16 at the time of the strike. She remembered of the visitors whom her mother put up in their home that:

> My mum took great pride, in that she was a trade unionist, she was a strong woman, but she took pride in cooking our family meals. But when these fucking feminists come from Oxford and Cambridge who was telling her that you know we shouldn't be doing that, you know, I remember, I hated them.[105]

One woman interviewed just after the strike said, '[w]e don't class ourselves as feminists. We've met a lot of feminists and we've been insulted by a lot of feminists. Not that they meant to insult us, but we still want to be married women. We still want to love our husbands. Love our kids.'[106] When asked whether she was a feminist, Kay Case answered, 'no. Family woman'.[107] For many coalfield women, the two identities appeared to be mutually exclusive, and they saw the strike as aiming to *defend*, not unsettle, family life. Like Liz French, Anne Kirby, and Kay Case, most of the coalfield women we interviewed had an ambivalent relationship with feminism. They believed in the equality of women, but often viewed 'feminism' as middle-class and pedantic, an ideology which placed the rights of women over the rights of men, and which criticised women's association with the domestic.[108]

Differences in habitus were potential sources of tension in interactions between working-class women and middle-class feminist supporters of the strike, as well as other activists from outside the coalfields. Humorous anecdotes about differences in food and clothes were often used to communicate and contain anxieties about class and cultural difference. Activist women from South Wales led the way in making connections with lesbian and gay supporters;[109] Siân James recalled with humour her support group's 'consternation' at being taken for a vegetarian meal in London when visiting Lesbians and Gays Support the Miners (LGSM), and recalled her relief when the first visitor from the group to Dulais, Mike Jackson, 'turned out to be a meat-eating northerner, thank God!' Yet Siân also emphasised how much women in her group felt they had in common with LGSM members from London: 'they understood what struggle was, they understood what fighting back was, they had years of experience of political activism. So they were our sort

---

[105] Lisa McKenzie, b. 1968, Nottinghamshire, interviewed by Florence Sutcliffe-Braithwaite and Natalie Thomlinson, 29 March 2016.
[106] Interviewee 8, unpublished book manuscript, 7BEH/1/2, papers of Betty Heathfield, Women's Library@LSE, London.
[107] Kay Case, b. 1948, South Wales, interviewed by Florence Sutcliffe-Braithwaite, 13 August 2018.
[108] Sutcliffe-Braithwaite and Thomlinson, 'Vernacular Discourses'.
[109] Daryl Leeworthy, 'For Our Common Cause: Sexuality and Left Politics in South Wales, 1967–1985', *Contemporary British History*, 30 (2016), 260–80, at 263.

of people.'¹¹⁰ As this suggests, despite some tensions, many women emphasised that a common cause united people across class and cultural divides, and recalled the positive experiences they had working with people from different backgrounds. Betty Cook, for example, remembered Jean McCrindle fondly as 'a very gentle person', who 'hadn't had the struggles we had' but 'whose education was broadened by mixing with us'.¹¹¹ Kay Case remembered the women she met in Devon who supported the strike 'being very colourful and dressed up in not hippy, clothes but, you know, that sort of style'; but also as 'always very helpful', offering tea, cake, and 'a chat'.¹¹² Doubtless many coalfield women did not want to appear ungrateful to their supporters. In Onllwyn, when the Scarlett Harletts, a London-based feminist theatre group, came to perform their show in support of the strike in January 1985, the *Valleys Star* newsletter instructed its readers, 'they are coming here especially to support our group, we must show our appreciation for such commitment. Please give them a full house!'¹¹³ But more than that, many of the more politically-engaged strike activists were committed to the idea of solidarity—that people, whatever their class background, race, or sexuality could be brought together in the service of what was right, and to support each other through struggle. To dwell on differences would not only undermine the idea of solidarity, but also the possibility of a more just future society in which people could transcend distinctions of class, race, and sexuality.

Most coalfield-based action groups did not, it must be stressed, make sustained connections with outside groups leading to mutual visits and longstanding friendships; and even in those groups that did, only a minority of women were generally involved in liaising with outside supporters. Few of our interviewees could remember any sustained discussion of feminism within their groups, and only a small number remembered anything of contact with feminists from outside the coalfields. The huge volume of support given by the trade union movement was the most obvious source of aid for groups, and tended to loom largest in our interviewees' accounts. Of course, feminists were part of these efforts as well, but they were not necessarily visible *as* feminists. When probed, most of our interviewees said that the focus of conversation was on the strike and their immediate activities to support it; Marie Price commented that 'the women hadn't got time' to talk about politics in her group.¹¹⁴ In Cortonwood, women from the action group recalled that:

> In our group, though we knew what was going on, what the government was trying to do, and so on, we weren't really that political. There were women in some of the other groups that were much more so. We were more for the

---

[110] Siân James.   [111] Cook, interviewed by Cohen.   [112] Kay Case.
[113] *Valleys Star*, 23 January 1985.
[114] Marie Price, b. 1935, Nottinghamshire, interviewed by Natalie Thomlinson, 29 May 2019.

support, not for the politics, in fact many of the 'politicians' were not miners' wives—they worked hard, but for different reasons; they were very intense, we liked to have a laugh.[115]

Betty Cook told us that in her soup kitchen, 'none of the women were political, they didn't want to go to meetings or rallies or anything—you go, you bring in the money, we're quite happy to work in the kitchen'.[116] Indeed, it was notable in our interviews that the names of many of the politicians most commonly discussed in relation to the strike—Neil Kinnock, Dennis Skinner, and Tony Benn—appeared only rarely, Thatcher being the one Westminster figure who was consistently named. The high politics of the dispute was rarely uppermost in the minds of women who agitated to support the strike, certainly at grassroots level. Those who did remember discussing political issues other than the strike itself suggested that feminism was rarely one of the topics raised. Kim Hickling and Wendy Minney pointed out that their mother Rita Wakefield's rich scrapbooks from the time did not contain anything about feminism, though they did contain information about other left-wing movements.[117]

When more overtly political discussion *was* brought to the fore in groups, reactions were mixed. Sheffield WAPC,—the umbrella group for all the support groups in the Sheffield area,—functioned as a forum in which women from mining villages met leftist strike supporters. Pat Smith recalled that 'you'd have all t'miners' wives, and then you'd have some that were quite gobby and then you'd have little ones that sat in t'background and said nothing, and, er, you know, it were just a whole new experience, mixing like-minded people but em, but on different levels if you like of politicalness'.[118] Kath Mackey—from a working-class background but one of the 'political' women involved in Sheffield WAPC—was more critical of the other 'political' women, recalling that they allowed their own concerns to dominate: 'some of the mining lasses from the villages, they didn't know what folks were talking about'.[119] One woman who attended the group from the mining village of Thurcroft concurred, suggesting, 'I found their meetings a bit boring...I'm not thick, but [sometimes] they were way over my head.' But another Thurcroft woman said, 'I got a lot out of them. I was learning through them, I was getting educated.'[120] Relationships between more and less explicitly political women could be fraught and shot through with mutual incomprehension; but they could also be an arena of genuine exchange and mutual education.

---

[115] Denise Fitzpatrick, Christine M. Nelson, May Cadwallader, and Edith Armitage, *10 Years On and Still Laughing* (Rotherham: Dearne Community Arts, 1994), 5.
[116] Betty Cook.
[117] Kim Hickling, b. 1962, Wendy Minney, b. 1964, and Rita Wakefield, b. 1943, all Nottinghamshire, interviewed by Natalie Thomlinson, 20 August 2018.
[118] Pat Smith.   [119] Kath Mackey, interviewed by Daisy Payling, 10 January 2014.
[120] David Gibbon and Peter Steyne, *Thurcroft. A Village and the Miners' Strike: An Oral History by the People of Thurcroft* (Nottingham: Spokesman, 1986), 182.

Coalfield women sometimes criticised 'political' supporters of all sorts from outside the coalfields for appearing to want to hijack the strike support movement for their own purposes. This accusation was particularly levelled at far-left groups. One of Meg Allen's interviewees from South Wales recalled:

> There were lots of groups that were around then, like the Workers' Revolutionary Party and Socialist Action, and those people came to all the areas and they started talking to the people to get them organised and that... A lot of these groups don't get any attention or credibility without disputes or strikes to work in and they touted for membership.[121]

It was telling that at NWAPC's conference in November, women agreed that '[w]e must not let ourselves be used by any political group who are trying to use the strike to further their own political ends'.[122] Given the avowedly political nature of many women in NWAPC, this suggested a suspicion of the particular groups who might be trying to 'use' the strike, rather than of having political goals per se. For some women, this suspicion went further than just far-left groups suspected of entryism. Anne Kirby, for example, thought that the feminist supporters who criticised her were 'jumping on the bandwagon'.[123] Catherine Paton Black complained, similarly, that 'it felt like every organisation that wanted attention was jumping on our bandwagon'.[124] Some coalfield women felt they were being used as pawns in political battles that were not their own.

As this suggests, coalfield-based strike activists had a complex and ambiguous relationship with the idea of the 'political'. In certain contexts, some activists were happy to call themselves political, and to claim the strike politicised them. This narrative is particularly evident in publications that were written during or shortly after the strike and aimed at a left audience. Margaret from the Lothian Women's Support Group, for example, said that 'I didn't think much about politics... Now, since the end of the strike, I've got politically motivated.'[125] Betty Cook was quoted in North Yorkshire Women Against Pit Closures' *Strike 84/85* as saying, 'I've had three months up to now on the picket lines and my political education is being acquired at a gallop.'[126] And Bobby from Bentley told Loretta Loach in her October 1984 article for *Spare Rib* that, '[b]efore we'd have never talked politics or religion now I'd have my say on both'.[127] This framing could be part of a

---

[121] Allen, 'Carrying on the Strike', 129.
[122] 'Conference of the National Women Against Pit Closures', n.d., DWSG 4/1, SWWSG papers.
[123] Anne Kirby.
[124] Catherine Paton Black, *At the Coalface: My Life as a Miner's Wife* (London: Headline, 2012), 303.
[125] Lothian Women's Support Group, *Women Living the Strike* (Dalkeith: Lothian Women's Support Group, 1986), 54.
[126] North Yorkshire Women Against Pit Closures, *Strike 84/85* (Leeds: North Yorkshire Women Against Pit Closures, 1985), 55.
[127] Loach, 'We'll be Here Right to the End and After'.

narrative of the strike which cast it as a moment of personal transformation, as we discuss in Chapter 8. It may have also been easier for those who had been active on the left for some time to discuss their political inclinations more freely in front of feminist or leftist audiences. But the moment of production of these texts is also significant. These accounts were often generated in dialogue with explicitly leftist or feminist actors: being asked by an overtly 'political' interlocutor whether the strike had changed their politics may have encouraged some activists who had not previously seen themselves as political to consider their participation in a different light. In other words, the very production of these texts could generate newly 'political' subjectivities.

While some strike activists were happy to present themselves as newly politicised, many others, however, were notably keen to divest themselves of any association with 'politics', including feminism, because of their desire to present themselves as 'ordinary'. The increasing valorisation of 'ordinariness' in postwar Britain has been much discussed by historians.[128] It was associated with common sense, and a lack of vested interests or partisan bias; as such, being 'ordinary' was often read as diametrically opposed to being 'political'.[129] The very arena of politics was increasingly seen in the postwar decades as a place for the already-privileged to pursue their own interests.[130] It is unsurprising, then, that many—certainly the majority—of strike activists described themselves as 'ordinary' and 'not political'. Sometimes this was a disingenuous rhetorical strategy, a deliberate distraction from their background in trade union organising and leftist political parties. No less than Anne Scargill told a crowd that, '[t]his is not a political protest. We are fighting for pits and jobs. We are fighting for communities and a future.'[131] Presenting the support movement as 'apolitical' also allowed activists to present the women and children of the coalfields as 'innocent victims', and to distance women from the violence associated with NUM picket lines, and from right-wing rhetoric—like that of Irene McGibbon—which delegitimised trade

---

[128] Florence Sutcliffe-Braithwaite, *Class, Politics, and the Decline of Deference in England, 1968–2000* (Oxford: Oxford University Press, 2018); Jon Lawrence, *Me, Me, Me? The Search for Community in Post-War England* (Oxford: Oxford University Press, 2019); Claire Langhamer, 'Who the Hell are Ordinary People? Ordinariness as a Category of Historical Analysis', *Transactions of the Royal Historical Society*, 28 (2018), 175–95; Mike Savage, *Identities and Social Change in Britain since 1940: The Politics of Method* (Oxford: Oxford University Press, 2010); Mike Savage, Gaynor Bagnall, and Brian Longhurst, 'Ordinary, Ambivalent and Defensive: Class Identities in the Northwest of England', *Sociology*, 35 (2001), 875–92.

[129] John Clarke, 'Enrolling Ordinary People: Governmental Strategies and the Avoidance of Politics', *Citizenship Studies*, 16 (2010), 637–50, at 642, quot. in Langhamer, 'Who the Hell are Ordinary People?', 188.

[130] Nick Clarke, Will Jennings, Jonathan Moss, and Gerry Stoker, *The Good Politician: Folk Theories, Political Interaction, and the Rise of Anti-Politics* (Cambridge: Cambridge University Press, 2018).

[131] Richard Kay, 'Scargill's Wife Goes Begging', *Daily Mail*, 31 July 1984, in Marsha Marshall scrapbook of cuttings from UK press during miners' strike, A-3951/G/3/7, papers of Barnsley Women Against Pit Closures, Barnsley Archives, Barnsley (hereafter Barnsley WAPC papers).

unions by presenting them as too 'political'. One newspaper in Barnsley talked of the activism of women's groups being:

> A cry for help—for children without shoes, for mothers with little or no food in the house, or even enought [sic] money for bus fares to get into town... whatever you may think of the miners' strike, children and wives should not have to suffer.[132]

In the same article, Anne Hunter, of Barnsley WAPC, was quoted as saying:

> Just because a few women were arrested on a picket line, some people think we are only out to cause trouble. You hear little coverage about the many food kitchens we have set up, or of the hundreds of food parcels we distribute. This is the side we would like people to see.[133]

There were thus powerful incentives to present the women's movement in an unthreatening light as 'ordinary', 'non-political', and 'respectable'.

Moreover, as Jean Spence and Carol Stephenson have argued, working-class women have often been required to perform a model of domestic femininity in order to demonstrate proof of their 'authentic' working-class identities.[134] Even Siân James, though already politically active before the strike and later to become an MP, was at pains to tell us that she had been 'very, very content as a housewife'.[135] During the strike, Spence and Stephenson suggest, working-class women had to emphasise they were housewives and mothers, and highlight their roles preparing food and care-giving, in order to show they were deserving of support and of a hearing in public.[136] They could not claim the right to speak as 'political' actors, but rather had to deploy the authority of their personal experience as 'ordinary' wives and mothers. Thus, Lorraine Bowler's speech at the Barnsley rally in May foregrounded her own ordinariness with talk of her domestic life ('He'd [her husband] rather do a month on nights than mind the kids!'), and gave no hint of her extensive political experience, or membership of the CPGB.[137] An emphasis on the ordinariness of those who supported the strike implicitly positioned the Tories as 'not-ordinary', driven by illegitimate political motives; this clearly suited the strategy pursued by those in the CPGB agitating

---

[132] 'Strike Brings out the Best in Them', unknown newspaper, in Marsha Marshall scrapbook of cuttings from UK press during miners' strike, A-3591/G/3/32, Barnsley WAPC papers.
[133] Ibid.
[134] Jean Spence and Carol Stephenson, 'Pies and Essays: Women Writing through the British 1984–5 Coal Miners' Strike', *Gender, Place & Culture: A Journal of Feminist Geography*, 20 (2013), 218–35.
[135] Siân James.   [136] Spence and Stephenson, 'Pies and Essays'.
[137] Barnsley Women Against Pit Closures, *Women Against Pit Closures, Volume 2* (Barnsley Women Against Pit Closures: Barnsley, 1984), 22.

for a popular front in the strike and against the Conservatives.[138] (In such a formulation, it was the Conservatives—and not the Labour Party or the left generally—who were condemned as 'ideological'.) This emphasis on ordinariness was also a rhetorical move deployed more widely across the left. Betty Cook described herself as 'a lowly housewife and mother' before the strike, obscuring her experience as a Labour Party member and her active engagement in her trade union.[139] As Anne Scargill recollected, 'it was a dirty word, politics'.[140]

Rank-and-file members of the support movement also consistently used this language of ordinariness, domesticity, and motherhood. In November 1984, Iris Preston, a member of Sheffield WAPC, visited Northern Ireland to raise money for the strike. In a speech while she was there, she described herself as:

> Just an ordinary housewife.
> Mother of two miners.
> Before strike I like many other women would see family off to work or school, in fact did all usual jobs women do for their families.
> Involved in no political activities.
> Except I never voted Tory.[141]

Many women, like Preston, claimed that they never voted Tory: as we discussed in Chapter 2, voting Labour was a powerful communal norm in the coalfields, and women could comply with it without seeing themselves as 'political'. (Indeed, not voting Tory was part of being 'ordinary' for them.) Looking back on the strike, Royston Drift WAPC wrote, in a similar vein to Preston:

> Ordinary women is what we were, though it is doubtful whether any of us had considered whether we were ordinary or not, we were all housewives, some of us had jobs as well, others hadn't. All of us were quiet, respectable and proud members of our community—proud of our ability to manage our families.[142]

It was deeply important to these women to emphasise they were 'ordinary', 'respectable' wives and mothers looking out for their families and communities. In doing so, they invoked a particular vision of the family based on heterosexual couples and traditional gender roles, and drew on a long tradition of progressive

---

[138] We would like to thank the anonymous reviewer of this book for this insightful point.
[139] Allen, 'Carrying on the Strike', 48–51. See also Triona Holden, *Queen Coal: Women of the Miners' Strike* (Stroud: Sutton, 2005), 69, for a typical view of Cook as a 'downtrodden housewife with little education or ambition' before the strike.
[140] Anne Scargill, b. 1941, Yorkshire, interviewed by Natalie Thomlinson, 16 March 2019.
[141] Iris Preston, Strike Journal, SxMOA 99/58/1, papers of Iris Preston, Mass Observation Archives, The Keep, Brighton.
[142] Royston Drift Women Against Pit Closures, *United by the Struggle*, unpublished manuscript, papers of Maureen Robinson, A-3440/G, Barnsley Archives, Barnsley.

maternalist politics which carved out a public role for women by suggesting that their 'natural' caring talents ideally suited them to promoting the health and wellbeing of working-class families and communities.[143] An attachment to what we might see as a 'conservative' way of life was not the prerogative of simply the Conservative Party; indeed, the women's support movement drew some of its power from the fact that it was able to contest Thatcherite economic policy with 'common-sense' ideas about the importance of maintaining traditional communities and the nuclear family—ideas which had appeal across the political spectrum. The defence of 'community' could carry different political valences—some more progressive, others conservative: it was the very elasticity of the concept that made it so effective as a banner for people to rally under. It was not a goal that necessarily entailed a reconfiguration of women's roles, even as women's strike activism did sometimes destabilise gender relations.

Women's investment in 'ordinariness' was not simply a rhetorical ploy, however. Claire Langhamer has pointed to the centrality of 'ordinariness' as a subject position for women in postwar Britain, and its associations with the private sphere, and lack of a public voice.[144] In this context, it is significant that women who undertook public speaking during the strike almost always emphasised that this was a new and terrifying realm of experience for them.[145] Despite participating in seemingly very 'political' activities in their support groups, many strike activists' subjectivities were constructed through the category of 'ordinariness', and their investment in this subject position made them reluctant to identify as 'political'. Catherine Paton Black, a striking canteen worker involved in the support movement in Ollerton, remembered that, having 'never previously been a political person', she was now 'becoming known as an activist'; but, she insisted, 'I didn't see it like that. I was just a mum and a miner's wife, who wanted to help keep her husband's job. We were just ordinary folk forced to do something extraordinary.'[146] Many of our interviewees made similar assertions. Aggie Currie told us, 'I'm not right political, me', despite having been arrested fourteen times during the strike and being a key player in the occupation of Markham Main colliery in the 1992–3 round of pit closures.[147] Kay Case recalled that, 'the majority of people were like me: not politically-minded. They didn't want to bring the government down, weren't trying to get Margaret Thatcher or the Conservatives,

---

[143] On the history of this approach, see Seth Koven and Sonya Michel, eds., *Mothers of a New World: Maternalist Politics and the Origins of Welfare States* (London: Routledge, 1993); Pat Thane, 'The Women of the British Labour Party and Feminism, 1906–1945', in Harold L. Smith, ed., *British Feminism in the Twentieth Century* (Amherst: University of Massachusetts Press, 1990), 124–43, at 129; Stephen Brooke, *Sexual Politics: Sexuality, Family Planning, and the British Left from the 1880s to the Present Day* (Oxford: Oxford University Press, 2011).

[144] Langhamer, 'Who the Hell are Ordinary People?'

[145] See, e.g., Janie Robertson, b. 1955, Scotland, interviewed by Florence Sutcliffe-Braithwaite, 20 November 2018; Aggie Currie, b. 1950, Yorkshire, interviewed by Victoria Dawson, 22 June 2018; Betty Cook.

[146] Paton Black, *At the Coalface*, 306.   [147] Aggie Currie.

we were basically fighting for the right to live, and that was it.'[148] The key discursive strategies through which working-class women could legitimise their political aspirations (coded as 'non-political') were rooted in conservative discourses of gender and the (heteronormative) family. To gain legitimacy as actors in the political sphere, ironically, coalfield women often had to disavow an explicitly political identity. Claims to be 'non-political' reflected the discourses through which working-class women were positioned as subjects, and which created the place from which they necessarily spoke.

The Moral Economy of the Strike

In November 1984, Cwmbach Miners' Relief Fund brought together three striking men and three striking miners' wives to discuss the strike. The discussion formed the basis of a pamphlet, *Cwmbach Miners and Women Speak Out*, published in December and sold for 50p, with proceeds going to the Relief Fund. It was just one of many publications—pamphlets, books, and newsletters—produced by the support movement to raise money and morale and to share information during the strike. Along with speeches, media appearances, placards, banners, and slogans, these publications were places where activists articulated a shared moral economy: that is, a shared framework for evaluating right and wrong, legitimate and illegitimate behaviour, the obligations and responsibilities different parties owed to one another within the sphere of the economy.[149] Thatcherite political economy held that the 'law' of the market admitted no appeal to morality: pits were uneconomic, therefore they must close; strikers had no basis for defying this 'law', and the immiseration of their families was the result of their defiance. Strikers and their supporters contested this liberal political economy: as Scargill said in 1982, he was determined to 'protect the coal industry from the ravages of the market mechanism'.[150] Strikers and women in the support movement collectively constructed an alternative moral economy that held that economic decisions should not be based solely on the profit motive, but made with reference to higher moral imperatives. They contested the right of the Thatcher government and the NCB to close pits, holding that efficiency could not trump the human value of communities. And they argued that it was the duty of miners and their families and communities to strike to honour the struggles of past generations of miners, and

---

[148] Kay Case. See also, e.g., Janet Slater, b. 1954, Nottinghamshire, interviewed by Natalie Thomlinson, 3 August 2018. Several project interviewees told us they were not political while also saying they habitually voted Labour, e.g., Ann, b. 1942, Yorkshire, interviewed by Victoria Dawson, 25 July 2018; Christina Bell, b. 1949, North East England/Nottinghamshire, interviewed by Victoria Dawson, 27 June 2018.
[149] See E. P. Thompson, 'The Moral Economy of the English Crowd in the Eighteenth Century', *Past & Present*, 50 (1971), 76–136, and, for discussion, Tim Rogan, *The Moral Economists: R. H. Tawney, Karl Polanyi, E. P. Thompson, and the Critique of Capitalism* (Princeton: Princeton University Press, 2017).
[150] Adeney and Lloyd, *Miners' Strike*, 37.

to defend jobs and communities for future generations. Their internalisation of this moral economy made it very difficult for activists to contemplate wavering in their support for the strike.

In the Cwmbach discussion, miner's wife Trish recalled that:

> My uncle was paralysed for 12 years through a pit accident, then died. My family, my grandparents, they've all contributed in some way to this community, not just Cwmbach, but Cefnpennar [another mining community nearby] too. They went down the pits, they went short, they had terrible conditions at work. It was those people who fought for better conditions for our men. So we're not just going to say, let's give up.[151]

Another miner's wife, Viv, agreed: '[t]here's men from the '26 strike coming to us now, saying "Don't give in"'.[152] During and after the strike, supporters often pointed to the generosity of pensioners, and this was something several of our interviewees remembered, too.[153] This served to emphasise that the elderly, living on small, fixed incomes, were willing to make significant personal sacrifices to support the strike. It also helped construct a line of continuity between the present strike and a longer history of working-class struggle, as well as the earlier generations of miners who had built up their communities and had fought for better safety practices, higher wages, trade unions, and nationalisation. Some saw the inheritance even more broadly: Brenda Greenwood emphasised when she was interviewed in February 1985 that she thought the workers of today must 'fight on every front in defence of all the rights and standards that have been won for us, in blood, sweat and tears by the working class of the past... it is our proud heritage to hold them in trust for future generations of our class'.[154] Other activists emphasised that the very wealth of the nation had been built on the backs of the miners.[155] Margaret, from North Gawber, wrote in 1985, 'I take pride in being a member of a community that has brought untold wealth and benefits to this country.'[156] Supporting the strike was, in this view, about honouring the work of earlier generations and continuing their struggle, particularly as mining tended to

---

[151] *Cwmbach Miners and Women Speak Out* (Cardiff: Everyday Printers, 1984), 10.
[152] Ibid.
[153] E.g. ibid., 2; 'Report on Ilkeston Solidarity Group', *Here We Go! Bulletin of the Nottinghamshire Women's Support Groups*, 5, August 1984, FWC/9/3/13, papers of Fred Westacott, Nottingham University Special Collections; Pam Thomas, 'A Miner's Wife's Story—Pam Thomas', in Ray Davies, *A Miner's Life: The 1984 Miners' Strike and the Rhymney Valley Miners Support Group* (Caerphilly: RTD Publishers, 2014). See also the reproduction, in books and pamphlets about the strike, of letters of support sent with donations from pensioners, e.g. Barnsley Women Against Pit Closures, *Women Against Pit Closures, Vol. 2*, 32. Among our interviewees, see Anne Kirby.
[154] *Women's Fightback. Paper of the Women's Campaign Labour Movement Fightback for Women's Rights*, 37 (dated February 1984 but evidently from 1985), 'Miners' Strike Papers'.
[155] Betty Long, 'Looking Back', *Valleys Star*, 29, 20 February 1985, South Wales Miners' Library.
[156] Barnsley Women Against Pit Closures, *Women Against Pit Closures, Vol. 2*, 28.

be an occupation passed down in families.¹⁵⁷ In an unpublished memoir, Annie Clarke—born in the 1920s, a member of Upton Families Support Group, and a miner's daughter, wife, and mother—wrote: '[w]hen I think of what my father and father-in-law sacrificed to get a union and a Labour party... I look all around at the single lads and the mining families who have stood solid for a year and rightly so, I am very proud of them for their guts and the honour they have shown to their forefathers.'¹⁵⁸

The 1926 General Strike and seven-month miners' lockout, which affected a million miners, was a touchstone in the moral economy of the strike. The first film in the radical Miners' Campaign Tapes series (over 4,000 copies of which were distributed in the UK, sent to both women's support groups and NUM lodges to spread the word, and sold or rented out to raise money for the strike) explicitly drew these links.¹⁵⁹ Entitled *Not Just Tea and Sandwiches*, it began with footage of the General Strike of 1926 and the Women's Hunger March of 1930, followed by footage of a women's march in 1984. Later in the film, one interviewee, Margaret Vallins, pointed out, over more images of 1930s hunger marches, that her generation had never 'actually been in the position where we've no food in the cupboard'—unlike many working-class people from earlier generations—but that now this was a reality for many.¹⁶⁰ This was an argument for sympathy from outsiders, but also a call to arms: if families today had never experienced such hardship before, it was at least in part because of the achievements of earlier generations. And if those past generations had fought for their communities and for the labour movement in the face of such hardship, miners and their wives should not shy from the struggle today. The moral capital of past generations was thus deployed to exhort others to remain strong. Sometimes this was quite literal: Pauline, from Woolley colliery, finished a strike poem: 'What would my Granddad say / Fight them, fight them all the way'.¹⁶¹

Activists also argued that the strike was not just about honouring the miners of yesterday, but about fighting for the miners of today, and, importantly, for future generations, too. Linda, from Park Mill, in Yorkshire, put it thus:

---

[157] On mining as an inheritance, see: Emily Peirson-Webber, 'Masculinity and Mining in the British Coal Industry: From Nationalisation to Pit Closures' (unpublished PhD thesis, University of Reading, 2022).

[158] Annie Clarke memoir, papers of Jill Page, FAN/JP/Box 1, Feminist Archive North. See also Gwen Newton, ed., *We are Women, We are Strong: The Stories of Northumberland Miners' Wives 1984–85* (Northumberland: The People Themselves, 1985), 66.

[159] *The Miners' Campaign Tapes 1. Not Just Tea and Sandwiches*, dir. Birmingham Film/Video Workshop and Platform Films, 1984; see *A Catalogue of Films and Videotapes Produced During the 1984/5 Miners' Strike* (Gateshead: Northern Film and Television Archive, 1986), 8–9, MacLeod papers; Roger Shannon, interviewed by Florence Sutcliffe-Braithwaite and Natalie Thomlinson, 9 November 2021.

[160] *The Miners' Campaign Tapes 1. Not Just Tea and Sandwiches*.

[161] Barnsley Miners' Wives Action Group, *We Struggled to Laugh* (Barnsley: Barnsley Miners' Wives Action Group, 1987), 15.

> this fight isn't just about coal
> I've three daughters at home that are growing up fast,
> And they don't want a life on the dole...
> So come on you working class women,
> You mothers and mothers to be
> This one's for our children and those yet unborn,
> It's not just for you and for me.[162]

The same point was made at the outset of the Channel 4 documentary *Coal Not Dole*, aired in early summer 1984. The programme opened with footage of two young miners' wives on a coach to a demonstration; one said, 'it's worth fighting to try and get jobs for your children—I mean, you see nowadays, anywhere you go, I mean, all these young kids leaving school and there's no jobs, I mean, it's just hopeless for them'.[163] Among our interviewees, several emphasised that this was the fundamental justification for the strike—an argument that was made all the more powerful, as they pointed out, by the subsequent impact of pit closures and the effect on young people's job prospects.[164] As Kay Case remembered, 'there's massive unemployment now ... I feel sorry for youngsters trying to find a decent living wage so they can get a home together.'[165]

As several scholars studying industrial communities in postwar Scotland have shown, a powerful discourse grew up in these areas that saw industry as an asset of the community. An industrial job was not seen as the possession of the individual currently doing that job, but was held in trust by him for future generations: a man taking redundancy was selling a job that did not, in fact, belong to him.[166] This view was not unique to Scotland but articulated in industrial communities in England and Wales, too. Miners and their wives supporting the strike across the country elaborated on this idea. Women emphasised that they were not simply supporting the strike for their husbands' sake, but for their children, as well. Men and women in the coalfields had complex attitudes towards work in the pit: they knew all too well that the work was hard, dirty, and dangerous, but also that the industry provided relatively well-paid and secure work, with a sense of fellowship and masculine camaraderie that was rare in lighter and safer jobs above ground.[167] These jobs provided a decent wage and allowed men and women to marry and to

---

[162] Ibid., 8.
[163] 'Coal not Dole', *People to People*, dir. Richard Anthony, Channel 4, 4 June 1984.
[164] Kay Case. [165] Ibid.
[166] Ewan Gibbs, 'The Moral Economy of the Scottish Coalfields: Managing Deindustrialization under Nationalization, c.1947–1983', *Enterprise & Society*, 19 (2018), 124–52; Jim Phillips, Valerie Wright, and Jim Tomlinson, *Deindustrialisation and the Moral Economy in Scotland since 1955* (Edinburgh: Edinburgh University Press, 2021).
[167] Richard King, *Brittle with Relics: A History of Wales, 1962–1997* (London: Faber & Faber, 2022), 100.

support families. The moral economy of the strike held that to fail to defend them would be to betray future generations.

Women also appreciated that strong communities required a steady economic base: this underpinned the widely-used slogan, 'Close a pit, kill a community'.[168] Women were all-too-aware of how the death of communities happened: they had seen many pits close, especially in the 1950s and 1960s, the years of NCB rationalisation and contraction. In County Durham, when the Save Easington Area Mines (SEAM) group sent out a leaflet urging women to get involved in supporting the strike, they asked:

> What future will there be for our children when they grow up? They will be forced to leave the area in their droves to find work, leaving an aging population with noone [sic] to take care of them... there will be a surplus of empty houses for sale with the consequent dramatic reduction in values (as witnessed in the Consett area), there will be an upsurge of bankruptcies particularly among small businesses and local shopkeepers, and so the inevitable decline will continue in a sickening and depressing cycle, UNLESS WE CAN RALLY TO SAVE THE PITS.[169]

Without the strong economic anchor of the pits, other local businesses and community infrastructure were likely to falter. But calling on women to rally to the cause to protect the value of their homes was hardly the leitmotif of radical politics: rather, it was about protecting existing communities.

The discourse that women in the support movement constructed to defend the strike was a powerful one. Woven into it was an insistence on the fundamental respectability of mining communities, echoing the way that women laid claim to respectability in their constructions of themselves as 'ordinary' mothers and housewives. Respectable communities, strike activists argued, should be protected, not persecuted, by the government. Publicity for the Miners' Families Christmas Appeal quoted from a report from the Dawdon Miners Distress Centre, in County Durham, which read:

> I cannot of course begin to tell you of the desolation we all feel, especially when we are talking about people who are basically honest, who have paid their taxes and debts to this society and who, in any circumstances, are honest citizens and by their nature, proud and caring parents.[170]

---

[168] See, e.g., the poster reproduced in Allen, 'Carrying on the Strike', 155.
[169] Pat McIntyre, 'The Response to the 1984–5 Miners' Strike in Durham County: Women, the Labour Party and Community' (unpublished PhD thesis, University of Durham, 1992), 188–9.
[170] 'Let's Make it a Happy Christmas and a Hopeful New Year in the Pit Villages', Press Release for Miners' Families Christmas Appeal, 1984, U DJS/1/57, papers of John Saville, Hull History Centre.

Similarly, rejecting Thatcher's claim that miners were the 'enemy within', prominent strike activist Betty Cook wrote in a poem about women's support for the strike: 'We have a brain we think and reason / We have never thought of treason / All we ask is a job for life / To enable the men to support a wife.'[171] The strike, again, was framed as a struggle to *maintain* a way of life. Drawing on longstanding working-class discourses valorising hard work, independence, and respectability, this rhetoric echoed elements of Thatcherism (work, self-reliance, and family values), but used these same ideals to attack the Thatcherite project. Particular gender roles were integral to this—as, of course, they had always been to constructions of working-class respectability. As Cook's poem suggests, men were constructed as virtuous here because they occupied the traditional masculine role of breadwinner and provider. Just as in the late nineteenth century, working men claimed admission to the franchise on the basis that they, like middle-class men, could be respectable householders, so in 1984-5 particular gender roles underpinned claims to respectability and justifications of the strike.

The moral economy of the strike distributed not only material but also psychic goods. Sue Petney, a member of Blidworth Action Group, articulated this sentiment when she wrote in a strike poem, 'We've only lost money / But you have lost your pride.'[172] On the day the strike was called off, Marlene Thompson wrote, 'With heads held high we'll struggle on / But a scab's a scab till the day he's gone.'[173] 'Scabs' were constructed not only as shamed, but as 'unmanned'. As we have seen, strike activists often deployed traditional gender ideologies in their rhetoric on picket lines, and the same was true in many other protests. At a demonstration in Stirling in September 1984, women carried a banner reading, 'Notts women strike back: Notts real men are striking'.[174] On a march in London in February 1985, Yorkshire women marched behind the words, 'Yorkshire miners wives behind their men. Notts scabs behind their women!' (see Figure 5.6). One cartoon in a benefit book published for WAPC even put a striking miner in bed with a busty working miner's wife; while his 'Coal Not Dole' placard rested against the bedroom wall, the caption below read '[s]troke of luck your husband being a working miner, Gladys'.[175] Jean Gittins, mother of two striking miners and a member of North Yorkshire WAPC, articulated the connection between taking strike action and normative gender roles in 'A Sad Tale of a Striker's Bride', one of her most popular poems, which imagined the thoughts of a young woman whose

---

[171] Barnsley Miners' Wives Action Group, *We Struggled to Laugh*, 27.
[172] Sue Petney, 'A Question of Loyalty', in Witham, *Hearts and Minds*, 131.
[173] Marlene Thompson, 'A Time of Sadness', 7JMC/A/20, McCrindle papers.
[174] Photograph in the papers of Janie Robertson, private collection. Janie Robertson, b. 1955, Scotland, interviewed by Florence Sutcliffe-Braithwaite, 20 November 2018. Another photo in the same collection has men holding a banner reading, 'Ruffords [sic] real men are on strike'.
[175] *Deep Digs! Cartoons of the Miners' Strike: A Benefit Book for Women Against Pit Closures* (London: Pluto, 1985), n.p.

Figure 5.6 Yorkshire women protest in London, February 1985. © Joanne O'Brien/Format.

wedding plans were disrupted by the strike; Gittins listed the compromises and cutbacks the young couple had had to make, but finished,

> So ah'll wait for my dream 'ome till later,
> Give 'im all the support that ah can,
> 'Cause when this lot's ower, ah'm glad ah can say
> Well, leastways ah married a man.[176]

This shared understanding of what 'real' men and 'real' women were supposed to do underpinned other protests, too: at a demonstration outside the Welsh Office, in Cardiff, in summer 1984, Welsh women carried placards reading 'Thatcher snatched our milk. Now she's stealing our bread' (see Figure 5.7). Thatcher had

---

[176] Jean Gittins, *Striking Stuff* (Bradford: 1 in 12 Club, 1986), 7.

Figure 5.7 Welsh women protest outside the Welsh Office in Cardiff, 1984.
© Martin Shakeshaft.

been labelled the 'milk snatcher' in 1971 when, as Education Secretary in Edward Heath's government, she ended free school milk for junior school children. The placards drew their power from the implication that Thatcher had transgressed her proper feminine role of providing care for children.

Activist women thus insisted that there were things that were more important than money: self-respect; the sense that you had stood up for what was right; the ability to hold your head up in your own community; the knowledge that your husband was a 'real' man. All this helped harden activists' resolve. As one recalled shortly after the end of the strike, '[i]t wasn't me that was bowing my head when I walked through the street. It was them. It wasn't me that was feeling guilty when I was filling my trolley...So I got to the stage where it didn't bother me.'[177] But there were, as we will see in Chapter 6, other ideas about what 'moral' behaviour looked like circulating in 1984–5; and, as the strike dragged on, some women and men would come to feel that these conflicting dictates of conscience justified a return to work. Even for those who remained on strike, it could be hard to live up to the moral economy they had articulated and internalised. In 1986, Monica Shaw and Mave Mundy interviewed a support group activist in North East England, 'Joan', who revealed that six months into the strike, she had asked her husband to go back. She explained that '[t]he half of me that wanted him to go back was

---

[177] Chrys Salt and Jim Layzell, *Here We Go! Women's Memories of the 1984/5 Miners Strike* (London: Co-operative Retail Services, 1985), 41.

because of the bairns... they were all good eaters, well you felt awful when you had to say "You can't have any more of that." It used to choke me.' Joan recalled going without meals herself and lying about it to her husband. Ultimately, though, she said she was 'pleased he stuck it out... because I don't think I would have liked neither myself nor him for going back because of the hassle the others got. I wouldn't have liked to think I was going around the village and them calling me a scab.'[178] She told this to Shaw and Mundy on the condition of anonymity: such stories were difficult to admit to in 1986, and have remained taboo in the years since. Inner conflicts like the one 'Joan' experienced would only get more common and more intense in the new year. It went against the ethical self that activists had constructed over the course of the strike to even consider breaking ranks: the very idea of contravening the moral economy of the strike created painful—sometimes almost intolerable—levels of cognitive dissonance.

Conclusion

The tide turned for the strike in autumn. Most communities outside of the Midlands remained reasonably solid, but increasing numbers returned to work everywhere. A very small number of women, most prominently Irene McGibbon, called publicly for men to go back to work, motivated by an ideological conviction that the strike was an illegitimate form of trade unionism, an undemocratic action fomented by left-wing extremists who wanted to bring down another Tory government. Unsurprisingly, these women found a sympathetic ally in Margaret Thatcher. Most of those who returned to work in this period, however, were almost certainly not motivated by such strong political beliefs. Anger, futility, and desperation were the key factors influencing most miners and their wives in taking the decision to return to work. Men, women, and children all had to deal with the consequences of strikebreaking, often becoming ostracised in their own neighbourhoods.

The women's support movement became ever more important as the NUM's ability to prosecute the strike diminished, particularly after the sequestration of NUM funds in autumn. NWAPC raised and distributed large sums of money in these months; its very presence was also important, in the light of McGibbon's 'Miners Wives Back to Work' organisation, in demonstrating that many miners' wives were still strongly pro-strike. The support movement mobilised ever greater numbers of activists over these months, and, as the next chapter shows, this ensured that many striking families remembered Christmas as a positive time. But the support movement also had its own difficulties, with internal divisions and

---

[178] Monica Shaw and Mave Mundy, 'Complexities of Class and Gender Relations: Recollections of Women Active in the 1984–5 Miners' Strike', *Capital & Class*, 29 (2005), 151–74, at 156–7.

splits. While some of these arose from personal conflicts, political divisions were also important. Many—almost certainly the majority of—activist women saw their work as defending communities, families, and a way of life, but there were also more 'political' women in the movement who hoped that it could ultimately pursue larger goals. NWAPC was also politically divided: women like Anne Scargill and Betty Cook saw its primary purpose as supporting the NUM and Scargill's strategy for the strike; others, like Jean McCrindle, had a more expansive view of what NWAPC could become politically, but also had an intense personal loyalty to Scargill. By contrast, a faction of Eurocommunist CPGB women hoped that NWAPC would form part of a popular front contesting Thatcherism, and opposed Scargill's strategy of winning the strike simply though the miners' collective industrial power.

Claims that the women's support movement represented a working-class feminism are unconvincing. Indeed, many activists were profoundly resistant to labelling themselves as 'political' at all, and were heavily invested in understanding themselves as 'ordinary' family women. They understood their actions within a moral economy which dictated that not supporting the strike would be deeply shameful, a betrayal of their communities, their forefathers, and their children. But as the dispute continued into the new year, the prospect of having to break this moral code and return to work began to loom ever larger, creating an unbearable dilemma for many of those involved in supporting the strike.

6
Flood Back to Defeat: Winter 1984–5

25 December 1984

The only way to explain Christmas, was, I'm talking of a village Christmas, I'm not talking about a family, individual Christmas, I'm talking about a village. You've seen how small our village is...for me, personally...it was the best Christmas we ever had, because everybody had exactly the same, and everybody had nothing. So it was Christmas. Everybody had their tree, because most of them had artificial trees, or they had a sprig of something, and the union provided a turkey, the vegetables, the pudding, a bottle of wine for every miner, and the children had a black dustbin—dustbin bag of whatever their age was. Wasn't what—little Johnny wanted this for Christmas, he wanted a bike, he got a toy soldier, and he got a gun, and he got a bat and ball, because that's what the donations were that came into the village from all over the—Europe and everywhere, you know. And it was, it was fantastic. And every child got a sack, with their name on...It was brilliant, absolutely brilliant.[1]

This was how Sue, who lived in a pit village in Kent with her husband and their daughter, remembered Christmas 1984. She was far from alone. Among our interviewees, many activist women recalled Christmas fondly. Aggie Currie recalled that it was the 'best Christmas we ever had', because, she explained, her children 'were so grateful for what they got, you know—erm, and I thought, that's just how I used to be...A stocking, two and six in it, and maybe a jigsaw puzzle—we never got a lot, but we were so grateful for what we got.'[2] Similar sentiments are found in writing from the time: Ann Musgrave, an activist from Yorkshire, for example, wrote that, 'Christmas 84 has been the best ever...Some of [the children] have started to believe in Santa again.'[3] With these accounts,

---

[1] Sue, b. 1956, Kent, interviewed by Florence Sutcliffe-Braithwaite, 14 July 2018.
[2] Aggie Currie, b. 1950, Yorkshire, interviewed by Victoria Dawson, 22 June 2018.
[3] Ann Musgrave, 'Christmas', 7JMCA/20, papers of Jean McCrindle, Women's Library@LSE, London (hereafter McCrindle papers).

Women and the Miners' Strike, 1984–1985. Florence Sutcliffe-Braithwaite and Natalie Thomlinson, Oxford University Press.
© Florence Sutcliffe-Braithwaite and Natalie Thomlinson 2023. DOI: 10.1093/oso/9780192843098.003.0006

women implicitly critiqued the materialism and individualism that they saw as characterising Britain in the aftermath of Thatcherism.

Activists tended to recall Christmas 1984 in a positive light because they were most tightly woven into community networks, networks which played a major part in boosting morale and warding off feelings of isolation and despair. Some had started planning for Christmas as early as August,[4] and their work only became more pressing when the National Coal Board (NCB) decided, in early November, to offer large bonuses to miners returning to work before Christmas.[5] Women knew the prospect of privations at Christmas could drive some men back to work. Support groups ran raffles, held jumble sales and collections (see Figure 6.1), made and sold Christmas cards, and undertook a vast array of other fundraising activities.[6] French, Belgian, and German trade unions sent lorry-loads

Figure 6.1 Women in Kent sort clothing during the strike. © Aylesham Heritage Centre and Kent Mining Heritage Foundation.

---

[4] See, e.g., report of women's meeting, Onllwyn Welfare Hall, 22 August 1984, Neath and District Miners' Strike Support Fund minute book, 6 May–22 September 1984, SWCC/MND/25/1, box 4 of 8, South Wales Coalfield Collection, Richard Burton Archive, Swansea (hereafter SWCC papers).
[5] David Felton, 'NCB Encourages Pre-Christmas Return to Work', *The Times*, 3 November 1984.
[6] Sheffield Women Against Pit Closures, *We are Women, We are Strong* (Sheffield: Sheffield Women Against Pit Closures, 1987), 12–14.

of toys, as well as chickens and turkeys.[7] Support groups outside the coalfields mobilised to supply food, toys, and money,[8] and the Mining Families' Christmas Appeal, instigated by National Women Against Pit Closures (NWAPC) brought in nearly £400,000.[9]

Women's groups in the coalfields organised presents for miners' children, extra food parcels, discos, pantomime trips, Santa's grottoes, and children's parties (Figure 6.2).[10] Though it seems more women from striking families got involved in support groups at this emotionally freighted time of year, the volume of work was still huge. Jackie Parkin of Save Easington Area Mines (SEAM) wrote an

Figure 6.2 Children enjoy a Christmas party at Frickley Colliery Miners' Welfare, with food donated from supporters, South Elmsall, West Yorkshire. © John Sturrock/reportdigital.co.uk.

---

[7] Pat McIntyre, 'The Response to the 1984–5 Miners' Strike in Durham County: Women, the Labour Party and Community' (unpublished PhD thesis, University of Durham, 1992), 224.

[8] Diarmaid Kelliher, *Cultures of Solidarity: London and the 1984–5 Miners' Strike* (London: Routledge, 2021).

[9] £394,678 at a cost of £17,300 for adverts in the national press: Jean McCrindle, 'The National Organisation of Women Against Pit Closures in the Miners' Strike of 1984–5' (unpublished PhD thesis, Oxford Brookes, 2001), 179.

[10] For parties, see, e.g. entry for 20 December 1984, Seafield/Frances Strike Committee (Dysart Strike Centre) Report Book 1, A/AAX/4/2/6, Fife Archives, Glenrothes. For Santa, see Barnsley Women Against Pit Closures, *Women Against Pit Closures, Volume 2* (Barnsley: Barnsley Women Against Pit Closures, 1985), 69. For food and presents, see minutes of meeting 9 December 1984, Neath and District Miners' Support Group minute book, 23 September 1984–17 February 1985, SWCC/MND/25/1, SWCC papers.

account of a week in her life in the run-up to Christmas: in addition to taking care of her home and son and helping run the soup kitchen at the colliery club, Friday saw her clearing up from the party the previous night, held for the SEAM women themselves, as well as making a trip to the toy shop and sweet shop ('weigh and bag about 15 tons of sweets'). On Saturday, Monday, Tuesday, Wednesday and Thursday Parkin was helping out at a Santa's grotto, and on Tuesday she also took a group of children to a pantomime. On Friday she was 'going to make up 120 food parcels, 1700 turkeys to dish out, 600 lunches and sweets to be made'.[11] The Annesley and Newstead Women's Support Group, in Nottinghamshire, gave out Christmas food parcels containing lemon curd, jam, mincemeat, jelly, fruit, Nescafé, corned beef, peas, sugar, pickles, three pounds of flour for baking, stuffing and a turkey, plus one big and three small presents for each child and a pound bar of chocolate.[12] In Blidworth, Nottinghamshire, 'a fantastic loaves & fishes miracle was carried out by the women's support group when nearly twice as many as expected turned up on Xmas day to enjoy their dinners together'.[13]

But not all women caught up in the strike recalled Christmas like this. Many relied mainly on family for food and presents, and their accounts of Christmas were less celebratory and more prosaic. Many went to parents' or other family members' houses.[14] Jeanette McComb was living in a small mining community in Ayrshire during the strike; she had moved there from Wolverhampton when she married her husband, who was a miner. At the time of Christmas 1984, they had a young daughter, and Jeanette was pregnant with their second child. The local support group provided a present and a selection box for Jeanette's daughter, but the family decided to go to stay with Jeanette's parents in Wolverhampton for several weeks, because, she recalled 'otherwise we wouldn't—or I couldn't have had a Christmas, you know, we wouldn't have had a meal or anything, kind of— well, we probably would have, but I couldn't have managed Christmas presents and things like that'.[15] Alison Anderson, from Fife, recalled that her son loved the party put on in the local club for miners' children, but her recollections of Christmas centred on her struggle to provide presents for him: she ordered a few small things from a catalogue, and her mother bought him a bike, which she gave Alison to say that it came from Santa.[16] Activists sometimes found that their efforts went unrewarded, too. Liz French, a prominent activist in Kent, recalled

---

[11] *The Last Coals of Spring: Poems, Stories and Songs by the Women of Easington Colliery* (Durham: Durham Voices, 1985), 42–3.
[12] Joan Witham, *Hearts and Minds: The Story of the Women of Nottinghamshire in the Miners' Strike, 1984–1985* (London: Canary, 1986), 117–19.
[13] *Here We Go! Bulletin of the Nottinghamshire Women's Support Groups*, January 1985, papers of Gwen MacLeod, private collection (hereafter MacLeod papers).
[14] E.g. Joyce Boyes, b. 1955, Yorkshire, interviewed by Victoria Dawson, 21 September 2018.
[15] Jeanette McComb, b. 1953, West Midlands/Scotland, interviewed by Victoria Dawson, 26 September 2018.
[16] Alison Anderson, b. 1959, Scotland, interviewed by Victoria Dawson, 29 August 2018.

spending twenty-four hours at the youth club sorting toys, allocating them to children and distributing them. But, she said:

> Bugger if we didn't go out Boxing Day, round the club and somebody went, 'I think you lot are a friggin' disgrace... my little 'un didn't get the right thing.' And I went, 'I'm ever so sorry.' 'Yes, only got this.' And I said, 'Well isn't it better than nothing?' 'Well, not really. Look at the state of it.'[17]

Liz and her husband were furious. Not everyone was grateful for what they had on Christmas Day 1984, and not everyone felt that community spirit trumped material things.

Christmas raised the spirits of many strikers. In Nottinghamshire, Janet Slater recalled, 'I think any war-time, disaster-time, Christmas, give[s] you a bit of a boost.'[18] But the period after Christmas was an increasingly grim one. There was no sign of movement from the NCB. More and more miners were going back to work all around the country. Figures were hotly contested—the number of miners returning to work could have a significant impact on whether strikers stayed out or went back, and the National Union of Mineworkers (NUM) and NCB each released their own figures. As the one-year anniversary of the start of the strike approached, questions began to circulate about whether the NCB would be able to sack all miners who were still out on strike after a year.[19] From January onwards, the South Wales Area NUM was pursuing its own strategy for ending the strike, with Kim Howells as its spokesman, arguing that a union-mandated return to work—even without a settlement—would at least save mining communities from the agony of a long, slow erosion of solidarity.[20] Defeat started to seem inevitable to more and more men and women. This chapter traces the experiences of committed supporters of the strike, those who were increasingly agnostic about whether it could go on, and those whose family members decided to return to work.

The Experience of Strikers

Janet Slater remembered that it was 'after Christmas' that she started to realise that the strike would probably be lost: 'some people had got *nothing*, I mean

---

[17] Liz French, b. 1950, Kent, interviewed by Florence Sutcliffe-Braithwaite, 6 July 2018.
[18] Janet Slater, b. 1954, Nottinghamshire, interviewed by Natalie Thomlinson, 3 August 2018.
[19] See minutes of meeting 3 February 1985, Neath and District Miners' Support Group minute book, 23 September 1984–17 February 1985, SWCC/MND/25/1, box 4 of 8, SWCC papers. '12-Month Strike Fears Shot Down', *The Miner, Journal of the NUM*, special issue, 7 February 1985, 3 refuted these rumours.
[20] Ben Curtis, *The South Wales Miners 1964–1985* (Cardiff: University of Wales Press, 2013), 240; Andrew Taylor, *The NUM and British Politics* (Aldershot: Ashgate, 2003), 247.

nothing... how long can you live like that, y'know, you've got to [unclear] for your children. You can only support your husband for so long... So, it started to become inevitable.'²¹ While in some ways the strike had become 'a way of life', in others Janet felt it could not 'go on for much longer':

> Christmas time comes around and you've all got this great big up-lift... 'Cause you get all this support coming in from outside and you suddenly feel, hang on, y'know, got to carry on, this is the right thing to do... but I think by that time it was, 'How long can this go on for?', y'know, I just couldn't see an end to it.²²

Linda Chapman, who was supporting her family with full-time work during the strike—even though she was devastated to be missing out on so much time with her young son—recalled that after Christmas:

> You'd seen MacGregor go into the talks and y'know, you'd sit there and yer'd think... hope... hope against hope they're going to come out and there'd be a solution, and there wasn't, and I just remember saying to him [her husband] at that point, it was probably around the February time, 'how much longer can this go on, before you have to go back and work?', and he just saying, 'I'll never go back.'²³

Linda felt both 'furious' and 'not furious' about this: her husband had 'always been very principled', and she felt 'it was the right thing to do'. Nevertheless, she went on to talk about how after the strike, she and her husband both came to feel as though they might have been pawns in a political game. Janet and Linda both articulated the ambivalence and inner conflict that many women who supported the strike experienced in its final months: feeling it was right to go on, but simultaneously anticipating defeat. This was a period of increasing hardship and a period of waiting. Both of the probable outcomes came at a heavy cost: either more and more miners would simply drift back to work, taking the painful individual decision to break the strike, or the action would be called off with no concessions from the NCB.

The idea of breaking the strike was intolerable to many women, and particularly activists, who had done the most to champion the moral economy of the strike. Norma Dolby, from Arkwright Town, Derbyshire, had become a committed activist in the strike, but she and her husband, she wrote in her strike diary, 'were now under great pressure. Even our own children seemed against us. They were fed up with having to do without; they kept on at their Dad to go back to work.'²⁴ By

---

²¹ Janet Slater. ²² Ibid.
²³ Linda Chapman, b. 1958, North East England, interviewed by Victoria Dawson, 18 July 2018.
²⁴ Norma Dolby, *Norma Dolby's Diary: An Account of the Great Miners' Strike* (London: Verso, 1987), 68.

February the support group Dolby was part of was making up only seventy parcels a week, including only four for the village itself.[25] Dolby wrote, '[d]eep down what I was really frightened of was that we too would have to give in, but the thought was killing us, how could we live with ourselves if we did?'[26] To contemplate breaking the strike went against the moral economy that the NUM and the support movement had constructed, which, as we saw in the previous chapter, framed it as the duty of all those in mining families to support the strike, not simply to defend the jobs of current miners, but also to honour the struggle of previous generations of miners, and to protect the communities of today and tomorrow. It went against the ethical self that women like Dolby had constructed and maintained over the past nine or ten months, and created painful—almost intolerable—levels of cognitive dissonance. And yet many women experienced this inner conflict frequently in these final months, as hardship grew even more severe. The moral capital claimed by strikers—the sense that strikers and their supporters could hold their 'heads high', while strikebreakers 'lost [their] pride'—was increasingly put in jeopardy.[27]

Relationships within communities were, for many women, another powerful block on even contemplating breaking the strike. In Kent, Lorraine Walsh—who said she would have divorced her husband if he had broken the strike—and her sister Linda Finnis commented that in a way, the men who broke the strike had to be 'brave': neither Linda nor Lorraine could imagine how they could cross the picket lines and look at the faces of their friends.[28] Anne Kirby, from Cowdenbeath, said similarly that strikebreakers must 'have had some guts to get on those buses and go', while members of their own community (Anne included) stood on the picket lines and shouted 'scab'.[29] Harassment of strikebreakers was not limited to picket lines, either (see Figure 6.3). In High Valleyfield, Fife, Alison Anderson, who was solidly behind the strike, nevertheless recalled there were 'loads of times' she wished her husband, Trapper, was working: 'you felt, oh, I just wished he was back at work and I had some money. Yeah. But you knew you couldn't—you knew you could never live in that community—that would have changed your life.'[30] Alison and Trapper recalled that another family was forced to leave High Valleyfield because of the levels of hostility towards them simply because they had been friends with a strikebreaker. Trapper remained out on strike throughout (indeed, his pit remained out even beyond the official end of the strike, only returning to work in late March). Within mining communities that were solid for the strike, social bonds—and the hostility and ostracism that

---

[25] Ibid., 67.   [26] Ibid., 60.
[27] Marlene Thompson, 'A Time of Sadness', 7JMCA/20, McCrindle papers; Sue Petney, 'A Question of Loyalty', in Witham, *Hearts and Minds*, 131. For more on this see Chapter 5.
[28] Linda Finnis, b. 1952, and Lorraine Walsh, b. 1959, both Kent, interviewed by Florence Sutcliffe-Braithwaite, 3 July 2018.
[29] Anne Kirby, b. 1955, Scotland, interviewed by Victoria Dawson, 16 November 2018.
[30] Alison Anderson.

Figure 6.3 A miner's wife attacks a 'scab' with her shoe after police flood the pit village of Rossington, near Doncaster, July 1984. © Peter Arkell/reportdigital.co.uk.

strikebreakers and their families faced—meant it was much harder to consider crossing the picket line.

But communities were increasingly divided, and the atmosphere in many mining areas grew worse and worse. Norma Dolby recorded that by December, 'gone was the feeling of togetherness; it [Arkwright Town] was now a village with a big black cloud over it'.[31] Jackie Keating, from Brampton Bierlow, in South Yorkshire, recalled that the 'atmosphere also changed' in the café where she worked: '[n]ow the strike never seemed to be out of the conversation'. On one occasion she heard her employer say 'quite venomously that he hoped that every miner would lose their job and he hoped that they would end up spending all their lives on the dole'. Another employee agreed that 'miners and their families were nothing but yobs and thugs', and 'hoped that the ones caught by the policemen would be sent to prison for a long time'. Keating wrote: 'I was totally devastated. So this was how they really thought of me and my family.'[32] Community support was extremely important to many striking miners: this meant not only the support of other mining families, but also the support of wider local networks. When local shops or market traders supported the dispute, it was significant not simply for practical reasons, but also because it suggested that the wider community did not

---

[31] Dolby, *Norma Dolby's Diary*, 53.
[32] Jackie Keating, *Counting the Cost: A Family in the Miners' Strike* (Barnsley: Wharncliffe Publishing, 1991), 86.

buy into narratives in the Thatcherite press demonising strikers as 'bully boys'. Thus when women no longer felt, in the streets, in shops, or at work, that the community was with them, it added yet another layer of emotional difficulty to the experience of being on strike.

In these final months, women deployed the same survival strategies they had used throughout the strike: women went out to work, children received free school meals, families claimed child benefit and supplementary benefit, mortgages and rent payments were suspended, family and friends offered help, meals were taken in soup kitchens, and food parcels accepted.[33] In the coldest months of winter, keeping warm was more important than ever: as Joyce Boyes recalled, 'dad sometimes brought us some wood, but you just sort of like contained yourself into one room...you just put extra clothes and things on, and got into bed early with the hot water bottle'.[34] Some heated their homes with electricity or gas, and here women struggled to find the money to pay their bills. Others relied on coal for heating and hot water, and, without their usual supplies from the NCB, had to look for other sources of fuel. Some went coal-picking, digging out coal from partially exposed seams, or gathering it from slag-heaps, though the police sometimes stopped miners and their families from doing this.[35] In Lothian, women recalled, 'we used to make a bit of a mixt and maxter from shingle and coal but the shingle didn't burn well'.[36] In North East England, miners gathered 'dross' from the coal reserves under the seabed which were cast up on the beaches, as Poppy Peacock* recalled: 'there was—sort of, big cave rock-pool areas and they used to have baskets and sacks and things. They used to go and—and just, basically, either get it off the beach or get it out the pools and things, wash it off.'[37] Dross would usually be placed over a coal fire to bank it up, ensuring that it remained lit at a low level overnight: it would not burn on its own, so Poppy remembered, 'all of a sudden there was no fences, there was no bannisters, various doors would go missing and—anything wooden would—was taken'.[38] In November 1984, brothers Paul and Darren Holmes, aged 15 and 14, were killed when a railway embankment in Goldthorpe, South Yorkshire, collapsed on them as they dug into it for coal, which they planned to sell for Christmas money.[39] Another teenage boy from nearby Upton, Paul Womersley, died in similar circumstances.[40] Striking miners referred to these tragedies in publications and

---

[33] See Chapter 4.   [34] Joyce Boyes.
[35] Barnsley Women Against Pit Closures, *Women Against Pit Closures, Vol. 2*, 64.
[36] Lothian Women's Support Group, *Women Living the Strike* (Dalkeith: Lothian Women's Support Group, 1986), 44.
[37] Poppy Peacock*, b. 1968, North East England, interviewed by Victoria Dawson, 28 June 2018.
[38] Ibid.
[39] Patricia Clough, 'Two Brothers Die Digging for Coal', *The Times*, 19 November 1984.
[40] Upton Miners, 'The Infant Support Group', in Raphael Samuel, Barbara Bloomfield, and Guy Boanas, eds., *The Enemy Within: Pit Villages and the Miners' Strike of 1984-5* (London: Routledge & Kegan Paul, 1986), 122-6, at 124.

evidently discussed them; these events brought home just how significant the risks were that men, women, and children ran when they went coal-picking.⁴¹

The cold, Joyce Boyes recalled, was 'one of the worst things':

> I remember being so cold it made you feel ill. You know, it were just—and it were no good putting electric fires and things on, because it just racked your bill up. I think we did sometimes put like a little fan heater on. And at the time, again I seem to remember paying my bill off a couple of pounds a week. There were electric board shops then, and there were one in Selby, and you just went down and paid a couple of pounds a week off. But you couldn't rack bills up with other heating, because you just didn't have the money to pay it, were just another debt when you'd finished.⁴²

Joyce supported her husband's decision to strike—indeed, she was proud that he had stayed out throughout the strike. But she also remembered the final months of the strike as a period when she felt they were coming to the end of what they could bear:

> After Christmas, it were about January, February...I know he never thought about going back. Another friend of mine at Castleford, her husband had gone back, em, but [my husband] didn't, he didn't want to go back, on principle of things. But I can remember saying to him, after the Christmas, '84, I said, 'I'm not prepared to lose the house.' I said, 'if this isn't finished before long, you'll have to go out and find something else to do.'⁴³

The strength of the culture of trade unionism and the psychic hold of the moral economy of the strike—the sense that it was simply the right thing to do—kept many miners on strike, despite the extreme hardship and mounting debts most families faced; but at this point, Joyce was close to insisting that her husband begin bringing in a wage again, whether as a miner or not. Significantly, Joyce and her husband did not live in a mining community; she did not get involved in a women's group and he was not a regular picket. They were therefore at one remove from the relationships which kept many supporters of the strike from contemplating anything other than fighting on until the end. As we have seen, many mining families did not live in 'traditional' pit villages in the 1980s, and only a minority of women—the Wintertons estimated around 5 per cent of women from mining families in Yorkshire—got involved in support movement activism.⁴⁴ The

---

⁴¹ *Cwmbach Miners and Women Speak Out* (Cardiff: Everyday Printers, 1984), 4.
⁴² Joyce Boyes.   ⁴³ Ibid.
⁴⁴ Jonathan and Ruth Winterton, *Coal, Crisis and Conflict: The 1984-5 Miners' Strike in Yorkshire* (Manchester: Manchester University Press, 1989), 122.

experiences and feelings of women like Joyce were thus likely to be replicated many times over in mining households, though they have not usually been considered in studies of women in the strike.

Activism Under Pressure

Women's groups worked to try to keep morale up, but they could only do so much. In Derbyshire, women's action group meetings bringing together all the women's support groups in the area were still happening in Chesterfield, and the women decided to 'have one last bash at keeping the strike alive', with Betty Heathfield leading them in a march around each pit in the county. But at group meetings in Chesterfield, Norma Dolby could feel the 'tension in the room. What we really wanted was for someone to say to us, "Do not worry, it will soon be over, the strike is coming to an end."'[45] Part of the problem was that no one close to Scargill could say publicly that the strike seemed increasingly likely to end in defeat. As a prominent NWAPC activist, and the wife of Scargill's lieutenant Peter Heathfield, Betty Heathfield toed the line, arguing that victory was within sight. NWAPC cleaved to the Scargillite line that the strike would be pursued to victory, releasing a statement to this effect which was publicised in *The Miner* in January, and implicitly criticising attempts by others with positions of influence in the NUM (like Kim Howells) to pursue the possibility of an end to the strike in any way other than total victory for the miners.[46] Levels of cognitive dissonance were likely to be high when leaders insisted victory was near but many activists feared that in fact, defeat was imminent. This was a time of tension, stress, and extraordinary effort for many women in support groups. Groups kept up their work to provide food, raise funds, attend morale-raising rallies and marches, and picket the increasing numbers of pits where men were working (Figure 6.4). Given the misery that the cold inflicted on striking families, many groups inevitably stepped up efforts in this area, by advising families on how they could claim one-off payments from the DHSS to cover the costs of extra fuel,[47] by seeking donations of 'fuel and heating appliances',[48] and by logging—that is, cutting trees or fallen branches into logs to supply fires.[49] The provision of fuel was not only a pragmatic

---

[45] Dolby, *Norma Dolby's Diary*, 68.

[46] McCrindle, 'National Organisation of Women Against Pit Closures', 184.

[47] Photocopied note giving information on how to claim extra benefits to cover cost of fuel in cold weather, Nottingham Centre for the Unemployed, MacLeod papers.

[48] *Here We Go! Bulletin of the Nottinghamshire Women's Support Groups*, January 1985, MacLeod papers.

[49] On Kent, see Linda Finnis and Lorraine Walsh; on South Wales, see minutes of meeting 20 January 1985, Neath and District Miners' Support Group minute book, 23 September 1984–17 February 1985, SWCC/MND/25/1, box 4 of 8, SWCC papers; on Scotland, see Margot Russell, interviewed by David Bell, March 2018, Oral History Collection, National Mining Museum Scotland, Newtongrange (hereafter Russell, interviewed by Bell).

Figure 6.4 Miners' wives picketing at Yorkshire Main, Edlington, 21 February 1985. © John Sturrock/reportdigital.co.uk.

choice: it was also symbolically important, a vital tactic in the battle to win the moral high ground. In a piece for the *New Statesman* published in December 1984, Michael Ignatieff intervened in long-running debates between the old left and the new about how to pursue political goals in the 1980s, criticising Scargill's strategy of using industrial muscle to win the strike, and writing that 'Arthur Scargill has appealed for the power workers to turn out the lights... Many workers believe that if the price of victory in this or any dispute is plunging old age pensioners huddled before single bar fires into the freezing dark, then the price is too high.'[50] In the context of hardening anti-trade union rhetoric in the right-wing press and from the Conservative Party in the 1970s and 1980s, trade unions had to walk a careful line to try to retain public support. For workers in a nationalised industry like coal, this required paying close attention to any groups that could be characterised as 'innocent victims' of their strike action. Just as the NUM wanted to construct Thatcher and the NCB as the ones who were harming the 'innocent' women and children of the coalfields, similarly, supporters of the strike wanted to claim for themselves the moral capital that came from being on the side of the powerless. Pensioners could not be left in the cold and deliveries of coal to hospitals could not be blocked. The miners knew this: Margot Russell commented, 'the guys were logging to make sure that pensioners—because you know coal supplies were starting to get a bit diminished—so we were supplying pensioners. That gave us

[50] Michael Ignatieff, 'Strangers and Comrades', *New Statesman*, 108, 14 December 1984, 25–7, at 26.

a wee bit of sympathy.'[51] Alice Samuel, from Glenrothes, Fife, recalled that the women held a demonstration to demand that the pit continue to give retired miners their coal allowance.[52]

The problem of ensuring funding was evenly distributed continued to recur in 1985.[53] At the January meeting of the NWAPC committee, the problem was raised again, and the committee reiterated its position that 'new twinning/adoption arrangements should not be encouraged', because they resulted in the uneven distribution of funds.[54] This issue made it even more important that NWAPC conduct its own fundraising.[55] A follow-up to the Christmas appeal was therefore planned, with the themes to be '(1) hardship (2) determination of the miners and (3) the waste of public money on the dispute'.[56] Jean McCrindle, Hilary Wainwright, and Peter Hain spearheaded the Miners Families' Appeal, asking for donations that would be distributed nationally via NWAPC. The appeal appeared in the *Guardian*, *Times*, and *Morning Star* in early February, and in the first week resulted in 3,000 letters and over £70,000 in donations.[57] By 16 February it had raised £100,000, which was being distributed to member groups as quickly as possible to bolster support for the strike; by 14 March the total was £169,726.80.[58] NWAPC was concerned about fairness in other areas of the movement's work, too. Over Christmas, requests from abroad to send miners' wives to speak and fundraise had grown, and NWAPC decided to attempt to share these out more evenly across the country; while Kent and South Wales had quite extensive links with other European countries already, other areas had fewer connections, and NWAPC wanted to encourage more miners' wives—particularly those who had not already been abroad—to take up these opportunities.[59] The issue of how to share out funding fairly continued to preoccupy NWAPC even after the strike, as they debated how best to support sacked and victimised miners.[60]

Where support groups were struggling, it was feared more miners would return to work. Other parts of the left, therefore, also took up the task of channelling resources to the groups with the lowest funds. The *Socialist Worker* ran a piece

---

[51] Russell, interviewed by Bell.
[52] Alice Samuel, b. 1958, Scotland, interviewed by Natalie Thomlinson, 1 August 2018.
[53] See Chapter 5.
[54] Minutes of NWAPC committee meeting 9 January 1985, DWSG4/1, papers of the South Wales Women's Support Group, Glamorgan Archives, Cardiff (hereafter SWWSG papers).
[55] McCrindle, 'National Organisation of Women Against Pit Closures', 178–9.
[56] Minutes of NWAPC committee meeting 9 January 1985, DWSG4/1, SWWSG papers.
[57] 'Don't Desert Them Now' poster, and press release, WAIN/1 file 4, papers of Hilary Wainwright, People's History Museum and Archive, Manchester (hereafter Wainwright papers).
[58] Minutes of NWAPC committee meetings 16 February 1985 and 16 March 1985, both in DWSG4/1, SWWSG papers.
[59] McCrindle, 'National Organisation of Women Against Pit Closures', 176; minutes of NWAPC committee meeting 9 January 1985, DWSG4/1, SWWSG papers.
[60] Minutes of NWAPC committee meeting 16 March 1985, DWSG4/1, SWWSG papers.

listing miners' support groups that were in need, encouraging readers to donate. The Sprotbrough and Brodsworth Mining Families' Support Group was listed as in danger, as it was not tied to a single pit and got no regular support from the NUM. It received at least six donations in response: £50 from a 'patient at Westminster Hospital', £60 from Clevedon Miners' Support Group, in Avon, a donation from Wadham College Miners' Support Group in Oxford, and three further donations from individuals.[61] Individual support groups and umbrella support groups within the coalfields also started to channel more funds to struggling groups. In January 1985, the Swansea, Neath and Dulais Valley Miners' Support Group (a mixed umbrella group bringing together support groups, mainly run by women, in nine communities in the area) was concerned about the lack of effective food provision in some other areas of South Wales. Hywel Francis, the group's chair, travelled to visit various groups and find out about the food parcel situation; the group subsequently promised, jointly with the Wales Congress, to send £2,000 a week to the Afan and Maesteg valleys, and quickly started distributing large sums.[62] There were ongoing debates, however, about where the group should direct its resources (both money and pickets); one man said at a meeting in early February that 'we should look after South Wales', but at the next it was agreed that each of the nine centres would 'contribute and send a vanfull [sic] of food' to Nottinghamshire, where strikers were reported as being in dire straits.[63]

The support movement was under strain. By February 1985, with intense pressure on the strike, there were complaints about some areas within the Swansea, Neath and Dulais Valley Miners' Support Group's purview not contributing enough: for example, '[p]eople in Crynant will not do anything'.[64] Other tensions surfaced: some women felt that non-activists in their communities were ungrateful (as Liz French's story about Christmas highlighted)—or that they were actually hostile towards the support movement. Dianne Hogg from Askern women's group recalled in 1986 that a

> lot of women in this village couldn't believe that there were maybe a dozen to twenty women willing to go down to that soup kitchen, to cook meals, to serve

---

[61] Letter from patient at Westminster Hospital, 10 January 1985; letter from Tom Archer, for Clevedon Miners' Support Group, Avon, 14 January 1985, and notes of moneys received, all in papers of Maureen Coates, private collection.

[62] Minutes of meeting 20 January 1985, Neath and District Miners' Support Group minute book, 23 September 1984–17 February 1985; letter from Hywel Francis, 1 February 1985; and minutes of meeting 10 February 1985, Neath and District Miners' Support Group minute book, 23 September 1984–17 February 1985, all SWCC/MND/25/1, box 4 of 8, SWCC papers.

[63] Minutes of meetings 3 February 1985 and 10 February 1985, Neath and District Miners' Support Group minute book, 23 September 1984–17 February 1985, SWCC/MND/25/1, box 4 of 8, SWCC papers.

[64] Minutes of meeting 17 February 1985, Neath and District Miners' Support Group minute book, 23 September 1984–17 February 1985, SWCC/MND/25/1, box 4 of 8, SWCC papers.

meals, to go round collecting, to do things—to do things for this village... And they weren't getting owt out of it. They couldn't believe that. All you got out of them were 'what are they getting out of it?'[65]

This accusation—that support group volunteers were getting more than their fair share of resources—surfaced repeatedly; unsurprisingly, activists were deeply offended by such claims.

As more miners returned to work, activists in the strike also began to face the difficult issue of what to do about fellow activists whose husbands became strikebreakers. In general, these women were not allowed to continue to participate in support groups. In the Thurcroft Women's Action Group, activists felt that strikebreakers' wives had 'been involved, often actively', with their husbands' decisions, and should be treated as such.[66] Many women supporters of the strike in the village felt bitter about instances where they thought strikebreakers' wives had been showing off their money with new perms or conspicuous consumption.[67] Even where strikebreakers' wives vocally denounced their husbands' decisions, it was usually too difficult to include them in activism. This had a painful effect on the close bonds that had grown up within groups. In February, the issue confronted NWAPC itself, when the group received the news that the husband of one of their regional delegates, Joyce Molyneux, from Lancashire, had returned to work. An alternative reserve delegate had been sent to the monthly NWAPC committee meeting, which had to discuss the issue of whether wives of men who had returned to work would be allowed, in theory, to be delegates to NWAPC. The National Committee agreed that it should 'not interfere in local matters', such as the election of delegates, but also that each area should 'ensure that it is not represented by a working miner's wife'.[68] McCrindle commented in her PhD thesis that it was 'painful' to have to exclude Molyneux, and that it demonstrated how closely NWAPC was affiliated to the Scargillite faction within the NUM.[69] The Scargillite line—absolute loyalty to the NUM President and to the strike—would brook no other option. But the difficulty of knowing what to do with the wives of men who had returned to work would produce profound tensions in the women's support movement after the strike, as well.

Support group activists continued to try to get more women involved. After Christmas, the Swansea, Neath and Dulais Valleys Miners' Support Group agreed on the need for a 'fresh push' to get more men to participate in the strike, and to

---

[65] Dianne Hogg, interviewed by unknown person, 14 January 1986, SY689/V/9/1, papers of Askern Women's Support Group, Sheffield City Archives, Sheffield.
[66] David Gibbon and Peter Steyne, *Thurcroft. A Village and the Miners' Strike: An Oral History by the People of Thurcroft* (Nottingham: Spokesman, 1986), 188.
[67] Ibid., 188–9.
[68] Minutes of NWAPC committee meeting 16 February 1985, DWSG 4/1, SWWSG papers.
[69] McCrindle, 'National Organisation of Women Against Pit Closures', 175.

involve more wives.⁷⁰ Activists knew that women who got involved felt less depressed and more committed to the strike, and that their participation could impact on their husbands, too. Women in Thurcroft actively tried to recruit the wives of men thought to be possible strikebreakers: '[w]e'd get the woman involved, then [the man] would think "I can't go back because she's down [at the Welfare]"'. Sometimes they would even pretend the kitchen was short staffed in order to persuade other women to help.⁷¹ By late February, however, even many support groups saw the end of the strike approaching.⁷²

Breaking the Strike

In early 1985, with no sign of movement from the NCB, and Nottinghamshire producing large quantities of coal, the drift back to work that had begun in autumn started to turn into a flood. By 21 January, NCB figures had 54.8 per cent of miners working in North Derbyshire, 29.0 per cent in Scotland, 23.1 per cent in the North East, and 9.6 per cent in Yorkshire. In South Wales it was just 1.5 per cent, but in Nottinghamshire it was as high as 94.9 per cent.⁷³ This made a significant difference to some non-militant miners who had supported the strike, but without high levels of ideological commitment. This was the case for Adrienne C.'s husband, who worked in the Selby coalfield. The fact that more and more miners were returning to work, Adrienne recalled, played a major part in his decision: 'you know I'd seen it all on the telly, about—'cause by that time people had started going back, and I think that's—that were part of his thinking as well, er—you know, it's now time for people to start making decisions for themselves'. Adrienne's husband returned 'a couple of months before the strike finished'.⁷⁴

Adrienne and her husband, she said, 'wanted to support it [the strike]—because you didn't want to cross picket lines', but also 'got on with our lives as well as we could' while it was happening, trying to protect their children from its effects. Adrienne contrasted this attitude with that of the couples at the heart of the mining community in their village, who were activists in the strike and in the support movement, and whose 'lives completely revolved around what was going on with the strikes'. Adrienne and her husband, though they would go to the village pub, had always felt they did not want to be part of a tight-knit mining

---

⁷⁰ Minutes of meeting 31 December 1984, Neath and District Miners' Support Group minute book, 23 September 1984–17 February 1985, SWCC/MND/25/1, box 4 of 8, SWCC papers.
⁷¹ Gibbon and Steyne, *Thurcroft*, 189.
⁷² See, for example, minutes of meeting 21 February 1985, Barnsley WAPC minute book, A-3590/G, papers of Jean Miller, Barnsley Archives, Barnsley.
⁷³ David Cross, '1,800 Return to Work in One Day', *The Times*, 22 January 1985. Figures for Kent are included in the South Midlands area, where 80.4 per cent were working; the percentage was certainly much lower in Kent, however, which was a highly militant coalfield.
⁷⁴ Adrienne C., b. 1956, Yorkshire, interviewed by Victoria Dawson, 26 June 2018.

community where families lived 'in each other's pockets'.⁷⁵ Adrienne's father was a hospital administrator, and her mother a nurse; her husband was the son of a miner but had worked in other industries before going into the pits, and in her interview, Adrienne said that though her background was working-class, she now saw herself as on the 'boundary' between 'upper-working-class' and 'lower-middle-class'. The family never went to a soup kitchen and did not receive food parcels. Their pre-existing values, their network of family and friends, and their distance from picketing and support group activism in the strike all helped make it possible for Adrienne's husband—who Adrienne emphasised loved his job as a miner—to decide to return to work, and for Adrienne to support his decision. Adrienne nevertheless felt 'really anxious' about the 'stigma' of being a 'scab' and being 'tarred with that for the rest of his life', and about the 'stones' and 'abuse' thrown at buses going through picket lines.⁷⁶

As Joanne's* testimony, discussed in Chapter 5, shows, women were right to be worried about what men might experience going into work—as Joanne recalled, listening to her father recount his first experience crossing the picket line was 'the only time I've ever, ever seen him cry'.⁷⁷ Adrienne's husband told her he did not feel 'intimidated'. She recalled that the fact that he went to the local pub to tell the strikers he was planning to go back meant that at least he was not perceived to have gone back 'sneakily'.⁷⁸ 'Scabs' had long been constructed in trade union culture as dishonest, low, and cowardly—as forfeiting masculine brotherhood and masculine pride.⁷⁹ It was, therefore, important to Adrienne's husband—and to Adrienne—to show that he had not been 'sneaky' or fearful: he had not lost his claim on authentic working-class masculinity. But though he had supported the strike for nine months, Adrienne's husband, like Adrienne, had never been deeply committed to the moral economy of the strike constructed by activists. The drift back to work meant they started to feel differently about supporting the strike. Adrienne's words are telling: where in the first nine months of the dispute, her husband had accepted the decision to strike—a decision made by a collective—he now began to feel that it was 'time for people to start making decisions for themselves'.

When Poppy Peacock's* father returned to work in North East England in early 1985, her parents did not even tell her about his decision. Poppy's father had spent much of the strike out at his allotment or collecting dross on the beach, so his absence from home each day was not a surprise. Since November 1984, as more men had started to go back, children at Poppy's school had gathered outside at the end of the day to watch buses carrying working miners go past and to 'pelt the

---

[75] Ibid.   [76] Ibid.
[77] Joanne*, b. 1973, North East England, interviewed by Victoria Dawson, 16 July 2018; see Chapter 5.
[78] Adrienne C.   [79] See, e.g., Jack London, 'The Scab', *The Atlantic*, January 1904.

buses, throw stuff, shout, scream, swear'. Though she did not participate, Poppy regularly witnessed the buses go by, and this was how she discovered that her father was back at work, sometime in the new year. Poppy confronted her father that night but he 'wouldn't talk': 'if he didn't want to have a conversation', she explained, 'he didn't have a conversation; you could shout and scream all you wanted and I did that night'. Her mother returned from work, Poppy recalled, and she demanded '"did you know he was back at work?" And, yes.'[80] Poppy thought that her parents considered her too young to discuss politics (she was in her mid-teens), and that her mother wanted to protect her from the hostility she might face as the daughter of a 'scab'. Poppy thought that by this time, it was clear to many people that the strike would be called off soon—and that this took the 'sting' out of it a little: she did not face abuse or shunning. Nevertheless, she was shocked: Poppy recalled that at the start of the strike, her parents were 'very much for... I don't remember anybody *not* being—it was just, it, it was definitely something that needed to be done'.[81] The shock when she saw her father on the pit bus was so profound that Poppy later rewrote it as the climactic moment of a short story, 'Frontline', transposing the moment of recognition to the picket line outside the pit, where her main character Millie has gone to make sketches for an A-level art project: Millie 'stumbles back' when she sees her father going into work, unwilling—perhaps even unable—to comprehend what she is seeing.[82]

In South Wales, Carol's* family faced overt hostility when her father returned to work three weeks before the strike ended. Carol was still at school during the dispute, and she remembered that from the start, her parents had conflicted feelings: they agreed with 'the principle of it', and knew that 'closing the mines' would be 'horrific for our whole town', but they 'didn't agree with how the strike happened'. At Carol's father's pit, a large majority voted against strike action, but they were picketed out by miners from elsewhere in the country: it was 'ingrained' in the men, Carol said, not to cross a picket line. Many men, however, including Carol's father, felt angry that there had not been UK-wide support for a strike in earlier years, when South Wales pits were being closed; they also felt that it was clear that 'the mines are closing, we already know that'.[83] The strike, therefore, seemed somewhat futile from the start. Carol recalled that her parents' overwhelming emotion that year was anger: 'I just remember them being really angry with everyone involved in the strike. You know, they were angry at Thatcher, really angry at Thatcher; angry at Scargill, you know, my mother couldn't even look at him on TV.'[84] Carol's mother worked part time, but they had several children still at home and the family struggled financially: her mother did not like

---

[80] Poppy Peacock*. [81] Ibid.
[82] Poppy Peacock, 'Frontline', published in *The Yellow Room*, private collection.
[83] Carol*, b. 1968, South Wales, interviewed by Natalie Thomlinson, 19 June 2018. On the closures in Wales in 1983 see Chapter 2.
[84] Carol*.

having to use food parcels 'at all', and Carol said that she could see the strike 'was destroying my father'. Her parents suspected that while they were struggling, activists in the strike and the support movement were getting the best of the donated food (the same accusation that Dianne Hogg faced in Askern), and other miners were 'doing hobbies' (taking jobs on the side), or claiming sickness benefit. Although Carol's family lived in a close-knit mining community, her parents' feelings about how the strike had begun, their sense of its futility, and their distance from and suspicion towards strike activists all created the context in which Carol's father considered returning to work.

In February 1984 'word had got out' in Carol's village that miners thinking of returning to work were going to meet in a pub to discuss it. Just under twenty men met and decided to return to work the following week; Carol's father was among them. Carol thought that, though her parents did not say anything to the children, her mother was probably 'having a nervous breakdown'. Her father asked the family, including his siblings (his brothers were also miners), 'would you have any issue if I went back, because you know this is just way, way too much, and the whole family said no—go'. Carol said:

> I admired him massively, because, to me, he had the biggest balls to do that, you know, to say, this is enough, you know, we're having nothing coming in, it's futile, it's totally futile... I admired him massively, and I still do, for having that steel and that resolve to make that decision.[85]

The weather was 'bitterly cold'; the NCB sent a taxi for her father and the police were stationed 'outside the door', anticipating 'that perhaps there would be some bother'. Carol recalled that her father was 'really scared', and, feeling she 'needed to look after him', rose before dawn to see him off:

> I would get up before my father, and light the fire, I'd light the coal fire, build it all up with the paper, and the stick and the coal, and light that, and cook him breakfast, and then wait until the taxi, and then I would be in the window, watching him go.[86]

After the first group of men started back at work, others soon followed; within weeks, the strike was called off. Carol recalled only a few incidents of abuse, mainly from children and teenagers, 'shouting scab, you know, at the house, throwing stones at the windows', but her father continued to feel 'very nervous' when out of the house that someone would shout 'scab': he was 'forever watching his back', and her mother felt the same.[87]

---

[85] Ibid. [86] Ibid. [87] Ibid.

These were very similar experiences to those of Joanne's* family after her father returned to work in North East England in autumn 1984. Indeed, the families of men who returned to work in majority-striking coalfields during the first drift back to work in autumn 1984 probably faced even more severe social penalties. Joanne's family experienced the full sanctions the community could bring to bear. Joanne recalled that the community 'changed overnight': 'all of these people who used to walk past on a Saturday night and speak—hiya, you know, all of that—they all became, like, the enemy, and they were all dishing out [abuse]'. Joanne's mother would stand at the door waiting for people to go by and shout at the house, so that she could shout back. They received 'silent phone calls'; Joanne was called a scab 'all the time' by other children, and the family had their kitchen window smashed. After a time the overt forms of hostility died down, but Joanne recalled that the community was never the same again.[88] Carol and Joanne both wanted to remain anonymous, and, indeed, most of the interviewees whose husbands or fathers broke the strike chose to go by a pseudonym or just their first names. The anxiety and fear they felt for their menfolk, their families and themselves in 1984–5—anxieties about physical attacks and social stigmatisation, but also emotional pain—were not entirely gone in the 2010s.

Some strikebreakers were defiant, but men and women breaking the strike in its final weeks were often agonised by their decision. In her autobiography, Catherine Paton Black recalled a fellow canteen-worker, Grace, who went on strike with Paton Black, but who returned to work in February, faced with the threat of being sacked from her job and repossession of her home. Paton Black described the scene when Grace came to tell her: Grace's 'arms folded around herself like a hug', and she could only speak in a whisper, 'not looking me in the eye'.[89] In Paton Black's telling, Grace embodied the implications of breaking with the moral code of the strikers: her voice and pose showed that she had not rejected this code, but been driven by desperation to go against it; her inability to look her friend in the eye demonstrated Grace's profoundly compromised sense of self. Paton Black recounted that other strikers condemned Grace when they heard about her return to work, but Paton Black herself defended Grace, arguing that she had stayed out for nearly a year, and had only been forced back to work by the threat of losing everything. The account was perhaps dramatised for the book, but nevertheless conveys how the moral economy of the strike worked to shape not only the decisions that supporters of the strike made, but also their emotions, their affect, and the way they were able to present themselves.

Jeanette McComb's husband, too, ended up returning to work shortly before the end of the strike. In early 1985, Jeanette had decided to return to her parents' house in Wolverhampton, where the whole family had spent Christmas, because

---

[88] Joanne*.
[89] Catherine Paton Black, *At the Coalface: My Life as a Miner's Wife* (London: Headline, 2012), 316.

they could not afford to heat their home in Ayrshire. Jeanette said that she could 'only imagine what the pressure was like on my husband, we never talked about it, and we never have'. She thought that it was harder for him: 'I think his conscience was bothering him, you know, what he was putting his family through.' She felt strongly that she would support him in striking or in returning to work:

> I just wanted the strike to end. I never wished for him to go back, I didn't want him to go back, if he didn't want to go back, but I wished the strike would end, and everybody would go back. Because I could see it was futile. I could see that—we—we were never gonna—they were never gonna win, we were never gonna win. You know, this is just, really, ba- they're just basically beating the life out of them, you know.[90]

By February, she said, 'I'd had enough'. By 7 February, the NCB claimed that only 105,000 NUM members, or 56 per cent of the total employed by the Board, were on strike.[91] (The NUM claimed that the figure was higher, with over 70 per cent of the workforce still out—around 138,000 miners.)[92] Jeanette thought there were 'a lot of us at that time who really were at the end of their tether, you know—this is just never going to end, we can't keep going this long'. Jeanette's testimony repeatedly returned to the desperation she and her husband felt: 'we were on our knees by then, you know, and—it were just—[he] said, "oh, I'm going back"'. Jeanette did not recall much antagonism from the community, just 'odd comments', though she thought her husband might have been on the receiving end of more hostility. But though she had 'had enough', her husband's return to work was still difficult. Although Jeanette and her husband had 'toughed it out for the best part of a year', they still felt they had 'given in': 'you felt a failure', Jeanette said.[93]

What role did women play in the drift back to work? Before the start of the strike, Jean McCrindle and Nell Myers had feared that women might be a conservative force, nagging their husbands back to work. The real picture, of course, was more complex. There were some families where it was the man's decision to return to work, some where the decision was shared or mutual, and some where wives exerted pressure on husbands. One of the interviewees for Gibbon and Theyne's oral history of the strike in Thurcroft reported: '[t]here's one down the street here. She said she was going to leave if he didn't go back. She hated Scargill. She thought that those who were going back to work were heroes. She thinks it's great her husband went back to work.'[94] Among our interviewees,

---

[90] Jeanette McComb.
[91] Paul Routledge, 'The Whiff of Defeat Creeps Closer', *The Times*, 7 February 1985.
[92] 'Strike News in Brief', *The Miner*, 7 February 1985, 3.   [93] Jeanette McComb.
[94] Gibbon and Steyne, *Thurcroft*, 187.

Jessica Gibson reported two women in her extended family who had pressured their husbands to return to work (though, importantly, she also reported many women offered vital support to their striking husbands). One of those who urged her husband to return to work, Jessica said, had threatened to leave him; he had a mortgage and was worried about losing the house, and he did not live in a mining village where there would be immediate and harsh social sanctions for strikebreakers.[95] Such second-hand stories need to be read with some care, though—strikers and supporters of the strike might have found it easier to pin the blame for strikebreaking on women rather than on those who were supposed to be brothers in struggle, in order to maintain a psychic investment in the idea of masculine camaraderie and solidarity. On the whole, wives seem to have supported their husbands rather than trying to coerce them into behaving a certain way. Their actions were probably informed by an increasing emphasis on marriage as a partnership of mutual support.[96] The hardships that striking inflicted on families were shared by both partners: husbands often found it hard to not be supporting their families; wives struggled to run the home without an adequate income. The penalties associated with strikebreaking would also be shared between both, but women often felt that men had the most to lose—both in terms of their sense of masculine pride, and their bonds with their fellow workers, men with whom they would have to work on a daily basis after the end of the strike.

It is unsurprising that only a small number of women whose husbands or fathers worked through the strike, or returned to work early, or who themselves worked through the strike, came forward to be interviewed for this project. In majority-striking coalfields, returning to work early carried a huge stigma at the time, a stigma which has only partly faded in the intervening years. In majority-working coalfields like Nottinghamshire, though there was not the same stigma from *within* the immediate community, working miners were called 'scabs' by their fellow miners on picket lines on a daily basis. The epithet is still used today in matches between Yorkshire and Nottinghamshire football clubs.[97] The destruction of the coal industry in less than a decade after the strike vindicated, for many, Scargill's claim that Thatcher wanted to destroy the industry, and public narratives of the strike from *Billy Elliot* to *Pride* have presented the strikers as heroic figures, albeit heroes of a tragic story.[98] In this context, tales of breaking the strike were hard to articulate. The evidence for understanding the experience of women whose husbands or fathers returned to work is, thus, not extensive. But the testimonies discussed here do shed important light on what they went through.

---

[95] Jessica Gibson, b. 1963, Scotland, interviewed by Florence Sutcliffe-Braithwaite, 26 November 2018.
[96] See Chapter 2.
[97] Jay Emery, 'Geographies of Belonging in the Nottinghamshire Coalfield: Affect, Temporality and Deindustrialisation' (unpublished PhD thesis, University of Leicester, 2018), 58, 200.
[98] *Billy Elliot*, dir. Stephen Daldry, 2000; *Pride*, dir. Matthew Warchus, 2014.

Though not numerous, they are lengthy and rich. They are testament to the powerful and difficult emotions women shared with their husbands and fathers, and to how they dealt with these emotions. They shed light on the intense anger which some striking men and their families came to feel about the position they had been put in, and how they sometimes directed that anger at both Thatcher and Scargill.

Pre-existing orientations to the mining industry, mining communities, networks of family, friends, and activists all shaped the conditions in which some men and women came to contemplate breaking the strike. Going back to work, even in what would turn out to be the strike's final weeks, left many men and women with profoundly difficult feelings of fear, anxiety, and shame. Often they had to significantly rewrite their internal stories about how they related to their communities and how they understood right and wrong, in order to be able to construct a coherent sense of self. For those who were not deeply involved in the life of the local community, or ideologically invested in the strike, such as Adrienne C., supporting their partners' return to work could feel like a relatively straightforward decision.[99] For other men and women, breaking the strike was far more emotionally and psychically painful: it required breaking community ties—and often family ties—that had been central to their lives, and it required rethinking the moral framework that had guided their actions for nearly a year. In a poem published after the strike, Betty Cook described how men and women who had been out on strike for nearly a year explained their decision to return to work:

> Women tell me they can't go on
> That they're still loyal to their Union
> But children are hungry and not well clad
> And they say their duty as a dad
> Is to provide for basic things
> You don't get much for a pawned wedding ring.[100]

Men and women now needed to articulate a different moral framework to justify their decision to support a return to work. Where the moral economy of the strike demanded that men and women make sacrifices now in order to honour the struggles of their forebears, and secure the futures of their children and their communities, in the final months of the strike, some began to articulate a sense that their duties as parents—for fathers, as breadwinners, and for mothers, as carers—had to take precedence. These stories of breaking the strike have been

---

[99] Adrienne C.
[100] Barnsley Miners' Wives Action Group, *We Struggled to Laugh* (Barnsley: Barnsley Miners' Wives Action Group, 1987), 38.

hard—sometimes almost impossible—to tell in the context of communities (and leftist discourses) which still stigmatise working miners. As Carol* said at the end of her interview for this project, recounting her memories had been like 'some kind of exorcism'.[101]

The End

As defeat came to seem inevitable to more and more strikers, what they and their families were being asked to do changed. Now, many felt like they were faced with an agonising choice between their self-respect and their families' material interests. By late February, nearly half of the workforce nationally had returned to work. In South Wales, the most solid area, 7.5 per cent were working by 28 February; in Yorkshire, it was 21 per cent.[102] Victory seemed impossible. But strikebreaking was unthinkable to many; as the chairman of Maerdy colliery lodge said, it 'would have been absolutely horrific if men in Maerdy had gone back to work without the decision of the lodge.'[103] Calling off the strike without a settlement would at least mean those still on strike did not face this choice, and on 3 March, a Special Delegate conference of the NUM voted 98–91 to do just that. In his speech to the conference, Scargill praised the support of the women's movement.[104]

Most strikers returned to work on 5 March; some stayed out several days longer. Kent miners initially decided not to return to work without protection for sacked miners, and sent pickets to South Wales and Yorkshire on 5 March, in some cases delaying the return to work there. However, with the support of the sacked miners themselves, the Kent miners called off their pickets and returned to work on 11 March.[105] Some strikers and some activist women wanted to keep the strike going: one woman said, in an interview shortly after the end of the strike, 'I was quite prepared for him to stop out as long as it took... We'd rather have stopped out that bit longer and for victory at the end of it.'[106] Another woman recalled, ten years after the strike, that the activists in her support group had 'withdrawal symptoms; for twelve months we had been on a high and we honestly thought that we would win'.[107] Kim Howells of the South Wales Area was widely seen as the foremost proponent of returning to work without a settlement, and

---

[101] Carol*. [102] Curtis, *South Wales Miners*, 242–3.
[103] Richard King, *Brittle with Relics: A History of Wales, 1962–1997* (London: Faber & Faber, 2022), 322–3.
[104] Winterton and Winterton, *Coal, Crisis and Conflict*, 205.
[105] 'Betteshanger Occupation Strike 1984–5' pamphlet, in WAIN/1 file 12, Wainwright papers.
[106] Chrys Salt and Jim Layzell, eds., *Here We Go! Women's Memories of the 1984-5 Miners Strike* (London: Co-operative Retail Services, 1985), 82.
[107] Denise Fitzpatrick, Christine M. Nelson, May Cadwallader, and Edith Armitage, *10 Years On and Still Laughing* (Rotherham: Dearne Community Arts, 1994), 38.

activists who wanted to push on with the strike often spoke of him with bitterness. But one woman in a discussion group in Blaengwynfi several months after the end of the strike suggested that she thought Howells had been

> made the sacrificial lamb because he actually had the courage to say what a lot of people... even though I know activists don't like to think that your ordinary, you know, miners were thinking that but I'm sure that, you know, really when it came down to it, he was just voicing the opinion of more than half...[108]

She noted that while on 4 March only four men in her village were back at work, if the strike had gone on for a month longer, it might well have been forty.

Activists, both male and female, worked hard to celebrate and honour the work that men and women had done to keep the strike going, and to try to temper the crushing weight of defeat. Women from Grimethorpe WAPC remembered that the final day on the picket line was 'really emotional': all the pickets gathered in front of the caravan from which the women served food and drink, and 'applauded and cheered our efforts. Many tears were shed that day. Some of sadness, but mainly of elation for a job well done.'[109] At pits where most miners were still on strike, they usually marched back to work together behind the union banner, sometimes accompanied by women's support groups and other supporters, and by music. In some places, as in Rossington, near Doncaster, women led the marches (Figure 6.5). At Bilston Glen and Monktonhall in Lothian, bands and pipers accompanied the marchers; at Bilston Glen the sacked men marched at the front carrying the union banner.[110] In Maerdy, the miners were joined by the Maerdy Women's Support Group and representatives from the groups which had supported them in the UK, Italy, and Denmark, to the accompaniment of the Tylorstown Colliery Band.[111]

When activist women wrote about the marches back, one image occurred over and over again: 'heads held high'. A poem by a Bilston Glen miner's wife included the lines, 'Four hundred men marched back, all with their heads held high... spare a thought for the real miners of the Glen'.[112] Jean Gittins, mother of two striking miners, wrote two poems about the end of the strike, such was the significance and emotion of the moment. One included the lines: 'So you're back at work mi darlin's / And the Unions [sic] in shreds / But you'll be marchin through the gates / Wi' proud uplifted heads'.[113] On 5 March 1985, Ann Musgrave, a miner's wife from Worsborough, wrote:

---

[108] Discussion Class—Blaengwynfi Group, 26 November 1985, AUD/506, '1984–85 Miners' Strike Study', South Wales Coalfield Collection, South Wales Miners' Library, Swansea.
[109] Barnsley Women Against Pit Closures, *Women Against Pit Closures, Vol. 2*, 92.
[110] Lothian Women's Support Group, *Women Living*, 50.   [111] King, *Brittle with Relics*, 328.
[112] Lothian Women's Support Group, *Women Living*, 50.
[113] 'March Back', in Jean Gittins, *Striking Stuff* (Bradford: 1 in 12 Club, 1986), 16.

Figure 6.5 Rossington Women's Support Group leading the march of striking miners returning to work, March 1985. © John Harris/reportdigital.co.uk.

> Today I marched, head held high with my husband and son, down the pit lane towards Houghton Main. Yes, it has been worth it. I am proud to have been a part of the longest dispute in British history. This is what I can tell my grandchildren. We have held on to our pride. We have not been defeated. The fight goes on.[114]

Maggie Stubbs marched back with her husband and the other strikers at Maltby, and said they all felt the marches back were vitally important: 'you've got to keep your head up'.[115] The moral economy that strikers and their supporters

---

[114] Ann Musgrave, 'Tues 5th March 1985', 7JMC/A20, McCrindle papers.
[115] Maggie Stubbs, b. c.1950, Jamaica/South Yorkshire, interviewed by Natalie Thomlinson, 13 September 2018.

constructed during the strike to contest the Thatcherite law of the free market had helped many find the resolve to go on for an entire year. In defeat, strikers and their families could at least feel they still had self-respect, that their menfolk were 'real' men. That this self-respect was the only thing strikers had won made it all the more important that the marches back to work emphasised the pride that miners and their families could feel in their heroic efforts: it was vital to counteract the overwhelming sense of defeat.

In Nottinghamshire, however, most miners had been working for many months, if not for the entire year. Here there could be no marches back behind union banners: strikers simply had to rejoin their workmates. When Jean Witham spoke to women from Nottinghamshire support groups in the months after the strike, she found that:

> No woman seemed able to find words to describe adequately what she felt when the announcement came that the strike was over ... they were thrown into a state of shock, numbed with sadness, even though they had known for weeks that events were moving rapidly towards the end.[116]

Gwen MacLeod recalled, 'I think we cried for about four weeks! Devastating. We just felt let down, we were lost, we were devastated.'[117] Wendy Minney, Kim Hickling, and their mother Rita Wakefield, all committed supporters of the strike, were angry and sad: Rita recalled that her husband 'just cried'. Having remained out on strike for the entire year despite being in a minority, they could not understand how miners' leaders in other areas took the increasing numbers returning to work as a sign that the strike could not go on.[118] These women had invested huge amounts of time, energy, and emotion in the strike, in the most difficult circumstances, and the decision to call it off was a crushing blow. For other activists, however, feelings were more mixed. In Scotland, Alice Samuel felt 'relief' mixed with sadness, watching the marches back to work on TV: 'in some respects, it was a victory, you know, they went back, their heads were held high, they didnae disgrace themselves in any way', she said; but at the same time, 'the fight that we were fighting ... was lost'. As Alice commented, the strike had been part of her life for a year and she was 'loving doing all the things that I was doing'.[119] Activism was hard work, but it also boosted women's morale, gave them new networks and new experiences. These disappeared in the aftermath of the strike: as we will see in the next chapter, most groups folded almost immediately,

---

[116] Witham, *Hearts and Minds*, 215. [117] Interview with Gwen MacLeod, MacLeod papers.
[118] Rita Wakefield, b. 1943, Kim Hickling, b. 1962, and Wendy Minney, b. 1964, all Nottinghamshire, interviewed by Natalie Thomlinson, 20 August 2018.
[119] Alice Samuel.

and many women were more focused on getting 'back to normal' than on continuing their political work.

While strike activists tried to salvage something positive from defeat, many women recalled that it was difficult for them to find solace in the shows of pride and solidarity. Claire*, from South Wales, remembered watching the march back to work in Maerdy on breakfast TV with her mother on the same day that her father returned to the pit, and 'crying, because although everyone said, "oh you're going back with your head held high, you know, you've got nothing to be ashamed of, you tried, you fought"—you knew that nothing would ever be the same again, and it wasn't'.[120] Alison Anderson's husband, Trapper, worked in the last pit in Scotland to return to work: the march back into the pit, accompanied by a piper, was shown on TV, and Alison said, 'I can remember it being on the news and sitting crying, and everything, you know, because they were away back in—because, you felt it was for nothing. You know, you've just gave up a whole year of your life, and sacrificed for—and we got nothing.'[121] Activist Anne Kirby, from Cowdenbeath, did not march behind the banner into the pit: she hesitated and faltered as she recalled that 'a lot of women went down to the—the—the—erm—marched in with the men to the—you know, the gate, but I—I wouldn't cause I—I just—it was a—a bit of a downer, actually'.[122]

Many women felt mingled sorrow and relief. Christina Bell's husband was chair of Shireoaks NUM lodge, and both had staunchly supported the strike; yet when asked how she felt when the strike was called off, Christina paused, and then said, 'well, I suppose I was relieved in a way, because it meant they were going back to work'. But, she continued, her feelings changed when her husband told her that 'these pits are not—these pits are not gonna stay open for long'.[123] When asked the same question, miner's wife Chloe*—who had not been involved in the women's support movement but who had supported her husband's strike action—said she felt:

> Great [laughter]. I don't know, it were like, how've we survived this? How've we done this? It's like how have we done this? I thought it were great them going back to work because I felt it were lost a long time before they actually went back. I didn't want him to go back like the Nottingham miners are, I didn't want him to go back as some had gone back and were called scabs—and still to this day I know where they live and who they are and people will still say today, 'you scabbed in t'strike', or, 'her dad scabbed in t'strike', so, er, and I never wanted him to do that anyway. I wanted, I, er, thought it went on longer than it should—there

---

[120] Claire*, b. 1969, South Wales, interviewed by Natalie Thomlinson, 11 August 2018.
[121] Alison Anderson.   [122] Anne Kirby.
[123] Christina Bell, b. 1949, North East England/Nottinghamshire interviewed by Victoria Dawson, 17 June 2018.

was more hardship than [there] needed to be, so I felt great when they went back, er he was really upset, his pit went back and they were really upset; it was, it was like a war weren't it, and they'd lost the war and, and it effectively—what they'd fought for had gone, hadn't it, 'cause all the pits were going to close and all the communities around them would suffer and the knock-on industries and everything, so yeah, but I thought it were lost long before that and so when they went back I thought, thank goodness we've got some sense somewhere to like put a stop, you know, and start from another perspective or something, so I were pleased.[124]

Chloe's complex feelings were probably similar to those felt by many miners' wives. Her laughter—like Christina's pause before she answered the question about how she felt at the end of the strike—suggested that there was something slightly difficult about articulating this sense of relief. How could one feel relieved about crushing defeat? Yet many women did understandably feel relieved that the end they had long felt was inevitable had finally arrived.

The situation was different, of course, for women whose husbands had been sacked or imprisoned: for them, the end of the strike did not mean they had their husbands' wages coming in again. Over 1,000 miners were dismissed during the strike, 800 in England and Wales, and 206 in Scotland; 280 of these miners in England and Wales were reinstated by May 1985, but none of those in Scotland had been.[125] In Lothian, three women whose husbands had been sacked spoke about their experiences shortly after the strike. Margaret F. said, '[y]ou begin to have rows over wee silly things. There's a mental strain with having them around the house constantly... You keep asking yourself "why us?" Your life becomes obsessed with it.' Eleanor agreed: '[s]ometimes I'm in bed listening to my husband pace up and down the room'. Margaret M. thought, '[i]t's the emotional side of it that's worse than the money. Every fortnight signing on. I never thought you could be so humiliated.'[126] Among our interviewees, Sue's husband had been sacked during the strike, and she recalled that even after most men had returned to work, there was still 'upheaval' in their home:

Because we was—still on—not on strike, but he didn't have a job, we didn't know what was happening. I'd say, the union was very good, they reinstated all our coal, and they paid, and everything, you know. But you still had the worry, you didn't know what the outcome was going to be.

---

[124] Chloe*, b. 1959, Yorkshire, interviewed by Victoria Dawson, 30 August 2018.
[125] Jim Phillips, 'Strategic Injustice and the 1984-85 Miners' Strike in Scotland', *Industrial Law Journal* (early online publication, 2022), 1–29, at 10.
[126] Lothian Women's Support Group, *Women Living*, 58.

Sue's husband was paid a partial wage by the NUM, but it was not until 1987 that he was reinstated and returned to work down the pit. As Sue said, 'our strike lasted three years, basically'.[127]

Conclusion

The final three months of the strike were a profoundly difficult time for all involved. Women's support groups struggled on, but tensions escalated in some groups, as more miners returned to work. While some contemporaries blamed women for supposedly nagging or driving their husbands back to work, it seems likely that in many cases, the decision to return was, in fact, taken by men, or by husbands and wives together; it could simply be psychologically easier for a male-dominated trade union to blame the breakdown of solidarity on women, rather than on male comrades. It is clear that some women in striking families were reaching breaking point in these months, as hardship intensified, and defeat started to look almost certain; however, many NUM members simply could not contemplate breaking the strike, because of their political principles and also because of the strength of their relationships with workmates, the social sanctions they would face within their communities, and the sense they had that their masculinity depended on standing strong. Many of our interviewees recalled that it was almost impossible for them to ask their husbands to break the strike, knowing the consequences for relations with workmates and within the community could be so severe. Many also had a profound sense that supporting the strike was simply their moral duty. The moral economy that activists in the strike had articulated and defended over the past year was a powerful one, and profoundly shaped the actions of both activists, and many striking families whose members did not become involved in activism. This strengthened the strike, but it also led to painful feelings of anxiety for women as it became evident to many that the strike was likely to end in defeat. Women and men who were less deeply integrated into mining communities, however, could draw on an alternative moral framework focused on defending the immediate interests of one's children, in order to make the case for breaking the strike. The stigma that men who returned to work early—and their families—faced meant that it was still difficult for many women to recall this experience, even thirty-five years later. But the bitter hardships of the final months of the strike meant that many women felt relief when it was called off, even if this feeling was often mixed with sadness and anger.

[127] Sue.

7
Aftermath

9 March 1985

On International Women's Day, just four days after the miners returned to work, women and men gathered for a rally in Chesterfield football stadium (see Figure 7.1). The *Morning Star* claimed 10,000 people were present; even if this was an exaggeration, the crowd was certainly large.[1] One woman who was there recalled that the banners were 'hung over the terraces', and that the atmosphere was 'electric'.[2] Another remembered, 'Arthur Scargill entered to cheers and shouts, everyone started singing, "We'll support you evermore". Feet were stamping... At last the noise subsided, Arthur was able to speak. He paid tribute to everyone who had supported the miners, a special thank you was given to Woman Against Pit Closures.'[3] Christine Worth, who became involved in supporting the strike through her local Labour Party women's section in Ambergate, Derbyshire, attended the rally, and she, too, recalled the intensity of emotion in her interview in 2018:

> I remember being a bit scared, because we made so much noise, 'cause we were stamping so loud, in this very flimsy football stadium...I remember Scargill saying, 'the first time I've ever been shut up by women', or something...
>
> *What were the emotions that day?*
>
> Well it was—it was a bit of mass hysteria as those things are, you know, and there's a lot of people in a confined space, and it's all over. I wouldn't think the— the shouting and cheering on that day were not—the same as the sort of general sadness and sense of—of defeat that we generally had.[4]

The National Women Against Pit Closures (NWAPC) committee had originally planned that the speakers would be women only, but ultimately this plan was

---

[1] Jean McCrindle, 'The National Organisation of Women Against Pit Closures in the Miners' Strike of 1984–5' (unpublished PhD thesis, Oxford Brookes, 2001), 186.
[2] Worsborough Community Group, *The Heart and Soul of It* (Huddersfield: Worsborough Community Group and Bannerworks, 1985), n.p.
[3] Barnsley Women Against Pit Closures, *Women Against Pit Closures, Volume 2* (Barnsley: Barnsley Women Against Pit Closures, 1985), 104.
[4] Christine Worth, b. 1952, Derbyshire, interviewed by Natalie Thomlinson, 2 August 2018.

Figure 7.1 The rally organised by National Women Against Pit Closures for International Women's Day at Saltergate Football Stadium, Chesterfield, 9 March 1985. © Raissa Page.

abandoned.[5] Arthur Scargill was invited to speak, alongside Ann Lilburn, Betty Heathfield, and Anne Scargill, plus an array of female speakers from a broad spectrum of the left, including Joan Ruddock from the Campaign for Nuclear Disarmament (CND), Margaret Prosser from the Transport and General Workers' Union (TGWU), and a representative from the South West Africa People's Organization (SWAPO).[6]

Arthur Scargill was upbeat, telling the meeting that the women had 'transformed their lives' through their activism.[7] When he finished, women started singing the song by Mal Finch that had become the women's support movement's unofficial theme tune: 'We are women, we are strong / We are fighting for our lives / Side by side with our men / Who work the nation's mines'.[8] Anne Scargill, too, was positive, concluding her speech with the words, 'total victory is inevitable'.[9] Some women certainly felt that the end of the strike was simply a staging post in a longer struggle. One anonymous writer penned the following lines about the day:

---

[5] Minutes of NWAPC committee meeting 9 January 1985, DWSG 4/1, papers of the South Wales Women's Support Group, Glamorgan Archives, Cardiff (hereafter SWWSG papers).
[6] McCrindle, 'National Organisation of Women Against Pit Closures', 185.
[7] *Morning Star*, 11 March 1985, quot. in ibid., 188.
[8] Barnsley Women Against Pit Closures, *Women Against Pit Closures, Vol. 2*, 104.
[9] McCrindle, 'National Organisation of Women Against Pit Closures', 187.

> this wasn't a miners
> rally, the strike ended
> days ago
> This was the women of Britain
> gathering to show, the rest
> of the world that the
> greater fight had only just
> begun, we may have lost
> a battle but the war
> has still to be won.[10]

Some thought the rally showed how effectively the strike had politicised coalfield women. One of the interviewees for Betty Heathfield's oral history project (conducted shortly after the end of the strike) felt the 'message of the day' was that the women present 'knew what they were doing' when they 'stood and cheered the oppressed women of the world' in a way that would have been 'unheard of' a year previously.[11] They cheered Scargill, she argued, when he said they were 'fighting for...an end to capitalism...and the fight for Socialism', and 'actually understood the struggle that SWAPO was putting forward...They understood that the Soviet Union was the first country in the world to have in its constitution that women were equal.'[12] This woman saw the Chesterfield rally as evidence for the case that the strike had occasioned a mass politicisation of female activists.

Not all women agreed, however. Marina Lewycka, another leftist and feminist activist who had supported the strike, and who was present at the rally, thought Arthur Scargill's boosterism was 'addressed to the writers of history, not the poor struggling people'.[13] While some recalled the strike as a moment of political awakening, there were many other coalfield women who wanted to go back to something like 'normal' in its aftermath. These women did not want to change their lives; rather they wanted to re-establish their old routines, focus on their families and their family finances, and revert to the gender roles of pre-strike days, where their husbands brought in the main family wage. 'Normal', it is important to stress, did not mean reverting to the sort of gender order described in *Coal is Our Life*: as we outlined in Chapter 2, on the eve of the strike many wives had part-time or even full-time jobs, many husbands helped out around the home and with the children, and many marriages operated more on a 'companionate' model than a patriarchal one. A process of gradual change in coalfield women's lives was

---

[10] Anonymous testimony, n.d., in 7JMC/A20, papers of Jean McCrindle, Women's Library, LSE, London (hereafter McCrindle papers).

[11] Interviewee 26, 7BEH/1/2, papers of Betty Heathfield, Women's Library, LSE, London (hereafter Heathfield papers).

[12] Ibid.

[13] Lewycka diary, quot. in McCrindle, 'National Organisation of Women Against Pit Closures', 188.

already underway before 1984, and developments in coalfield communities in the decades after the strike would contribute further to shifts in patterns of women's work, the domestic division of labour, and women's engagement in politics in the coalfields. In the long term, the loss of the strike, and the swift closure of pits in the years that followed, accelerated many of the changes—in women's work, for example—that were already in train before the strike. This chapter takes up the story of activist groups, as well as the experiences of individual women and of coalfield communities, in the months and years after the strike.

The Women's Support Movement

During the strike there were confident assertions that the many women's groups that had formed would continue after its end. One miner's wife interviewed in summer 1984 in South Wales said:

> When the strike is over the women's support group will stay together. We're preparing things now. There's a conference being arranged which will be held every year for groups throughout the country, and we're going to have monthly meetings. We will keep in contact, and stay together as a women's action support group, and whatever we can fight, we'll fight; whoever's in difficulty, we'll help them. There's no way we'll ever go behind the kitchen sink again. No way.[14]

In the crucible of the strike, when enthusiasm for the immense achievements of the women's movement was high, many women activists were reluctant to lose the new networks and experiences that activism had brought them.[15] Leftist and feminist activists felt that the energy of the new women's movement forged in the strike must not be allowed to dissipate.

In fact, though, most women's support groups seem to have folded as soon as, or very shortly after, the strike ended. Many seem not even to have considered doing otherwise: they saw their job as supporting the strike, and without the strike, they had no reason to exist. Only 9 per cent of women surveyed for Allen and Measham's study in coalfield communities in West Yorkshire in 1986 were aware of women's groups that had continued after the strike.[16] Some groups kept going for a few weeks after 3 March, to distribute their remaining food and money and

---

[14] Welsh Campaign for Civil and Political Liberties and NUM South Wales Area, *Striking Back* (Cardiff: Welsh Campaign for Civil and Political Liberties and NUM South Wales Area, 1985), 32.
[15] E.g. Alice Samuel, b. 1958, Scotland, interviewed by Natalie Thomlinson, 1 August 2018.
[16] Fiona Measham and Sheila Allen, 'In Defence of Home and Hearth? Families, Friendships and Feminism in Mining Communities', *Journal of Gender Studies*, 3 (1994), 31–45, at 39.

Figure 7.2 Dalkeith Miners Women's Support Group float passes Canongate Kirk, en route to Holyrood Park, in Edinburgh, demonstrating against the victimisation of sacked and imprisoned miners after the end of the strike, in 1985. © National Mining Museum Scotland.

help miners waiting for their first paycheques to arrive.[17] A small number of others did continue in the longer term, and their main goals were usually to support the National Union of Mineworkers (NUM), to oppose further pit closures, and to aid in the struggle to reinstate sacked and victimised miners (see Figure 7.2). Over 1,000 miners were dismissed during the strike,[18] and groups took part in lobbying and protesting to demand their reinstatement—the Scottish Area Women's Support Group, for example, took part in lobbies of the National Coal Board (NCB) offices in Edinburgh, of the Scottish Trades Union Congress Annual Congress in Inverness and of Parliament in 1985.[19] Women's groups also raised funds; the Bentley Women's Action Group in Doncaster even funded the first issue of the *Rank and File Miner*, which campaigned for sacked miners, in June 1985.[20] In areas where the Union of Democratic Mineworkers (UDM) was

---

[17] For groups in Barnsley and Doncaster, see McCrindle, 'National Organisation of Women Against Pit Closures', 194–5. For groups in the Swansea, Neath and Dulais Valleys, see *Valleys Star*, 33, 20 March 1985, South Wales Miners' Library, Swansea.

[18] Jim Phillips, *Collieries, Communities and the Miners' Strike in Scotland, 1984-85* (Manchester: Manchester University Press, 2012), 152.

[19] *Coalfield Woman*, 1, July 1985, 7JMC/C, McCrindle papers.

[20] The activities of various groups are detailed in: *Coalfield Woman*, 2, October 1985, 7JMC/C, McCrindle papers; *Rank and File Miner*, 1, June 1985, WAIN 1/11, the papers of Hilary Wainwright, People's History Museum, Manchester (hereafter Wainwright papers).

challenging the NUM, women also campaigned against the breakaway union, which was formed in 1985 by miners who had worked through the strike, and was particularly prominent in Nottinghamshire.[21]

Some groups also had broader aims, hoping to continue with the work of political mobilisation and education that had begun during the strike. They continued to campaign, not only on the pressing issues of sacked miners and the UDM, but also on larger issues affecting coalfield communities, and for other left causes. They supported other trade unionists who had shown solidarity during the strike, as well as groups such as CND and the Greenham Common women's peace camp, and anti-racist and internationalist causes like the fight against apartheid.[22] Women from the movement helped the wives of Silentnight strikers to set up a support group in 1986, and in 1996 advised the wives of striking dockers in Liverpool on forming a group.[23] As part of the push for political education, several regional groups held their own conferences. In June 1985, the first conference of the South Wales Women's Support Groups, held in Aberdare, attracted over 100 women. There were talks about issues relating to the mining industry, like the European Economic Community's proposals for the future of coal; the conference resolutions focused on opposing pit closures and the devastating 'social consequences to the mining communities', fighting for the reinstatement of sacked miners, and building up NWAPC to 'combat the unabated attacks on the miners and all sections of the working class'.[24]

Sheffield WAPC also held a conference after the strike, with workshops on 'The Way Forward' for the women's groups and the 'Campaign for Coal', as well as—indicating a more explicitly feminist influence—a workshop on 'Women's Health', a feminist bookstall, and a 'Violence Against Women' stand.[25] One member of Sheffield WAPC, Iris Preston, whose sons were miners, recorded the debates at the planning meeting for the conference in her diary, and her comments suggest tensions about how the group's energies were best spent. One woman advocated setting up a women's centre, but Iris disagreed, writing that 'in the short term, there is too much hardship, and [too] many sacked miners for us to divert our strength'. Iris resisted the idea that the group's political agenda should simply focus on the needs of women:

[21] On Nottinghamshire groups, see *Coalfield Woman*, 2, October 1985, 7JMC/C. On North Staffordshire groups, see NWAPC meeting minutes 25 January 1986, DWSG4/1, SWWSG papers. On the UDM, see David Amos, 'The Nottinghamshire Miners, the Union of Democratic Mineworkers and the 1984-5 Miners' Strike: Scabs or Scapegoats' (unpublished PhD thesis, University of Nottingham, 2011).
[22] See *Coalfield Woman*, 1, July 1985, and unnumbered, January 1988, both 7JMC/C, McCrindle papers.
[23] Meg Allen, 'Carrying on the Strike: The Politics of Women Against Pit Closures' (unpublished PhD thesis, University of Manchester, 2001), 29-30.
[24] *Coalfield Woman*, 1, July 1985, 7JMC/C, McCrindle papers.
[25] Iris Preston strike journal, 3 April, SxMOA 99/58/1, papers of Iris Preston, Mass Observation Archives, The Keep, Brighton.

> We as a group should not lose our identity, and should try to encourage 4 day week for the miners better working conditions for them and their wives creches for the children. Better playing facilities, + surroundings for the children, better medical facilities for the men, safety education etc. Maybe sponsored places at universities for the 25-40 age group. Dreams—well maybe. But with determination I believe the women could make this happen.[26]

It would be hard to find a more fulsome expression of the political direction that the more community-oriented strand of WAPC wanted the organisation to take: a politics that focused on preserving (and improving) a community, rather than one which focused on the special needs of women. Such a politics had its immediate roots in the strike, but was clearly part of a much longer tradition of maternalist progressive politics, in which women's 'special interests' in children, health, and education were to be directed into improving family and community life.[27]

Iris Preston was far from the only activist who wanted to focus on projects that continued working practically in and for their communities. Education was often central to such ventures—this was not so much political education, as education and training designed to build up the confidence and skills of participants, often in order to enable them to enter the labour force or develop their careers. Gwent Fund Support Group campaigned after the strike for a Community Project Centre with a day centre, training workshops, a creche, and community centre, in Llanhilieth.[28] A group of women from the Yorkshire area of WAPC got financial support from their local authority to set up the Castleford Women's Centre, and solicited suggestions for what educational provision local women wanted; soon they began running courses on a wide range of topics, as well as a creche; the centre ran for over thirty years.[29] Women in the Swansea, Neath and Dulais Valleys who wanted to build on the achievements of the women's mobilisation in the strike started the DOVE Workshop, a community education and training provider and community enterprise. Mair Francis, the wife of Hywel Francis, the labour historian (and later Labour MP) who took over the chair of the Swansea, Neath and Dulais Valleys Support Group during the strike, helped to set up DOVE, along with some of the women who had been activists in the support movement. Mair explained her motivations: 'my view was, they are going through

---

[26] Ibid.
[27] See Seth Koven and Sonya Michel, eds., *Mothers of a New World: Maternalist Politics and the Origins of Welfare States* (London: Routledge, 1993); Pat Thane, 'The Women of the British Labour Party and Feminism, 1906-1945', in Harold L. Smith, ed., *British Feminism in the Twentieth Century* (Amherst, MA: University of Massachusetts Press, 1990), 129; Stephen Brooke, *Sexual Politics: Sexuality, Family Planning, and the British Left from the 1880s to the Present Day* (Oxford: Oxford University Press, 2011).
[28] *Coalfield Woman*, 2, October 1985, 7JMC/C, McCrindle papers.
[29] 'Castleford Women's Centre', JP Box 2 12/05, papers of Jill Page, Feminist Archive North, Leeds (hereafter Page papers).

this struggle, but when it ends, what's going to happen? You can't struggle for a year and not put it into something positive that's permanent... The strike was a catalyst to help us set up DOVE.'[30] The workshop gained substantial funding from central and local government, and eventually took over the Banwen Offices of the NCB Opencast Executive, opening a crèche and running courses on subjects from machine knitting and computer skills to welfare rights and Italian cities; it is still running today.[31]

There were also creative projects. A group of women from Worsborough who had organised short courses at Northern College before the strike, and who set up a support group during the dispute, created a theatre group and toured their shows around the region.[32] North Staffs Miners' Wives Action Group produced a show called 'There's No Going Back', 'a collection of songs and stories about the determination and courage of a group of women from the pit community who came together during the miners' strike... and who have stuck together through thick and thin ever since'; they received financial support from West Midlands Arts and the Cadbury Trust, as well as professional support from Banner Theatre, and were still performing in 1991.[33]

Many of the long-lasting initiatives that came out of the strike were projects like the DOVE Workshop and Castleford Women's Centre that were able to get state funding and 'professionalise'. This was not always the case though: a group of women who had supported the strike in Brampton Bierlow felt afterwards that they wanted to 'form a community centre to keep the people together'.[34] They organised it with no input from the local council (indeed, the women felt that their local councillors had been downright unhelpful). The idea for a community centre had been floated before the strike, but it was only after the strike, with support from two local churches, finance from charitable foundations, and the fundraising and organising of women from the local support group, that Cortonwood Comeback Community Centre took shape. It opened in October 1986, and operated a drop-in advice centre, focusing particularly on unemployment, as well as offering meals, hosting groups such as a disability group and a senior citizens group, and courses like machine knitting and first aid. Ten years after the strike began, the group published a book outlining their work, and the centre is still operating today.[35]

[30] Mair Francis, b. 1948, South Wales, interviewed by Florence Sutcliffe-Braithwaite, 17 July 2018.
[31] Mair Francis, *Up the DOVE! The History of the Dove Workshop in Banwen* (Cardigan: Iconau, 2008). The capitalisation of DOVE is original.
[32] Worsborough Community Group, *Heart and Soul*, n.p.
[33] North Staffs Miners' Wives Action Group, 'There's No Going Back' leaflet, and Lancashire Women Against Pit Closures poster, 'An Evening of Solidarity with the Miners', 23 November 1991, both in EVT/MINESTRIKE/2, 'Miners' Strike 1984–1985 Support Groups Collection', Working Class Movement Library, Salford.
[34] Denise Fitzpatrick, Christine M. Nelson, May Cadwallader, and Edith Armitage, *10 Years On and Still Laughing* (Dearne Valley Community Arts: Rotherham, 1994), 39.
[35] Ibid.; and see https://cortonwoodcomeback.com/.

One group of women who were certainly determined to keep the movement going after the strike were the organisers of NWAPC, and their goals were resolutely political. They started a newsletter, *Coalfield Woman*, to network groups around the country, and began planning a national conference for summer 1985. They faced a number of pressing organisational issues, however. The first was the question of whether working miners' wives could participate in the movement, and on 31 March 1985, the national committee held a 'long discussion' on this question. Delegates from areas like Nottinghamshire and Leicestershire, where strikers had always been in the minority, 'agreed that they would find it difficult to work with women who had been responsible for their husbands losing their jobs, being put in prison, losing seniority, etc etc'. But delegates from places like north Derbyshire and Northumberland, where the final weeks and months of the strike had seen a significant return to work, 'felt that we had to try and rebuild unity and communities'.[36] As one woman interviewed shortly after the end of the strike said, 'in the long term... if the NUM is to be successful it needs the solidarity of the whole of the membership of the Union. So at some time in the future it needs those people.'[37] This was an intractable issue, and the committee decided to allow a 'cooling off period' before taking any final decision on it. Individual groups were allowed to admit working miners' wives as members if they wanted to, but these women could not hold office.[38] The discussion illuminated how difficult activism on behalf of 'mining communities' would be in many areas after the strike: many communities had been profoundly fractured by strikebreaking, particularly the mass returns to work in the final weeks and months of the strike.

The second important organisational issue discussed on 31 March 1985 was NWAPC's relationship to the NUM. The idea of giving women's groups 'associate membership' had been floated, and Arthur Scargill was supportive.[39] This form of membership would not give women's groups the ability to vote at conferences, but it would be a powerful symbol of the NUM's commitment to work with the women's movement, and would give women access to NUM educational events. On 4 July, WAPC groups from Yorkshire, Derbyshire, and the Midlands lobbied the NUM conference in favour of the rule change, holding placards that read: 'Don't cut off the hands that fed you'.[40] But the vote went against them: many NUM officials wanted the union to remain a predominantly male space, and NWAPC was also implicated in intra-NUM factional politics. In the aftermath of the strike, the NUM was riven by factional divides which remained deep for years,

---

[36] Minutes of NWAPC special meeting 31 March 1985, DWSG4/1, SWWSG papers.
[37] Chrys Salt and Jim Layzell, eds., *Here We Go! Women's Memories of the 1984-5 Miners Strike* (London: Co-operative Retail Services, 1985), 42.
[38] Minutes of NWAPC special meeting 31 March 1985, DWSG4/1, SWWSG papers.
[39] *Coalfield Woman*, 2, October 1985, 7JMC/C, McCrindle papers.
[40] *Coalfield Woman*, 1, July 1985, 7JMC/C, McCrindle papers.

if not decades. NWAPC was seen by some as a potential site for far-left entryist groups, and by others as too closely aligned to Scargill, whose leadership was controversial within the union.[41] (The rapturous reception the women had given Scargill at the Chesterfield rally on 9 March probably did not help; moreover, many prominent figures in WAPC, like Anne Scargill and Jean McCrindle, were indeed close to Scargill, and the organisation would support Scargill in his campaign for re-election as President of the NUM in 1988.)[42] The Scottish Area NUM gave Scottish women's support groups associate membership at local level in 1985, but it was not until 1987 that associate membership was added to the NUM rulebook at national level.[43] By this time, few women's groups were left and it seems few, if any, women applied for associate membership.[44]

Disappointment about the associate membership vote was one cause of pessimism at NWAPC's conference at Sheffield City Hall in August 1985, which was attended by over 100 women, and which proved so fractious that at a lunchtime committee meeting, many women were 'crying' and wanted to 'pack up and go home'.[45] The problems stemmed in part from rushed organisation, but also from underlying divisions within the movement. There was a lack of clear 'direction' now the strike was over.[46] The conference began with a motion from South Wales women that the discussion of 'aims, draft proposals and future action', planned for the morning, should be moved to the afternoon and held in a closed session, where 'contentious issues'—particularly relations with the NUM and the use of money in the support fund—could be discussed without the press present. Ann Lilburn, in the chair, was heckled from the floor, and a disputatious debate was held on the motion. The discussion swiftly branched out to encompass the broader purpose of NWAPC now the strike was over. One delegate argued that the proposed 'aims' were 'too vague': suggestions for 'education are all well and good', but NWAPC should not be 'a national network of education groups... ready to be used as an N.U.M.H auxiliary in the next strike (applause)'. This delegate's group felt NWAPC should be 'organising and arguing for the necessity of a new national strike'.[47] There were thus major disagreements about what NWAPC should stand for after the dispute that had brought it into existence was over.

That question was closely connected with the continuing debate over *who* NWAPC was for. The Sheffield conference debated yet again the 75 per cent

---

[41] Florence Sutcliffe-Braithwaite and Natalie Thomlinson. 'National Women Against Pit Closures: Gender, Trade Unionism and Community Activism in the Miners' Strike, 1984–5', *Contemporary British History*, 32 (2018), 78–100, at 92.
[42] Letter from Arthur Scargill to Lyn Dennett, 7 December 1987, DWSG4/1, SWWSG papers.
[43] *Coalfield Woman*, 2, October 1985, 7JMC/C, McCrindle papers.
[44] McCrindle, 'National Organisation of Women Against Pit Closures', 214 ff.
[45] Pete Carter, 'Women Against Pit Closures Meeting, Friday 20 Sept 1985', for Women's Advisory Committee, 23 September 1985, in CP/CENT/WOM/5/2, papers of the Communist Party, People's History Museum and Archive, Manchester (hereafter CP papers).
[46] Ibid.   [47] Partial transcript of 17 August 1985 conference, DWSG4/1, SWWSG papers.

rule: should 75 per cent of a group's members be required to be miners' *wives*, *related* to miners, or *closely* related to miners—or should the rule be got rid of altogether, as delegates from the Communist Party of Great Britain (CPGB) Eurocommunist faction desired?[48] CPGB women wanted to open up NWAPC, to use the movement to radicalise coalfield women, and to pursue broader political aims—to 'introduce a feminist perspective'.[49] This was precisely the same ideological division that had dogged NWAPC from the start.[50] Just as they had during the strike, the attempts of outside leftist and feminist activists to turn NWAPC to their ends provoked anger from some coalfield women: one conference delegate commented, '[i]t looks as though some Women's Support Groups have been hijacked by these outside groups'.[51] If NWAPC was simply an auxiliary force for Scargill or the NUM, its politics would be narrow and it would lack autonomy; but if it was to serve larger political goals, then it would be difficult to unite the diverse membership behind a single vision of what those goals should be. In this respect, NWAPC faced a dilemma common to single-issue campaigns that aim to broaden their scope beyond that one issue.

In the four years after 1985, NWAPC continued to hold meetings and conferences, publish *Coalfield Woman*, support the Justice for Mineworkers campaign, meet foreign delegations, send women on trips abroad, and take the WAPC banner to marches and galas.[52] But the same problems continued to surface. As the strike faded into the past, women drifted away and local and regional groups folded. The overall goals of NWAPC, its membership, and its relationship to the NUM continued to be debated. On 17 October 1987, an Extended Conference in Sheffield discussed the name and future direction of the organisation, in the end concluding that the name should be retained, and that the movement should remain 'coalfield based'. More communication between groups and more money were needed.[53] When the national committee met soon after the conference, its members agreed that 'we have to regenerate the organisation'.[54] Though there were fundraising efforts, they were not enough to keep *Coalfield Woman*, the most important tool for networking the movement, going. After its last issue, in January 1988, the dwindling movement fragmented even further. Later that year, the Scottish delegate, Ella Egan, a longstanding member of the national committee, resigned from the chair, because the Scottish group had now disbanded.[55] In autumn 1989, there were angry discussions about the use of funds left in the will of

[48] Amendments to draft proposals, Women's Conference, August 1985, WAIN/1/3, Wainwright papers; photocopy of 'Draft Proposals for a Women's Organisation Associated with the NUM', CP/CENT/WOM/5/2, CP papers.
[49] Ibid.   [50] See Chapter 5.
[51] *Coalfield Woman*, 2, October 1985, 7JMC/C, McCrindle papers.
[52] McCrindle, 'National Organisation of Women Against Pit Closures', 217.
[53] *Coalfield Woman*, 6, January 1988, 7JMC/C, McCrindle papers.
[54] Minutes of NWAPC meeting 21 November 1987, DWSG4/1, SWWSG papers.
[55] Minutes of NWAPC meeting 17 September 1988, DWSG4/1, SWWSG papers.

activist Liz Hollis for the education of women in the coalfields: some committee members thought that the money had been wrongly paid to the Castleford Women's Centre. The delegates from North Yorkshire WAPC, who were also involved in the Castleford Centre, insisted that this was incorrect, and that the Centre had simply been allocated some funding from the bequest to run a day school for coalfield women. Some delegates felt 'that moves were afoot to move National WAPC up to Castleford Women's Centre and away from the NUM'; the delegates from North Yorkshire complained that 'there has been a lot of hostility which has seemed to be directed at them'.[56] Personal as well as political disagreements were causing serious problems within the dwindling movement. Within four or five years after the end of the strike, National WAPC had fragmented and faded as a political force.

The networks and the organisational skills that women had developed during the strike remained, however, and the strength of the connections made by activist women was demonstrated by the swiftness with which they were re-activated in late 1992, when the Tory government announced the imminent closure of thirty-one of the remaining fifty deep coal mines in Britain. Aggie Currie, a prominent activist in Markham Main Wives' Action Group, took direct action in the House of Commons as part of the campaign:

That's when I got kicked out.

What did you get kicked out for?

'Cause, erm, Michael Heseltine was speaking, and I chucked flour, they thought it were anthrax.

[Laughter]

Were you in the public gallery bit?

Mm.

And what—what was the flour?

Plain flour.

Plain flour—and how did you get that in?

In my knickers.[57]

In January 1993, NWAPC approved the setting up of 'pit camps' at threatened collieries, 'on the style of the Greenham Common Women's Camps'.[58] 'Neither of

---

[56] Minutes of NWAPC meetings 2 September 1989 and 4 November 1989, DWSG4/1, SWWSG papers.
[57] Aggie Currie, b. 1950, Yorkshire, interviewed by Victoria Dawson, 22 June 2018.
[58] Minutes of NWAPC meeting 9 January 1993, quot. in Jean Spence, 'Women, Wives and the Campaign against Pit Closures in County Durham: Understanding the Vane Tempest Vigil', *Feminist Review*, 60 (1998), 33–60, at 54.

the pit camps would have happened without Greenham', remembered Caroline Poland, who had been active in Sheffield WAPC, gone to Greenham in the 1980s, and played a key role in the Houghton Main pit camp in the Dearne Valley, alongside other Sheffield WAPC members.[59] The camp at Markham Main, Armthorpe, was organised by women from Doncaster and Barnsley WAPC, including Betty Cook, Anne Scargill, and Aggie Currie, all of whom had visited Greenham and been impressed with what they saw; Aggie called visiting Greenham 'an experience of a lifetime'.[60] The camps, which continued until late spring or summer 1993, were set up around caravans or portacabins, sometimes supplied by local authorities; they offered a meeting point for miners and activists, and made local, national, and international links, in order to raise awareness of the damage pit closures would do to local communities and families. The Houghton Main pit camp sent up a hot air balloon in March to raise awareness of the threat to pits and to encourage NUM, National Association of Colliery Overmen, Deputies and Shotfirers (NACODS), and rail union members to vote for strike action in support of the campaign against closures.[61] Lancashire WAPC, which had been dormant from 1987, revived to set up a camp at the sole remaining pit in the county, Parkside.[62] There were also camps at Grimethorpe (organised by Barnsley Miners Wives' Action Group), Rufford (organised by Nottinghamshire WAPC), Trentham (organised by the North Staffs Miners' and Wives' Action Group), and Vane Tempest colliery, in County Durham (organised by Seaham WAPC).[63]

The context for this activism was very different: there was no major NUM strike, and therefore no immediate hardship faced by mining families—indeed, miners were being offered generous redundancy packages if they agreed to pit closures. Thus, as Jean Spence has suggested, many, perhaps most, of the women activists were motivated by political conviction and fear for the long-term future of their communities, rather than being catapulted into activism by the circumstances in which they found themselves.[64] As the links between the pit camps and Greenham suggest, the influence of feminist activism was more explicit in the 1992–3 round of pit closures. Those who took part tended to be those who had been most heavily involved in 1984–5, and groups in 1992–3 probably had a larger contingent of women who were not closely related to miners than the women's support groups of 1984–5 had. Indeed, Spence, who was part of the Vane Tempest

[59] Caroline Poland, b. 1949, South East England/Yorkshire, interviewed by Natalie Thomlinson, 5 February 2019.
[60] Aggie Currie.
[61] *You Can't Kill the Spirit! Houghton Main Pit Camp, South Yorkshire: The Untold Story of the Women Who Set Up Camp to Stop Pit Closures* (Sheffield: Northend Creative Print Solutions, 2018), 98.
[62] Karen Beckwith, 'Lancashire Women Against Pit Closures: Women's Standing in a Men's Movement', *Signs*, 21 (1996), 1034–68.
[63] *You Can't Kill the Spirit!*, 122–8; Spence, 'Women, Wives, and the Campaign'.
[64] Spence, 'Women, Wives, and the Campaign', 41.

Vigil, critiqued the way that the women had to present themselves as, or at least allow themselves to be seen as, miners' wives in order to appear 'authentic'. In fact, a minority of women involved in the camp were from the village of Seaham, and a minority of women were miners' wives—only two women were both miners' wives and living in Seaham, and both of these were in full-time work.[65] Spence herself, though from a mining family, was not married to a miner, and thought that the adoption of the image of 'miners' wives' was limiting, forcing the women to obscure the feminist and socialist principles which had brought many of them into the struggle. This suggests the continuing difficulties that women who were read as 'working-class' had in presenting themselves as 'political' to the world—difficulties, that, as we saw in Chapter 5, had been present throughout the strike.

Getting 'Back to Normal'

Many women caught up in the strike—including many strike activists—wanted more than anything else to get 'back to normal' once the strike was over.[66] In the three months following the strike, Jean Witham interviewed women in Nottinghamshire about their activism, but found that some were unwilling to speak to her: 'many were desperately tired by this time, in some cases near to exhaustion, both mentally and physically'.[67] The loss of the strike—with no concessions at all from the NCB—was profoundly demoralising to many men and women. The women Witham spoke to in Nottinghamshire were anxious about debts, and wanted 'to re-establish a familiar pattern to their lives and to provide some stability for their children'.[68] 'Interviewee 25', an activist from Nottinghamshire, interviewed soon after the strike for Betty Heathfield's oral history project, thought that 'a lot of the older women are just dying to get back to the regular wage packet, the regular shopping, and just get back to normal'.[69] Margot Russell commented that '[s]ome of the ladies' who helped in the kitchen for Dalkeith Miners' Support Group 'seemed to be quite happy I suppose in a sense—grateful their husbands were back at work, getting a wage again and kind of getting their life back—so they were quite happy just to go back to what they did previously'.[70] This desire to get 'back to normal' is hardly surprising, particularly given that many activists had emphasised throughout the strike that their goal was to defend communities and a whole 'way of life'.[71]

---

[65] Ibid., 52.   [66] Allen, 'Carrying on the Strike', 23.
[67] Joan Witham, *Hearts and Minds: The Story of the Women of Nottinghamshire in the Miners' Strike, 1984–1985* (London: Canary, 1986), 113.
[68] Ibid.   [69] Interviewee 25, unpublished book manuscript, 7BEH/1/2, Heathfield papers.
[70] Margot Russell, interviewed by David Bell, March 2018, Oral History Collection, National Mining Museum Scotland, Newtongrange (hereafter Russell, interviewed by Bell).
[71] See esp. Chapter 5.

The wives of striking miners knew, however, that their husbands would often face a very different work environment down the pit once the strike was over. Prominent strike militants were sometimes victimised. Pat Smith's husband, Dave, who had been NUM branch President at Dinnington pit during the dispute, was punished afterwards for his leadership of the strike: Pat recalled, 'he got given a really disgusting job, working in t'sump, which is under t'cage—yeah. So it's under, under where t'cage goes down, and it fills up wi' water, and he got sent down to clean that out on a regular basis.'[72] Camaraderie underground had, in many pits, been fatally undermined by the divisions between men who had returned to work early and those who stayed out. In Derbyshire, Norma Dolby's husband had remained out until the end, but many men in the area had gone back; when he returned from his first shift back at work, Dolby recalled he was 'visibly shaken':

> When our men arrived at the area in which they were to work, it was as if they were not there. They were just ignored. They were the ones who were made to feel guilty. Friends Terry had known for years were turning their backs on him. They just did not have the guts to speak. Perhaps if they had, Terry might not have answered them, who knows?[73]

In communities, too, the divisions between those who had broken the strike and those who had stayed out until the end were often profound. In Kent, Sue's daughter remembered that her father 'would walk out of a pub after the strike, if there was a scab in there, for many, many years'; Sue herself recalled that she did not speak to a local strikebreaker for a long time: 'even now', she said, 'it's still in here', indicating that she still remembered in 2018.[74] The loss of the strike meant that men's jobs were not secure. As we saw in Chapter 6, Christina Bell felt 'relieved, in a way', when she heard the strike was over, but also knew that things were unlikely to go back to normal for long: her husband 'said to me, we're going back to work but I don't know for how long, 'cause, he says, these pits are not—these pits are not gonna stay open for long'.[75] Many women were, thus, anxious for their husbands, whether about the atmosphere they might face at work, the fractures in once-friendly communities, or the strains placed on men by looming pit closures and redundancies.

Paying off the debts they had accrued in the strike was the most pressing priority for many. In March 1985, women who had rent arrears, deferred mortgage payments, and unpaid utility bills received demands for payment. Others

---

[72] Pat Smith, b. 1949, Yorkshire, interviewed by Victoria Dawson, 8 June 2018.
[73] Norma Dolby, *Norma Dolby's Diary: An Account of the Great Miners' Strike* (London: Verso, 1987), 79.
[74] Sue, b. 1956, Kent, interviewed by Florence Sutcliffe-Braithwaite, 14 July 2018.
[75] Christina Bell, b. 1949, North East England/Nottinghamshire interviewed by Victoria Dawson, 27 June 2018.

owed money to local businesses, family and friends, even local authorities. A study of Armthorpe, near Doncaster, after the strike found that among the men and women interviewed (who tended to be committed activists in the strike), 'the average "Strike" deficit (as distinct from normal, ongoing debts), was £2,420'.[76] Joyce Boyes and her husband had to start making normal repayments on their mortgage plus a third; she recalled that they still had to 'cut their cloth' and restrain their spending. Joyce's husband took any overtime he could get, and they had no holidays. The repercussions lasted for at least another eighteen months, Joyce recalled, and the psychological effect of this was powerful:

> It were a time when—I weren't miserable, crying and moaning, it were just, everything were just stood still, you couldn't really plan for any future, you just had to get your nose down and get on with it and—and get your money back into t'bank and—do it like that. But it weren't really a particularly happy time; the strike were miserable, let's face it, who wouldn't be, you couldn't—it were just day-in day-out drudgery, really.[77]

Both Mig Weldon and Jeanette McComb recalled being unpleasantly surprised to discover that money they had respectively received from Fife and Strathclyde councils to help them during the strike was considered to be a loan rather than a gift, and needed to be paid back.[78] Alison Anderson, from Fife, recalled, 'I was in a lot, a lot of debt for a lot of years. Paying up—paying for carpets, paying for food vouchers, paying for clothing, paying electric arrears, paying for rent arrears. Everything.'[79] It was only when her husband was made redundant when his pit closed a few years after the strike that the redundancy money finally allowed them to pay off their remaining debts.[80] Anne Kirby, from Cowdenbeath, also recalled that it took 'years' to recover financially from the strike: she and her husband were still 'picking up the pieces' four years later, when Anne started part-time work.[81]

In fact, the end of the strike was the occasion for the first 'really big argument' Anne and her husband had, 'when he got his first wage'. Anne recalled that she was 'worried about the—the arrears, and the—the bills, and everything', while her husband felt, 'we'd worked hard, and we'd had a hell of a time, and he just wanted to relax'. Ironically, they had 'spent this whole year and a bit sort of like not arguing, and just getting on with life, and then, he went back to work, and

---

[76] John Murphy, 'Community and Struggle: A Sociological Study of a Mining Village in the 1980s' (unpublished PhD thesis, University of Warwick, 1989), 397.
[77] Joyce Boyes, b. 1955, Yorkshire, interviewed by Victoria Dawson, 21 November 2018.
[78] Mig Weldon, b. 1950, Scotland, interviewed by Victoria Dawson, 29 August 2018; Jeannette McComb.
[79] Alison Anderson, b. 1959, Scotland, interviewed by Victoria Dawson, 29 August 2019.
[80] Ibid.
[81] Anne Kirby, b. 1955, Scotland, interviewed by Victoria Dawson, 26 November 2018.

his—our first major argument was over the pay'.[82] For the past year, for many couples, disagreements had been subordinated to a shared sense of purpose in the face of very serious hardship. That changed with the end of the strike. It was not the end of the pressure on marriages and families, but rather a moment when the pressures changed. Joyce Boyes, Alison Anderson, and Anne Kirby all felt a sense of pride that they and their husbands had survived the strike, and stayed solid behind it; but after the strike their most immediate priority was, as Alison put it, 'picking up the pieces'.[83]

Long-Term Change in Mining Areas

In the eight years after the end of the strike, the mining industry was decimated. On the eve of the dispute, there were 170 NCB pits operating; by the end of 1993 there were just seventeen.[84] The closure of pits was nothing new, but this severe contraction of the industry came in the context of UK-wide deindustrialisation, and a new, Thatcherite insistence that it was not the government's job to prop up manufacturing employment in areas of job losses.[85] Unemployment in coalfield areas had become a significant issue by the mid-1990s. In a survey of miners made redundant in the early 1990s, the Coalfield Communities Campaign found that 46 per cent of men were still unemployed a year later.[86] The true level of joblessness was disguised by the numbers of former miners who were put onto disability rather than unemployment benefit, a phenomenon at its peak in the 1990s.[87] The job opportunities that opened up for men in the 1990s, 2000s, and 2010s were often less well-paid and less secure than mining jobs, and offered little of the camaraderie of the pit, or the sense of masculine pride and purpose many miners had derived from their work.[88] By 2017, the authors of a report on unemployment in Britain's 'older industrial towns' (of which coalfield areas formed a very significant part) suggested that the main problem in such areas was not the lack

---

[82] Ibid.   [83] Alison Anderson.
[84] Historical Coal Data: Coal Production, 1853 to 2019: https://www.gov.uk/government/statistical-data-sets/historical-coal-data-coal-production-availability-and-consumption.
[85] Ewan Gibbs, *Coal Country: The Meaning and Memory of Deindustrialization in Postwar Scotland* (London: University of London Press, 2021).
[86] David Waddington, Chas Critcher, Bella Dicks, and David Parry, *Out of the Ashes: The Social Impact of Industrial Contraction and Regeneration on Britain's Mining Communities* (London: The Stationery Office in association with the Regional Studies Association, 2001), 59–60.
[87] Christina Beatty and Steve Fothergill, 'Labour Market Adjustment in Areas of Chronic Industrial Decline: The Case of the UK Coalfields', *Regional Studies*, 30 (1996), 637–50; Beatty and Fothergill, *The Contemporary Labour Market in Britain's Older Industrial Towns* (Sheffield: Sheffield Hallam University Centre for Economic Research/Joseph Rowntree Foundation, 2018), 28–30; Huw Beynon and Ray Hudson, *The Shadow of the Mine: Coal and the End of Industrial Britain* (London: Verso, 2021), 258–62.
[88] Waddington et al., *Out of the Ashes*, 49–52.

of jobs, but 'finding suitable work with acceptable pay and conditions'.[89] Local authorities in ex-mining areas such as Blaenau Gwent, Merthyr Tydfil, Rhondda Cynon Taf, Caerphilly, Torfaen, Mansfield, North and East Ayrshire, Barnsley, and Rotherham were all in the top fifty districts (out of 378) in terms of estimated real unemployment rates.[90] Many of our interviewees resented the fact that their sons were forced to move away if they wanted to find the sort of reasonably well-paid industrial labour that was coded as 'men's work'. This was particularly pronounced in the South Wales valleys, where many echoed Christine Harvey's sentiments that 'most people have to leave the valley to find work'.[91] Some women used the phrase 'industrial gypsies' to describe such men.[92] Siobhan McMahon, interviewed by Ewan Gibbs in 2014, described the changes in Bellshill, North Lanarkshire thus: 'the jobs aren't coming to the area anymore. And when they do come, it's what I would, it's not, it's not the same type of jobs, not the skilled jobs that you required to keep people'.[93]

Many miners who were made redundant experienced stress, anxiety, boredom, and loss of a sense of purpose: one reported to Waddington et al. in the early 1990s that '[w]hen I was working, my life was sort of arranged. Whereas, when I finished, all that arrangement in my life had gone and there was a bit of a hole to fill that was normally filled at the pit. I sort of hit the bottle.'[94] In some cases, pit closures propelled men into a crisis of masculinity. One of Waddington et al.'s interviewees in Brodsworth, near Doncaster, described the 'constant agitation' of worrying about money now that he was unemployed, and described his response to the stress:

I stopped smoking for five years and I've started again... Everybody says, 'My dad's grumpy.' If I'm that way inclined, I just go barmy with them all—if they don't move a cup, or knife, or anything like that, I go absolutely crazy... Very, very irrational in my behaviour, temper-wise.[95]

The fact that his wife was 'keeping' him added yet another layer of anxiety and anger, and the researchers suggested that they had found similar reactions in many of the men they interviewed. Unemployment had implications not only for families' living standards, but also for men's sense of self-worth—and their relationships with their wives.

Patterns of women's paid labour changed in these years, along with men's. Women are rarely prominent in accounts of deindustrialisation and its victims;

---

[89] Beatty and Fothergill, *Contemporary Labour Market*, 33. [90] Ibid.
[91] Christine Harvey, b. 1950, South Wales, interviewed by Florence Sutcliffe-Braithwaite, 14 August 2018.
[92] Janice Bartolo, b. 1957, Margaret Davis, b. 1949, and Kay Sutcliffe, b. 1949, all Kent, interviewed by Florence Sutcliffe-Braithwaite and Natalie Thomlinson, 5 March 2016.
[93] Gibbs, *Coal Country*, 97.   [94] Waddington et al., *Out of the Ashes*, 38.   [95] Ibid., 40.

but female employment was also dealt a blow by pit closures. Female NCB employees in colliery offices and canteens were, of course, made redundant, and some felt the loss of their jobs deeply. One anonymous woman from Askern who had worked in the pit canteen there told Waddington et al. that her new life was 'boring beyond belief':

> It's just the same jobs every day... I just wouldn't have left the pit. I couldn't have wished for a better job... If you've got troubles now, there's no-one to help you through them. Everything happened at once—my dad died, his mum died, and then [my husband] had his heart attack—all at once. The men kept me going because they knew you, they know your life, they know your relations. You've still got friends but it's not the same... If they could open that canteen up tomorrow, it would make my life worth living; but they're not going to. I wish it had never shut.[96]

Men were not the only ones to miss the camaraderie of the pit. Moreover, men made redundant from the pits moved into manufacturing jobs, crowding out women from such employment, and pushing them into the service sector, where jobs were often less secure and less well-paid.[97] With pit closures came general economic decline, which impacted women's work in local shops and other businesses. These effects were most obvious in areas that had been heavily dependent on the pits: miners and their families living in more mixed areas were likely to have access to a greater variety of employment options. Waddington et al. found that female employment had declined substantially in the three mining villages in Yorkshire, Nottinghamshire, and Derbyshire that they examined in the late 1980s. In 1984, 39 per cent of women were in paid employment, but by 1988 it was just 29 per cent, and almost all of these were working part-time.[98]

Across the period from shortly after the end of the Second World War to the present, the rate of married women's participation in the paid labour force has followed an upward trajectory across Britain as a whole. As we saw in Chapter 2, working motherhood was normalised to a significant extent in the coalfields by 1984.[99] Unsurprisingly, then, even if the closure of pits hit women's employment in the short-term, over time, as the loss of industry in the coalfields decreased men's employment opportunities, more women entered the workforce in order to

---

[96] Ibid., 97.
[97] Fernando M. Aragón, Juan Pablo Rud, and Gerhard Toews, 'Resource Shocks, Employment, and Gender: Evidence from the Collapse of the UK Coal Industry', *Labour Economics*, 52 (2018), 54–67.
[98] David Waddington, Maggie Wykes, and Chas Critcher, *Split at the Seams? Community, Continuity and Change after the 1984–5 Coal Dispute* (Milton Keynes: Open University Press, 1991), 78.
[99] Helen McCarthy, *Double Lives: A History of Working Motherhood* (London: Bloomsbury, 2020); see also Chapter 2.

shore up their families' living standards. When Waddington et al. revisited the Doncaster coalfield in 1992–3, they found that 50 per cent of the wives of present and past miners in their survey were in paid employment, and just 45 per cent were housewives—a significant increase in employment levels compared with the late 1980s data, and in step with the national trend in the same period.[100] Women's employment clustered in low-paid jobs, and particularly in the service sector. Some women found more secure and better-paid work in administrative roles, or in the expanding welfare state and third sector, including, from 1999 onwards, in organisations funded by the Coalfields Regeneration Trust (CRT), which was created to tackle the economic and social problems created by the loss of the mining industry. Most women's work, however, was in unskilled and semi-skilled jobs. In Waddington et al.'s survey in the early 1990s, of the wives currently in employment, 58.8 per cent were in caring, catering, or retail jobs, 21.7 per cent were doing domestic labour, factory work, or other labouring or manual work, and the remaining 19.5 per cent were doing managerial or office work, or were self-employed or in another form of work.[101] Women's work did not make up for the loss of well-paid men's jobs in mining. Waddington et al. concluded in 2001 that 'women's employment opportunities in mining communities remain restricted and cannot be expanded to compensate for the loss of male jobs'.[102] After the closure of the pits, coalfield areas like Easington and the local authorities in the South Wales valleys emerged as among the top ten most deprived places in the UK.[103]

As we will see in Chapter 8, the strike was framed by some women, particularly activists, as a moment which propelled them into new employment afterwards. In fact, there were many factors distinct from strike activism which could effect such a change. At the start of 1984, Pippa Morgan*, from South Wales, was married, with a young son, and a 'really controlling' husband.[104] The pressure on their family finances led to a gradual role reversal during the strike, however, as Pippa's husband took over the childcare, while she took on more work as an Avon rep, and got two new jobs—one as a carer, the other as a supermarket worker. Pippa recalled that working in the supermarket with older women, she began to discover that 'there's a big world out there'. After the strike she continued to work, but had to resume responsibility for the home and childcare. She felt strongly, however, that her experiences in the strike had given her a sense that 'you could do things outside, you could do—there was a life', and that she 'wanted to do more'. Several years after the strike she divorced her husband and subsequently had an interesting and varied career.[105] The strike, here, was the trigger for later changes in

---

[100] Waddington et al., *Out of the Ashes*, 55. (The sample included 196 women. The other 5 per cent were unemployed, in education, or retired.)
[101] Ibid., 56.   [102] Ibid., 57.   [103] Beynon and Hudson, *Shadow of the Mine*, 266.
[104] Pippa Morgan*, b. 1962, South Wales, interviewed by Natalie Thomlinson, 13 August 2018.
[105] Ibid.

Pippa's life, but rather than activism, it was the more prosaic experience of paid labour, earning her own money, and dealing with bills, that made the difference.

Several strike activists—perhaps unsurprisingly given the commitment to their communities they had displayed during the dispute—went into community work of one sort or another after the strike's end. Anne Kirby, for example, a dedicated activist in Cowdenbeath, ultimately went on to work for youth support service Connexions, in a homelessness unit, for social justice charity Nacro, working with young people who had dropped out of school or been to prison, and for Cumbria County Council, working on restorative justice.[106] It should be noted, however, that being a strike supporter or strike activist was far from the only route into work in community development or youth engagement. One of our interviewees, Robyn*, who had in fact worked through the strike in an administrative role at the NCB, later worked for the CRT.[107] Striking miner's wife 'Charlotte', interviewed in 2007 for Yvette Taylor's 'Coalface to Carpark' project, was hostile to the strike and the women's support movement, but far from unsupportive of her local community—in 2007 she worked in community development in her area.[108] Activists and non-activists, supporters and opponents of the strike were all caught up in the general trend pushing more coalfield women into paid employment in the late twentieth and early twenty-first centuries. Inevitably, some coalfield women found work tackling the very social problems that the closure of pits and loss of employment bred.

Sociologists studying mining communities in the years immediately after the strike concluded that changes in gender roles within the home during the strike had been, in the main, temporary. The project led by Waddington et al. in the 1980s found that, in the three villages in Yorkshire, Nottinghamshire, and Derbyshire that they surveyed in 1987–8, most women thought things had gone 'back to the old ways'.[109] During the strike, only 10–11 per cent of women in each village reported changes in gender roles in the home.[110] Afterwards, the team found six women in 'Yorksco' who had been supporters of the strike and who felt that there had been domestic changes because of their activism: of these, however, five felt that after the strike gender roles had reverted to normal; in 'Derbyco' seven out of nine felt roles had reverted back; and in 'Nottsco' four out of five.[111] When men were back in work, the division of paid and domestic labour tended to revert to what it had been before—that is, a strongly gendered division of labour, though, as Waddington et al. emphasised, before 1984, there was already 'a degree of male

---

[106] Anne Kirby; see also, e.g., Theresa Gratton*, b. 1955, North East England, interviewed by Florence Sutcliffe-Braithwaite, 22 February 2020.
[107] Robyn*, b. 1963, Yorkshire, interviewed by Victoria Dawson, 26 July 2018.
[108] 'Charlotte', interview 009, in Yvette Taylor, 'From the Coalface to the Car Park? The Intersection of Class and Gender in Women's Lives in the North East, 2007–2009' (data collection), 2012, UK Data Service, SN: 7053.
[109] Waddington et al., *Split at the Seams?*, 89.   [110] Ibid., 82–4.   [111] Ibid., 195.

involvement in domestic life at variance with the stereotype of the traditional miner'.[112] Dennis Warwick and Gary Littlejohn's study of four mining communities in the Featherstone and Hemsworth areas of West Yorkshire came to similar conclusions. In their post-strike surveys, 29 per cent of women said there had been a change during and since the strike in the division of labour in their households, but of these, less than half—46 per cent—attributed it to the strike, while the others gave reasons like ill-health, retirement, and taking up employment.[113] Changes were slightly more common among women who had agreed with the strike, but no more likely among those who had been activists compared with those who had not been.[114] Even where women started going out to work, men were likely to take on only a small portion of the domestic labour—as one study found, women still did the housework, but less often and to a less high standard.[115]

Sometimes changes in patterns of childcare were generational as much as gendered: Tim Strangleman found that in Easington District, older miners who were made redundant in the 1990s sometimes helped out their own children by taking on more responsibility for grandchildren, to enable their sons and daughters to work more hours and make up for the loss of secure earnings from the pit.[116] Overall, it seems likely that the division of domestic labour has shifted only a limited extent in response to growing levels of women's paid labour. We know that nationally, men generally do more around the house than they did thirty years ago, but women still take on the majority of the work and the responsibility for the work of childcare, cooking, and cleaning; it is probable that the same is true in coalfield communities.[117]

As we saw above, developing women's skills in order to enable them to start their own small businesses or take up new job opportunities was one of the key goals of organisations like the DOVE Workshop and Castleford Women's Centre that grew out of women's strike organising. After the strike, many activists saw education as a key need of coalfield women, and several of our interviewees discussed returning to education in the aftermath of the strike.[118] In doing so, they were swimming with the general tide: the period from the 1970s to the mid-1990s was a 'golden age' for women—particularly working-class women—returning to further and higher education as mature students.[119] It was free, and grants were available. Women from the baby boom generation often looked back

---

[112] Ibid., 82.
[113] Dennis Warwick and Gary Littlejohn, *Coal, Capital and Culture: A Sociological Analysis of Mining Communities in West Yorkshire* (London: Routledge, 1992), 194.
[114] Ibid.
[115] Measham and Allen, 'In Defence', 40–1 (this is based on data from Warwick and Littlejohn's study).
[116] Tim Strangleman, 'Networks, Place and Identities in Post-Industrial Mining Communities', *International Journal of Urban and Regional Research*, 25 (2001), 253–67, at 260, 262.
[117] McCarthy, *Double Lives*, 154–5.   [118] E.g. Pat Smith; Anne Kirby.
[119] Eve Worth, 'Women, Education and Social Mobility in Britain during the Long 1970s', *Cultural and Social History*, 16 (2019), 67–83.

with regret on the shortcomings of the education they had received at school, and, given their tendency to have children early and limit their family size, many found themselves without heavy caring responsibilities by the time they were in their late thirties or forties. Furthermore, faced with an increasingly difficult labour market, many women recognised that gaining new skills would be a way to find better-paid and more rewarding work.

The loss of the pits affected social infrastructure, with the decline of working men's clubs, miners' welfares, and community organisations like brass bands; the lack of a strong local economic base had a knock-on effect on shops, pubs, and other local businesses.[120] The much-discussed 'decline of the high street' has been a general trend in deindustrialising Britain, and although this has not been caused only by the loss of industry—the growth of car-ownership, women's paid labour, and out-of-town shopping centres have all been significant factors, too—ex-mining areas have often been hit particularly hard; many women saw this as emblematic of the decline of their communities.[121] Theresa Gratton* remembered of County Durham, where she had lived all her life, that:

> Horden... was a vibrant, thriving community and now, you have to walk down the streets and they're boarded up and it's just incredibly depressing and when I go down Easington front street... I go past the shops and I just want to cry. It looks like the land of the lost, it looks depressed, it looks disadvantaged and it is.[122]

Similarly, Kay Case remembered of Treharris that:

> We haven't got a community in Treharris anymore. A lot of the shops have shut, the men have drifted, a lot of them didn't work again, they went to work in other industries, but Treharris itself, I don't know that I'm any different but Treharris itself is certainly different. It isn't the community it was when we... up until they closed the pits. Down there now, if you go down there now, I think we've got about four or five kebab, Chinese and chip shops. The Co-op is still there, but right along we had... there was a lot of shops at the time of the strike, a lot of shops. They may have shut anyway because... different reasons, out-of-town shopping, I don't know, but they seemed to me to fade away after the... we lost the colliery.[123]

---

[120] John Tomaney, Lucy Natarajan, and Florence Sutcliffe-Braithwaite, *Sacriston: Towards a Deeper Understanding of Place* (London: UCL Bartlett School of Planning, 2021).
[121] Ibid.
[122] Theresa Gratton*, b. 1955, North East England, interviewed by Florence Sutcliffe-Braithwaite, 22 February 2020.
[123] Kay Case.

In line with the general trend in the UK in the 1980s and 1990s, inequality in coalfield areas has also increased. Pit closures entailed the loss of relatively well-paid manual work. Subsequently, a degree of economic polarisation took place within these communities, as some ex-miners and their wives did relatively well—going into secure jobs in the public sector, for example, or starting their own businesses—while others were trapped on benefits or in low-paid and insecure work. Pit villages also fared differently depending on where they were: isolated villages often suffered serious decline, but those with an attractive location, particularly with good road or rail links, saw new developments of private housing spring up. The houses in these developments were often attractively priced to relatively affluent outsiders, whose lifestyles were often primarily car-based, and who had little interest in spending time or money in the villages where they lived.[124]

Residents of former mining communities suffered disproportionately from poor health. Mining left a legacy of health issues, including pneumoconiosis, caused by coal dust damaging the lungs, myocarditis, TB, bronchitis, emphysema, and asthma.[125] In 2011, 10 per cent of residents in South Wales, and 9 per cent of those in County Durham, said that their health was 'bad or very bad', compared to just 4 per cent in South East England.[126] 'Diseases of despair' also disproportionately affected former coalfield areas; in 2013, one in every six residents of Blaenau Gwent was on anti-depressants.[127] Chronic substance abuse also became a significant problem. In the early twenty-first century, the MP for the former mining district of Bassetlaw, in Nottinghamshire, John Mann, claimed that research he had commissioned showed that one in three households in the area had been directly affected by heroin addiction, through either the addiction of a household member, or through being the victim of drug-related crime.[128]

With the loss of the strike, the power of the NUM, which in 1974 had brought down Ted Heath's Conservative government, was severely diminished. It faced the challenge of the breakaway UDM. As pits closed and the workforce dwindled, the NUM's significance as a political force in coalfield areas declined; 1992 was the last year in which it sponsored Labour Party MPs. The period from the 1970s onwards saw a gradual 'dealignment' in class voting patterns across the UK, including in the coalfields.[129] The strength of Labour Party support in coalfield areas in its mid-twentieth-century heyday was such that for many years, most ex-mining areas continued to elect Labour MPs; but the beginnings of the shift that culminated in

---

[124] Tomaney et al., *Sacriston*.   [125] Beynon and Hudson, *Shadow of the Mine*, 275.
[126] Ibid., 257.   [127] Ibid., 258.
[128] 'Mining Towns Hit Hard by Heroin', BBC, 18 October 2002: http://news.bbc.co.uk/1/hi/england/2338623.stm. See also, e.g., Matthew Beard, 'Agencies in Dock over Mining Villages Ravaged by Heroin, *Independent*, 18 September 2002; Martin Wainwright, 'Former Pit Towns Say No to Drug Addiction', *Guardian*, 21 July 2004.
[129] Bo Särlvik and Ivor Crewe, *Decade of Dealignment: The Conservative Victory of 1979 and Electoral Trends in the 1970s* (Cambridge: Cambridge University Press, 1983); see also Chapter 2.

2019 with the so-called 'crumbling of the red wall' were already evident before the strike.[130] In 2019, many constituencies like Don Valley, in South Yorkshire—which had been represented by NUM-sponsored MPs until 1992—turned blue; but the change had been a long time coming. Where, between 1945 and 1966, over 70 per cent of votes at General Elections in Don Valley had been for Labour, thereafter Labour MPs were elected with much smaller majorities, and on lower turnouts—in 2010, Caroline Flint was elected with under 40 per cent of the vote.

In parallel with dealignment in class voting patterns, the late twentieth and early twenty-first centuries saw a 'feminisation' of politics, particularly of left-wing politics, as feminists demanded that the left take seriously women's issues, and ultimately entered into the Labour Party, aiming to change its predominantly masculine culture.[131] In the aftermath of the strike, there were some high-profile examples of women entering Labour Party politics. Most dramatically, Siân James attended university and eventually became MP for Swansea East.[132] As we have seen, Siân was keen to emphasise in her interview with us that she had been 'very, very content as a housewife'; she constructed her story within a heroic narrative framework of the strike as an emancipation and a political awakening. It is important to recognise that Siân had, in fact, been involved in politics—both in the Labour Party and in CND—before the strike. Yet Siân clearly did feel strongly that her engagement with politics after the strike was qualitatively different to her engagement with politics before it. Her story was hardly typical, but other women also became more actively involved in electoral politics. Margot Russell, a member of Dalkeith Miners and Women's Support Group, had got to know NUM official Eric Clarke during the strike, and volunteered for his campaign to be elected as MP for Midlothian in 1992; Clarke subsequently asked Russell to go to work for him, and she also became a local councillor in 1999.[133] Others did not stand for election, but got involved in other ways: Aggie Currie, for example, went canvassing for Labour after the strike.[134] Meg Allen also found that, among the forty-five deeply-involved strike activists she interviewed, engagement in politics increased after the strike (though it also seemed to have faded somewhat over time). All the women Allen interviewed continued to be active in politics in some way after the strike, and among her sample, Labour Party membership increased from nine women before the strike to twenty-one afterwards.[135] For a small minority of women, involvement in the strike could change or at least develop their sense of

---

[130] See James Kanagasooriam and Elizabeth Simon, 'Red Wall: The Definitive Description', *Political Insight*, 12 (2021), 8–11.

[131] Sarah Perrigo, 'Gender Struggles in the British Labour Party from 1979 to 1995', *Party Politics*, 1 (1995), 407–17.

[132] Siân James, b. 1959, South Wales, interviewed by Florence Sutcliffe-Braithwaite, 5 February 2019.

[133] Russell, interviewed by Bell; see also Ian MacDougall, *Voices from Work and Home: Personal Recollections of Working Life and Labour Struggles in the Twentieth Century by Scots Men and Women* (Edinburgh: Mercat Press, 2000), 146–7.

[134] Aggie Currie. [135] Allen, 'Carrying on the Strike', 75–6.

themselves, allowing them to see themselves as people who *could* play a significant role in the 'political' arena.

Some strike activists also continued to engage in politics in other ways, outside electoral politics. One member of Lothian Women's Support Group got involved in the local unemployed workers' centre.[136] Among our interviewees, Rita Wakefield and her daughters Wendy Minney and Kim Hickling all developed an interest in animal welfare and became vegetarians; Wendy attended CND marches and helped set up an anti-poll tax union.[137] Meg Allen found that, among her forty-five interviewees, the number of women involved in community campaigns increased from nine to thirteen, and in social movement activism from three to ten, including involvement in 'Mines not Missiles', and environmental campaigns about opencast mining. There was also a small increase in activism on 'feminist' issues, with one woman becoming involved in the Rape Crisis Centre set up in Barnsley after the strike.[138] Jean Spence and Carol Stephenson found, in research conducted between 2002 and 2004 with a small group of women who had been deeply involved in strike activism in North East England, that levels of political engagement had remained high. The authors acknowledged that these were the women who were most likely to have remained politically active, but pointed out, significantly, 'their continuing commitment to an ideal of community activism focused on the traditional female location in the neighbourhood': where they got involved in formal politics, these women tended to favour the role of parish councillor (a role that is often not party-political) focusing their work on the hyper-local, the neighbourhood and immediate community.[139]

Conclusion

The end of the strike did not bring an immediate easing of the pressures and difficulties that most striking families faced: far from it, many women and men now faced the prospect of having to repay the debts they had accrued. It is perhaps unsurprising that many coalfield women wanted to get 'back to normal' for their families. Even among strike activists who wanted to build on the political work and education they had begun to develop during the strike, there was a recognition that not all their fellow activists felt the same. Small numbers of activists wanted to keep the movement going, and worked hard to keep NWAPC alive,

---

[136] Lothian Women's Support Group, *Women Living the Strike* (Dalkeith: Lothian Women's Support Group, 1986), 54.
[137] Rita Wakefield, b. 1943, Kim Hickling, b. 1962, and Wendy Minney, b. 1964, all Nottinghamshire, interviewed by Natalie Thomlinson, 20 August 2018.
[138] Allen, 'Carrying on the Strike', 75–6.
[139] Jean Spence and Carol Stephenson, 'The Politics of the Doorstep: Female Survival Strategies and the Legacy of the Miners' Strike 1984–5', *Community, Work and Family*, 10 (2007), 309–27, at 314.

either to continue the work of supporting the NUM, or as a broader-based movement to campaign for coalfield communities. But the project faltered within a few years. The challenges of keeping such a movement going—of determining its goals in the aftermath of the loss of the strike, of keeping women motivated and engaged once the urgent pressure to organise self-help in the strike was gone— were simply too great. The legacy of the activism was seen, however, seven years later, when some of the women who had been involved in the movement mobilised quickly to set up pit camps to contest the final major round of pit closures proposed by John Major's government.

In the decades after the strike, coalfield communities suffered from high levels of unemployment, inadequate numbers of secure, reasonably well-paid manual jobs, poor health, and problems with addiction. They endured significant levels of economic deprivation and decaying social infrastructure. In all this, the coalfields mirrored the many other areas of the UK where the industrial base had collapsed in the 1980s and 1990s. Because mining communities were often distant from major cities—the locus of much economic growth in the late twentieth and early twenty-first centuries—they tended to fare particularly badly.[140] In line with the UK as a whole, coalfield areas became far more unequal, and, also in line with the rest of the UK, their politics changed, with a gradual dealignment between class and voting. All these changes had complex knock-on effects for women. Women's employment levels were reduced in the years immediately after the strike, but ultimately continued on their pre-strike upward trajectory, and gender roles within the home were impacted by that change (though the gendered division of labour was generally not radically re-engineered). Some miners' wives took up opportunities in education and in politics after the strike. In all this, coalfield women were in line with general trends affecting working-class women in Britain in this period. As we will see in Chapter 8, some strike activists framed their experiences in the strike as transformative, drawing on culturally-dominant narratives that emphasised the strike as a driver of change in women's lives. But we should not lose sight of the fact that many of the changes in women's lives in the coalfields in the decades after the strike had roots in pre-strike trends, and that the experiences of women, families, and communities were profoundly shaped by the implications of the closure of pits, which rippled through the coalfields and caused so much pain.

---

[140] On cities as engines of growth, see: Ron Martin, Peter Sunley, Peter Tyler, and Ben Gardiner, 'Divergent Cities in Post-Industrial Britain', *Cambridge Journal of Regions, Economy and Society*, 9 (2016), 269–99.

8
Remembering the Strike

11 September 2014

Maureen Coates, the first interviewee for this project, welcomes us warmly into her Doncaster home alongside her husband Jimmy. He is on oxygen for severe emphysema, a legacy of his time at Brodsworth pit. The area is familiar to Natalie, who grew up a five minute walk away; Maureen is the aunt of a family friend who has kindly put us in touch, knowing of our desire to find women willing to talk about their experiences during the strike. We do not quite know what we will find; we know that Maureen was active in supporting the strike, but not about her life before or since. The hours we spend with her in many ways prefigure the next eighty or so interviews we will conduct alongside our postdoctoral research associate, Victoria Dawson: Maureen gives generously of her time to tell us of her life and her strike experiences, remembering events both happy and sad, at pains to try to give us an account that conveys her feelings about the things she went through, and the truth as she sees it.

How did women remember the strike and its aftermath? For Maureen, as for many women, the process of remembering these events was shot through with ambivalence. She told us that, 'it were a bad time, but it were a good time, because everybody pulled together'.[1] For those who had been involved in activism, the emotional intensity of the experience often made it one of the stand-out events of their lives: 'the best of times and the worst of times' as one interviewee put it.[2] A number of women even felt that their lives had been transformed by the experience. But there was little doubt of the stress that the dispute had imposed upon individuals, families, and communities. Some women—particularly those who had not been involved in supporting the strike—found it difficult to look back on the year with any fondness.

Immediately after the strike, many groups from the women's support movement created and published their own accounts of their activism, in order to write the achievements of the movement into history. In the media and in popular culture, women's experiences have only become more prominent over the years in

---

[1] Maureen Coates, b. 1942, Yorkshire, interviewed by Florence Sutcliffe-Braithwaite and Natalie Thomlinson, 11 September 2014.
[2] Margaret Holmes, b. 1942, Kent, interviewed by Florence Sutcliffe-Braithwaite, 26 July 2018. This formulation was also used by George, husband of Christina Bell, b. 1949, North East England/ Nottinghamshire, interviewed by Victoria Dawson, 27 June 2018.

representations of the miners' strike. These representations have usually focused on activism, and have constructed a heroic narrative of miners' wives emancipated through their work in support groups. This narrative impacted on how many of our interviewees—particularly those who were involved in activism—remembered their own experiences: some women used this narrative as a way of articulating what they felt to be the significance of the strike, and the changes they had seen in their lives since. This narrative, however, was never hegemonic, and other women—both supporters and opponents of the strike—contested it, drawing on a range of alternative cultural discourses to give an account of themselves.

Most coalfield women we interviewed felt the mining communities they had grown up in had now changed beyond recognition. For some, the strike has become a symbol through which the wider changes that deindustrialisation has wrought on communities can be articulated. The deep sense of loss that was expressed in many testimonies was palpable; almost all our interviewees talked of the pain they felt about the closure of the pits and the loss of a certain version of community, whether they were for or against the strike. Joblessness and attendant social issues such as chronic ill health, crime, and addiction, have bedevilled coalfield areas since the 1980s, and on almost all measures over the last thirty years, such communities have ranked as some of the most deprived in Britain. There was good reason why activists had claimed during the strike that to 'close a pit' was to 'kill a community'. Yet laments for the loss of community have been a common trope not just for decades, but for centuries.[3] We need to recognise, as Jon Lawrence has argued, the ways in which community has evolved rather than disappeared in the twenty-first century, while taking seriously the incipient political critiques in these complaints.[4]

Writing the Story of the Strike

After the strike, many groups in the women's support movement wrote their own stories, and these books became important conduits through which narratives of the strike became politically embedded within leftist circles. During the strike, women's creativity had been celebrated in the large quantities of strike poetry and songs that were produced: these were often performed at meetings and shared in newsletters and broadsides, and filmmaker Ken Loach also produced a film of miners and their wives performing strike poetry and songs, shown on Channel 4.[5] A few groups, like Barnsley Women Against Pit Closures (WAPC), published

---

[3] Stefan Ramsden, *Working Class Community in the Age of Affluence* (London: Routledge, 2017); Jon Lawrence, *Me, Me, Me? The Search for Community in Post-War England* (Oxford: Oxford University Press, 2019), 1–18.

[4] Ibid.

[5] See Jean McCrindle, 'The National Organisation of Women Against Pit Closures in the Miners' Strike of 1984–5' (unpublished PhD thesis, Oxford Brookes, 2001), 182, for Loach's film. For discussion

accounts of their work while the strike was still ongoing.⁶ After its end, there was an outpouring of books and pamphlets about women's strike activism, based on women's written and oral accounts. These were often produced as part of the campaign for sacked and victimised miners: publications were sold at local political events and in radical bookshops to raise funds for the cause. But women's writing was also often motivated by a larger leftist project: it was an attempt to ensure that the mobilisation of women in the strike had a lasting legacy of education and politicisation, and to ensure that the achievements of the women's groups were recognised and recorded.

One of the biggest and most consciously political projects aiming to capture the experiences of activist coalfield women was that which resulted in the 1986 publication *The Cutting Edge*, led by left activist and Sheffield Polytechnic lecturer Vicky Seddon. Women from across the coalfields gathered at Northern College to help produce the work, which emphasised the struggles women had had with men in the National Union of Mineworkers (NUM) and the lasting achievements of activist women, claiming 'communities have been forced to accede to them a right to gather together in public places and to organise themselves'.⁷ Seddon wrote in her introduction that the movement represented the 'flowering of the mining women' and 'the fruit of the current phase of the movement for women's liberation' (though other contributors were more sceptical of the framing of the support movement as 'feminist').⁸ The London Region Co-operative Retail Services Political Committee also funded a major book, *Here We Go!*, charting and celebrating the women's movement, based on interviews with women from Yorkshire, Kent, Derbyshire, Nottinghamshire, and South Wales.⁹ Researched by Chrys Salt and edited by Salt and Jim Layzell, the book told the story of the movement through a patchwork of unattributed excerpts from the interviews, organised and introduced by the editors.¹⁰ Like Seddon's collection, Salt and Layzell painted a complex, but ultimately celebratory picture of the women's support movement. They showed, for example, that women had ambiguous views of 'feminism', quoting one as saying, '[w]e've become feminists in our own kind of way but

---

of poems, their sale and circulation, see Jean Spence and Carol Stephenson, 'Pies and Essays: Women Writing through the British 1984-5 Coal Miners' Strike', *Gender, Place & Culture: A Journal of Feminist Geography*, 20 (2013), 218-35.

⁶ Barnsley Women Against Pit Closures, *Barnsley Women Against Pit Closures, Volume 2* (Barnsley: Barnsley Women Against Pit Closures, 1985), 35. North Yorkshire Women Against Pit Closures, *Strike 84/85* (Leeds: North Yorkshire Women Against Pit Closures, 1985) was also written in the final months of the strike.

⁷ Vicky Seddon, ed., *The Cutting Edge: Women and the Pit Strike* (London: Lawrence & Wishart, 1986), 12.

⁸ Ibid., 15; Sandra Taylor, 'Grub Up for the Miners!', in Seddon, ed., *Cutting Edge*, 79-96.

⁹ Chrys Salt and Jim Layzell, *Here We Go: Women's Memories of the 1984-5 Miners Strike* (London: Co-operative Retail Services, 1985).

¹⁰ Some of the interviews for the book are held in the Betty Heathfield collection in the Women's Library@LSE, and Heathfield wrote the final chapter, 'The Way Forward'.

we're not true feminists'—yet still entitled the chapter in which they cited this quote, 'Grass Roots Feminism'.[11]

Individual women's groups and regional networks also produced their own accounts; it is difficult to put an exact figure on the number of books of this kind that were produced, but there were at least several dozen. They were generally much shorter than the substantial works edited by Seddon and Salt and Layzell, and usually published by local radical presses that were part of the worker-writer and community publishing movement, which often gave significant aid in the writing and production of these books.[12] The Normanton and Altofts Support Group's book was produced with the aid of local community publishing group Artivan, with the women noting in the text that 'without their help we would never have written and published *Striking Figures*'.[13] A few of these works centred on communities, encompassing the experiences of men and women in the strike, but the majority focused on women alone.[14] Some were produced by a single author, usually an activist with a high level of education, who interviewed women, and constructed the narrative.[15] But most were produced collectively, and took the form of collage, often including prose, poetry, drawings, and photos, giving a platform to a range of women's voices. These books often followed a formula, interspersing potted biographies of group members with retellings of key events in a group's history, such as the start of the strike, setting up soup kitchens, the daily work of feeding and fundraising, the exhilaration of marches and rallies, standing on picket lines, organising for Christmas, trips abroad, and the end of the strike. They described not only the activism women had undertaken but the impact of the strike—and of their activism—on women's home life, their emotions, and their sense of self, mixing descriptions of collective action with individual women's testimonies. These books generally had a less overtly political framework

---

[11] Salt and Layzell, *Here We Go!*, 78.

[12] E.g. Lothian Women's Support Group, *Women Living the Strike* (Dalkeith: Lothian Women's Support Group, 1986); Barnsley Miners' Wives Action Group, *We Struggled to Laugh* (Barnsley: Barnsley Miners' Wives Action Group, 1987); Gwen Newton, ed., *We are Women, We are Strong: The Stories of Northumberland Miners' Wives 1984–85* (Northumberland: The People Themselves, 1985); North Yorkshire Women Against Pit Closures, *Strike 84/85*; Sheffield Women Against Pit Closures, *We are Women, We are Strong* (Sheffield: Sheffield Women Against Pit Closures, 1987); *The Last Coals of Spring: Poems, Stories and Songs by the Women of Easington Colliery* (Durham: Durham Voices, 1985); Joan Witham, *Hearts and Minds: The Story of the Women of Nottinghamshire in the Miners' Strike, 1984–1985* (London: Canary, 1986). On the explosion of the worker-writer and community publishing movement, see Tom Woodin, *Working-Class Writing and Publishing in the Late Twentieth Century: Literature, Culture and Community* (Manchester: Manchester University Press, 2018).

[13] Janine Head, Mavis Watson, and Teresa Webb, *Striking Figures: The Story of Normanton and Altofts Miners Support Group 1984-5* (Huddersfield: Artivan and Striking Figures, 1986), 30, 33.

[14] For an example looking at women and men, see: Worsborough Community Group, *The Heart and Soul of It* (Huddersfield: Worsborough Community Group and Bannerworks, 1985).

[15] E.g. Jane Thornton, *All the Fun of the Fight* (Doncaster: Doncaster Library Service, c.1987), produced as part of a writer's placement by the Yorkshire Arts Service; Witham, *Hearts and Minds*, produced by a lecturer in education who had been involved in Newark Miners' Support Group and the Nottinghamshire Women's Support Group.

than *The Cutting Edge* or *Here We Go!*; they often related tales of working closely with the NUM, and some did not even mention feminism or women's liberation. Though they gave space to a range of perspectives, collectively, they played an important role in celebrating and cementing a particular heroic narrative of the women's movement.

Within the potted biographies, activists tended to be presented as 'ordinary' women: Mavis Watson from Normanton recounted that, '[b]efore the strike I was a typical wife and mother. My husband worked shifts and I was there breakfast, dinner, tea. I'd clean the house, bake, sew, walk the kids to and from school, I didn't think I had time for anything else.'[16] The strike was often presented as a moment which occasioned deep personal change. An Ashington woman whose memories were recorded in a collection of stories from Northumberland miners' wives said:

> at one time I wouldn't dream of doing or saying half the things that I do now. I've got the confidence now to go out and just do whatever I'm thinking of. I could never give a speech or anything like that or even take over the chair but now I have that confidence.[17]

These books often presented the women's support movement as a more-or-less spontaneous uprising of working-class women. Sally from the Coventry Miners' Wives Support Group remembered that:

> This is to me the best way where I can answer about the change in women.
>
> It is the only occasion during the strike where women came out of every corner of Great Britain and for the first time we could see where our solidarity stood.
>
> 40 000 women left their homes, families and roles as housewives to let their sisters know what they too were doing in their areas about this long and hard fight.
>
> You can only see your small area and look at a friend and smile inside, 'My God, she's actually sticking up for herself', or that woman helping in the kitchen thinking, 'How the hell do we manage to cook for all these people', or 'Oh look at her and she was the quiet one, good on you.'[18]

In North Yorkshire WAPC's *Strike 84/85*, one woman remembered that:

---

[16] Head et al., *Striking Figures*, 26; see also Newton, ed., *We are Women, We are Strong*, 14.
[17] Ibid., 48.
[18] Coventry Miners' Wives Support Group, *Mummy... What Did You Do in the Strike?* (Coventry: Coventry Miners' Wives Support Group, 1986), 56.

> When this strike began, it was only a matter of a few weeks before the women saw that it didn't just concern the men it also concerned the women and our children. Maggie got a big shock. She expected the women to sit back begging for our men to go back to work. But we didn't. We stood up and shouted, 'Don't dare threaten our miners' jobs! Don't dare threaten our mining communities! And don't dare threaten our children's futures!'[19]

Coalfield women were presented as standing up, as emerging into the public sphere—as *becoming visible* for the first time as political agents. Though feminism was rarely mentioned, the strike was generally configured as a moment of, if not women's collective liberation, then at least *personal* liberation and—perhaps most importantly—as a moment in which working-class women became politically visible. It is important that we read these accounts not simply as a transparent description of what had happened during the strike: rather, they were *an active attempt to construct working-class women as new political agents, and orchestrate their demands.*[20] The figure of the politically-conscious coalfield woman who emerged during the strike was—if not precisely *created* by these books—then at least considerably fleshed out. These books thus helped render these women legible as political subjects, creating a new discursive position for them to occupy and from which they could make claims.

Not all of the personal stories included in these books were constructed around a dramatic tale of political awakening. Some of the narratives highlighted more subtle shifts in women's habitus during the strike. In the second volume of Barnsley WAPC's account of the group's strike activism, one 'retired miner's wife' recounted how one day in summer 1984, another activist phoned to ask if she could go to London the next morning: '[t]hat is impossible I replied. I always go shopping to supermarket [sic] on Thursday morning. My friend replied, what happened to the women [sic] that enjoys doing unplanned things? This was a challenge! I drew breath and asked, "how, why, what time?"'[21] They were going to join the lobby of Parliament in support of the Miners' Day of Action. The author described the 'flood' of coaches, the 'feeling of optimism' on the march, and the 'ecstatic' reception of Arthur Scargill's speech. She concluded that it was a 'day I saw solidarity in action', and added, 'P.S. I went to the supermarket the day after'.[22] This ending, while undoubtedly humorous, served to emphasise just how significant it was to this woman to break with her established routine. Stories like this constructed the strike as a moment when working-class women were able to assert more independence, and to subtly shift their understanding

[19] North Yorkshire Women Against Pit Closures, *Strike 84/85*, 85.
[20] On the construction of political discourses and political constituencies, see: Gareth Stedman Jones, *Languages of Class: Studies in English Working Class History, 1832-1982* (Cambridge: Cambridge University Press, 1983).
[21] Barnsley Women Against Pit Closures, *Women Against Pit Closures, Vol. 2*, 19.   [22] Ibid.

of themselves, from a relational mode of selfhood to a more autonomous sense of self.

The compilation of books about their activities was another stage in the claiming of a voice for working-class women. Thus activist women (in conjunction with left-wing and feminist organisations keen to see something good coming out of the strike) constructed a powerful story of women's transformation. These books and pamphlets were an attempt to secure a place in history for the strike and the women's support groups, and to underline the importance of the latter to the former. Indeed, the Normanton and Altofts group began their book *Striking Figures* with the words '[t]he Striking Figures of this book are not famous people, politicians or great explorers, they are...'; the book then listed the names of twenty-six women and men who had been locally active. The list was finished with the words, '[t]hey took it upon themselves to stand up and be counted, alongside thousands of ordinary women and men throughout the country, against this uncaring government'.[23] This concern to inscribe the historical significance of the women's support movement can be seen in the title of Coventry Miners' Wives Support Group's *Mummy... What Did You Do in the Strike?*, which drew on one of Britain's most famous First World War posters ('Daddy, what did YOU do in the Great War?') to evoke a powerful sense of the struggle and the heroic achievement of the women. Through the act of producing these works, women were quite literally writing themselves into the historical record, and making a claim for the significance of working-class women as historical actors. Their accounts have been instrumental in how the women's support groups have been remembered and memorialised.

Popular Culture, Public Memory, and the Strike

If activist accounts laid the foundations of a story of women's triumph and transformation in the strike, then popular culture has helped cement this narrative, ensuring that it has in subsequent years become culturally embedded, particularly on the left. Countless films, books, plays, documentaries, and newspaper and magazine articles on the strike have been produced since the dispute's end. Most of the early plays and documentaries were made by sympathetic left-wingers, who often worked in conjunction with striking communities, and who reproduced many of the key heroic narratives about women and the strike that were, as we have seen, established quite early on in the dispute.[24] The initial swathe of documentaries about the strike, including *The Miners' Campaign Tapes*, Ken Loach's *Which Side Are You On*, and 'Please Don't Say We're Wonderful', a

---

[23] Head et al., *Striking Figures*, n.p.   [24] See Chapter 1, 'Writing the Strike'.

1986 episode of Channel 4 documentary strand *People to People*, were overwhelmingly supportive of striking miners, and included coverage of the women's movement.[25] Also sympathetic were plays such as David Thacker and Ron Rose's *The Enemies Within*, Peter Cox's *The Garden of England*, and Jane Thornton's *Amid the Standing Corn*, all produced in conjunction with mining communities themselves and using verbatim testimonies: Peter Cox gathered material for *The Garden of England* from men and women in Kent over three months during the strike, and *Amid the Standing Corn* was based on several days the production team spent with Barnsley WAPC during the strike.[26]

Early cultural productions about the strike almost always made some space for women. In the '1984' episode of landmark 1990s BBC TV drama *Our Friends in the North*, women are shown on the picket lines and working in support groups; *Brassed Off* (1996)—though about the 1992–3 round of pit closures—has several female characters involved in activism, though this is not a narrative focus of the film.[27] As Katy Shaw has noted, filmmakers and writers in the 1990s turned away from the strike somewhat, and towards other subjects of social and political concern.[28] But with the turn of the millennium, the release of *Billy Elliot* (2000) heralded a new wave of productions about the strike, perhaps the most creative being Jeremy Deller's 2001 artwork The Battle of Orgreave, shown on Channel 4, which recreated the eponymous encounter using battlefield re-enactors.[29] In *Billy Elliot*, Billy first encounters the dancing class because the hall where the class used to rehearse has been taken over by women activists, and mining families are shown (in the background) eating at soup kitchens. Even the book written to accompany Deller's artwork, *The English Civil War Part II*, included a substantial interview with WAPC activist Stephanie Gregory, despite the fact that the event the artwork was recreating was an almost all-male affair.[30] Women were rarely centre-stage in these dramas and documentaries, but their role in the strike was acknowledged.

The press was less sure about covering the strike in the first decade after its end. In 1985, the *Guardian*'s John Torode, while disdaining the 'gloating' of Ian

---

[25] *The Miners' Campaign Tapes*, dir. Platform Films, 1984; *Which Side Are You On? Songs, Poems and Experiences of the Miners' Strike, 1984*, dir. Ken Loach, Channel 4, 9 January 1985; 'Please Don't Say We're Wonderful', *People to People*, dir. Jessica York, 27 July 1986, Channel 4.

[26] On *The Enemies Within*, see Kat Dibbits, 'Play Preview: The Enemies Within in Bolton', *Lancashire Telegraph*, 4 December 2009, https://www.lancashiretelegraph.co.uk/leisure/stage_/news/4778303.play-preview-enemies-within-bolton/. On *The Garden of England* and *Amid the Standing Corn*, see 'Peter Cox, The Garden of England'; letter from Anne Louise Wirgman, Joint Stock Theatre, to Jean McCrindle, 8 January 1985, both 7JMC/B/11, papers of Jean McCrindle, Women's Library@LSE, London. Thornton was also author of *All the Fun of the Fight*.

[27] '1984', *Our Friends in the North*, dir. Simon Cellan-Jones, 26 February 1996; *Brassed Off*, dir. Mark Herman, 1996.

[28] Katy Shaw, *Mining the Meaning: Cultural Representations of the 1984–5 UK Miners' Strike* (Newcastle upon Tyne: Cambridge Scholars Publishing, 2012), 177.

[29] *Billy Elliot*, dir. Stephen Daldry, 2000; The Battle of Orgreave, dir. Jeremy Deller, 2001.

[30] Jeremy Deller, *The English Civil War Part II: Personal Accounts of the 1984–85 Miners' Strike* (London: Artangel, 2001).

MacGregor, had asked his readers, 'who can feel anything but a mild shiver of pleasure at the humbling of King Arthur?'[31] During the tenth anniversary of the strike, in 1994–5, the *Guardian* ran just a handful of articles about the dispute, which made little or no mention of women.[32] The *Times* also mentioned nothing, and, perhaps more surprisingly, local newspapers such as the *Barnsley Chronicle* and the *Doncaster Free Press* also contained very little coverage. Dave Hill went so far as to issue a plea in the *Guardian* that the strike should be 'keenly remembered'.[33] Ten years later, it very much was—and the story of women in the strike had become much more prominent.

The year 2004 saw two twentieth-anniversary documentaries, Channel 4's *Strike: When Britain Went to War*, and BBC2's *The Miners' Strike*.[34] The former featured interviews with Anne Scargill and Betty Cook; the voiceover confidently informed the viewer that, 'before the strike, the mining families lived a very traditional life. The men went to work while the wife stayed at home', picking up on, and reinforcing, an important cultural narrative about the strike. The BBC's 2005 drama *Faith* was the fictional tale of two sisters, Linda and Michelle, and their husbands, a striking miner and a policeman respectively.[35] Michelle, the wife of the striking miner, was a WAPC activist; the drama was directed by David Thacker, the director of *The Enemies Within*, who also revived the play in Bolton in 2009.[36] More recently, 2014's *Pride* centred on the story of Lesbians and Gays Support the Miners and their relationship with a women's support group in the Dulais Valley.[37] Interest in the strike and in women's experiences has not faltered in recent years. The Corbyn-aligned Labour Party fringe festival The World Transformed staged another reading of *The Enemies Within* in 2017, and the 2022 BBC crime drama *Sherwood* took a community divided by the strike in Nottinghamshire as its setting, with an undercover 'spy cop' shown infiltrating the local women's strike support group.[38]

In the press, too, there was an increased focus on the strike, and on women's roles in it, in the twenty-first century: in 2004–5 there were no less than nine *Guardian* articles about the dispute's twentieth anniversary, including one specifically on

---

[31] John Torode, 'Who Won the Miners' Strike for Maggie?', *Guardian*, 18 March 1985.
[32] E.g. Dave Hill, 'A Fight to the Death', *Guardian*, 5 March 1994; Seumas Milne and Keith Harper, 'Thatcher was One Day Away from Defeat', *Guardian*, 7 March 1994. The right-wing 'paper of record' *The Times* ran very little on any of the major anniversaries of the strike, save reviews of cultural productions around the event.
[33] Hill, 'A Fight to the Death'.
[34] *The Miners' Strike*, 27 January 2004, BBC2; *Strike: When Britain Went to War*, Channel 4, 24 January 2004. This was criticised by Katy Shaw for its 'selective focus' and by Eamonn Kelly for 'trivialising' the dispute: Shaw, *Mining the Meaning*, 173–7; Kelly, 'Channel 4's *Strike: When Britain Went to War* (2004): Trivialisation, Popular Culture, and the Miners' Strike', in Simon Popple and Ian W. Macdonald, eds., *Digging the Seam: Popular Cultures of the 1984-5 Miners' Strike* (Newcastle upon Tyne: Cambridge Scholars, 2012), 203–16.
[35] *Faith*, dir. David Thacker, BBC1, 28 February 2005.
[36] Dibbits, 'Play Preview'.
[37] *Pride*, dir. Matthew Warchus, 2014.
[38] *Sherwood*, dir. Lewis Arnold and Ben Williams, BBC1, 13 June 2022.

women, and a host of others that mentioned the strike incidentally. An article on women's activism started with Betty Cook's story:

> Twenty years ago, Betty Cook was a miner's wife and a miner's mother. She stayed at home bringing up children till they were old enough to go down the pit. Hers was not, by any means, an empty life but one she now says was 'unfulfilled'.
>
> Then, something happened that changed it completely: the 1984 miners' strike. It was during this year-long struggle that Cook found that there was another world beyond the doorstep of her house in the village of Woolley, near the Yorkshire town of Barnsley.
>
> A woman who went off to make a cup of tea when the news came on, returning when the programmes were back, suddenly became engrossed in politics and current affairs. The strike got her watching the news and going out of the house, it brought her new horizons and new friends. Like many others, Cook became part of a movement that emerged from the ashes of the strike, a coming together and an empowering of working-class women all across the country.[39]

No mention was made of the fact that even before the strike Cook had been a shop steward for USDAW.[40] In 2014–15, for the thirtieth anniversary of the strike, the *Guardian* ran ten articles focusing on the strike, including two on women, and many others mentioning the strike—not least because the film *Pride* was released in 2014. The first *Guardian* article focusing on women's activism again repeated a narrative of emancipation, this time starting with the story of Staffordshire WAPC activist Brenda Proctor:

> Brenda Proctor was once 'a typical miner's wife, staying at home, bringing up the kids and making sure food was on the table when my man came back from work'. But the strike of 30 years ago not only transformed the industrial landscape of Britain, it radically changed her life as well as those of thousands of other women.[41]

The *Barnsley Chronicle*, which ran no commemorative pieces in 2004–5, carried a full page spread in 2014, with one column tellingly entitled 'Women Found their Voices and Grew in Confidence'.[42]

---

[39] Audrey Gillan, 'I was Always Told I was Thick: The Strike Taught Me I Wasn't', *Guardian*, 10 May 2004.
[40] Betty Cook, b. 1938, Yorkshire, interviewed by Natalie Thomlinson, 16 March 2019.
[41] Harriet Sherwood, 'The Women of the Miners' Strike: "We Caused a Lot of Havoc"', *Guardian*, 7 April 2014.
[42] Gail Robinson, 'Women Found their Voices and Grew in Confidence', *Barnsley Chronicle*, 7 March 2014. The *Doncaster Free Press* ran a dozen or so articles in the year about the strike, but none were about women.

As this shift in newspaper coverage suggests, popular and political memories of the strike have grown more nostalgic and more positive over the decades: today, there is less focus on violent pickets, and more focus on the violence of police, the hardship faced by striking families and communities, and the noble solidarity shown by striking miners and their wives. The closure of most of Britain's deep coal mines in the decade after the strike has undoubtedly reshaped ideas about the dispute: though Scargill remains a deeply controversial figure, his claim that the government planned to destroy the mining industry was proven to be correct, helping to change perceptions of the strikers' cause. Though women's experiences have grown in prominence in accounts of the strike over the decades, it is notable that the story that is usually told about women and the strike has changed remarkably little. As the articles on women's activism in the *Guardian* suggest, the story has been one of 'ordinary' miners' wives coming out from behind the kitchen sink, banding together to defend their communities, and emancipating themselves in the process: precisely the same narrative that leftist journalists and activist groups constructed during and immediately after the strike. This narrative provided one framework through which women involved in support group activism could tell their stories, and inevitably structured the way some—though not all—of our interviewees recounted their experiences. Indeed, it is not possible to pull apart the cultural discourses that have constructed the memory of the strike from the 'real' experiences of the women who went through it: they made sense of their experiences *through* the narrative resources available to them.

Deploying the Heroic Narrative

Many activists used the framework of 'transformation' in telling the story of the strike. They suggested that their new experiences in the strike had changed them, made them more 'self-confident', given them a new 'voice', and made them determined that they would not (as one put it in an interview shortly after the strike) 'go back to how it was'.[43] Activist women sometimes had a strong psychic investment in the heroic narrative of the strike: to be able to place themselves in this narrative conferred legitimacy on their political activism, bolstered their self-worth, and, in a more existential sense, gave meaning to their life-stories. Many of our interviewees presented the strike as a moment of liberation—as, for example, with Alice Samuel. Born in 1958 and raised in Hamilton, South Lanarkshire, Alice married aged 19, while in the second year of her nurse training, and was pregnant by the time she qualified. She and her husband, a miner, and their young family moved to Fife just a few weeks before the start of the strike in 1984, a period

---

[43] Interviewee 25, unpublished book manuscript, 7BEH/1/2, papers of Betty Heathfield, Women's Library@LSE, London.

during which Alice was not in paid employment. For her, getting involved in her local strike centre was a way of getting involved in the community as a whole, and breaking out of the isolated position she was in as a newcomer—a 'weegie' from the west coast of Scotland—in Fife. Alice became deeply involved in the strike in a huge range of ways: she helped in the strike centre, travelled to marches and rallies, spoke at fundraisers in Aberdeen and Dundee, represented Fife Miners' WAPC in the national WAPC organisation, and participated in a sit-in at Seafield colliery. When asked how much of an impact the strike had on her life, Alice said that it had been huge: she thought that many of the decisions she made after its end had been possible because of the confidence she gained during the dispute. She went back to work as a nurse, which she felt 'was a massive big thing for me, I didnae know how I was going to cope with it'. She thought she probably would not have left her ex-husband, but would have stayed with him as a good provider and 'put up with his crap', if it had not been for the strike. 'A lot of the choices and decisions that I've made since then are probably because of the confidence I gained in that time', she told us.[44]

Likewise, Anne Kirby, a dedicated strike activist in Cowdenbeath, told us in her interview that the strike had given her confidence as well as new skills, and played an important role in her decision to return to work once her youngest child was in school. She worked part-time as a cleaner for seven years, before returning to education to take an HND in social sciences and a careers advice qualification, a process which, she said, led her to be 'more independent of him' (her husband). Moving away from home to take up a placement ultimately led to the dissolution of her first marriage. Anne said several times in her interview that she would not have decided to take these opportunities had it not been for her experiences in the strike. She told us that the strike's impact on her was that: 'I found my voice, I found a platform, I became more politically aware. I found skills I never had, or didn't think I had.'[45] For both Alice and Anne, the strike was the prism through which they understood the subsequent trajectory of their lives. It is, of course, rarely possible to definitively attribute life trajectories to any one experience. The strike doubtless played a part in changing some women's orientation to their lives; but it is just as important to appreciate the significance of the 'heroic' strike narrative: this allowed—even encouraged—women to think of the strike as a transformative event, enabling them to frame their life-stories in a way which positioned the dispute as *the* motor of personal change. It is notable that, like Alice, several women who divorced their husbands years—or in the case of Anne, more than a decade—after the strike, still attributed the decision to part from their husbands to the dispute.

---

[44] Alice Samuel, b. 1958, Scotland, interviewed by Natalie Thomlinson, 1 August 2018.
[45] Anne Kirby, b. 1955, Scotland, interviewed by Victoria Dawson, 26 November 2018.

Of course, if the strike played a role in these women's decisions to divorce, so did other events in the intervening years. As we suggested in Chapter 7, deindustrialisation, the rise of the service sector, the normalisation of married women's paid work, and significant cultural shifts in gender norms all played a major role in changing women's lives and gender roles in coalfield communities—as elsewhere in Britain—in the late twentieth and early twenty-first centuries. But this should not lead us to completely dismiss the idea of transformation through the strike. Penny Summerfield has suggested that while the idea that women's work in the Second World War was liberating was something of a myth, it was a myth that came retrospectively to influence how many women told their own stories.[46] The myth itself became a facilitator for changes in women's perceptions of themselves. The same could be said to be true of the heroic narrative of women's experiences in the strike. In the late twentieth and early twenty-first centuries, an increasing cultural emphasis was placed on personal autonomy and individual agency, and individuals were encouraged to seek self-fulfilment through self-help and the ideas of the psy-sciences.[47] In this context, the narrative of liberation in the strike was a useful one for women to deploy in constructing a story of increasing self-confidence and personal growth. Tanya Dower even made a comparison between women's strike experiences and women's work in the Second World War in her discussion of how the strike had affected her mother. Tanya thought the strike was an 'emancipation' for her mother, just as in the war—when they had to work and struggle on the home front while men were away fighting—'women took up the reins, and did—just got on with it'.[48]

While some women described the strike as an important moment propelling them into further education, new careers, or new political roles, many interviewees also told stories of more subtle shifts in outlook. Born in 1935, Marie Price from Nottinghamshire recalled that before the strike she had done everything for her husband, Alan, who two decades earlier had forced her to give up her work after they had children. In the strike, however, she became a committed activist in the divided Nottinghamshire coalfield, and afterwards, she said, 'I was no longer just a housewife': if Alan asked her for a cup of tea, she'd say 'kettle's in there', which she 'never would before'. Marie said that, 'I was a different person, and Tracy [her daughter] saw that, and she always says it was that that gave her the go

---

[46] Penny Summerfield, *Reconstructing Women's Wartime Lives: Discourse and Subjectivity in Oral Histories of the Second World War* (Manchester: Manchester University Press, 1998).

[47] Mathew Thomson, *Psychological Subjects: Identity, Culture, and Health in Twentieth-Century Britain* (Oxford: Oxford University Press, 2006); Florence Sutcliffe-Braithwaite and Natalie Thomlinson, 'Vernacular Discourses of Gender Equality in the Post-War British Working Class', *Past & Present*, 254 (2022), 277–313.

[48] Tanya Dower, b. 1967, South Wales, interviewed by Victoria Dawson, 13 August 2018. Maggie Stubbs, b. c.1950, Jamaica/Yorkshire, interviewed by Natalie Thomlinson, 13 September 2018, also drew this comparison.

to go to university. You know, she was more assertive.'[49] Marie used the strike as the turning point in a story of a shift from a relational to a more autonomous and independent sense of self, a break with an older culture which saw women as first and foremost helpmeets to men, their lives inscribed within a routine of care for others. This break was not dramatic—Marie was not leaving her husband, simply asking him to make his own cup of tea—but this story, nevertheless, was invested with a great deal of significance.

Activists who had been interviewed many times before, and who had appeared in national media talking about their experiences, were most likely to emphasise the heroic nature of women's activism in the strike in the oral histories for this project. For these women, their work in the strike was central to their sense of self, and was a source of self-esteem; it is unsurprising, therefore, that they had chosen to frequently retell their stories. Aggie Currie told us explicitly that, 'I always enjoy talking about it. I want it to go down in history.'[50] Many of those who had been particularly involved in activism told us that they would repeat the experience: Aggie, for example, said she would 'do it again in a heartbeat'; Betty Cook said she would 'do it all again', and Liz French told us, 'glad I was there. Glad I done it. Glad I met all them people.'[51] In telling their stories, these women gave composed accounts of themselves; that is, accounts with which they were comfortable, which fitted in with dominant cultural discourses, which could help to further their political beliefs in the present—and perhaps gain them a place in history.

Complicating the Heroic Narrative

The heroic narrative of women's transformation in the strike was not, however, completely hegemonic within our interview sample. Even some strike activists were downbeat about how the dispute should be remembered: Margaret Holmes, from Kent, told us, 'I wouldn't say it was a fantastic time; I would say it was a time we lived through.'[52] Anne Kirby said she 'wouldn't have thought there was a lot to celebrate. Because I shouldn't think there was a lot of happy men walking through that gate the day they went back.'[53] Tanya Dower thought it was important to 'learn' from the strike rather than celebrate it.[54] Others were more positive about the strike, but still contested some of the narratives about the changes it had occasioned. Pat Smith did see the strike as an important turning-point in her life: though she had done various jobs as well as adult education courses before the strike, afterwards, she did an access course, went to university, and ultimately got

---

[49] Marie Price, b. 1935, Nottinghamshire, interviewed by Natalie Thomlinson, 29 May 2019.
[50] Aggie Currie, b. 1950, Yorkshire, interviewed by Victoria Dawson, 22 June 2018.
[51] Ibid.; Betty Cook; Liz French, b. 1950, Kent, interviewed by Florence Sutcliffe-Braithwaite, 6 July 2018.
[52] Margaret Holmes.   [53] Anne Kirby.   [54] Tanya Dower.

involved in local politics. But when asked if her husband did more around the house during the strike, Pat explained:

> he [Dave] always likes to tell the story himself that erm, he, er, it were said that— during t'strike, that er, it took women away from t'kitchen sink, and he always says *she never was behind it*, I mean I've already told you I wasn't particularly keen on cooking, so er, erm, I—I've never been a number one er proud-houseproud sort of person, d'you know what I mean, it's er, erm, obviously keep it tidy and you keep it clean, but erm, it—me aim in life hasn't been to make sure there weren't a speck of dust everywhere, it's like, life's for living and enjoying, in't it.[55]

Both Pat and Dave were aware of the emancipatory strike narrative, and both contested it. Janet Slater, similarly, complicated the straightforward narrative of liberation. Like Tanya Dower, Janet drew a comparison with women's work in the Second World War, but she suggested that the strike was the occasion not of widespread transformation, but 'more like, like in the war...when women were called upon to do the jobs that only the men could do...but then after the war they had to go back to their roles, and I felt it was more that'. While she thought the strike did change 'some women', she concluded that 'for me personally it didn't have that effect'.[56]

For many interviewees, the strike was one important life event among several. There were few who did not see it as significant in some respect (such women would be unlikely to volunteer for the project), but there were women for whom the strike was certainly not the fulcrum on which the story of their lives turned. 'It was one phase of my life', mused Joyce Boyes, 'for all that it was important at the time, as time's gone on, it's become less and less important'.[57] Joan Holden said that, 'it was just something that happened'; 'it's been and gone, and I don't dwell on it'. She attributed her lack of emotional investment in the strike to the fact 'that I didn't belong there' (Joan was originally from Blackpool rather than from a mining community).[58] Adrienne C. called it a 'blip' in her and her family's lives, and said, 'I don't think it's anything I'd want to celebrate or commemorate.'[59] Ann Robertson, who, like Adrienne, disagreed with the strike, recalled:

> It wasn't a time that either my husband or I looked back on with any fond memories of any sort. We never talked about it once it was over. That was it. It was a period of our lives that we didn't particularly enjoy. And I think the sadness

[55] Pat Smith, b. 1949, Yorkshire, interviewed by Victoria Dawson, 8 June 2018.
[56] Janet Slater, b. 1954, Nottinghamshire, interviewed by Natalie Thomlinson, 3 August 2018.
[57] Joyce Boyes, b. 1955, Yorkshire, interviewed by Victoria Dawson, 21 September 2018.
[58] Joan Holden, b. 1937, Lancashire/Yorkshire, interviewed by Victoria Dawson, 23 July 2018.
[59] Adrienne C., b. 1955, Yorkshire, interviewed by Victoria Dawson, 26 June 2018.

of it was, it was the wretchedness of a strike that achieved nothing. It was the futility of it all that depressed me. You know, for what?[60]

These less dramatic narratives have been less audible in works on the strike, but it is likely that many women would have agreed with Ann and Adrienne.

The strike left some women feeling depressed and disempowered. Ann McCracken worked as a secretary in the NHS, and in a local pub, during the strike, in order to pay her family's mortgage and bills, and the family also received parcels of food and clothing—though this was difficult for Ann, because, she said, you 'never see yourself taking parcels'.[61] She spoke eloquently about the psychological impact of the hardship of the strike on her and her family:

> everything you'd built up, and been—through my childhood been taught, and been taught to, you know, get on wi' life and make the best in life and all of a sudden it comes along and just sweeps it away from under your feet, and there's nothing you can do about it.

Ann felt that, because of the strike, she 'lost all my confidence', and it was only slowly that she began to regain it, after divorcing, returning to Scotland from Yorkshire, where she lived during the strike, and studying for a degree.[62] The psychological impact of the strike—the feelings of stress and helplessness it induced—lasted beyond the end of the action for some women. It was hard for women like Ann to inscribe the strike with meaning: in fact, for her, the strike had destroyed the structures that had given her a sense of meaning and agency. Unlike activists, who usually had strong networks of mutual support during the strike, and who often looked back on the strike as a difficult time but also a moment of personal and collective achievement, women who were relatively isolated from such activist networks often saw the strike as more purely destructive: destructive of the stability of their families, their communities, and their sense of their place in the world.

Even some women from mining villages where there was strong community support during the strike found it painful to recall: this seems to have been particularly the case where women disagreed with what had become the dominant narratives about the dispute in their communities. The voices of women like this are hard to find, because they are, of course, unlikely to come forward for projects like ours, but we can catch glimpses of such testimonies in other research projects less explicitly about the strike. 'Charlotte', born in 1950 and interviewed in 2007 for Yvette Taylor's 'Coalface to Carpark' project in North East England, suggested

---

[60] Ann Robertson, b. 1934, London/Kent, interviewed by Florence Sutcliffe-Braithwaite, 5 November 2018.
[61] Ann McCracken, b. 1954, Scotland/Yorkshire, interviewed by Victoria Dawson, 6 December 2018.
[62] Ibid.

why some women from mining communities felt negatively about the strike. When it was first mentioned, Charlotte tried to move on the discussion, saying, 'I don't like talking about the strike.'[63] She explained that she thought it was 'totally and completely wrong', a 'political' struggle (the implication of 'political' being that it was illegitimate, a sectional struggle waged for ideological reasons). Her husband had been a miner, and had gone on strike in 1984–5, but Charlotte said that 'we just got on with our lives and ignored everybody else and what was going on'. Charlotte was 'mortifyingly embarrassed' to see miners accepting handouts. She drew on two discourses in her discussion of the strike: an anti-politics discourse, and—as we discuss in Chapter 4—a powerful discourse that associated 'charity' with shame. Charlotte, drawing on these framings, saw the strike as a moment of humiliation for her community, and a fundamentally illegitimate action. For women like her, the strike had little meaning, and no redemptive qualities—in some cases, it was actively destructive of the things they valued. They wanted to put it behind them, not to remember it. In fact, Charlotte complained that '[s]ome people just go on and on and on about it [the strike] and I don't like that at all': the women who had worked in the kitchen, she said, 'talk about it today, Oh one of the proudest things I did was make the dinners in the kitchens for the people during the strike and I'm thinking oh my god. And they're so proud, you can't say a word against them you know.'[64] Charlotte's feelings about the strike seemed to be particularly difficult for her to articulate because she lacked an obvious 'cultural script' she could draw on in giving her account, and she ultimately asked the interviewer if they could move on.

Another woman whose story went against predominant community narratives was Carol*, from South Wales. Carol, who had never spoken of her experience in any sort of public forum or project before, had deeply mixed feelings about the strike. As we discussed in Chapter 6, her father had returned to work three weeks before the end. The complexity of her own feelings about the strike was in evidence when she said of public discourse about the dispute:

> It's either pro the strike, or against the strike, and I say d'you know what, there's a whole bunch of people that are caught in this whole middle part as well, that's never talked about. And I think it's always, you know, really upset me, that my father even, you know, now, there's probably a few people that would look at my father and in their head they're going 'scab'.[65]

---

[63] 'Charlotte', interview 009, in Yvette Taylor, 'From the Coalface to the Car Park? The Intersection of Class and Gender in Women's Lives in the North East, 2007–2009' (data collection), 2012, UK Data Service, SN: 7053.
[64] Ibid.   [65] Carol*, b. 1968, South Wales, interviewed by Natalie Thomlinson, 19 June 2018.

Carol felt that both miners who stayed out until the end *and* those who had returned to work had been misunderstood; she told us that she felt she had to take part in the project as soon as she saw it advertised. As we have seen, she described the process of being interviewed as an 'exorcism'.

Women whose husbands or fathers worked through the strike in coalfields like Nottinghamshire also found their stories difficult to tell. Jay Emery has observed that 'a culture of silence surrounding the miners' strike still pervades north Nottinghamshire',[66] and indeed, three of the women we spoke to from the county who had working husbands or fathers initially cancelled their interviews. They appeared to be more reluctant to reminisce, perhaps knowing that they had been cast—at least in some strike histories—as the villains rather than the heroes of the hour. What happened after the strike added another layer of complexity to how working miners and their wives looked at the dispute: many of those working through the strike in Nottinghamshire believed that their pits—highly productive, and producing coal that was ideal for the domestic energy market—had a secure long-term future. The fact that most of these pits did, in fact, close in the eight years after the strike meant that many came to feel they had been lied to by the National Coal Board (NCB). The strike was, therefore, still likely to be a locus of painful feelings for the wives of working miners in areas like Nottinghamshire. Polly*, one such woman, claimed in her interview that had she known that the strike was to save pits, she would have supported it, telling us:

> Well, you see with hindsight, if we'd have known that, then—that's why I'm so angry with Scargill for not going about it the right way and giving us the chance to vote for a strike, because then we would have been all in it together, and what would have happened may never have possibly happened.[67]

Given Polly's political engagement, it is difficult to believe that she did not know at the time that Scargill framed the strike as a fight to save jobs. She conflated two separate issues here—the reasons for which the strike was being fought, and the (deeply controversial) question of whether a national ballot should have been held. Yet Polly did not appear to be being disingenuous; more likely, it was simply too painful to acknowledge that striking miners—whom she had opposed so vigorously—were correct in their fears for the future of pits, and that she had simply not believed that Nottinghamshire collieries were at risk. As Emery has suggested, 'miners in north Nottinghamshire on both sides of the strike continue to struggle to come to terms with their coalfield's own role in that history'.[68]

---

[66] Jay Emery, 'Belonging, Memory and History in the North Nottinghamshire Coalfield', *Journal of Historical Geography*, 59 (2018), 77–89, at 88.

[67] Polly*, b. 1944, Lincolnshire/Nottinghamshire, interviewed by Natalie Thomlinson, 7 September 2018.

[68] Emery, 'Belonging, Memory and History', 88.

Polly* and Carol* both explicitly condemned Conservative governments' policies towards mining communities after the strike; both had an emotional investment in being part of a mining community in a way that was not true for women like Ann Robertson or Adrienne C., who more easily and straightforwardly drew on contemporaneous discourses that condemned the strike. Such complex subject positions were difficult to fashion out of the discursive resources available to Polly and Carol: there was no readily available cultural script allowing them to be both critical of the strike *and* of the Conservative government. It is thus unsurprising that these interviewees found it more difficult to narrate a 'composed' story; it was very clear that, unlike some of the pro-strike activists we interviewed, these women had not told their stories before. They were trying to make sense of their lives and experiences in the strike within the moment of the interview itself, and the oral history interview here became a process capable of generating new narratives. For strike activists, the interview was a process that reified narratives long established, with little room for alternative interpretations of events to arise: it worked to psychically secure their identities. But for those women whose feelings towards the dispute were more ambivalent or hostile, the interview was often a more difficult exploration of how their own memories and feelings could be reconciled within a dominant cultural paradigm that tends to valorise the strike.

Nevertheless, it is significant that these women did want their stories to be heard. Several interviewees told us they felt their stories had been marginalised, and that through speaking to us, they hoped to ensure their experiences were part of the historical record. As we saw above, Carol* thought that the experiences of those who had ambivalent or conflicted feelings about the strike were 'never talked about'.[69] Rebecca Shirt*, who did not get involved in activism during the strike but simply focused on getting through it, found her interview 'challenging': she reflected that she now felt that it was a bit of a 'let down' that she did not get involved in the support movement, but thought that though she and her family had a 'very minor story', it was nevertheless important to tell it.[70] Chloe*, who supported her husband's strike action, but who also did not get involved in activism, felt that discussions of the strike were 'always about the miners that were in the strike or the mining communities', or at best about the most dramatic forms of female activism:

> But not everybody had the chance to be that, not, people's lives don't always give you a chance to fight for others, sometimes you're too busy fighting for yourself and to get by. So it's for them, for those females that I'd like it to be heard, 'cause

---

[69] Carol*.
[70] Rebecca Shirt*, b. 1956, Yorkshire, interviewed by Victoria Dawson, 12 October 2018.

there's a lot of them and the strike was a lot about how things were kept going and, erm, working together and just, you know er, dealing with something that we couldn't control...we're always written out.[71]

The prominence of activism in accounts of women and the strike is understandable—the support movement was dramatic and dynamic—but it has rendered other stories sometimes difficult to articulate, or to be publicly heard.

Communities after Coal

One of the most prominent themes that emerged from our interviews was the decline of communities. Women's testimonies on this point were often remarkably similar, and infused with melancholy: the decay of physical infrastructure, unemployment, anti-social behaviour, and substance abuse all figured heavily. As we saw in Chapter 2, interviewees reminisced nostalgically about growing up in what they remembered as friendly, safe, and homogeneous communities in the 1950s, 1960s, and 1970s: many recalled that children were able to play out all day, and families were all 'the same'. Kay Case, from Treharris, South Wales, told us: 'when I moved in here I knew absolutely everybody, every man and his dog in the street, all the children's names, everything'.[72] Of course, these recollections obscured as much as they revealed. 'Sameness' could feel comfortable, but could also mean rigid gender roles and heteronormativity; the sense of 'safety' was maintained by the suppression of the knowledge of domestic violence and child sexual abuse;[73] Move and not everyone was 'the same' in any case: working-class communities had long been fractured by distinctions between the 'rough' and the 'respectable'. Furthermore, as we have seen, mining communities were not static, ethnically homogeneous, and unchanging places, but shaped by migration, particularly from within the four nations of the UK and from Eastern Europe (though—as Maggie Stubbs' journey from Jamaica to Maltby reminds us—migrants sometimes came from further afield as well). But a flattened idea of what mining communities were like in the past worked in interviewees' recollections as a way of critiquing the present.

The mining communities of the past were also remembered as economically secure. As we saw in Chapter 2, work was recalled as easy to come by: the claim that you could 'leave one job on Friday and have another on Monday morning'

---

[71] Chloe*, b. 1959, Yorkshire, interviewed by Victoria Dawson, 30 August 2018.
[72] Kay Case, b. 1948, South Wales, interviewed by Florence Sutcliffe-Braithwaite, 13 August 2018.
[73] Pippa Morgan*, b. 1962, South Wales, interviewed by Natalie Thomlinson, 13 August 2018, and Liz French both gave frank discussions of domestic violence in their interviews; Polly* discussed childhood sexual abuse.

was made over and over again.[74] Interviewees described their areas as thriving before the strike: as Marjorie Simpson, from Stainforth, South Yorkshire, put it, 'life was pretty good prior to March 1984—we were buying houses and new cars, etc.; everybody knew each other, we were happy and content'.[75] For Marjorie, the dispute functioned as a placeholder through which to articulate many of the larger changes that the community saw; and a stark sense of mining towns 'before' and 'after' was present in many of the interviews we undertook. This was perhaps most obviously exemplified by Marie Price, who said grimly that the experience of the past three decades, 'just proves that what the men did was right. It's [i.e. pit closures] killed this country.'[76] Carol Willis described Ashington as a 'boom town' in the decade before the strike, and described the collective nostalgia expressed on the Facebook page 'Ashington Remembered': 'it's full of people my age going "oh, do you remember—the high street was so full of shops, and there was specialist shops—do you remember the Disc, and do you remember the Landlight club, and Fleetwood Mac playing there!"' But things had changed now: 'it's awful nostalgia for a time which has gone forever', Carol said.[77] Polly*—who was not a supporter of the strike—nevertheless told us with deep sadness of her village in Nottinghamshire after its pit closed: 'so many men lost their jobs, and women, at the pit canteen. The pub up there, lost… the welfare got closed down. It affected the whole community.'[78] Rebecca Shirt* talked of 'ghost towns' in South Yorkshire;[79] Kay Case remembered, 'Treharris just isn't the same, it's not the same feeling, it's not the same… it's not the same place anymore';[80] and Myra Dakin told us simply that 'we had everything, we had everything. There's nothing now.'[81]

Not only had high streets decayed and affluence disappeared—the social fabric was seen to have frayed, too. Many interviewees lamented no longer knowing their neighbours. Kay Case, who recalled knowing 'everybody' when she first moved to Treharris, told us: 'I don't know hardly anybody here now.'[82] Aggie Currie remembered of Armthorpe that, 'when I was fetched up, everyone were aunty and uncle. It's not like that anymore.'[83] Jessica Gibson complained that 'you hardly ken [know] anybody now' in Gilmerton, Midlothian, and that there was 'no community spirit'.[84] In a similar vein, Christine Harvey, from the Cynon Valley in South Wales, told us that:

---

[74] E.g. Janice Bartolo, b. 1957, Kent, interviewed by Florence Sutcliffe-Braithwaite and Natalie Thomlinson, 5 March 2016; Joyce Boyes; Mandy Slater, b. 1937, Yorkshire, interviewed by Victoria Dawson, 8 August 2018.
[75] Marjorie Simpson, b. 1938, Yorkshire, interviewed by Victoria Dawson, 23 May 2018.
[76] Marie Price.
[77] Carol Willis, b. 1952, North East England/Manchester, interviewed by Victoria Dawson, 3 April 2019.
[78] Polly*.   [79] Rebecca Shirt*.   [80] Kay Case.
[81] Myra Dakin, b. 1959, Yorkshire, interviewed by Victoria Dawson, 16 August 2018.
[82] Kay Case.   [83] Aggie Currie.
[84] Jessica Gibson, b. 1963, Scotland, interviewed by Florence Sutcliffe-Braithwaite, 26 November 2018.

there's not the same feel, I don't think. The coming together isn't as strong as it was. There are still community things, of course. But I don't think they're as strong. I think sometimes people are more selfish. They've become more splintered, things have become more splintered.[85]

As Jo-Anne Welsh, who grew up in Wath-upon-Dearne, South Yorkshire, said, 'if you kind of rob a whole community of its infrastructure and its status, it's hard to kind of keep that [i.e. community spirit] going'.[86] Several interviewees discussed drug abuse and rising crime rates in a register of despair, often connecting these phenomena to the loss of work in the pits and a sense among young people that there was little to look forward to. Pauline C. tied these issues together when over the course of two minutes in her interview she asked 'what prospects have young people got?', before complaining about anti-social behaviour from local youths—'they go out, and you just see...it's mostly young men, just doing what they want...they don't care about our community'—moving on to discuss crime and 'the big drug culture' in her local community in Northumberland.[87] Sociologists of their own communities, Pauline and others recognised that these problems were not discrete but interconnected.

As we saw in Chapter 7, there was a real empirical base for such anguish. After the mining industry disappeared, coalfield areas suffered from high levels of unemployment, a lack of attractive job opportunities, particularly for men, and economic and social deprivation. Nevertheless, we should not simply take our interviewees' statements about what had happened to the areas they lived in at face value. They were shaped by pervasive cultural tropes about the decline of community, and often expressed emotional rather than literal truths.[88] How, then, should we interpret these strongly-held feelings? Valerie Walkerdine has pointed to the affective dimensions of such pronouncements, interpreting them through the lens of psychoanalysis to suggest that community can function as an 'ego-skin', holding those within in it as a baby would be held. The perceived destruction of community is thus felt as a visceral trauma, variously expressed as anxieties about safety and death.[89] Certainly, the 'safety' of knowing your neighbours—and the corollary of the danger of strangers—appeared to be implicit in much of the testimony we heard. Some of the statements interviewees made about the decline of community also echoed discourses demonising classed 'others'. Robyn*, when asked what the South Yorkshire mining village she grew up in was like now, responded:

---

[85] Christine Harvey.
[86] Jo-Anne Welsh, b. 1967, Yorkshire, interviewed by Florence Sutcliffe-Braithwaite, 9 June 2018.
[87] Pauline C., b. 1949, Northumberland, interviewed by Victoria Dawson, 19 November 2018.
[88] Ramsden, *Working Class Community*; Lawrence, *Me, Me, Me?*, introduction.
[89] Valerie Walkerdine, 'Communal Beingness and Affect: An Exploration of Trauma in a Post-Industrial Community', *Body and Society*, 16 (2010), 91–116, esp. 102.

Now I think it's more—is it fair to say—they're a more—it's a more residual class—there's people there that are put there 'cause they may be troubled families and that's a shame because there's still a core which are very hard working and take pride in where they live and wanna, yes, look after their community, but I suppose it's like anywhere, isn't it, y'know, you get things that looks like it probably hasn't moved on since the strike, really, but I remember it very close-knit, very happy, everybody knew one another.[90]

Here, a rough 'residual' class threatened the former 'respectability' of the 'hard-working' mining community; Robyn was not alone in making such comments, and the anxiety she articulated probably points in part to the precarity of the 'respectability' of miners and mining families, which was never as secure as such recollections implied. This form of nostalgia problematically situates a 'good' and 'respectable' working class in the past, implicitly criticising the working classes of the present.[91] And while we heard few explicitly racist sentiments voiced during our interviews, it is not difficult to see how some of these 'othering' discourses could take on a racial dimension.

On the other hand, a much more progressive strand of critical nostalgia can be read into these recollections, where an idealised past in which social relations were harmonious—and where communities were undergirded by values of mutual aid and cooperation—was invoked to criticise the apparently selfish and individualistic society of the present. As John Tomaney has noted in relation to the Durham Miners' Gala, '[n]ostalgia is a social emotion, typically the product of current fears and anxieties, a way of maintaining solidarities in the face of disruption and pain and the erosion of hard-won social gains'.[92] This was perhaps most clearly articulated by Alice Samuel, who told us:

> We've got a society now where it's 'I'm alright Jack'...I feel sorry for my children that they're never going to have that sense of you know—sense of community, and sense of—you do a day's work, you get paid a day's work, you get paid a decent living wage...We have lost so much that was hard fought for, you know—first of all with the suffragettes and everything, and before that with trade unionism and things, and a lot of that's all lost now, and there's not that sense of let's stick together and do these things.[93]

---

[90] Robyn*, b. 1963, Yorkshire, interviewed by Victoria Dawson, 26 July 2018.
[91] Steph Lawler, 'Heroic Workers and Angry Young Men: Nostalgic Narratives of White Working-Class Life', *European Journal of Cultural Studies*, 17 (2014), 701–20.
[92] John Tomaney, 'After Coal: Meanings of the Durham Miners' Gala', *Frontiers in Sociology*, 5 (2020), n.p.
[93] Alice Samuel.

As this suggests, a leftist critique of contemporary politics was also part of this critical nostalgia. Jessica Gibson told us that 'communities have been decimated. You've got mass unemployment that the Tories try and cover up, and you've got people going to food banks... there is nae social housing now'.[94] She was wistful for the time before the strike, when, she told us, 'communities were all together, like, hand in hand'.[95] Liz French also told us that she felt 'sorry' for young people today, giving her reasons as 'jobs, housing, y'know... can't even put your name on the council list'.[96]

Jim Phillips argues that for those who actively supported the strike—as Alice, Liz, and Jessica all did—the dispute often came to be seen as a moment when communities were cohesive and mutualistic.[97] Many of our interviewees remembered the strike in this way: Ann, from South Yorkshire, said, for example, that it 'brought people together'.[98] These sentiments were often voiced in recollections of Christmas, as when Sue, from Kent, recalled that Christmas 1984 was 'brilliant', because 'everybody had exactly the same, and everybody had nothing'.[99] The strike figured here as a last hurrah for the tightly-knit, solidaristic coalfield communities that Thatcherism was in the process of destroying. As Phillips points out, such communities had been gradually changing over the decades prior to the strike, under the influence of pit closures, suburbanisation, and increasingly affluent and privatised lifestyles.[100] Nostalgic recollections of togetherness, however, highlighted the damage Thatcherism had done to Britain's industrial heartlands.

Finally, we should heed Jon Lawrence's argument that community has not disappeared in the twenty-first century, even if the forms it takes are different and less often based on physical proximity and face-to-face interactions than they once were.[101] Indeed, some of our interviewees offered more nuanced visions of community, suggesting that it had changed rather than disappeared. Christina Bell remembered that, 'the communities were very close then, up there in—in the north east. *I think they still are, actually*, but, like I say, er, modern times now, people don't mix as much as they used to.'[102] Despite her sorrow for the loss of community, Alice Samuel also told us that, in London, where she moved in the 1990s, 'I do see a lot of social conscience that goes on in this area.'[103] Claire* leavened her lament for the decline of the valley she grew up in with the suggestion that the community there was still 'close-knit'; indeed that it could, at times, be 'claustrophobic'.[104] As Lawrence has suggested, as early as the 1950s and 1960s,

---

[94] Jessica Gibson. [95] Ibid. [96] Liz French.
[97] Jim Phillips, 'The Meanings of Coal Community in Britain since 1947', *Contemporary British History*, 32 (2018), 39–59.
[98] Ann, b. 1942, Yorkshire, interviewed by Victoria Dawson, 25 July 2018.
[99] Sue, b. 1956, Kent, interviewed by Florence Sutcliffe-Braithwaite, 14 July 2018.
[100] Phillips, 'Meanings of Coal Community', 41. [101] Lawrence, *Me, Me, Me?*
[102] Christina Bell. [103] Alice Samuel.
[104] Claire*, b. 1969, South Wales, interviewed by Natalie Thomlinson, 11 August 2018.

there were suggestions that some working-class families were opting for more 'elective' forms of belonging where newfound affluence allowed them to, choosing who to mix with, and not relying on close neighbours and kin for mutual material aid.[105] These interviewees suggested that by the early twenty-first century, this form of community was more pervasive.

Many community organisations have endured, too. Christine Worth gave a positive account of her local community in Ambergate, Derbyshire, telling us that 'even now, this is a fairly safe community where most people know each other. We had the carnival we had last weekend. We had huge numbers down on the recreation ground, all had a great time dancing 'til the evening.'[106] Christine was a district councillor, and may therefore have wished to present the local community positively, but such testimony still suggests the continuation of close and positive social bonds. Indeed, it is notable how many women we interviewed lamented the death of community while at the same time being deeply involved in a range of local groups, the existence of which suggests that at least some of the traditional associational life of coalfield communities has kept going after the loss of the pits. This fits with the findings of Waddington et al., who, in 2001, argued that despite worries about jobs, infrastructure, and crime, residents in ex-mining communities in the Doncaster area still tended to rate their locales highly on scores of neighbourliness.[107] Former coalfield communities have certainly been heavily affected by the closure of pits; but their obituaries have perhaps been published too prematurely.

Conclusion

The strike has become an event overflowing with meaning. It has come to stand for something *more than itself*. For some of the women we interviewed, the dispute functioned as a fulcrum around which they could narrate large-scale changes that they had experienced in their personal lives, in the community around them, and in the country at large. The strike symbolised many things to the women who lived through it. Activists commonly focused on it as a moment that had transformed them personally and politically, an understanding structured by the prevalence of cultural discourses making this claim. For some, it was a moment when life in Britain changed for women. For many, it was the moment in which the working class was dealt a definitive blow.

---

[105] Lawrence, *Me, Me, Me?*, 14, 38.
[106] Christine Worth, b. 1952, Derbyshire, interviewed by Natalie Thomlinson, 2 August 2018.
[107] David Waddington, Chas Critcher, Bella Dicks, and David Parry, *Out of the Ashes: The Social Impact of Industrial Contraction and Regeneration on Britain's Mining Communities* (The Stationery Office in association with the Regional Studies Association, 2001), ch. 4, 71–94.

Longer-term shifts in society, such as deindustrialisation, women's increasing entry into the paid labour force, greater mobility, and the changing nature of community, were all, ultimately, much more significant drivers of change in coalfield women's lives than the strike, or women's activism during the strike. In oral history testimony, popular writing, and academic analysis, the support movement has sometimes been figured as a simple way of explaining the causes of socio-economic changes which are enormously hard to disentangle. The support movement was, in fact, more a result than a cause of long-term shifts. Working-class women mobilised in new ways and on a relatively large scale in 1984–5, in comparison with a period like the 1926 miners' lockout, precisely because miners' wives' lives—their experiences in education, at work, and in the home, as well as their very sense of self and place in the world—had changed so dramatically since the interwar period. The emphasis that many activists placed on the dispute as a motor of personal change can work to obscure the many other social changes that Britain witnessed in the postwar era. The dominance of a heroic narrative of women's activism has, as we have seen, masked the diversity of strike experiences. It is, therefore, crucial to pay attention to the voices of non-activists—the majority among coalfield women—if we are to understand both the strike and the various shifts in women's lives it is sometimes claimed to have occasioned. Restoring these voices to the historical record helps us to better understand the impact of the strike; as the dispute was not at the centre of these women's stories, exploring their testimony helps us to understand the importance of these longer-term shifts in producing change in coalfield women's lives.

Nevertheless, the women's support movement *was* a significant moment in modern British history, if not in precisely the ways it is most often assumed to be. Analysing it illuminates the contours of change in British women's lives, and, indeed, in British politics more broadly. That the movement happened at all is itself revealing. While this was not the first time that women from the coalfields had been involved in political activism, the scale of involvement was new. Working-class women *had* been configured as political subjects before, through appeals to them as housewife citizens, or as activists in the tradition of maternalist socialism, or as members of trade unions taking strike action themselves, as in the disputes at Ford, Trico, and Grunwick in the 1960s and 1970s.[108] Yet during the miners' strike, working-class women were configured anew as defenders of industrial communities against the Thatcherite onslaught: a more expansive role. Women who were active in the support movement were able to carve out an independent space for activism; they were able in (limited) ways

---

[108] Caitríona Beaumont, *Housewives and Citizens: Domesticity and the Women's Movement in England, 1928–64* (Manchester: Manchester University Press, 2016); Stephen Brooke, *Sexual Politics: Sexuality, Family Planning, and the British Left from the 1880s to the Present Day* (Oxford: Oxford University Press, 2011); Jonathan Moss, *Women, Workplace Protest and Political Identity in England, 1968–85* (Manchester: Manchester University Press, 2019).

to challenge male-dominated institutions such as the NUM, and sometimes travelled significant distances in the cause of activism, leaving their striking husbands to keep the home-fires burning. The very visibility of the movement, and the media attention it attracted, helped to create this political space for coalfield women, even if some of those media reports were based on an exaggerated sense of the numbers involved. And the movement's legacy facilitated the creation of a cultural memory of working-class women's political participation which itself helped to enlarge understandings of women's roles, and made some activists think differently about their own life trajectories. Thus the support movement reflected significant shifts in women's lives, helped create a new space in which working-class women could be politically active, and in turn could sometimes foster a new sense of self among activists. For such women, activism created an opening through which personal autonomy could be achieved; it was a potential outlet for the popular individualism that was becoming more apparent in British society in the postwar period, and particularly from the 1970s onwards.[109]

It is easy to be despairing about the aftermath of the strike. The NUM was broken; trade unions have never since wielded so much power in Britain. Even if the decline of community has been overstated, there is no doubt that pit closures were economically devastating for mining districts, and economic dislocation brought with it a host of social problems. At the time of writing, the political battles which strike activists saw themselves as fighting for—the right to well-paid jobs, to dignity in labour, for working-class communities to have a future as well as a past—seem in many ways to have been lost. Most of the women we interviewed felt these losses heavily; indeed, a number of interviewees contested heroic readings of the strike precisely because they felt it had achieved nothing, and occasioned huge hardship for no apparent end. Yet for some women—particularly those who had been committed activists—the strike was still the stand-out experience of their lives. The drama of the dispute—and the extensive media coverage it received—gave them, probably for the first time, a sense that they were participating in something of global significance, that their actions impacted on the lives of others, *that they too could make history*.

Such women's testimonies are not transparent windows onto the experiences they had in the strike: rather, they were constructed through a culturally-embedded 'heroic narrative' of the strike. Nevertheless, the political power that this narrative has is enormous, and many women were keen for the positive aspects of their experience to be remembered as a source of education and inspiration for future generations. Janet Slater laughingly told us that in fifty

---

[109] Emily Robinson, Camilla Schofield, Florence Sutcliffe-Braithwaite, and Natalie Thomlinson, 'Telling Stories about Post-War Britain: Popular Individualism and the "Crisis" of the 1970s', *Twentieth Century British History*, 28 (2017), 268–304.

years' time, what she would like people to take from the strike was 'to stand up for what you believe in [and] don't let the bastards grind you down!'[110] Caroline Poland told us that she would like people to remember 'the spirit of solidarity. The building up of understanding of different lives, the building up of respect for people, you know, from different lives.'[111] And Christina Bell told us that she wanted people in the future to know that 'we stood up to the establishment. Alright, we might not have won it, but we stood up for what we've believed in, we stood up for what we thought was right, and it's worth remembering that people can still—people still do this.'[112]

As Christina's words suggest, supporting the strike gave women a sense of agency in extremely challenging circumstances—circumstances very much not of their own making. While this could not entirely compensate for the failure of the strike, it is clear that activism had its own rewards, and allowed women to feel that they were not simply passive victims of the political order or of global economic shifts, but could have some hand in making the future of their communities. The enthusiasm of many activist women for their political experiences in the dispute was infectious; their optimism that strike activism still has something to teach us all about how the world could be better sounded a note of political hope at a moment when such hope seemed in short supply. It is doubtless this which makes their stories so attractive to many of those who are interested in the politics of social justice, and which explains why the strike, and women's role in it, remains so culturally prominent today.

---

[110] Janet Slater.
[111] Caroline Poland, b. 1949, South East England/Yorkshire, interviewed by Natalie Thomlinson, 5 February 2019.
[112] Christina Bell.

APPENDIX 1

Details of Project Interviewees

These interviews are archived at the National Coal Mining Museum for England, Wakefield. Note that some interviewees wished to be known by first name only, or by first name and surname initial; we therefore alphabetise by first name in this list. In the table, * denotes a pseudonym, and † denotes an interview is embargoed for a period of time (time periods differ across interviews).

Name/pseudonym	Year of birth	Strike location	Interviewer	Date of interview	Catalogue reference
Adrienne C.	1956	North Yorkshire	Victoria Dawson	26/06/2018	WMS84-011†
Aggie Currie	1950	South Yorkshire	Victoria Dawson	22/06/2018	WMS84-022
Alice Samuel	1958	Fife	Natalie Thomlinson	01/08/2018	WMS84-060
Alison Anderson	1959	Fife	Victoria Dawson	29/08/2018	WMS84-001
Angela	1958	Oxford	Florence Sutcliffe-Braithwaite	09/07/2018	WMS84-053
Angela Jones	1965	Cynon Valley, South Wales	Victoria Dawson	02/09/2018	WMS84-038
Ann	1942	South Yorkshire	Victoria Dawson	25/07/2018	WMS84-059
Ann McCracken	1954	South Yorkshire	Victoria Dawson	06/12/2018	WMS84-079
Ann Robertson	1934	Kent	Florence Sutcliffe-Braithwaite	05/11/2018	WMS84-056
Ann Wilson	1945	Cynon Valley, South Wales	Victoria Dawson and Florence Sutcliffe-Braithwaite	11/08/2018	WMS84-081
Anne Kirby	1955	Fife	Victoria Dawson	26/11/2018	WMS84-043
Anne Scargill	1941	South Yorkshire	Natalie Thomlinson	16/03/2019	WMS84-018†
Anne Watts	1949	Cynon Valley, South Wales	Florence Sutcliffe-Braithwaite	23/05/2019	WMS84-073
Betty Cook	1938	West Yorkshire	Natalie Thomlinson	16/03/2019	WMS84-018†
Brooke*	1959	London	Natalie Thomlinson	20/07/2018	WMS84-028†

Continued

APPENDIX 1

Name/pseudonym	Year of birth	Strike location	Interviewer	Date of interview	Catalogue reference
Carol*	1968	South Wales	Natalie Thomlinson	19/06/2018	WMS84-042†
Carol Willis	1952	Manchester	Victoria Dawson	03/04/2019	WMS84-080
Carole Hancock	1938	South Yorkshire	Victoria Dawson	26/06/2018	WMS84-034
Caroline Poland	1949	South Yorkshire	Natalie Thomlinson	05/02/2019	WMS84-051
Chloe*	1959	South Yorkshire	Victoria Dawson	30/08/2018	WMS84-064
Christina Bell	1949	Nottinghamshire	Victoria Dawson	27/06/2018	WMS84-004
Christine Harvey	1950	Cynon Valley, South Wales	Florence Sutcliffe-Braithwaite	14/08/2018	WMS84-035
Christine Wooldridge	1941	Nottinghamshire; worked South Yorkshire	Victoria Dawson	25/05/2018	WMS84-082
Christine Worth	1952	Derbyshire	Natalie Thomlinson	02/08/2018	WMS84-083
Clair	1972	Kent	Florence Sutcliffe-Braithwaite	14/07/2018	WMS84-058†
Claire Erasmus	1970	Rhymney Valley, South Wales	Victoria Dawson	01/09/2018	WMS84-027
Colette Butterly	1968	Nottinghamshire	Natalie Thomlinson	08/11/2018	WMS84-010
Connie Dixon	1948	Midlothian	Victoria Dawson	07/12/2018	WMS84-067
Diane Jarratt	1945	South Yorkshire	Victoria Dawson	20/11/2018	WMS84-003†
Elizabeth Ann*	1943	South Wales	Victoria Dawson	12/08/2018	WMS84-068†
Erica Stevenson*	1959	South Yorkshire	Victoria Dawson	01/08/2018	WMS84-006†
Eve Featherstone	1955	London	Natalie Thomlinson	20/07/2018	WMS84-028†
Jane Petrie	1955	South Yorkshire	Victoria Dawson	16/11/2018	WMS84-050
Janet Slater	1954	Nottinghamshire	Natalie Thomlinson	03/08/2018	WMS84-062
Janice Bartolo	1957	Kent	Natalie Thomlinson and Florence Sutcliffe-Braithwaite	05/03/2016	WMS84-085
Janie Robertson	1955	Stirlingshire	Florence Sutcliffe-Braithwaite	20/11/2018	WMS84-057
Jean Shadbolt	1948	Nottinghamshire	Natalie Thomlinson	23/07/2018	WMS84-041

APPENDIX 1   251

Jeanette McComb	1953	Ayrshire	Victoria Dawson	26/09/2018	WMS84-046
Jennifer Llewellyn	1962	Cynon Valley, South Wales	Victoria Dawson	02/09/2018	WMS84-038
Jenny*	1961	Nottinghamshire	Natalie Thomlinson	02/08/2018	WMS84-071†
Jessica Gibson	1963	Midlothian	Florence Sutcliffe-Braithwaite	26/11/2018	WMS84-033
Jill Whitaker	1973	South Yorkshire	Victoria Dawson	06/09/2018	WMS84-076
Jo-Anne Welsh	1967	South Yorkshire	Florence Sutcliffe-Braithwaite	09/06/2018	WMS84-075
Joan Holden	1937	West Yorkshire	Victoria Dawson	23/07/2018	WMS84-037
Joanne*	1973	North East England	Victoria Dawson	16/07/2018	WMS84-066†
Josie Warner*	1952	London	Victoria Dawson	13/06/2018	WMS84-078
Joyce Boyes	1955	North Yorkshire	Victoria Dawson	21/11/2018	WMS84-007†
Judy*	1947	South Yorkshire	Victoria Dawson	20/11/2018	WMS84-003†
Karmen Thomas	1956	Carmarthenshire	Florence Sutcliffe-Braithwaite	12/08/2018	WMS84-069
Kath Court	1943	London	Florence Sutcliffe-Braithwaite	26/04/2019	WMS84-019
Kay Case	1948	Taff Bargoed Valley, South Wales	Florence Sutcliffe-Braithwaite	13/08/2018	WMS84-012
Kay Sutcliffe	1949	Kent	Natalie Thomlinson and Florence Sutcliffe-Braithwaite	05/03/2016	WMS84-085
Kerry Smith	1972	Nottinghamshire	Natalie Thomlinson	23/07/2018	WMS84-041
Kim Hickling	1962	Nottinghamshire	Natalie Thomlinson	28/08/2018	WMS84-036
Linda Chapman	1958	Tyne and Wear	Victoria Dawson	18/07/2018	WMS84-014
Linda Conway	1955	Fife	Victoria Dawson	28/08/2018	WMS84-017
Linda Finnis	1952	Kent	Florence Sutcliffe-Braithwaite	03/07/2018	WMS84-030
Lisa McKenzie	1968	Nottinghamshire	Natalie Thomlinson and Florence Sutcliffe-Braithwaite	29/03/2016	WMS84-084

Continued

APPENDIX 1

Name/pseudonym	Year of birth	Strike location	Interviewer	Date of interview	Catalogue reference
Liz Crowther	1958	West Yorkshire	Victoria Dawson	17/08/2018	WMS84-020
Liz French	1950	Kent	Florence Sutcliffe-Braithwaite	06/07/2018	WMS84-032
Lorraine Walsh	1959	Kent	Florence Sutcliffe-Braithwaite	03/07/2018	WMS84-030
Madeline (Mandy) Slater	1937	South Yorkshire	Victoria Dawson	08/08/2018	WMS84-024
Maggie Stubbs	c.1950	South Yorkshire; worked Nottinghamshire	Natalie Thomlinson	13/09/2018	WMS84-065
Mair Francis	1948	Dulais Valley, South Wales	Florence Sutcliffe-Braithwaite	17/07/2018	WMS84-031
Margaret Davis	1949	Kent	Natalie Thomlinson and Florence Sutcliffe-Braithwaite	05/03/2016	WMS84-085
Margaret Holmes	1942	Kent	Florence Sutcliffe-Braithwaite	26/07/2018	WMS84-039
Margaret Whitaker	1942	South Yorkshire	Victoria Dawson	06/09/2018	WMS84-077
Marie Price	1935	Nottinghamshire	Natalie Thomlinson	29/05/2019	WMS84-052
Marjorie Simpson	1938	South Yorkshire	Victoria Dawson	23/05/2018	WMS84-061
Mary*	1945	South Yorkshire	Victoria Dawson	20/11/2018	WMS84-003†
Mary Hole	1935	Cynon Valley, South Wales	Victoria Dawson	02/09/2018	WMS84-038
Maureen Coates	1942	South Yorkshire	Natalie Thomlinson and Florence Sutcliffe-Braithwaite	11/09/2014	WMS84-016
Maxine Penkethman	1967	Staffordshire	Victoria Dawson	03/08/2018	WMS84-049
Mig Weldon	1950	Fife	Victoria Dawson	29/08/2018	WMS84-074
Myra Dakin	1959	West Yorkshire; worked South Yorkshire	Victoria Dawson	16/08/2018	WMS84-048
Nicola Field	1960	London	Florence Sutcliffe-Braithwaite	24/07/2018	WMS84-029

Name	Year	Location	Interviewer	Date	ID
Pat Smith	1949	South Yorkshire	Victoria Dawson	08/06/2018	WMS84-063
Pauline C.	1949	Northumberland	Victoria Dawson	19/11/2018	WMS84-023
Philip Brown (interview focuses on mother, Cath Brown, b. 1924)	1955	Tyne and Wear	Victoria Dawson	18/07/2018	WMS84-008
Pippa Morgan*	1962	Cynon Valley, South Wales	Natalie Thomlinson	13/08/2018	WMS84-070
Polly*	1944	Nottinghamshire	Natalie Thomlinson	07/11/2018	WMS84-045†
Poppy Peacock*	1968	North East England	Victoria Dawson	28/06/2018	WMS84-055
Rachel Johnson	1970	Nottinghamshire	Natalie Thomlinson	23/07/2018	WMS84-041
Rebecca Shirt*	1956	South Yorkshire	Victoria Dawson	12/10/2018	WMS84-072†
Rita Wakefield	1943	Nottinghamshire	Natalie Thomlinson	20/08/2018	WMS84-036
Robyn*	1963	South Yorkshire	Victoria Dawson	26/07/2018	WMS84-009
Roni Chapman	1941	South Yorkshire	Victoria Dawson	11/06/2018	WMS84-013
Sara C.	1971	South Yorkshire	Victoria Dawson	25/06/2018	WMS84-015
Sarah Andrews	1949	Kent	Florence Sutcliffe-Braithwaite	20/06/2018	WMS84-002
Sharron Dewhurst	1960	South Yorkshire	Victoria Dawson	08/08/2018	WMS84-024
Shelan Holden	1970	West Yorkshire	Victoria Dawson	23/07/2018	WMS84-037
Siân James	1959	Swansea Valley, South Wales	Florence Sutcliffe-Braithwaite	05/02/2019	WMS84-040†
Sue	1956	Kent	Florence Sutcliffe-Braithwaite	14/07/2018	WMS84-058
Tanya Dower	1967	Cynon Valley, South Wales	Victoria Dawson	13/08/2018	WMS84-025
Theresa Gratton*	1955	County Durham	Florence Sutcliffe-Braithwaite	22/02/2020	WMS84-086†
Tracy Bell	1971	Nottinghamshire	Victoria Dawson	12/06/2018	WMS84-005
Veronica*	1946	Nottinghamshire	Natalie Thomlinson	29/05/2019	WMS84-054†
Victoria*	1946	South Yorkshire	Victoria Dawson	20/11/2018	WMS84-003†
Virginia O'Reilly	1953	Dublin	Natalie Thomlinson	12/08/2018	WMS84-047
Wendy Minney	1964	Nottinghamshire	Natalie Thomlinson	20/08/2018	WMS84-036

APPENDIX 2
Details of Key Sociological Studies of the Strike and Aftermath

Allen, Meg, 'Carrying on the Strike: The Politics of Women Against Pit Closures' (unpublished PhD thesis, University of Manchester, 2001). Allen's research was based on the published writings of women's support group activists, and interviews with 45 activists, all deeply committed to the cause, 36 of whom were related by family or marriage to miners.

Measham, Fiona, and Sheila Allen, 'In Defence of Home and Hearth? Families, Friendships and Feminism in Mining Communities', *Journal of Gender Studies*, 3 (1994), 31–45. This study is based on the interviews carried out in 1986 for Warwick and Littlejohn's *Coal, Capital and Culture*; 123 women and 31 men from 124 households (which had been randomly selected), in Warwick and Littlejohn's four mining areas in West Yorkshire, were interviewed. Men and women were interviewed separately. Interviewees came from mining families and non-mining families. Thirty-nine of the women came from households containing an NCB employee (though not all of these were on strike), and 84 from other households; 44 came from a 'mining household' (defined as having or having recently had an immediate family member employed in mining) and 75 from other households (with four women uncategorised on this metric).

Waddington, David, Chas Critcher, Bella Dicks, and David Parry, *Out of the Ashes: The Social Impact of Industrial Contraction and Regeneration on Britain's Mining Communities* (London: The Stationery Office in association with the Regional Studies Association, 2001). The central three chapters of the book (2–4) are based on a comparative study of four Doncaster mining communities, Askern, Brodsworth, Hatfield, and Rossington, carried out in 1992 and 1993, and encompassing: (1) a questionnaire survey of 340 miners/ex-miners and their partners, plus a sub-sample of 40 miners who had taken voluntary redundancy and their partners, plus a sub-sample of 80 Rossington residents not involved in mining; (2) in-depth follow-up interviews with 30 miners/ex-miners and their partners; (3) in-depth interviews with 60 key informants such as social workers.

Waddington, David, Maggie Wykes, and Chas Critcher, *Split at the Seams? Community, Continuity and Change after the 1984-5 Coal Dispute* (Milton Keynes: Open University Press, 1991). The study examined 'Yorksco', a strongly pro-strike village, 'Nottsco', a Nottinghamshire village where 4–11 per cent of the workforce was on strike at different times in the dispute and 'Derbyco', a Derbyshire village where, at the height of the strike, half the workforce was striking. The methodology involved semi-structured interviews with 125 people—both those involved in the strike, and 'outsiders' like social workers—plus a sample survey of 400 people from the three communities, stratified based on age, gender, and employment in the mining community. Fieldwork was carried out 1987–8.

Warwick, Dennis, and Gary M. Littlejohn, *Coal, Capital and Culture: A Sociological Analysis of Mining Communities in West Yorkshire* (London: Routledge, 1992). This research began in 1978 and covered four communities in the Featherstone and Hemsworth areas. In 1981 and 1984, the researchers conducted over 70 biographical interviews, mainly in one of the research locations, 'Ashby'. While the strike was ongoing in 1984 they also interviewed 80 men and women about the strike. They then conducted 324 interviews in a randomly selected sample of households in all four locations in 1986 and 1987, plus a small follow-up survey in some of these households in 1989.

Winterton, Jonathan, and Ruth Winterton, *Coal, Crisis and Conflict: The 1984–5 Miners' Strike in Yorkshire* **(Manchester: Manchester University Press, 1989).** This study was conducted during and immediately after the strike, and based on: documentation of NUM bodies; participant observation at locations like picket lines and strike centres; interviews with an expert informant from each Yorkshire pit; and a questionnaire distributed to individuals through colliery contacts and women's action groups. The questionnaire was completed by 1,830 respondents (it was sent out to 6,000), and by using participation rates calculated on the basis of the interviews, the questionnaire responses were weighted to correct for the overrepresentation of strike activists in the responses.

APPENDIX 3

Chronology

Before the Strike

1926	General Strike and miners' lockout
1939–45	Second World War
1945	Labour Party under Clement Attlee elected in landslide General Election victory
1945	National Union of Mineworkers (NUM) formed out of Miners' Federation of Great Britain
1947	Britain's deep coal mines taken into national ownership; National Coal Board (NCB) formed to run the industry
1957–67	243,000 jobs lost in mining industry
1972	First national miners' strike since nationalisation; Battle of Saltley Gate; miners win major pay increase
1974	Second national miners' strike since nationalisation; miners victorious; Conservative Prime Minister Ted Heath calls a General Election and loses, returning a Labour government
1977–8	Area Incentive Scheme introduced in coal industry: productive Areas can win high wages
1979	Margaret Thatcher's first General Election victory, returning Conservative Party to power
1981	NCB agrees to major increase in miners' wages to head off potential strike
1982	Arthur Scargill becomes NUM President
1982	National ballot fails to return a mandate for NUM strike action
1983	Further national ballot fails to return a mandate for NUM strike action
1983	Margaret Thatcher's second General Election victory
1983	Ian MacGregor becomes NCB Chairman

The Strike

1 March 1984	NCB announces the closure of Cortonwood colliery, South Yorkshire
5 March 1984	Collieries in South Yorkshire strike or are picketed out in response; collieries in other Areas later follow suit
12 March 1984	99 pits employing over 96,000 men are closed for production
15–16 March 1984	Nottinghamshire Area NUM votes 73.5 per cent against striking

March 1984	Women's groups begin to form in the coalfields to support the strike
12 May 1984	First national women's march and rally held in Barnsley, South Yorkshire
14 May 1984	Anne Scargill arrested on the picket line at Silverhill colliery, Nottinghamshire
17–20 June 1984	Occupation of Betteshanger colliery, Kent
18 June 1984	Battle of Orgreave
21–22 July 1984	Inaugural conference of National Women Against Pit Closures (NWAPC) held at Northern College, South Yorkshire
11 August 1984	NWAPC march in London
18 September 1984	Thatcher meets the 'Miners Wives Back to Work Campaign'
12 October 1984	IRA bomb targets Thatcher at Conservative Party Conference in Brighton
31 October 1984	Final round of talks between the NUM and NCB collapses
10–11 November 1984	NWAPC holds second national conference in Chesterfield
3 March 1985	NUM Special Delegate conference calls off the strike
5 March 1985	Most striking miners return to work; some remain out for several days more before returning
9 March 1985	NWAPC International Women's Day rally at Chesterfield football stadium

After the Strike

17 August 1985	Third NWAPC conference held in Sheffield
1987	Associate membership for women's groups added to NUM national rulebook
1988	Last issue of *Coalfield Woman*, NWAPC newsletter, produced
1992–3	John Major's Conservative government announces closure of 31 out of 50 remaining pits; Women Against Pit Closures groups set up pit camps to contest closures
1994	Privatisation of remaining nationalised coal mines
2015	Closure of Kellingley colliery, Yorkshire, the last deep mine to close in the UK

Bibliography

Archival Collections

Barnsley Archives, Barnsley
The Papers of Barnsley Women Against Pit Closures (including material relating to Barnsley Miners' Wives Action Group).
The Papers of Maureen Robinson.

Bishopsgate Archive, London
Format Photographers Collective collection.

British Library, London
National Life Stories.
Sisterhood and After Collection.

Feminist Archive North, Leeds
The Papers of Jill Page.

Fife Archives, Glenrothes
'Reports and Papers relating to the 1984–1985 Miners' Strike'.

Glamorgan Archives, Cardiff
The Papers of Aberdare Miners' Relief Fund.
The Papers of the South Wales Women's Support Group.
The Papers of Violet John.

Hull History Centre, Hull
The Papers of John Saville.

London Metropolitan University Special Collections, London
TUC Collection.

Mass Observation Archives, The Keep, Brighton
The Papers of Iris Preston.

The National Archives, London
The Records of the Prime Minister's Office.

National Mining Museum for Scotland, Newtongrange
Oral History Collection.

Nottingham University Special Collections, Nottingham
The Papers of Fred Westacott.

People's History Museum and Archive, Manchester
'The Miners' Strike Papers'.
The Papers of the Communist Party.
The Papers of Hilary Wainwright.

Richard Burton Archive, Swansea
The Papers of Raissa Page.
South Wales Coalfield Collection.

Sheffield City Archives, Sheffield
The Papers of Askern Women's Support Group.
The Papers of Lesley Boulton.
The Papers of Rossington Women's Support Group.

South Wales Miners' Library, Swansea
South Wales Coalfield Collection.

Women's Library@LSE, London
The Papers of Betty Heathfield.
The Papers of the Essex Road Women's Centre.
The Papers of Jean McCrindle.

Working Class Movement Library, Salford
'Miners' Strike 1984–1985 Support Groups Collection'.
Oral History Collection.

Online Archives

Archive of Market and Social Research, https://www.amsr.org.uk/.
Margaret Thatcher Foundation (MTF) website, http://www.margaretthatcher.org.

Unarchived Oral History Interviews

Claire* interviewed by Natalie Thomlinson, 11 August 2018.
Stewart B. interviewed by Emily Peirson-Webber, 26 August 2020.
Hugh Dixon interviewed by Florence Sutcliffe-Braithwaite, 21 February 2020.
Kath Mackey interviewed by Daisy Payling, 10 January 2014.
Jean McCrindle interviewed by Florence Sutcliffe-Braithwaite and Natalie Thomlinson, 29 September and 13 November 2015.
Roger Shannon interviewed by Florence Sutcliffe-Braithwaite and Natalie Thomlinson, 9 November 2021.

Data Collections

1971 Census, UK Data Service, https://casweb.ukdataservice.ac.uk/.
National Child Development Study: Childhood Data from Birth to Age 16, Sweeps 0–3, 1958–1974 (data collection), 3rd edition, National Children's Bureau, National Birthday Trust Fund (original data producer), Institute of Education, Centre for Longitudinal Studies, University of London (2020), UK Data Service, SN: 5565.
National Child Development Study: Age 23, Sweep 4, 1981, and Public Examination Results, 1978 (data collection), 2nd edition, National Children's Bureau (original data producer), Institute of Education, Centre for Longitudinal Studies, University of London (2020), UK Data Service, SN: 5566.
Yvette Taylor, 'From the Coalface to the Car Park? The Intersection of Class and Gender in Women's Lives in the North East, 2007–2009' (data collection) (2012), UK Data Service, SN: 7053.

Private Collections

The Papers of Gwen MacLeod, in the collection of Lisa McKenzie.
The Papers of Janie Robertson.
The Papers of Maureen Coates.
The Papers of Penny Green.
The Papers of Poppy Peacock*.

Other

Hansard, House of Commons Debates.

Film and Television Programmes

'1984', *Our Friends in the North*, dir. Simon Cellan-Jones, BBC2, 26 February 1996.
Billy Elliot, dir. Stephen Daldry, 2000.
Brassed Off, dir. Mark Herman, 1996.
'Coal not Dole', *People to People*, dir. Richard Anthony, Channel 4, 4 June 1984.
The Battle of Orgreave, dir. Jeremy Deller, 2001.
Faith, dir. David Thacker, BBC1, 28 February 2005.
Look North, BBC1, 10 February 2022.
The Miners' Campaign Tapes 1. Not Just Tea and Sandwiches, dir. Birmingham Film/Video Workshop and Platform Films, 1984.
The Miners' Strike, BBC2, 27 January 2004.
'Please Don't Say We're Wonderful', *People to People*, dir. Jessica York, Channel 4, 27 July 1986.
Pride, dir. Matthew Warchus, 2014.
Sherwood, dir. Lewis Arnold and Ben Williams, BBC1, 13 June 2022.

Smiling and Splendid Women, dir. Gail Allen, 1986.
Strike: When Britain Went to War, Channel 4, 24 January 2004.
Which Side Are You On? Songs, Poems and Experiences of the Miners' Strike, 1984, dir. Ken Loach, Channel 4, 9 January 1985.
'Women in Line', *World in Action*, ITV, 16 April 1984.

Newspapers and Magazines

'12-Month Strike Fears Shot Down', *The Miner*, 7 February 1985.
'Diary', *Guardian*, 18 September 1984.
'"I'm Proud of Her"—Scargill', *Daily Mail*, 17 May 1984.
'Miner's Wife Wins Cheer with Tales of Harassment', *Globe and Mail* (Toronto), 10 October 1984.
'Petticoat Pickets', *Nottingham Evening Post*, 10 March 1984.
'Scargill should be Sued for Overtime, says an Angry Wife', *Daily Mail*, 10 January 1984.
'Strike News in Brief', *The Miner*, 7 February 1985.
'Strike Stalemate as Miners Wait for Talks', *The Times*, 17 April 1984.
'Striking Miner's Wife Defies the Pickets', *Daily Mail*, 24 January 1972.
Beard, Matthew, 'Agencies in Dock over Mining Villages Ravaged by Heroin', *Independent*, 18 September 2002.
Brown, Maggie, 'A Flying Leap onto the Picket Line', *Guardian*, 28 May 1984.
Campbell, Beatrix, 'The Other Miners' Strike', *New Statesman*, 27 July 1984.
Clough, Patricia, 'Two Brothers Die Digging for Coal', *The Times*, 19 November 1984.
Cross, David, '1,800 Return to Work in One Day', *The Times*, 22 January 1985.
Dibbits, Kat, 'Play Preview: The Enemies Within in Bolton', *Lancashire Telegraph*, 4 December 2009.
Disney, Anthea, 'We're Not Asking for Damn Cake', *Daily Mail*, 16 February 1972.
Felton, David, 'Coal Strike Threat Spreads as NCB Insists on Closures', *The Times*, 7 March 1984.
Felton, David, 'NCB Encourages Pre-Christmas Return to Work', *The Times*, 3 November 1984.
Foster, Dawn, 'Margaret Thatcher Didn't Expect it, but Miners' Wives Galvanised the '84 Strike', *Guardian*, 12 March 2014.
Gillan, Audrey, 'I was Always Told I was Thick: The Strike Taught Me I Wasn't', *Guardian*, 10 May 2004.
Head, Joanna, 'Miners' Wives', *New Statesman*, 15 June 1984.
Hill, Dave, 'A Fight to the Death', *Guardian*, 5 March 1994.
Hollingsworth, Mark, 'Using Miners to Bust the Union', *New Statesman*, 14 December 1984.
Ignatieff, Michael, 'Strangers and Comrades', *New Statesman*, 14 December 1984.
Jones, Tim, 'Strike Ballot by Welsh Miners', *The Times*, 24 February 1983.
Jones, Tim, 'Close Result Likely in Welsh Pit Strike Call', *The Times*, 25 February 1983.
Jones, Tim, 'Anger and Despair at Doomed Pit', *The Times*, 11 March 1983.
Jones, Tim, 'Bitter Strikers Set to Go Back', *The Times*, 12 March 1983.
Keel, P., 'Pit Sit-in Ends as Two Miners Quit Work', *Guardian*, 21 June 1984.
Loach, Loretta, 'We'll be Here Right to the End and After', *Spare Rib*, 147, October 1984.
London, Jack, 'The Scab', *The Atlantic*, January 1904.
Long, Betty, 'Looking Back', *Valleys Star*, 29, 20 February 1985 (the *Valleys Star* is archived at the South Wales Miners' Library, Swansea and the Glamorgan Archives, Cardiff).

McGibbon, Irene, 'Talks as Bar to Return to Pits', *The Times*, 24 October 1984.
Martin, Gill, 'Cowley Militants "Gag Moderates"', *Daily Mail*, 2 May 1974.
Milne, Seumas, and Keith Harper, 'Thatcher was One Day Away from Defeat', *Guardian*, 7 March 1994.
Mullins, Joseph, 'Fury as the Picket Line Wives go into Action', *Daily Mail*, 8 February 1972.
Oldfield, Stephen, 'Why Women are Against the Strikes', *Daily Mail*, 12 March 1984.
Robinson, Gail, 'Women Found their Voices and Grew in Confidence', *Barnsley Chronicle*, 7 March 2014.
Routledge, Paul, 'Miners Vote "No" and Push Union into Policy Crisis', *The Times*, 9 March 1983.
Routledge, Paul, 'Militant Picketing Spreads Coal Strike to 100 Pits', *The Times*, 13 March 1984.
Routledge, Paul, 'Colliery Officials may Quit NUM', *The Times*, 18 January 1985.
Routledge, Paul, 'The Whiff of Defeat Creeps Closer', *The Times*, 7 February 1985.
Sherwood, Harriet, 'The Women of the Miners' Strike: "We Caused a Lot of Havoc"', *Guardian*, 7 April 2014.
Torode, John, 'Who Won the Miners' Strike for Maggie?', *Guardian*, 18 March 1985.
Wainwright, Martin, 'Former Pit Towns Say No to Drug Addiction', *Guardian*, 21 July 2004.
Wintour, Patrick, 'Woman's Place is on the Picket', *Guardian*, 17 May 1984.

Published Sources

Ackers, Peter, 'Gramsci at the Miners' Strike: Remembering the 1984–1985 Eurocommunist Alternative Industrial Relations Strategy', *Labor History*, 55 (2014), 151–72.
Adeney, Martin, and John Lloyd, *The Miners' Strike, 1984–5: Loss without Limit* (London: Routledge & Kegan Paul, 1986).
Andrews, Geoff, *Endgames and New Times: The Final Years of British Communism, 1964–1991* (London: Lawrence & Wishart, 2004).
Aragón, Fernando M., Juan Pablo Rud, and Gerhard Toews, 'Resource Shocks, Employment, and Gender: Evidence from the Collapse of the UK Coal Industry', *Labour Economics*, 52 (2018), 54–67.
Arnold, Jörg, *The British Miner in the Age of De-Industrialization: A Political and Cultural History* (Oxford: Oxford University Press, 2023).
Ashworth, William, *The History of the British Coal Industry. Volume 5, 1946–1982: The Nationalized Industry* (Oxford: Clarendon Press, 1986).
Barnsley Miners' Wives Action Group, *We Struggled to Laugh* (Barnsley: Barnsley Miners' Wives Action Group, 1987) (copies can be found in the papers of Raissa Page, Richard Burton Archives, Swansea, and in the TUC Collection, London Metropolitan University Special Collections, London).
Barnsley Women Against Pit Closures, *Women Against Pit Closures, Volume 2* (Barnsley: Barnsley Women Against Pit Closures, 1985).
Barron, Hester, *The 1926 Miners' Lockout: Meanings of Community in the Durham Coalfield* (Oxford: Oxford University Press, 2010).
Beaton, Lynn, *Shifting Horizons* (London: Canary, 1985).
Beatty, Christina, and Steve Fothergill, 'Labour Market Adjustment in Areas of Chronic Industrial Decline: The Case of the UK Coalfields', *Regional Studies*, 30 (1996), 637–50.

Beatty, Christina, and Steve Fothergill, *The Contemporary Labour Market in Britain's Older Industrial Towns* (Sheffield: Sheffield Hallam University Centre for Economic Research/Joseph Rowntree Foundation, 2018).

Beaumont, Caitríona, *Housewives and Citizens: Domesticity and the Women's Movement in England, 1928–64* (Manchester: Manchester University Press, 2016).

Beckwith, Karen, 'Lancashire Women Against Pit Closures: Women's Standing in a Men's Movement', *Signs*, 21 (1996), 1034–68.

Bennett, Katy, Huw Beynon, and Ray Hudson, *Coalfields Regeneration: Dealing with the Consequences of Industrial Decline* (Bristol: Policy Press, 2000).

Benney, Mark, *Charity Main: A Coalfield Chronicle* (London: George Allen & Unwin, 1946).

Beynon, Huw, ed., *Digging Deeper: Issues in the Miners' Strike* (London: Verso, 1985).

Beynon, Huw, and Terry Austrin, *Masters and Servants: Class and Patronage in the Making of a Labour Organisation: The Durham Miners and the English Political Tradition* (London: Rivers Oram Press, 1994).

Beynon, Huw, and Ray Hudson, *The Shadow of the Mine: Coal and the End of Industrial Britain* (London: Verso, 2021).

Boanas, Guy, 'Interviews at Grimethorpe', in *The Enemy Within: Pit Villages and the Miners' Strike of 1984-5*, ed. Raphael Samuel, Barbara Bloomfield, and Guy Boanas (London: Routledge & Kegan Paul, 1986), 202–15.

Booth, Alan, 'The Economy of Kent: An Overview', in *Kent in the Twentieth Century*, ed. Nigel Yates (Woodbridge: Boydell Press, 2001), 27–58.

Booth, Alan, and Roger Smith, 'The Irony of the Iron Fist: Social Security and the Coal Dispute of 1984–5', *Journal of Law and Society*, 12 (1985), 365–74.

Borland, Katherine, '"That's Not What I Said!" Interpretive Conflict in Oral Narrative Research', in *Women's Words: The Feminist Practice of Oral History*, ed. Sherna Berger Gluck and Daphne Patai (New York: Routledge, 1991), 63–75.

Bradshaw, Jonathan, and Alan Deacon, *Reserved for the Poor: The Means Test in British Social Policy* (Oxford: Blackwell, 1983).

Brooke, Stephen, *Sexual Politics: Sexuality, Family Planning, and the British Left from the 1880s to the Present Day* (Oxford: Oxford University Press, 2011).

Bruley, Sue, 'The Politics of Food: Gender, Family, Community and Communal Eating in the General Strike and Miners' Lockout in South Wales in 1926', *Twentieth Century British History*, 18 (2007), 54–77.

Buckley, Sheryl Bernadette, 'Making Miners Militant? The Communist Party of Great Britain and the National Union of Mineworkers, 1956-85', in *Waiting for the Revolution: The British Far Left from 1956*, ed. Evan Smith and Matthew Worley (Manchester: Manchester University Press, 2017), 107–24.

Bulmer, Martin, 'Sociological Models of the Mining Community', *Sociological Review*, 23 (1975), 61–92.

Campbell, Alan, *The Scottish Miners, 1874-1939, I: Industry, Work and Community* (Aldershot: Ashgate, 2000).

Campbell, Alan, Nina Fishman, and David Howell, *Miners, Unions and Politics, 1910–47* (Aldershot: Scholar Press, 1996).

Campbell, Beatrix, *Wigan Pier Revisited: Poverty and Politics in the Eighties* (London: Virago, 1984).

Campbell, Beatrix, 'Proletarian Patriarchs and the Real Radicals', in *The Cutting Edge: Women and the Pit Strike*, ed. Vicky Seddon (London: Lawrence & Wishart, 1986), 249–82.

Carruth, Alan A., and Andrew J. Oswald, 'Miners' Wages in Post-War Britain: An Application of a Model of Trade Union Behaviour', *Economic Journal*, 95 (1985), 1003–20.

Church, Roy, *The History of the British Coal Industry. Volume 3, 1830–1913: Victorian Pre-Eminence* (Oxford: Clarendon Press, 1986).

Clark, Paul F., 'Introducing Productivity Incentives in the British Coal-Mining Industry', *Industrial Relations Journal*, 11 (1980), 24–36.

Clarke, John, 'Enrolling Ordinary People: Governmental Strategies and the Avoidance of Politics', *Citizenship Studies*, 16 (2010), 637–50.

Clarke, Nick, Will Jennings, Jonathan Moss, and Gerry Stoker, *The Good Politician: Folk Theories, Political Interaction, and the Rise of Anti-Politics* (Cambridge: Cambridge University Press, 2018).

Collins, Marcus, *Modern Love: An Intimate History of Men and Women in Twentieth-Century Britain* (London: Atlantic, 2003).

Corrigan, Suzanne, Cath Cunningham, and Margo Thorburn, 'Fife Women Stand Firm', in *The Cutting Edge: Women and the Pit Strike*, ed. Vicky Seddon (London: Lawrence & Wishart, 1986), 30–49.

Coventry Miners' Wives Support Group, *Mummy... What Did You Do in the Strike?* (Coventry: Coventry Miners' Wives Support Group, 1986).

Cowan, David, '"Modern" Parenting and the Uses of Childcare Advice in Post-War England', *Social History*, 43 (2018), 332–55.

Curtis, Ben, *The South Wales Miners 1964–1985* (Cardiff: University of Wales Press, 2013).

Cwmbach Miners and Women Speak Out (Cardiff: Everyday Printers, 1984).

Darlington, Ralph, 'There is No Alternative: Exploring the Options in the 1984–5 Miners' Strike', *Capital & Class*, 87 (2005), 71–95.

Daunton, Martin, 'Down the Pit: Work in the Great Northern and South Wales Coalfields, 1870–1914', *Economic History Review*, 34 (1981), 578–97.

Davidoff, Leonore, and Catherine Hall, *Family Fortunes: Men and Women of the English Middle Class* (London: Routledge, 1988).

Davies, Jane, and Shirley James, 'Women from the Valleys Turn Activist', in *The Cutting Edge: Women and the Pit Strike*, ed. Vicky Seddon (London: Lawrence & Wishart, 1986), 16–29.

Davies, Ray, *A Miner's Life: The 1984 Miners' Strike and the Rhymney Valley Miners Support Group* (Caerphilly: RTD Publishers, 2014).

Dawson, Graham, *Soldier Heroes: British Adventure, Empire and the Imagining of Masculinities* (London: Routledge, 1994).

Deep Digs! Cartoons of the Miners' Strike: A Benefit Book for Women Against Pit Closures (London: Pluto, 1985).

Deller, Jeremy, *The English Civil War Part II: Personal Accounts of the 1984–85 Miners' Strike* (London: Artangel, 2001).

Dennis, Norman, Fernando Henriques, and Clifford Slaughter, *Coal is Our Life: An Analysis of a Yorkshire Mining Community* (London: Eyre & Spottiswoode, 1956).

Dolby, Norma, *Norma Dolby's Diary: An Account of the Great Miners' Strike* (London: Verso, 1987).

Dorey, Peter, 'Weakening the Trade Unions, One Step at a Time: The Thatcher Governments' Strategy for the Reform of Trade-Union Law, 1979–1984', *Historical Studies in Industrial Relations*, 37 (2016), 169–200.

Drabble, Barbara, 'Office Workers Take Action', in *The Cutting Edge: Women and the Pit Strike*, ed. Vicky Seddon (London: Lawrence & Wishart, 1986), 109–23.

Edgerton, David, *The Rise and Fall of the British Nation: A Twentieth Century History* (London: Penguin, 2019).
Elliott, Jane, 'Demographic Trends in Everyday Life, 1945–87', in *Marriage, Domestic Life and Social Change: Writings for Jacqueline Burgoyne (1944–88)*, ed. David Clark (London: Routledge, 1991), 85–110.
Emery, Jay, 'Belonging, Memory and History in the North Nottinghamshire Coalfield', *Journal of Historical Geography*, 59 (2018), 77–89.
Feickert, Dave, *Britain's Civil War Over Coal: An Insider's View* (Newcastle upon Tyne: Cambridge Scholars Publishing, 2021).
Fitzpatrick, Denise, Christine M. Nelson, May Cadwallader, and Edith Armitage, *10 Years On and Still Laughing* (Rotherham: Dearne Community Arts, 1994).
Flinn, Michael W., David Stoker, and Roy A. Church, *The History of the British Coal Industry. Volume 2, 1700–1830: The Industrial Revolution* (Oxford: Clarendon Press, 1984).
Francis, Hywel, *History on Our Side: Wales and the 1984–5 Miners' Strike* (London: Lawrence & Wishart, 2015).
Francis, Mair, *Up the DOVE! The History of the Dove Workshop in Banwen* (Cardigan: Iconau, 2008).
Gibbon, Peter, 'Analysing the Miners' Strike of 1984–5', *Economy and Society*, 17 (1988), 139–94.
Gibbon, Peter, and David Steyne, *Thurcroft. A Village and the Miners' Strike: An Oral History by the People of Thurcroft* (Nottingham: Spokesman, 1986).
Gibbs, Ewan, 'The Moral Economy of the Scottish Coalfields: Managing Deindustrialization under Nationalization, c.1947–1983', *Enterprise & Society*, 19 (2018), 124–52.
Gibbs, Ewan, *Coal Country: The Meaning and Memory of Deindustrialization in Postwar Scotland* (London: University of London Press, 2021).
Gier-Viskovatoff, J. J., and A. Porter, 'Women of the British Coalfields on Strike in 1926 and 1984: Documenting Lives Using Oral History and Photography', *Frontiers*, 19 (1998), 199–230.
Gildart, Keith, *North Wales Miners, 1945–1996: A Fragile Unity* (Cardiff: University of Wales Press, 2001).
Gittins, Jean, *Striking Stuff* (Bradford: 1 in 12 Club, 1986).
Goldthorpe, J. H., D. Lockwood, F. Bechhofer, and J. Platt, *The Affluent Worker in the Class Structure* (Cambridge: Cambridge University Press, 1969).
Goodwin, Jeff, James M. Jasper, and Francesca Polletta, eds., *Passionate Politics: Emotions and Social Movements* (Chicago: University of Chicago Press, 2001).
Graves, Pamela M., *Labour Women: Women in British Working-Class Politics, 1918–1939* (Cambridge: Cambridge University Press, 1994).
Green, Penny, *The Enemy Without: Policing and Class Consciousness in the Miners' Strike* (Milton Keynes: Open University Press, 1990).
Gregory, Roy, *The Miners and British Politics, 1906–1914* (Oxford: Oxford University Press, 1968).
Gunn, Simon, 'People and the Car: The Expansion of Automobility in Urban Britain, c.1955–70', *Social History*, 38 (2013), 220–37.
Hall, Richard, 'Being a Man, Being a Member: Masculinity and Community in Britain's Working Men's Clubs, 1945–1960', *Cultural and Social History*, 14 (2017), 73–88.
Hall, Valerie Gordon, 'Contrasting Female Identities: Women in Coal Mining Communities in Northumberland, England, 1900–1939', *Journal of Women's History*, 13 (2001), 107–31.

Harrison, Roydon, ed., *Independent Collier: The Coal Miner as Archetypal Proletarian Reconsidered* (Hassocks: Harvester Press, 1978).
Head, Janine, Mavis Watson, and Teresa Webb, *Striking Figures: The Story of Normanton and Altofts Miners Support Group 1984-5* (Huddersfield: Artivan and Striking Figures, 1986).
Hedley, Margaret, *Women of the Durham Coalfield in the 20th Century: Hannah's Daughter* (Cheltenham: The History Press, 2020).
Hill, Brian, and Lesley Sutcliffe, *Let them Eat Coal: The Politics of Social Security during the Miners' Strike* (London: Canary, 1985).
Hilliard, Christopher, *English as a Vocation: The Scrutiny Movement* (Oxford: Oxford University Press, 2012).
Holden, Triona, *Queen Coal: Women of the Miners' Strike* (Stroud: Sutton, 2005).
Hudson, Janet, 'Holding it Together', in *The Cutting Edge: Women and the Pit Strike*, ed. Vicky Seddon (London: Lawrence & Wishart, 1986), 63-78.
Hume, Bob, 'The Hatfield Main Welfare Organisation', in *The Enemy Within: Pit Villages and the Miners' Strike of 1984-5*, ed. Raphael Samuel, Barbara Bloomfield, and Guy Boanas (London: Routledge & Kegan Paul, 1986), 128-38.
Humphries, Jane, 'Protective Legislation, the Capitalist State, and Working-Class Men: The Case of the 1842 Mines Regulation Act', *Feminist Review*, 7 (1981), 1-35.
Jackson, Ben, and Robert Saunders, eds., *Making Thatcher's Britain* (Cambridge: Cambridge University Press, 2012).
Jackson, Brian, and Dennis Marsden, *Education and the Working Class: Some General Themes Raised by a Study of 88 Working-Class Children in a Northern Industrial City* (London: Routledge & Kegan Paul, 1962).
Joannou, Maroula, '"Fill a Bag and Feed a Family": The Miners' Strike and its Supporters', in *Labour and the Left in the 1980s*, ed. Jonathan Davis and Rohan McWilliam (Manchester: Manchester University Press, 2017), 172-91.
John, Angela V., *By the Sweat of their Brow: Women Workers at Victorian Coal Mines* (London: Croom Helm, 1980).
Jolly, Margaretta, *Sisterhood and After: An Oral History of the UK Women's Liberation Movement, 1968-Present* (Oxford: Oxford University Press, 2019).
Jones, Gareth Stedman, *Languages of Class: Studies in English Working Class History, 1832-1982* (Cambridge: Cambridge University Press, 1983).
Joshi, Heather, and P. R. Andrew Hinde, 'Employment after Childbearing in Post-War Britain: Cohort-Study Evidence on Contrasts within and across Generations', *European Sociological Review*, 9 (1993), 203-27.
Kanagasooriam, James, and Elizabeth Simon, 'Red Wall: The Definitive Description', *Political Insight*, 12 (2021), 8-11.
Kay, Diana, and Robert Miles, 'Refugees or Migrant Workers? The Case of the European Volunteer Workers in Britain (1946-1951)', *Journal of Refugee Studies*, 1 (1988), 214-36.
Kay, Janet, and Kila Millidine, 'Intruders not Peacekeepers', in *The Cutting Edge: Women and the Pit Strike*, ed. Vicky Seddon (London: Lawrence & Wishart, 1986), 176-202.
Keating, Jackie, *Counting the Cost: A Family in the Miners' Strike* (Barnsley: Wharncliffe Publishing, 1991).
Kefford, Alistair, 'Housing the Citizen-Consumer in Post-War Britain: The Parker Morris Report, Affluence and the Even Briefer Life of Social Democracy', *Twentieth Century British History*, 29 (2018), 225-58.
Kelliher, Diarmaid, *Cultures of Solidarity: London and the 1984-5 Miners' Strike* (London: Routledge, 2021).

Kelly, Eamonn, 'Channel 4's *Strike: When Britain Went to War* (2004): Trivialisation, Popular Culture, and the Miners' Strike', in *Digging the Seam: Popular Cultures of the 1984-5 Miners' Strike*, ed. Simon Popple and Ian W. Macdonald (Newcastle upon Tyne: Cambridge Scholars, 2012), 203-16.

Kerr, Clark, and Abraham Siegel, 'The Interindustry Propensity to Strike: An International Comparison', in *Industrial Conflict*, ed. Arthur Kornhauser, Robert Dubin, and Arthur M. Ross (New York: McGraw-Hill, 1954), 189-212.

King, Laura, *Family Men: Fatherhood and Masculinity in Britain, 1914-1960* (Oxford: Oxford University Press, 2015).

King, Richard, *Brittle with Relics: A History of Wales, 1962-1997* (London: Faber & Faber, 2022).

Knight, Iris, 'Upton, the Infants' Support Group', in *The Enemy Within: Pit Villages and the Miners' Strike of 1984-5*, ed. Raphael Samuel, Barbara Bloomfield, and Guy Boanas (London: Routledge & Kegan Paul, 1986), 122-6.

Koven, Seth, and Sonya Michel, eds., *Mothers of a New World: Maternalist Politics and the Origins of Welfare States* (London: Routledge, 1993).

Labour Research Department, *Solidarity with the Miners* (London: LRD, 1985).

Langhamer, Claire, *The English in Love: The Intimate Story of an Emotional Revolution* (Oxford: Oxford University Press, 2013).

Langhamer, Claire, 'Who the Hell are Ordinary People? Ordinariness as a Category of Historical Analysis', *Transactions of the Royal Historical Society*, 28 (2018), 175-95.

The Last Coals of Spring: Poems, Stories and Songs by the Women of Easington Colliery (Durham: Durham Voices, 1985).

Lawler, Steph, 'Heroic Workers and Angry Young Men: Nostalgic Narratives of White Working-Class Life', *European Journal of Cultural Studies*, 17 (2014), 701-20.

Lawrence, Jon, *Me, Me, Me? The Search for Community in Post-War England* (Oxford: Oxford University Press, 2019).

Leeworthy, Daryl, 'For Our Common Cause: Sexuality and Left Politics in South Wales, 1967-1985', *Contemporary British History*, 30 (2016), 260-80.

Lockwood, David, 'Sources of Variation in Working-Class Images of Society', *Sociological Review*, 14 (1966), 249-67.

Lothian Women's Support Group, *Women Living the Strike* (Dalkeith: Lothian Women's Support Group, 1986).

McCarthy, Helen, 'Women, Marriage and Paid Work in Post-War Britain', *Women's History Review*, 26 (2017), 46-61.

McCarthy, Helen, *Double Lives: A History of Working Motherhood* (London: Bloomsbury, 2020).

McCrindle, Jean, and Sheila Rowbotham, 'More than Just a Memory: Some Political Implications of Women's Involvement in the Miners' Strike, 1984-85', *Feminist Review*, 23 (1986), 109-24.

MacDougall, Ian, *Voices from Work and Home: Personal Recollections of Working Life and Labour Struggles in the Twentieth Century by Scots Men and Women* (Edinburgh: Mercat Press, 2000).

McDowell, Linda, and Doreen Massey. 'A Woman's Place?', in *Geography Matters! A Reader*, ed. Doreen Massey and John Allen (Cambridge: Cambridge University Press, 1984), 128-47.

McGrail, Steve, and Vicky Patterson, *For as Long as it Takes: Cowie Miners in the Strike, 1984-5* (Cowie: S. McGrail and V. Patterson, c.1985).

Mackey, Kath, 'Women Against Pit Closures', in *The Cutting Edge: Women and the Pit Strike*, ed. Vicky Seddon (London: Lawrence & Wishart, 1986), 50–62.
McKibbin, Ross, *The Evolution of the Labour Party, 1910–1924* (Oxford: Oxford University Press, 1975).
Mandler, Peter, 'Educating the Nation I: Schools', *Transactions of the Royal Historical Society*, 24 (2014), 5–28.
Mandler, Peter, *The Crisis of the Meritocracy: Britain's Transition to Mass Education since the Second World War* (Oxford: Oxford University Press, 2020).
Marshall, Liz, 'A Canteen Worker on Strike', in *The Cutting Edge: Women and the Pit Strike*, ed. Vicky Seddon (London: Lawrence & Wishart, 1986), 97–108.
Martin, Ron, Peter Sunley, Peter Tyler, and Ben Gardiner, 'Divergent Cities in Post-Industrial Britain', *Cambridge Journal of Regions, Economy and Society*, 9 (2016), 269–99.
Massey, Doreen, and Hilary Wainwright, 'Beyond the Coalfields: The Work of the Miners' Support Groups', in *Digging Deeper: Issues in the Miners' Strike*, ed. Huw Beynon (London: Verso, 1985), 149–168.
Mauss, Marcel, *The Gift: The Form and Reason for Exchange in Archaic Societies* (London: Routledge, 2001; originally published Paris, 1925).
Measham, Fiona, and Sheila Allen, 'In Defence of Home and Hearth? Families, Friendships and Feminism in Mining Communities', *Journal of Gender Studies*, 3 (1994), 31–45.
Millar, Grace, 'This is Not Charity: The Masculine Work of Strike Relief', *History Workshop Journal*, 83 (2017), 176–193.
Miller, Jean, 'Barnsley', in *The Cutting Edge: Women and the Pit Strike*, ed. Vicky Seddon (London: Lawrence & Wishart, 1986), 227–40.
Miller, Susan, '"The Best Thing that Ever Happened to Us": Women's Role in the Coal Dispute', *Journal of Law and Society*, 12 (1985), 355–64.
Mitchell, Juliet, 'Women: The Longest Revolution', *New Left Review*, I/40 (1966), 11–37.
Morgan, Steffan, '"Stand by your Man": Wives, Women and Feminism during the Miners' Strike 1984–85', *Llafur*, 9 (2005), 59–71.
Moss, Jonathan, *Women, Workplace Protest and Political Identity in England, 1968–85* (Manchester: Manchester University Press, 2019).
Newson, John, and Elizabeth Newson, *Patterns of Infant Care in an Urban Community* (Harmondsworth: Penguin Books, 1965).
Newson, John, and Elizabeth Newson, *Four Years Old in an Urban Community* (London: Allen & Unwin, 1968).
Newton, Gwen, ed., *We are Women, We are Strong: The Stories of Northumberland Miners' Wives 1984–85* (Northumberland: The People Themselves, 1985).
Nocon, Andrew, 'A Reluctant Welcome? Poles in Britain in the 1940s', *Oral History*, 24 (1996), 79–87.
North Yorkshire Women Against Pit Closures, *Strike 84/85* (Leeds: North Yorkshire Women Against Pit Closures, 1985).
O'Hara, Glen, *Governing Post-War Britain: The Paradoxes of Progress, 1951–1973* (Basingstoke: Palgrave Macmillan, 2012).
Orwell, George, *The Road to Wigan Pier* (London: Victor Gollancz, 1937).
Paterson, Laura, '"I Didn't Feel Like My Own Person": Paid Work in Women's Narratives of Self and Working Motherhood, 1950–1980', *Contemporary British History*, 33 (2019), 405–26.
Paton Black, Catherine, *At the Coalface: My Life as a Miner's Wife* (London: Headline, 2012).

Payling, Daisy, *Socialist Republic: Remaking the British Left in 1980s Sheffield* (Manchester: Manchester University Press, 2023).

Perrigo, Sarah, 'Gender Struggles in the British Labour Party from 1979 to 1995', *Party Politics*, 1 (1995), 407–17.

Phillips, Jim, *Collieries, Communities and the Miners' Strike in Scotland, 1984–85* (Manchester: Manchester University Press, 2012).

Phillips, Jim, 'The Meanings of Coal Community in Britain since 1947', *Contemporary British History*, 32 (2018), 39–59.

Phillips, Jim, *Scottish Coal Miners in the Twentieth Century* (Edinburgh: Edinburgh University Press, 2019).

Phillips, Jim, 'Strategic Injustice and the 1984–85 Miners' Strike in Scotland', *Industrial Law Journal* (early online publication, 2022), 1–29.

Phillips, Jim, Valerie Wright, and Jim Tomlinson, *Deindustrialisation and the Moral Economy in Scotland since 1955* (Edinburgh: Edinburgh University Press, 2021).

Popular Memory Group, 'Popular Memory: Theory, Politics, Method', in *Making Histories: Studies in History Writing*, ed. Richard Johnson, Gregor McLennan, Bill Schwarz, and David Sutton (London: Hutchinson, 1982), 205–52.

Portelli, Alessandro, *The Death of Luigi Trastulli and Other Stories: Form and Meaning in Oral History* (Albany, NY: State University of New York Press, 1991).

Power, Chris, and Jane Elliott, 'Cohort Profile: 1958 British Birth Cohort (National Child Development Study)', *International Journal of Epidemiology*, 35 (2006), 34–41.

Preston, Iris, 'A Strike Diary: Brookhouse, South Yorkshire', in *The Enemy Within: Pit Villages and the Miners' Strike of 1984–5*, ed. Raphael Samuel, Barbara Bloomfield, and Guy Boanas (London: Routledge & Kegan Paul, 1986), 100–17.

Ramsden, Stefan, *Working Class Community in the Age of Affluence* (London: Routledge, 2017).

Rees, Gareth, 'Coal, Crisis and Conflict: The 1984–85 Miners' Strike in Yorkshire', *Sociology*, 27 (1993), 307–12.

Rees, Jeska, '"Are You a Lesbian?": Challenges in Recording and Analysing the Women's Liberation Movement in England', *History Workshop Journal*, 69 (2010), 177–87.

Richards, Andrew, *Miners on Strike: Class Solidarity and Division in Britain* (Oxford: Berg, 1996).

Rieger, Bernhard, 'British Varieties of Neoliberalism: Unemployment Policy from Thatcher to Blair', in *The Neoliberal Age? Britain since the 1970s*, ed. Aled Davies, Ben Jackson, and Florence Sutcliffe-Braithwaite (London: UCL Press, 2021), 112–34.

Roberts, Elizabeth, *A Woman's Place: An Oral History of Working-Class Women 1890–1940* (Oxford: Blackwell, 1984).

Roberts, Elizabeth, *Women and Families: An Oral History, 1940–1970* (Oxford: Blackwell, 1995).

Roberts, Robert, *The Classic Slum: Salford Life in the First Quarter of the Century* (Manchester: Manchester University Press, 1971).

Robinson, Emily, Camilla Schofield, Florence Sutcliffe-Braithwaite, and Natalie Thomlinson, 'Telling Stories about Post-War Britain: Popular Individualism and the "Crisis" of the 1970s', *Twentieth Century British History*, 28 (2017), 268–304.

Rogan, Tim, *The Moral Economists: R. H. Tawney, Karl Polanyi, E. P. Thompson, and the Critique of Capitalism* (Princeton: Princeton University Press, 2017).

Salt, Chrys, and Jim Layzell, *Here We Go: Women's Memories of the 1984–5 Miners Strike* (London: Co-operative Retail Services, 1985).

Samuel, Raphael, Barbara Bloomfield, and Guy Boanas, eds., *The Enemy Within: Pit Villages and the Miners' Strike of 1984-5* (London: Routledge & Kegan Paul, 1986).

Särlvik, Bo, and Ivor Crewe, *Decade of Dealignment: The Conservative Victory of 1979 and Electoral Trends in the 1970s* (Cambridge: Cambridge University Press, 1983).

Saunders, Jack, *Assembling Cultures: Workplace Activism, Labour Militancy and Cultural Change in Britain's Car Factories, 1945-82* (Manchester: Manchester University Press, 2019).

Saunders, Jonathan, *Across Frontiers: International Support for the Miners' Strike* (London: Canary, 1989).

Savage, Mike, *Identities and Social Change in Britain since 1940: The Politics of Method* (Oxford: Oxford University Press, 2010).

Savage, Mike, Gaynor Bagnall, and Brian Longhurst, 'Ordinary, Ambivalent and Defensive: Class Identities in the Northwest of England', *Sociology*, 35 (2001), 875-92.

Schoon, Ingrid, Andrew McCulloch, Heather E. Joshi, Richard D. Wiggins, and John Bynner, 'Transitions from School to Work in a Changing Social Context', *YOUNG*, 9 (2001), 4-22.

Scott, Joan, 'The Evidence of Experience', *Critical Inquiry*, 17 (1991), 773-97.

Seddon, Vicky, ed., *The Cutting Edge: Women and the Pit Strike* (London: Lawrence & Wishart, 1986).

Segal, Lynne, *Is the Future Female? Troubled Thoughts on Contemporary Feminism* (London: Virago, 1987).

Shaw, Katy, *Mining the Meaning: Cultural Representations of the 1984-5 UK Miners' Strike* (Newcastle upon Tyne: Cambridge Scholars Publishing, 2012).

Shaw, Monica, and Mave Mundy, 'Complexities of Class and Gender Relations: Recollections of Women Active in the 1984-5 Miners' Strike', *Capital & Class*, 29 (2005), 151-74.

Sheffield Women Against Pit Closures, *We are Women, We are Strong* (Sheffield: Sheffield Women Against Pit Closures, 1987).

Skeggs, Beverley, *Formations of Class and Gender: Becoming Respectable* (London: Sage, 1997).

Smith, George, 'Schools', in *Twentieth Century British Social Trends*, ed. A. H. Halsey and J. Webb (London: Routledge, 2000), 179-220.

Smith, Helen, 'Working-Class Ideas and Experiences of Sexuality in Twentieth-Century Britain: Regionalism as a Category of Analysis', *Twentieth Century British History*, 29 (2018), 58-78.

Spence, Jean, 'Women, Wives and the Campaign against Pit Closures in County Durham: Understanding the Vane Tempest Vigil', *Feminist Review*, 60 (1998), 33-60.

Spence, Jean, and Carol Stephenson, 'Female Involvement in the Miners' Strike 1984-1985: Trajectories of Activism', *Sociological Research Online*, 12 (2007), 1-11.

Spence, Jean, and Carol Stephenson, 'The Politics of the Doorstep: Female Survival Strategies and the Legacy of the Miners' Strike 1984-5', *Community, Work and Family*, 10 (2007), 309-27.

Spence, Jean, and Carol Stephenson, '"Side by Side with Our Men?" Women's Activism, Community, and Gender in the 1984-1985 British Miners' Strike', *International Labor and Working-Class History*, 75 (2009), 68-84.

Spence, Jean, and Carol Stephenson, 'Pies and Essays: Women Writing through the British 1984-5 Coal Miners' Strike', *Gender, Place & Culture: A Journal of Feminist Geography*, 20 (2013), 218-35.

Stead, Jean, *Never the Same Again: Women and the Miners' Strike 1984-85* (London: Women's Press, 1987).

Steedman, Carolyn, *Landscape for a Good Woman: A Story of Two Lives* (London: Virago, 1986).

Steedman, Carolyn, 'State Sponsored Autobiography', in *Moments of Modernity: Reconstructing Britain, 1945–1964*, ed. Becky Conekin, Frank Mort, and Chris Waters (London: Rivers Oram, 1999), 41–54.

Stevenson, George, *The Women's Liberation Movement and the Politics of Class in Britain* (London: Bloomsbury Academic, 2019).

Strangleman, Tim, 'Networks, Place and Identities in Post-Industrial Mining Communities', *International Journal of Urban and Regional Research*, 25 (2001), 253–67.

Strangleman, Tim, 'Mining a Productive Seam? The Coal Industry, Community and Sociology', *Contemporary British History*, 32 (2018), 18–38.

Summerfield, Penny, *Reconstructing Women's Wartime Lives: Discourse and Subjectivity in Oral Histories of the Second World War* (Manchester: Manchester University Press, 1998).

Supple, Barry, *The History of the British Coal Industry. Volume 4, 1913–1946: The Political Economy of Decline* (Oxford: Clarendon Press, 1987).

Sutcliffe-Braithwaite, Florence, *Class, Politics, and the Decline of Deference in England, 1968–2000* (Oxford: Oxford University Press, 2018).

Sutcliffe-Braithwaite, Florence, and Natalie Thomlinson, 'National Women Against Pit Closures: Gender, Trade Unionism and Community Activism in the Miners' Strike, 1984–5', *Contemporary British History*, 32 (2018), 78–100.

Sutcliffe-Braithwaite, Florence, and Natalie Thomlinson, 'Vernacular Discourses of Gender Equality in the Post-War British Working Class', *Past & Present*, 254 (2022), 277–313.

Szreter, Simon, 'The Genesis of the Registrar-General's Social Classification of Occupations', *British Journal of Sociology*, 35 (1984), 522–46.

Szreter, Simon, *Fertility, Class and Gender in Britain, 1860–1940* (Cambridge: Cambridge University Press, 1996).

Taylor, Andrew, *The NUM and British Politics* (Aldershot: Ashgate, 2003).

Taylor, Sandra, 'Grub Up for the Miners!', in *The Cutting Edge: Women and the Pit Strike*, ed. Vicky Seddon (London: Lawrence & Wishart, 1986), 79–96.

Thane, Pat, 'The Women of the British Labour Party and Feminism, 1906–1945', in *British Feminism in the Twentieth Century*, ed. Harold L. Smith (Amherst: University of Massachusetts Press, 1990), 124–43.

Thatcher, Margaret, *The Downing Street Years* (London: HarperCollins, 1993).

Thomlinson, Natalie, *Race, Ethnicity and the Women's Movement in England, 1968–1993* (Basingstoke: Palgrave Macmillan, 2016).

Thomlinson, Natalie, '"I was Never Very Clever, but I Always Survived": Educational Experiences of Women in Coalfield Communities in Post-War Britain', in *Education, Work and Social Change in Britain's Former Coalfield Communities: The Ghost of Coal*, ed. R. Simmons and K. Simpson (Basingstoke: Palgrave Macmillan, 2022), 173–96.

Thompson, E. P., 'The Moral Economy of the English Crowd in the Eighteenth Century', *Past & Present*, 50 (1971), 76–136.

Thompson, E. P., 'Rough Music', in Thompson, *Customs in Common* (London: Merlin Press, 1991), 467–531.

Thomson, Mathew, *Psychological Subjects: Identity, Culture, and Health in Twentieth-Century Britain* (Oxford: Oxford University Press, 2006).

Thomson, Mathew, *Lost Freedom: The Landscape of the Child and the British Post-War Settlement* (Oxford: Oxford University Press, 2013).

Thornton, Jane, *All the Fun of the Fight* (Doncaster: Doncaster Library Service, c.1987).

Tinkler, Penny, '"Are You Really Living?" If Not, "Get with It!"', *Cultural and Social History*, 11 (2014), 597–619.
Todd, Selina, 'Affluence, Class and Crown Street: Reinvestigating the Post-War Working Class', *Contemporary British History*, 22 (2008), 501–18.
Todd, Selina, and Hilary Young, 'Baby-Boomers to "Beanstalkers": Making the Modern Teenager in Post-War Britain', *Cultural and Social History*, 9 (2012), 451–67.
Tomaney, John, 'After Coal: Meanings of the Durham Miners' Gala', *Frontiers in Sociology*, 5 (2020).
Tomaney, John, Lucy Natarajan, and Florence Sutcliffe-Braithwaite, *Sacriston: Towards a Deeper Understanding of Place* (London: UCL Bartlett School of Planning, 2021).
Tomlinson, Jim, 'De-Industrialization Not Decline: A New Meta-Narrative for Post-War British History', *Twentieth Century British History*, 27 (2016), 76–99.
Turner, Royce, 'Post-War Pit Closures', *Political Quarterly*, 56 (1985), 167–74.
Upton Miners, 'The Infant Support Group', in *The Enemy Within: Pit Villages and the Miners' Strike of 1984–5*, ed. Raphael Samuel, Barbara Bloomfield, and Guy Boanas (London: Routledge & Kegan Paul, 1986), 122–6.
Vickery, Amanda, 'From Golden Age to Separate Spheres: A Review of the Categories and Chronologies of English Women's History', *Historical Journal*, 36 (1993), 383–414.
Vinen, Richard, 'A War of Position? The Thatcher Government's Preparation for the 1984 Miners' Strike', *English Historical Review*, 134 (2019), 121–50.
Waddington, David, Chas Critcher, Bella Dicks, and David Parry, *Out of the Ashes: The Social Impact of Industrial Contraction and Regeneration on Britain's Mining Communities* (London: The Stationery Office in association with the Regional Studies Association, 2001).
Waddington, David, Maggie Wykes, and Chas Critcher, *Split at the Seams? Community, Continuity and Change after the 1984–5 Coal Dispute* (Milton Keynes: Open University Press, 1991).
Walkerdine, Valerie, 'Communal Beingness and Affect: An Exploration of Trauma in a Post-Industrial Community', *Body and Society*, 16 (2010), 91–116.
Warwick, Dennis, and Gary M. Littlejohn, *Coal, Capital and Culture: A Sociological Analysis of Mining Communities in West Yorkshire* (London: Routledge, 1992).
Welsh Campaign for Civil and Political Liberties and NUM South Wales Area, *Striking Back* (Cardiff: Welsh Campaign for Civil and Political Liberties and NUM South Wales Area, 1985).
Westlake, Martin, *Kinnock: The Biography* (London: Little, Brown, 2001).
Wilson, Dolly Smith, 'A New Look at the Affluent Worker: The Good Working Mother in Post-War Britain', *Twentieth Century British History*, 17 (2006), 206–29.
Winterton, Jonathan, and Ruth Winterton, *Coal, Crisis and Conflict: The 1984–5 Miners' Strike in Yorkshire* (Manchester: Manchester University Press, 1989).
Witham, Joan, *Hearts and Minds: The Story of the Women of Nottinghamshire in the Miners' Strike, 1984–1985* (London: Canary, 1986).
Woodin, Tim, *Working-Class Writing and Publishing in the Late Twentieth Century: Literature, Culture and Community* (Manchester: Manchester University Press, 2018).
Worsborough Community Group, *The Heart and Soul of It* (Huddersfield: Worsborough Community Group and Bannerworks, 1985).
Worth, Eve, 'Women, Education and Social Mobility in Britain During the Long 1970s', *Cultural and Social History*, 16 (2019), 67–83.

You Can't Kill the Spirit!: Houghton Main Pit Camp, South Yorkshire: The Untold Story of the Women Who Set Up Camp to Stop Pit Closures (Sheffield: Northend Creative Print Solutions, 2018).

Zweig, Ferdynand, *Men in the Pits* (London: Victor Gollancz, 1949).

Webpages

1958 National Child Development Study; https://cls.ucl.ac.uk/cls-studies/1958-national-child-development-study/.

Coal Miners of African Carribean Heritage, Archive Oral History Collection; Norma Gregory; Black Miners Museum; https://blackcoalminers.com/oral-history-archives/.

Historical Coal Data: Coal Production, Availability and Consumption 1853 to 2020; Department for Business, Energy & Industrial Strategy; published 22 January 2013, updated 28 July 2022; https://www.gov.uk/government/statistical-data-sets/historical-coal-data-coal-production-availability-and-consumption.

'Mining Towns Hit Hard by Heroin', BBC, 18 October 2002; http://news.bbc.co.uk/1/hi/england/2338623.stm.

Regional Ethnic Diversity; published 1 August 2018; https://www.ethnicity-facts-figures.service.gov.uk/uk-population-by-ethnicity/national-and-regional-populations/regional-ethnic-diversity/latest#download-the-data.

Unemployment rate (aged 16 and over, seasonally adjusted); https://www.ons.gov.uk/employmentandlabourmarket/peoplenotinwork/unemployment/timeseries/mgsx/lms.

Unpublished PhD Theses

Allen, Meg, 'Carrying on the Strike: The Politics of Women Against Pit Closures' (University of Manchester, 2001).

Amos, David, 'The Nottinghamshire Miners, the Union of Democratic Mineworkers and the 1984–5 Miners' Strike: Scabs or Scapegoats' (University of Nottingham, 2011).

Davies, Rebecca, 'Not Just Supporting but Leading: The Involvement of the Women of the South Wales Coalfield in the 1984–5 Miners' Strike' (University of Glamorgan, 2010).

Emery, Jay, 'Geographies of Belonging in the Nottinghamshire Coalfield: Affect, Temporality and Deindustrialisation' (University of Leicester, 2018).

McCrindle, Jean, 'The National Organisation of Women Against Pit Closures in the Miners' Strike of 1984–5' (Oxford Brookes University, 2001).

McIntyre, Pat, 'The Response to the 1984–5 Miners' Strike in Durham County: Women, the Labour Party and Community' (University of Durham, 1992).

Murphy, John, 'Community and Struggle: A Sociological Study of a Mining Village in the 1980s' (University of Warwick, 1989).

Peirson-Webber, Emily, 'Masculinity and Mining in the British Coal Industry: From Nationalisation to Pit Closures' (University of Reading, 2022).

Shaw, Monica, 'Women in Protest and Beyond: Greenham Common and Mining Support Groups' (University of Durham, 1993).

Index

For the benefit of digital users, indexed terms that span two pages (e.g., 52–53) may, on occasion, appear on only one of those pages.

1926 General Strike 5–6, 18–19, 75–6, 86–7, 112–14, 135–6, 156, 246
1972 Miners' Strike 4–7, 36, 61, 72–3, 75–6
1974 Miners' Strike 4–5, 28, 36, 61, 75–6, 78, 217–18

Aberdare 112–13, 132–4, 215–16
Ammanford 92–3, 117–22, 142–3
Amid the Standing Corn 228–9
Anderson, Alison 45–6, 66–7, 117, 167–8, 170, 191, 209–10
Apartheid 199
Ashfield Women's Support Group 145–6
Askern 85–8, 104–6, 136
Askern Women's Support Group 83–4, 87–8, 106, 108, 126, 136, 177–8
Attlee, Clement 33–4
Aylesham Women's Support Group 62, 75–6, 78–80, 92–3

'Baby Boom' generation 11, 36–43, 215–16
Barnsley (*see also* Barnsley Women Against Pit Closures)
    Barnsley Chronicle 76–7, 228–30
    Barnsley Miners' Wives Action Group (BMWAG) (*see also* Barnsley Women Against Pit Closures) 19, 140–1
    Northern College 28–30, 76–7, 96–7, 201, 223–4
    Rally, 12th May 1984 (*see also* 'rallies') 92–4
Battle of Orgreave 107–8, 228
Bell, Christina 11–12, 84, 191, 208, 244–5, 247–8
Bell, Trevor 73–4
Benn, Caroline and Tony 78, 148
Bentley, South Yorkshire 131, 142, 198
Betteshanger 78–80, 103, 127–8
Billy Elliot 185–6, 228
Boulton, Lesley 107–9, 113, 122, 142–3
Bowler, Lorraine 97, 140–1, 151–2
Boyes, Joyce 43, 54–5, 109, 172–4, 208–10, 235
Brampton Bierlow 59, 171–2, 201, 228–9
British Broadcasting Corporation (BBC) 78–80, 128, 228–9

Calverton 67–70, 75–6, 85–6, 103, 136
Campaign for Nuclear Disarmament (CND) 55, 142–3, 194–5, 199, 218–19
Campbell, Beatrix 17–19, 104–5
Case, Kay 39, 48, 50–1, 61–2, 72–3, 80–1, 89, 112, 146–7, 153–4, 157, 216, 240–1
Castleford 43, 173
Castleford Women's Centre 201, 204–5, 215–16
Chapman, Linda 44, 64, 112, 115–16, 118, 169
Chapman, Roni 71, 73–4
Charity (attitudes towards) 25, 113, 121–4, 130, 214, 236–7
Children
    Childhood 36–42
    Experiences during strike 164–9
Christmas (1984) 26, 30, 49, 65, 110, 126–7, 129–30, 134, 158, 162–9, 172–3, 176–9, 183–4, 224–5, 244
Coalfields Regeneration Trust (CRT) 212–14
Coalfield Woman 202, 204–5
Coal House 71–2
Coal Industry Social Welfare Organisation (CISWO) 34
Coal is Our Life: An Analysis of a Yorkshire Mining Community (1956) (*see also* 'traditional mining community' stereotype) 32–3, 46–7, 196–7
Coates, Maureen 1–2, 55–6, 84, 106–7, 131, 221
Community
    Coalfield women's understandings of (*see also* 'Moral economy') 3, 15–16, 24–5, 51–4, 146, 152–62, 165–6, 173–4, 192, 200, 206–10, 222, 240–5, 247–8
    Feminists' understandings of (*see also* 'feminist depictions of the 1984–5 strike') 17–18, 101, 206–7
    Coalfield communities after the strike 240–5
    Community attitudes towards strike 112–15, 165–6, 171–2
    Community hostility to women's support movement 177–8, 181–2, 214
    'Traditional mining community' stereotype 17–18, 22, 24–5, 30–6, 44, 50–1, 56–7, 229

INDEX

Cortonwood 19–20, 59–60, 76–7, 106, 140–1, 147–8, 201
Communist Party of Great Britain, the (CPGB) 6–7, 77–8, 97, 139–41, 147, 151–2
  Eurocommunist faction 6–7, 97–8, 139–41, 162–3, 203–4
Conservative Party, the 4–5, 126, 128–9, 152–4, 174
Cook, Betty 16–17, 19, 21–2, 88, 132–4, 139–41, 146–52, 159, 162–3, 186, 205–6, 229–30, 234
Cowdenbeath 83–4, 170–1, 191, 209, 214, 232
Currie, Aggie 39–40, 93, 105–7, 153–4, 164–5, 205–6, 218–19, 234, 241
Cwmbach Miners and Women Speak Out (1984) 154–5
Cwmbach Miners' Relief Fund 154–5
Cynheidre Colliery, occupation of 136–9
Cynon Valley 87–8

Daily Mail, The 30, 68, 70, 96
Daily Mirror, The 95–6
Dalkeith 48–9, 198
Dalkeith Miners and Women's Support Group 207, 218–19
Debt arising from 1984–5 strike 25, 117–18, 124, 173–4, 207–10
Deindustrialisation 4, 7–9, 24, 157–8, 191–2, 210–19, 233, 240–6
Dennet, Lynne 56
Department for Health and Social Security (DHSS) 119–21, 174
Dixon, Connie 112–13
Dolby, Norma 169–72, 174–6, 208
Doncaster 13–15, 71, 114–15, 131, 188, 198, 205–6, 211–13, 221, 228–9, 245
Don Valley 54, 217–18
DOVE Workshop 200–1, 215–16
Dower, Tanya 112, 134, 233–5

Easington 49, 54, 86–8, 131–2, 138, 212–13, 215–16
Education, secondary 39–41, 57–8
Enemies Within, The 227–9
European Economic Community 199

Family
  After the strike 207–10
  Approaches to parenting in post-war period 13, 39, 196–7
  Experiences of marriage in the post-war period 43–4, 57–8, 63–4, 196–7
  During strike 24–5, 112, 146, 154–62, 167–8, 172–3

  in interwar period 31–2, 45–6
  in post-war period 37–8, 41–2, 45–6, 50–1
  Marriage rates 42–3
  Opposition to NUM policy among the wives of miners 29–30, 92, 184–5, 235–7
  Parenting 45–7
Far-left entryism 149, 202–4
Feminism
  Attitudes of coalfield women towards 3, 19–22, 24, 55–6, 141–2, 145–8, 163, 199–200, 206–7, 223–5
  Feminist depictions of the 1984–5 strike (*see also* 'media depictions of women's support groups') 16–19, 23–4, 142–5, 149–50, 223–4
  'Feminist transformation' during 1984–5 miner's strike (*see also* 'heroic narrative of women's involvement in the strike') 15–16, 20–2, 24, 142, 149–50, 196, 225–34
  Involvement of feminists with supporting strike 15–16, 142, 145–7
  Women's Liberation Movement 8–9, 29, 55–8, 82–3, 224–5
Fjaelberg, Jane 125–8
Food parcels and vouchers: *see* women's support movement, services offered
Francis, Hywel 176–7, 200–1
French, Liz 61–2, 83–6, 145–6, 167–8, 234, 244
Full Employment 4, 34–7
Fundraising 87–8, 132–4, 139, 165, 176–7, 204–5, 224–5

Gibson, Jessica 184–5, 241, 244
Gormley, Joe 5–6
Greenham Common peace camps (*see also* Houghton Main pit camp) 142–3, 199, 205–6
Grimethorpe 85–6, 107, 188, 205–6
Guardian, The 17–18, 119–20, 176, 228–31

Heath, Edward 4–5, 28, 36, 217–18
Heathfield, Peter 92–3, 95, 97, 174–6
Heathfield, Betty 78, 95–7, 134, 139–40, 174–6, 194–5, 207
Here We Go! 223–5
'Heroic' narrative of women's involvement in strike 3, 13–20, 23–4, 70, 196, 218–19, 221–34, 246–8
Heseltine, Michael 205
Hickling, Kim 148, 190–1, 219
Hogg, Dianne 136, 177, 181–2
Holden, Joan 84, 235
Hole, Mary 45–6, 112, 117
Holmes, Margaret 234–5
Houghton Main pit camp 189, 205–6

Housework
    Changes during strike 214–15
Housing
    Council housing 37–8, 45
    Privately rented housing 37–8, 45
    Tied housing 22, 30–2, 37–8

'Identity'-based politics 6–7, 139–40
    Black power politics 6–7
    Gay liberationist politics 6–7
    Intersectional socialism 18–19
Individual women's opposition to 1984–5 strike (*see also* Miners' Wives Back To Work Campaign) 3, 10, 26, 60–1, 64, 67–70, 129
Industrial policy 4–5
    Nationalised Industries Policy Group 4–5
    Privatisation 4
International support for strike 134–5, 164–5, 176, 188, 224–5
International Women's Day 194
Irish Republican Army (IRA), The 126

James, Siân 61–2, 98–9, 135–42, 146–7, 151–2, 218–19

Keating, Jackie 59, 106–7, 140–1, 171–2
Kinnock, Neil 6–7, 148
Kirby, Anne 83–4, 103–4, 145–6, 149, 170–1, 191, 209–10, 214, 232, 234–5

Labour Party, the
    'Feminisation' after the 1984–5 strike 218–19
    Masculine culture 31–2
    Local parties' support for 1984–5 strike 87–8, 118–19, 194
    National party's position on the 1984–5 strike 6–7
    Place in local coalfield politics 20–1, 54–5, 217–19
    Post-war rhetoric of 'fair shares' 8–9
    Research Department 134
Lesbians and Gays Support the Miners (LGSM) 146–7, 229
Lothian Women's Support Group 149–50, 219

MacGregor, Ian 4–5, 59, 106, 136–9, 169, 228–9
Mackey, Kath 97–8, 148
Marches (*see also* rallies) 12–13, 20–1, 24–5, 78–80, 174–6, 204–5, 224–5
Marital relationships 12–13, 17–18, 22, 24–5, 32–3, 41–51, 53–8, 63–4, 74, 167–8, 183–5, 232

Marshall, Liz 74, 104–5
McComb, Jeanette 50–2, 61, 64, 118, 121, 167–8, 183–4, 209
McCracken, Ann 116, 236
McCrindle, Jean 17–18, 28–30, 56–8, 65, 76–7, 92–100, 119–20, 139–41, 143–4, 146–7, 162–3, 176, 178, 184, 202–3
McGibbon, Irene 125–9, 150–1, 162
Memory of the strike (*see also* 'heroic narrative' of women's involvement)
    Loss 221–2
    Grassroots and radical oral histories and anthologies of the strike 223–5
    Strike verse 222–4
Miller, Jean 77–8, 80, 97, 140–1
Miner, The 15–16, 29, 174–6
Mines and Collieries Act (1842) 30–1
Miners' Campaign Tapes series (1984) 156, 227–8
Miners' strike, 1984–5
    Causes of 59–61
    End 187–93
    Media depictions of 17–18, 80–1, 174, 228–9
    Political reaction to 6–7, 125–7
    Return to work 126–7
Miners' Federation of Great Britain (MFGB) 5–6, 31–2, 54
Miners' Wives Back to Work Campaign (*see also* Individual women's opposition to 1984–5 strikes) 125–9
Mining industry
    Decline 34–6
    In relation to trade unionism 4–5
    Kent 35–6
    Nationalisation 5–6, 33–4
    Nottinghamshire 35–6
    Inefficiency of 4–5
    South Wales 35–6
    Yorkshire 35–6
Minney, Wendy 44, 148, 190–1, 219
Moral economy 3, 24–5, 120–1, 127, 154–62, 169–70, 180, 183, 189–90
Morning Star, The 6–7, 176, 194
Musgrave, Ann 164–5, 188–9
Myers, Nell 29, 57–8, 65, 80, 96–7

National Association of Colliery Overmen, Deputies and Sheriffs, (NACODS) 72–3, 126–7, 205–6
National Association for Freedom (NAFF) 128
National Child Development Study (1958) 12–13, 36–43, 45–7

278 INDEX

National Coal Board (NCB) 2–6, 19, 28, 33–5, 59, 72–4, 125–7, 129, 136–9, 154–5, 158, 165–6, 168, 172–3, 179, 184, 194, 207, 214, 238
   Area Incentive Scheme (1977-8) 6–7, 28–9, 150–1
National Working Miners' Committee 128
National Union of Mineworkers (NUM) 2–7, 15–20, 22–3, 28, 30, 34–6, 54, 71–2, 77, 80, 82–4, 87–9, 94, 97–9, 125–9, 136, 139–42, 162–4, 168–70, 174–8, 184, 187, 192–3, 197–9, 202–6, 217–19, 223–5
   Colliery Officials and Staff Area (COSA) 60–1, 71–5
   Decline after 1984-5 strike 217–18
   Exclusion of women 29, 31–2, 101–2, 202–3, 246–7
   Kent Area 28, 59–60, 78–80, 187–8
   Nottinghamshire Area 6–7, 26, 48, 59–60, 101–2, 238
   Regional tensions between coalfields 6–7, 29–30
   Scotland Area 134, 202–3
   South Wales Area 28, 59–60, 65–6, 118–19, 130–1, 168, 187–8
   South Yorkshire Area 28, 59, 65–6, 118–19, 187
National Women Against Pit Closures (NWAPC) 22–3, 95–101, 134, 139–42, 145–6, 149, 162–3, 165, 174–6, 178, 194–5, 199–200, 202–6
   1985 conference in Sheffield 202–3
   Barnsley WAPC (*see also* Barnsley Miners' Wives Action Group) 77–8, 80, 140–1, 151, 225, 227–8
   Sheffield WAPC 77–8, 108, 140–3, 148, 152, 199, 205–6
New Left 6–7, 16–17
New Left Review 8–9
New Statesman 56, 174

Oakdale 80, 104–5, 109, 114–15
Ollerton 21–2, 82, 102, 136, 153–4
Oral history
   Intersubjectivity 14–15
   Methodology of this study 26
   Oral history theory 13–15, 238–9
'Ordinariness' 150–4, 158, 163
Orwell, George 30–1

Paid employment, women
   Low levels during interwar period 30–1
   In postwar period 1–2, 7–8, 11–12, 21–2, 41, 46–51, 57–8, 196–7, 233, 246
   During strike 3, 10, 24–5, 115–17, 169, 172–3, 181–2
   After the strike 211–14
   Relationship with deindustrialisation 8–9, 21–2, 211–14, 246
Paton Black, Catherine 74, 80–1, 149, 153–4, 183
Pattison, Irene 110, 121
Paxton, Jane 67–8, 70
Picketing of coalfield women 12–13, 24–5, 101–9, 135–6, 174–6, 224–5, 231
Plan for Coal (1974) 36
Poland, Caroline 143–4, 205–6, 247–8
Policing of the 1984-5 strike 105–6, 172–3, 182
   Arrest of women activists 105–6, 136
   Police violence on pickets 105–6, 136, 231
   Over-policing of the strikes 4–5, 72, 103, 136
Popular individualism 8–9, 55–6, 246–7
Postwar migration 35–6
Preston, Iris 152, 199–201
Price, Marie 41–2, 50, 54, 62–3, 83–4, 147, 233–4, 240–1, 243
Pride (2014) 2–3, 185–6, 229–30
Protests 28, 108, 120–1, 135–9, 159–60, 231–2

Rallies (*see also* marches) 29, 78–80, 92–4, 99, 106, 174–6, 194–7, 224–5
Respectability, politics of 152–3, 158
Right to Buy 4, 11–12
Robertson, Ann 61, 65, 83, 122–3, 235–6, 239
Rossington 114–15, 188
Rowbotham, Sheila 17–18
Russell, Margot 174, 207, 218–19
Ruskin College 101–2, 145

Sacriston 52, 88
Samuel, Alice 61–2, 174, 190–1, 231–2, 243–5
Sankey Report (1919) 30–1
Save Easington Area Mines (SEAM) 78, 98–9, 158, 166
Scargill, Anne 95–8, 101–2, 140–1, 150–2, 162–3, 194–5, 202–3, 205–6, 229
Scargill, Arthur 4–7, 18–19, 22–3, 28–30, 56–61, 65, 68, 77, 92–4, 96–100, 141–2, 154–5, 162–3, 174–6, 178, 181–2, 184–7, 194–7, 202–4, 226–9, 231, 238
Seddon, Vicky 19, 223–4
Selby 179
Shadbolt, Jean 74–5, 94
Skeggs, Bev 55–6, 145
Skinner, Dennis 148
Slater, Janet 83–4, 93, 97–8, 168–9, 235, 247–8
Slater, Mandy 117
Smith, Pat 62, 83–4, 86–9, 118, 148, 234–5

Snowdown Women's Support group (see: Aylesham Women's Support Group)
Social contract 4
Socialism 3–4, 18–19
Sociologists' account of the strike 20–2
Soup kitchens: see women's support movement, services offered
South Wales Women's Support Group 98–9, 199
South West Africa People's Organization (SWAPO) 98–9, 194–6
Spare Rib 17–18, 142, 149–50
Sprotbrough and Brodsworth Mining Families' Support Group 1–2, 84, 131, 176–7
State benefits 4, 8–9, 172–3
Strikebreaking 3, 14–15, 71, 74–5, 107–9, 129–31, 135, 170, 178–87
Stubbs, Maggie 11–12, 44, 51–2, 115, 139, 189–90, 240
Substance abuse 217, 240
Sutcliffe, Kay 62, 78, 80, 99
Swansea, Neath and Dulais Valleys' Support Group 110, 130–2, 146–7, 176–9, 200–1

Thatcher, Margaret (*see also* 'Thatcherism') 4, 6–8, 30, 106, 120–1, 125–7, 148, 153–4, 159–60, 162, 181–2, 185–6
Thatcher government (*see* Thatcher, Margaret)
Thatcherism (*see also* 'Margaret Thatcher') 6–8, 126–7, 152–5, 159, 162–3, 165–6, 189–90, 210–11
Thatcherite (*see* Thatcherism)
The Cutting Edge (1986) 223–5
Thurcroft 80, 107–8, 112, 148, 178–9, 184–5
Times, The 128–9, 176, 229
Trade unions
  Attitudes towards 4, 66–7
  Coalfield women's trade unionism 8–9, 17–18, 20–1, 31–2, 50–1, 55, 71, 75–8, 84, 146, 204–5
  Place in British life 4, 7–8, 66–7, 217–18, 247
  Power of 4–5

Transport and General Workers' Union (TGWU) 127–8, 194–5
Treharris 72–3, 80, 89–90, 216

Unemployment 4, 210–11
Union of Democratic Mineworkers 198, 217–18
Upton Ladies' Action Group 80

Wakefield, Rita 148, 190–1, 219
Wainwright, Hilary 176
Walsh, Lorraine and Finnis, Linda 39, 45, 109, 117, 170–1
Washington, Tyne and Wear 115
Weldon, Mig 118–20, 209
Whitaker, Margaret 63
Willis, Carol 106, 240–1
Women's personal support for their striking husbands 63–4
Women's support movement 2–3, 17–18, 22–3, 75–90, 142–54, 162–3, 174–6
  After the strike 197–207
  Formation of groups 2–3, 43, 76–90
  Membership size 85–6
  Organisation 2–3
  Media depictions of (*see also* 'feminist depictions of the strike') 2–3, 6, 13–14, 16–17, 92
  Services offered by 2–3, 22–3, 80, 84–7, 110–12, 121, 131–2, 165–8, 172–4, 224–5
  Tensions with the NUM 88–90, 92, 103–5, 162–3, 203
  Tensions within the movement 101, 106, 140–1, 162–3, 174–8, 203–5

Wooldridge, Christine 72, 74
World in Action 62, 67, 78–80
Working-class masculinity 180, 189–90, 210–11
Worth, Christine 101–2, 194, 245

The manufacturer's authorised representative in the EU for product safety is Oxford University Press España S.A. of El Parque Empresarial San Fernando de Henares, Avenida de Castilla, 2 – 28830 Madrid (www.oup.es/en or product.safety@oup.com). OUP España S.A. also acts as importer into Spain of products made by the manufacturer.

Printed in the USA/Agawam, MA
November 5, 2025

895578.033